The
Manager's
Bookshelf

FIFTH EDITION

The Manager's Bookshelf

A Mosaic of Contemporary Views

Jon L. Pierce
University of Minnesota, Duluth

John W. Newstrom
University of Minnesota, Duluth

PRENTICE HALL, Upper Saddle River, New Jersey 07458

Senior Editor: David Shafer
Editorial Assistant: Kim Marsden
Editor-in-Chief: Natalie Anderson
Assistant Editor: Michele Foresta
Editorial Managing Editor: Jennifer Glennon
Marketing Manager: Michael Campbell
Director of Production: Michael Weinstein
Production Manager: Gail Steier de Acevedo
Production Coordinator: Maureen Wilson
Permissions Coordinator: Monica Stipanov
Manufacturing Buyer: Natacha St. Hill Moore
Senior Manufacturing Manager: Vincent Scelta
Cover Design: Lorraine Castellano
Cover Art/Photo: Salem Krieger
Full Service Composition: UG / GGS Information Services, Inc.

Library of Congress Cataloging-in-Publication Data

The manager's bookshelf: a mosaic of contemporary views/[collected
    by] Jon L. Pierce, John W. Newstrom.—5th ed.
        p.   cm.
    Includes bibliographical references and index.
    ISBN 0-321-01714-5
    1. Management literature—United States.   I. Pierce, Jon L. (Jon
Lepley)   II. Newstrom, John W.
HD70.U5M32 2000
658—dc21   99-43083
                                                                        CIP

Prentice-Hall International (UK) Limited, London
Prentice-Hall of Australia Pty. Limited, Sydney
Prentice-Hall Canada, Inc., Toronto
Prentice-Hall Hispanoamericana, S.A., Mexico
Prentice-Hall of India Private Limited, New Delhi
Prentice-Hall of Japan, Inc., Tokyo
Prentice-Hall (Singapore) Pte Ltd.
Editora Prentice-Hall do Brasil, Ltda., Rio de Janerio

Printed in the United States of America

10 9 8 7 6 5 4 3 2

We dedicate this book to two VIPs—
our highly valued partners, Janet Pierce and Diane Newstrom

Contents

Lance H. K. Secretan

Preface

The last decade was marked by an intense fascination with, and a continued proliferation of, books on management, managers, and organizations. Bookstores around the country featured a larger number than ever before of management books, and many of these books found themselves on, or close to, the "best-sellers" list. Clearly, both managers and the general public are intrigued by, and searching for answers in, the popular business literature.

The Manager's Bookshelf: A Mosaic of Contemporary Views was prepared both for managers and management students. A significant number of individuals in both of these groups do not have sufficient time to read widely, yet many people find themselves involved in conversations where someone else refers to ideas like vision, self-directed workteams, or superleadership. We believe that a laudable goal for managers as well as all students of management is to remain current in their understanding of the views being expressed about organizational and management practices. To help you become a better informed organizational citizen, we prepared *The Manager's Bookshelf*, which introduces you to more than forty recently popular management books.

The Manager's Bookshelf, as a book of concise readings, does not express the views of one individual on the management of organizations, nor does it attempt to integrate the views of several dozen authors. Instead, *this book is a collage*—a composite portrait constructed from a variety of sources. It provides you with insights into many aspects of organizational management from the perspectives of a diverse group of management writers, including some highly regarded authors like Douglas McGregor, Stephen Covey, Bill Byham, Thomas Peters, Margaret Wheatley, John Case, Peter Senge, and Judy Rosener. Through this collection we will introduce you to the thoughts, philosophy, views, and experiences of a number of authors whose works have captivated the attention of today's management community.

This book contains a rich array of pieces. From a topical perspective there are inclusions that focus on ethics, global perspectives, participative practices, environmental trends, organizational culture, managing diversity, strategy, and managerial/leadership styles. This collection includes the views from a variety of individuals—some practitioners, some philosophers, some management consultants, and some management educators. The selections reflect a wide variety in terms of their tone and tenor, as well as the bases for their conclusions. Indeed, critics have characterized some of the authors' works as passionate, invaluable, and insightful, whereas others have been attacked as overly academic, superficial, or unrealistic.

The nature and source of the ideas expressed in this collection are diverse. Some inclusions are prescriptive in nature, whereas others are descriptive; some are philosophical, whereas others report on personal or organizational experiences; some of these works represent armchair speculation, whereas others are based on empirical study. Finally, the selections take a variety of forms. Some of the readings are excerpts extracted from the original book, some of the readings are articles written by the book's author in which part of their philosophy on management is revealed, and some of the inclusions are descriptive summaries of popular books that have been specially prepared for inclusion in *The Manager's Bookshelf.*

This collage can provide you with some useful insights, stimulate your thinking, and spark some stimulating dialogue with your colleagues about the management of today's organizations. We hope these readings will prompt you to raise questions of yourself and your peers about the viability of many of the ideas expressed by these authors regarding the practice of organizational management. If these goals are met, our purpose for assembling this collection will be realized.

Acknowledgments

We would like to express our sincere and warm appreciation to several colleagues who read and prepared summaries of the contemporary books contained in this edition of *The Manager's Bookshelf*. Their commitment and dedication to students of organizations and management, coupled with their efforts, made this edition possible.

We would also like to express our appreciation to our late friend and colleague, Larry L. Cummings (Carlson School of Management at the University of Minnesota, and The Institute) for his "reflections on the best-sellers" that is contained in the introduction to our book. We thank Larry for taking the time to reflect on this part of the organization and management literature and to offer an update to the insightful observations that he prepared for the earlier editions. He will always be remembered and valued for his friendship.

New to this Edition

The following individuals prepared book summaries for this edition of *The Manager's Bookshelf:*

INTRODUCTION
Brad Jackson, Victoria University of Wellington—Micklethwait and
    Woolridge's *The Witch Doctors*

MANAGEMENT PARADIGMS
Brian Kalhbaugh, Hertz—Barker's *Paradigms: The Business of Discovering
    the Future*
Robert Marx, University of Massachusetts, Amherst—Bolman and Deal's
    Reframing Organizations

BEST-SELLER "CLASSICS"
William B. Gartner, Georgetown University and **M. James Naughton,**
    Expert-Knowledge Systems, Inc.—Deming's *Out of the Crisis*
Charles C. Manz, University of Massachusetts, Amherst—Blanchard and
    Johnson's *The One Minute Manager*

Gayle Porter, Rutgers University—McGregor's *The Human Side of Enterprise*

HIGH-PERFORMING ORGANIZATIONS

Steve Gildersleeve, Carlson Florist and Greenhouses—Hammer and Champy's *Reengineering the Corporation*

Gary P. Olson, Center for Alcohol and Drug Treatment—Galbraith and Lawler's *Organizing for the Future*

ORGANIZATIONAL, VISION, GOALS, AND STRATEGY

Gayle Baugh, The University of West Florida—Nanus' *Visionary Leadership*

Michael Roche—Goldratt's *The Goal*

MOTIVATION

Gayle Porter, Rutgers University—Daniels' *Bringing Out the Best in People*

Kelly Nelson, Armco's Mansfield Operations—Pfeffer's *The Human Equation*

EMPOWERMENT AND PARTICIPATION

Constance Campbell, Georgia Southern University—Byham and Cox's *Zapp! The Lightning of Empowerment*

Jack Hoggatt, University of Wisconsin–Eau Claire—Byham and Cox's *HeroZ: Empower Yourself, Your Co-workers, Your Company*

Connie J. Christenson, St. Louis County, Minnesota—Case's *Open-Book Management*

Cheri L. Stine—Case's *The Open-Book Experience*

TEAMS AND TEAMWORK

R. Warren Candy, Minnesota Power—Katzenbach and Smith's *The Wisdom of Teams*

Gary P. Olson, Center for Alcohol and Drug Treatment—Katzenbach and Smith's *Teams at the Top*

Cathy Hanson, M & M Mars Company—Wellins, Byham and Wilson's *Empowered Teams*

LEADERSHIP

Chris Graves, Salomon, Smith, Barney—Daft and Lengel's *Fusion Leadership*

Scott L. Newstrom, Harvard University—Wheatley's *Leadership and the New Science*

Robert C. Ford, The University of Central Florida—Block's *Stewardship*

MANAGING DIVERSITY

Scott L. Newstrom, Harvard University—Barrentine's *When the Canary Stops Singing*

Kristina A. Bourne, University of Massachusetts, Amherst—Rosener's *America's Competitive Secret: Women Managers*

ORGANIZATIONAL CHANGE AND RENEWAL

Jane Giacobbe-Miller, University of Massachusetts, Amherst—Peters' *The Tom Peters Seminar*

Chris Edwardson, University of Minnesota, Duluth's Natural Resource Research Institute—Dunlap's *Mean Business*

ORGANIZATIONAL LEARNING AND KNOWLEDGE-DRIVEN ORGANIZATIONS

Dorothy Marcic, Vanderbilt University—Senge's *The Fifth Discipline*

Jean A. Grube, University of Wisconsin-Madison—Argyris' *Overcoming Organizational Defenses*

David A. Wyrick, University of Minnesota, Duluth—Watson's *Strategic Benchmarking*

Michael D. Kull, George Washington University—Davenport and Prusak's *Working Knowledge*

ETHICAL MANAGEMENT

Gregory Fox, University of Minnesota, Duluth—Kouzes and Posner's *Credibility*

GLOBAL DECISIONS

Robert R. Wharton—Ohmae's *The Borderless World*

Kelly Nelson, Armco's Mansfield Operations—Naisbitt's *Global Paradox*

MANAGING PERSONAL EFFECTIVENESS

Stephen Rubenfeld, University of Minnesota, Duluth—Covey's *Principle-Centered Leadership*

Dorothy Marcic and Marilyn Crawford, Vanderbilt University—Marcic's *Managing with the Wisdom of Love*

R. Warren Candy, Minnesota Power—Secretan's *Reclaiming Higher Ground*

We would like to express our appreciation to a number of individuals who provided us with a great deal of assistance and support for the preparation of this book. Many of our management colleagues took the time and effort to contribute to this book by carefully reading and preparing a summary of one of the selected books. Many of these individuals wanted to offer their personal opinions, offer their endorsements or criticisms, and surface elements of their own management philosophies, but they stuck to their task. To them we express our thanks for their time, energy, and commitment to furthering management education. To those who reviewed our proposal for this Fifth Edition and a draft of the final manuscript, we appreciate your recommendations. To Connie Johnson and Laura Habert, who patiently helped us prepare the manuscript, we want to say *thank you* for helping us complete this project in a timely fashion. We appreciate the supportive environment provided by our colleagues in the Department of Management Studies here at the University of Minnesota, Duluth. We especially appreciate the continued project commitment and editorial assistance that we have received from Michael Roche.

Jon L. Pierce
John W. Newstrom

About the Editors

Jon L. Pierce is Professor of Management and Organization in the School of Business and Economics at the University of Minnesota, Duluth. He received his Ph.D. in management and organizational studies at the University of Wisconsin, Madison. He is the author of more than sixty papers that have been published or presented at various professional conferences. His publications have appeared in the *Academy of Management Journal, Academy of Management Review, Journal of Management, Journal of Occupational Behavior, Journal of Applied Behavioral Science, Organizational Dynamics, Organizational Behavior and Human Decision Processes,* and *Personnel Psychology.* His research interests include sources of psychological ownership, employee ownership systems, and organization-based self-esteem. He has served on the editorial review board for the *Academy of Management Journal, Personnel Psychology,* and *Journal of Management.* He is the coauthor of five other books—*Management, Managing,* and along with John W. Newstrom, *Alternative Work Schedules, Windows into Management,* and *Leaders and the Leadership Process* (second edition).

John W. Newstrom is Professor of Human Resource Management in the School of Business and Economics at the University of Minnesota, Duluth. He completed his doctoral degree in management and industrial relations at the University of Minnesota and then taught at Arizona State University for several years. His work has appeared in publications such as *Personnel Psychology, California Management Review, Journal of Management, Academy of Management Journal,* and *The Journal of Occupational Behavior.* He has served on the editorial review boards for the *Academy of Management Review, Academy of Management Journal, Academy of Management Executive, Human Resource Development Quarterly,* and *The Journal of Management Development.* He is the coauthor of nineteen books, including *Organizational Behavior: Human Behavior at Work* (tenth edition, with Keith Davis), *Supervision* (eighth edition, with Lester Bittel), *Transfer of Training* (with Mary Broad), and *The Complete Games Trainers Play* (with Ed Scannell).

*The
Manager's
Bookshelf*

PART ONE

Introduction

Part 1 contains three pieces. The first, "Understanding and Using the Best-Sellers," prepared by the editors of *The Manager's Bookshelf*, provides insight into why such a large number of management-oriented books have found themselves in the downtown bookstores, on our coffee tables, and on the bookshelves of those who manage today's organizations. Pierce and Newstrom discuss the rationale for this mosaic of contemporary views on organizations and management, and they provide you with insight into the nature and character of *The Manager's Bookshelf: A Mosaic of Contemporary Views*. They challenge you to read and reflect upon this collection of thoughts and experiences. They invite you to debate the ideas and philosophies that are presented here. They encourage you to let these contemporary management books stimulate your thinking, to motivate you to look more systematically into the science of organizations and management, and to provide you with the fun of learning something new.

As a result of their concern that these contemporary books will be seen as "quick and dirty" cures for organizational woes, Pierce and Newstrom encourage you to read books such as Ralph H. Kilmann's *Managing Beyond the Quick Fix*.

Several years ago Ralph Kilmann, in his earlier book *Beyond the Quick Fix: Managing Five Tracks to Organizational Success*, provided us with a valuable message, one that should serve as the backdrop to your consumption and assessment of the myriad of purported "one minute" cures for organizational problems and for the management of today's complex organizations. Kilmann encourages managers to stop perpetuating the myth of organizational and management simplicity and to develop a more complete and integrated approach to the management of today's complex organizations.

Many other writers have echoed these thoughts. *Fad-Free Management* (Richard G. Hamermesh) charges that managers engage in "bumper-car management," in which companies bounce from one fad to another; *Instant Management* (Carol Kennedy) provides a (presumably tongue-in-cheek) "idiot's guide to management gurus"; *Business Week* (June 23, 1997, p. 47) argues that "some of the most popular management remedies draw the highest rates of dissatisfaction"; and Craig Dreilinger (*Business Horizons*, November–December 1994) acknowledges that although management fads can (and sometimes do) work, they soon pass out of fashion and often result in more disappointment than success.

In an explicit attempt to provoke your critical thinking about management fads, we have included (as Reading 2) a summary of *The Witch Doctors*. After systematically and objectively reviewing a wide array of popular management books, Micklethwait and Wooldridge conclude that managers must become critical consumers of these products. This means being suspicious of the faddish contentions, remaining unconvinced by simplistic argumentation by the authors, being selective about which theory might work for you, and becoming broadly informed about the merits and deficiencies of each proposal.

Currently two types of voices create "messages" relevant to management education. One is the organizational scholar (e.g., Edward Lawler, Lyman Porter, Charles Perrow), who offers us rich theories of management and organization and rigorous empirical observations of organizations in action. The other source includes management consultants and management practitioners (e.g., Andy Grove, Jack Welch, Tom Peters, Stephen Covey, Bill Gates) who offer us perspectives from their lives on the "organizational firing line."

Traditional academics—students of tight theory and rigorous empirical study of organizational behavior—often find a large disparity between these two perspectives on management and organization. Confronted with the increasing popularity of the "best-sellers," the editors of *The Manager's Bookshelf* began to ask a number of questions about this nontraditional management literature. For example:

- Is this material "intellectual pornography," as some have claimed?
- Do we want our students to read this material?
- Should managers of today's organizations be encouraged to read this material and to take it seriously?
- What contributions to management education and development come from this collection of management books?
- How should this management literature be approached?

For answers to these questions we turned to colleague and friend Professor Larry L. Cummings

We asked Professor Cummings to reflect upon the current and continuous popularity of this literature. Professor Cummings was a distinguished management scholar, organization and management consultant, and educator of MBA and Ph.D. students. The questions we asked Professor Cummings are intended to help us frame, and therefore critically and cautiously consume, this literature. Professor Cummings' reflections on the role of the popular books in management education is presented as Reading 3 in this introductory chapter.

READING 1

Understanding and Using the Best-Sellers

Jon L. Pierce and John W. Newstrom

For several decades now, there have been a large number of books treating various aspects of management. These books have been in high demand at local bookstores. Several individuals have authored books that have sold millions of copies, among them Tom Peters (e.g., *In Search of Excellence*), Bill Byham (e.g., *Zapp! The Lightning of Empowerment*), Stephen Covey (e.g., *Seven Habits of Highly Effective People*), Lee Iacocca (e.g., *Iacocca: An Autobiography*), and Kenneth Blanchard and Spencer Johnson (e.g., *The One Minute Manager*). Some of their books have stayed on "best-seller" lists for many weeks and even years. What are the reasons for their popularity? Why have business books continued to catch the public's attention as we move into the twenty-first century? Frank Freeman of the Center for Creative Leadership suggests simply that we are living in the "business decade."[1] Corporate America, he says, is back in good standing with the public, and there has been a resurgence of pride and hope in the business community.

We have heard stories about, and many have felt the shock waves of, downsizing, restructuring, and reengineering of the organization. We have all heard stories about the success of foreign organizations. We have continued to watch bigger and bigger portions of our markets being dominated by foreign-owned and controlled organizations. And we have witnessed foreign interests purchase certain segments of America. Perhaps in response to these trends, a tremendous thirst for *American* success stories has arisen. In essence, the public is receptive and the timing is right for the writing, publication, and sale of popular management books at bookstores everywhere.

A second reason for the upsurge in management books stems from another form of competition. Many management consultants, fighting for visibility, have written books they hope will become best-sellers.[2] Through the printed word they hope to provide a unique take-home product for their clients, communicate their management philosophies, gain wide exposure for themselves or their firms, and occasionally profit handsomely.

Third, the best-sellers also provide an optimistic message to a receptive market. In difficult economic times, managers may be as eager to swallow easy formulas as sick patients are to drink their prescribed medicine. Sensing this, the authors of the best-sellers (and of many other books with lesser records) often claim, at least implicitly, to present managers with an easy cure for their organizational woes, or with an easy path to personal success. In a world characterized by chaos, environmental turbulence, and intense global competition, managers are driven to search for the ideas provided by others that might be turned into a competitive advantage.

Fourth, we are witnessing an increased belief in and commitment to proactive organizational change. An increasing number of managers are rejecting the notion that "if it ain't broke, don't fix it," and instead are adopting a *bias toward action*. These managers are seriously looking for and experimenting with different approaches toward organizational management. Many of the popular books provide managers with the insights into new and different ways of managing.

In their search for the "quick fix," generations of American managers have adopted a series of organizational management concepts, such as management by objectives, job enlargement, job enrichment, flextime, and a variety of labor-management participative schemes (such as quality circles and quality of work-life programs).[3] Each has been widely heralded, frequently implemented, and sometimes later abandoned and replaced by another emerging management technique. As a consequence of this managerial tendency to embrace ideas and then soon discard them, many viable managerial techniques have received a tarnished image. For example, many of the Japanese participative management systems that are being copied by American managers today found their way into the garbage cans of an earlier generation of American managers. With the demand for quick fixes, there is a ready market for new, reborn, and revitalized management ideas. We encourage you to read and seriously reflect on the probability of finding a legitimate quick fix. The search for solutions to major organizational problems in terms of "one-minute" answers reflects a Band-Aid® approach to management, one that is condemned in a couple hundred pages by us and destined to ultimate failure.

We alert you to this managerial tendency to look for "new" solutions to current organizational problems. The rush to resolve problems and take advantage of opportunities frequently leads to the search for simple remedies for complex organizational problems. Yet very few of today's organizational problems can be solved with any single approach. High-involvement management, the learning organization, and corporate culture advocated in today's generation of popular management books may also join the list of tried-and-abandoned solutions to organizational woes. We especially hope that the quick fix approach to organizational problem solving that characterizes the management style of many will not be promoted as a result of this mosaic (i.e., *The Manager's Bookshelf*) of today's popular business books.

RATIONALE FOR THIS BOOK

The business world has been buzzing with reference to terms like *vision, paradigms, stewardship*, the *learning organization*, the *spirit of work* and the *soul of business, transformational and charismatic leaders, knowledge management, high-involvement management and organizations*, and *corporate cultures*. On the negative side, these new terms feed the management world's preoccupation with quick fixes and the perpetuation of management fads. On the positive side, many of these concepts serve as catalysts to the further development of sound management philosophies and practices.

In earlier decades a few books occasionally entered the limelight (e.g., *Parkinson's Law, The Peter Principle, My Years with General Motors, The Money Game*), but for the most part they did not generate the widespread and prolonged popularity of the current generation of the business books. Then, too, many were not written in the readable style that makes most contemporary books so easy to consume.

Managers find the current wave of books not only interesting but enjoyable to read. A small survey conducted by the Center for Creative Leadership found that a significant number of managers who participated in a study of their all-around reading selections chose one or more *management* books as their favorite. Of the 179 business or management books identified in total, *In Search of Excellence* accounted for more than half of the books that were read by managers.[4] In essence, many of the popular management books *are* being read by managers—probably because the books are often supportive of their present management philosophies! Many managers report that these books are insightful, interestingly presented, and seemingly practical. Whether or not the prescriptions in these books have had (or ever will have) a real and lasting impact on the effective management of organizations remains to be determined.

Despite best-sellers' overall popularity, some managers do not read any current management books, and many other managers have read only a limited number or small parts of a few.* Similarly, many university students studying management have heard about some of these books but have not read them. *The Manager's Bookshelf: A Mosaic of Contemporary Views* presents perspectives from (but not a criticism of) a number of those popular management books. The book is designed for managers who are interested in the books but do not have time to read them in their entirety and for students of management who want to be well informed as they prepare for entry into the work world. Reading about the views expressed in many of the best-sellers will expand the knowledge of both groups and enable them to engage in meaningful conversations with their managerial colleagues.

Although reading the 45 summaries provided here can serve as a useful introduction to this literature, they should *not* be viewed as a substitute for immersion in the original material, nor do they remove the need for further reading of the more substantive management books and professional journals. The good news is that the popularity of these books suggests that millions of managers are reading them and they are exhibiting an interest in learning about what has worked for other managers and firms. This is an important step toward the development of an open system paradigm for themselves and for their organizations.

We strongly advocate that both managers and students be informed organizational citizens. Therefore, we believe it is important for you to know and understand what is being written about organizations and management. We also believe that it is important for you to know what is being read by the managers who surround you, some of which is contained in best-sellers, much of which is contained in more traditional management books, as well as in professional and scientific journals.[5]

---

*For a discussion on incorporating these types of management books into management training programs, see J. W. Newstrom and J. L. Pierce, "The Potential Role of Popular Business Books in Management Development Programs," *Journal of Management Development*, 8 (2, 1989) 13–24.

CONTENTS OF THE BEST-SELLERS

What topics do these best-selling books cover, what is their form, and what is their merit? Although many authors cover a wide range of topics and others do not have a clear focus, most fall into several categories. Some attempt to describe the more successful and unsuccessful companies and identify what made them successes or failures. Others focus on "micro" issues in leadership, motivation, or ethics. And yet others turn their attention toward broad questions of corporate strategy and competitive tactics for implementing strategy. Some focus on pressing issues facing the contemporary organization such as social responsibility, globalism, workforce diversity, and the "virtual workplace."

In terms of form, many contain apparently simple answers and trite prescriptions. Others are built around literally hundreds of spellbinding anecdotes and stories. Some have used interviews of executives as their source of information, and others have adopted the parable format for getting their point across. As a group their presentation style is rich in diversity.

Judging the merits of best-sellers is a difficult task (and one that we will leave for readers and management critics to engage in). Some critics have taken the extreme position of calling these books "intellectual wallpaper" and "business pornography." Certainly labels like this, justified or not, should caution readers. A better perspective is provided by an assessment of the sources, often anecdotal, of many of the books. In other words, much of the information in best-sellers stems from the experiences and observations of a single individual and is often infused with the subjective opinions of that writer. Unlike the more traditional academic literature, these books do not all share a sound scientific foundation. Requirements pertaining to objectivity, reproducibility of observations, and tests for reliability and validity have not guided the creation of much of the material. As a consequence, the authors are at liberty to say whatever they want (and often with as much passion as they desire).

Unlike authors who publish research-based knowledge, authors of best-sellers do not need to submit their work to a panel of reviewers who then critically evaluate the ideas, logic, and data. The authors of these popular management books are able to proclaim as sound management principles virtually anything that is intuitively acceptable to their publisher and readers. Therefore, *readers need to be cautious consumers.* The ideas presented in these books need to be critically compared with the well-established thoughts from more traditional sources of managerial wisdom.

CRITIQUING THESE POPULAR BOOKS

Although the notion of one-minute management is seductive, Jim Renier, former chief executive officer (CEO) of Honeywell, notes that "there are no fast-acting cures for what ails business." Recognizing that simple solutions are not likely to be found and that the best-sellers frequently present (or appear to present) quick fixes and simple solutions, we strongly encourage readers to read these popular books, looking less for simple solutions and more toward using them to stimulate their thinking and challenge the way they go about doing their business. We encourage you to not only achieve comprehension and understanding, but to ultimately arrive at the level of critique and synthesis.

To help you approach these works more critically, we encourage you to use the following questions to guide your evaluation[6]:

- **Author credentials:**

  How do the authors' background and characteristics uniquely qualify them to write this book? What relevant experience do they have? What unique access or perspective do they have? What prior writing experience do they have, and how was it accepted by others? What is their research background (capacity to design, conduct, and interpret the results of their observations)?

- **Rationale:**

  Why did the authors write the book? Is their reason legitimate?

- **Face validity:**

  On initial examination of the book's major characteristics and themes, do you react positively or negatively? Are you inclined to accept or reject the author's conclusions? Does it fit with your prior experience and expectations, or does it rock them to the core?

- **Target audience:**

  For whom is this book uniquely written? What level of managers in the organizational hierarchy would most benefit from reading the book and why?

- **Integration of existing knowledge:**

  A field of inquiry can move forward only if it draws on and extends existing knowledge. Was this book written in isolation of existing knowledge? Do the authors demonstrate an awareness of and build upon existing knowledge?

- **Readability/interest:**

  Do the authors engage your mind? Are there relevant, practical illustrations that indicate how the ideas have been or could be applied?

- **Internal validity:**

  To what degree do the authors provide substantive evidence that the phenomenon, practice, or ideas presented actually produce a valued result? Is there an internally consistent presentation of ideas that demonstrates the processes through which causes for their observations are understood?

■ Reliability:
To what degree do the author's conclusions converge with other sources of information or methods of data collection?

■ Distinctiveness:
Is the material presented new, creative, and distinctive, or is it merely a presentation of "old wine in new bottles"?

■ Objectivity:
To what extent do the authors have a self-serving or political agenda, or have the authors presented information that was systematically gathered and evaluated? Have the authors offered both the pros and cons of their views?

■ External validity:
Will the ideas work in my unique situation, or are they bound to the context within which the authors operate?

■ Practicality:
Are the ideas adaptable? Do the authors provide suggestions for application? Are the ideas readily transferable to the workplace in such a way that the typical reader could be expected to know what to do with them a few days later at work?

These are only some of the questions that should be asked as you read and evaluate any popular management book.

NATURE OF THIS BOOK

This is the fifth edition of *The Manager's Bookshelf*. The first edition was published in 1988. Recent editions have appeared in Italian and Chinese, pointing to the international popularity of these books. The fifth edition includes many books that were not previously summarized, representing a substantial revision. *The Manager's Bookshelf* provides a comprehensive introduction to many of the major best-sellers in the management field during recent years.

Some authors have achieved such a level of market success with their first book that they have been driven to follow up their earlier success with one or more additional books. In response to this trend, this edition of *The Manager's Bookshelf* includes summaries of multiple books written by the same author. This feature provides readers with a deeper and richer understanding of the range of perspectives a single author has, as well as changes in their views of appropriate managerial practices across time.

The selections contained in this book are of two types: excerpts of original material and summaries prepared by a panel of reviewers. In some cases, we provide the reader with not only the main ideas presented by the author of a best-seller, but also the flavor (style or nature) of the author's approach. For some selections, we obtained permission to excerpt directly a chapter from the original book, particularly chapters that are the keystone presentation of the author's major theme. In other cases, the author's original thoughts and words were captured by selecting an article (representing part of the book) that the author had written for publication in a professional journal. Here again, the reader will see the author's ideas directly, though only sampled or much condensed from the original source.

The other major format chosen for inclusion is a comprehensive summary of the best-seller prepared by persons selected for their relevant expertise, interest, and familiarity. These summaries are primarily descriptive, designed to provide readers with an overall understanding of the book. These summaries are not judgemental in nature, nor are they necessarily a complete or precise reflection of the authors' management philosophy.

Determining what constituted a best-seller worthy of inclusion was easy in some cases and more difficult in others. From the hundreds of books available for selection, the ones included here rated highly on one or more of these criteria:

1. *Market acceptance*: Several books have achieved national notoriety by selling hundreds of thousands, and occasionally millions, of copies.
2. *Provocativeness*: Some books present thought-provoking viewpoints that run counter to "traditional" management thought.
3. *Distinctiveness*: A wide variety of topical themes of interest to organizational managers are presented.
4. *Representativeness*: In an attempt to avoid duplication from books with similar content within a topical area, many popular books were excluded.
5. *Author reputation*: Some authors (e.g., Peter Drucker, Edward Lawler III) have a strong reputation for the quality of their thinking and the insights they have historically generated, and therefore, some of their newer products were included.

AUTHORS OF THE BEST-SELLERS

It is appropriate for a reader to inquire of a best-seller, "Who is the author of this book?" Certainly the authors come from varied backgrounds. Some have previously developed a respected academic and professional record and have subsequently integrated their thoughts into book form. Others have spent their entire careers working in a single organization and now share their reflections from that experience base.

Some of the authors have been described as self-serving egotists who have little to say constructively about management, but who say it with a flair and passion such that reading their books may be very exciting. Some books are seemingly the product of armchair humorists who set out to entertain their readers with tongue in check. Other books on the best-seller lists have been written with the aid of a ghost writer (i.e., by someone who takes information that has been provided by another and then converts it into the lead author's story). In summary, it may be fascinating to read the "inside story" as told by the CEO of a major airline or oil conglomerate, but the reader still has the opportunity and obligation to challenge the author's credentials for making broad generalizations from that experience base.

CONCLUSIONS

We encourage you to read and reflect on this collection of thoughts from the authors of today's generation of management books. We invite you to expand and enrich your insights into management as a result of learning from this set of popular books. We challenge you to question and debate the pros and cons of the ideas and philosophies that are presented by these authors. We hope you will ask when, where, how, and why these ideas are applicable. Examine the set of readings provided here, let them stimulate your thinking, and, in the process, learn something new. You'll find that learning can be fun and addictive!

Notes

1. Frank Freeman, "Books That Mean Business: The Management Best Sellers," *Academy of Management Review*, 1985, 345–350.
2. Dan Carroll, "Management Principles and Management Art." Paper presented to the Academy of Management annual meeting, Chicago, August 1986.
3. "Business Fads: What's In—and Out." *Business Week* (January 20, 1986). W. W. Armstrong, "The Boss Has Read Another New Book!" *Management Review* (June 1994), 61–64.
4. Freeman, "Books That Mean Business."
5. See, for example, a report on executive reading preferences by Marilyn Wellemeyer in "Books Bosses Read," *Fortune* (April 27, 1987).
6. See John W. Newstrom and Jon L. Pierce, "An Analytic Framework for Assessing Popular Business Books," *Journal of Management Development*, 12, (4, 1993) 20–28.

READING 2

The Witch Doctors: What the Management Gurus Are Saying, Why It Matters, and How to Make Sense of It

John Micklethwait and Adrian Wooldridge
Summary prepared by Brad Jackson

> **Brad Jackson** is Senior Lecturer in the School of Business and Public
> Management at Victoria University in Wellington, New Zealand. He is
> currently completing his doctoral thesis, "The Management Guru and
> Management Fashion Phenomenon: A Dramatistic Inquiry," at the
> Management School at Lancaster University, United Kingdom. He has
> published papers on the work of three prominent management gurus:
> Stephen Covey, Michael Hammer, and Peter Senge.

The growing "management theory industry" has had, and continues to have, an enormous impact on how we live our lives. It is also a relatively immature discipline that has many contradictions and limitations. In view of the discrepancy between its significance and its underdeveloped state, it is important to gain a better understanding of how the industry that produces management theory works or does not work. *The Witch Doctors* was written to help both managers and nonmanagers pull out the good from the bad, and the relevant from the irrelevant, in management theory.

THE RISE AND RISE OF THE MANAGEMENT THEORY INDUSTRY

The management theory industry is one of the world's largest and most rapidly growing industries. Its foot soldiers are the 100,000 or so management consultants who promote new management programs and oversee their introduction into companies across all industries and sectors. In America alone the total annual bill for consulting activity tops $15 billion. Business schools have also profited from the industry in their role as intellectual gatekeepers. In addition to providing the faculty who originate much of the new management theory, they also produce the 75,000 MBAs who graduate annually

John Micklethwait and Adrian Wooldridge, *The Witch Doctors: Making Sense of the Management Gurus*.
New York, NY: Times Business, 1996.

from America's 700-plus business schools and become the ready-made consumers for the industry's products and services.

The business book remains the industry's primary unit of production. Each year 2,000 business books are released in the United States. These generate more than $750 million in revenue even before they are turned into seminars, tapes, and videos. The best-selling business book authors are accorded management guru status, which entitles them to earn up to $60,000 for a day-long seminar. Perched at the top of the management theory industry are Peter Drucker and Tom Peters. Widely recognized as the "gurus' guru," Drucker has had a formidable impact on the world as the inventor of privatization, the apostle of a new class of knowledge workers, and the champion of management as a serious intellectual discipline that is not just confined to business but to all organizations. Peters is singled out not so much for what he has said but because he has been a central figure in launching and defining the management guru boom. His phenomenal sense of timing, marketing savvy, and trend-spotting instincts have inspired managers throughout the world to question the status quo, embrace change, and thrive on chaos.

The management theory industry has grown because it speaks to two primal human instincts: fear and greed. For those wishing to get ahead, new management ideas can provide a means by which they can readily distinguish themselves from the rest of the pack. Increasingly, knowledge of management theory is being viewed as an essential prerequisite for organizational survival. Under the threat of downsizing, many managers have become dependent on the gurus to help them make sense of an increasingly complicated world and to provide guidance about what they should be doing as managers.

Because of this dependence, the management theory industry has tended to drive management rather than being driven by it. Specifically, it has been responsible for driving three revolutions that have had far-reaching effects in the workplace: the reinvention of companies, the reinvention of careers, and the reinvention of government. Despite its significance, management theory remains widely disrespected for the following reasons:

- It is seemingly incapable of self-criticism. There is a tremendous vested interest in hyping the gurus and their wares, and almost nobody is criticizing them.
- Management theory uses language that is confusing and riddled with jargon. It seems designed more to impress than to inform.
- It rarely rises above common sense. Management gurus tend to predict a future that has already arrived. Although there is nothing wrong with stating the obvious, the industry should not promise more than it can necessarily deliver.
- Management theory is remarkably faddish. The increasingly short attention span of its consumers coupled with the built-in obsolescence of its ideas means that the typical life cycle of a new management idea currently lasts only a year, compared with a decade 30 years ago.
- The advice that management gurus give frequently pulls organizations and the individuals that work within them in conflicting directions. This has invariably led to increased frustration and worsening of morale.

THE GREAT DEBATES IN MANAGEMENT

Designing the New Company

A growing band of management thinkers has encouraged companies to transform from a corporate model based on control to one based on entrepreneurialism. The much-copied command and control model that was originally articulated by Alfred Sloan, the legendary president of General Motors, has disintegrated in the face of increased uncertainty and the need for timeliness and flexibility. The new horizontal corporate model is built on core competencies defined by Gary Hamel and C. K. Prahalad as the skills and capabilities that give a company its unique flavor, which cannot be easily imitated by a rival. The company also needs to continually pursue a process of renewal by designing the organization to encourage entrepreneurialism and networking. The structureless company is held together by culture, the intangible quality that allows managers and workers to trust each other and work productively together. Despite its obvious appeal, the new model is by no means free of problems. First, it places a great deal of importance on the presence of a charismatic leader. Second, these complex organizational forms are exceedingly difficult to manage effectively. Third, the shift from formal to informal management structures exposes the company to substantial financial risk as it loses its basic ability to control employees and their decisions.

Integrating Knowledge, Learning, and Innovation

Popular management theorists such as Peter Senge and Ikujiro Nonaka have done a great deal to promote *learning* and *knowledge* as important buzzwords associated with corporate success. The new emphasis on learning, knowledge, and innovation has challenged managers to create organizations that not only actively foster the dissemination and sharing of learning but also attract and retain knowledge workers who are critical to wealth generation. Recognizing their importance and worth, knowledge workers are dictating the terms of their employment, which includes being treated with respect and being given opportunities to continue to develop and, thereby, become even more marketable. Many organizations are developing innovative free agent contracts to accommodate these needs. The critical management challenge must, therefore, be finding ways to produce and disseminate knowledge while leaving employees in no doubt where the real power resides.

Making Strategy Work

Management guru Henry Mintzberg has been at the vanguard of management opinion that actively discredits strategic planning. Although elegant in theory, strategic planning rarely leads to strategic thinking, let alone strategic practice. It has in many companies degenerated into an annual corporate ritual that amounts to little more than a numbers game. Because it relies to a great extent on projecting current practices into the future, strategic planning is inevitably conservative and reactive. Management theorists have recast strategy as "vision," which provides a company with a sense of mission without entailing the costs and constraints of central planning. The most influential of these, Gary Hamel and C. K. Prahalad, insist that organizations should have the strategic architecture in place that will allow for 'stretch' (i.e., trying for huge gains without telling people how to get there) and is based on a clear and widely held understanding of the company's core competencies. This new approach to strategy is epitomized by Jack Welch's "Work-Out" program at General Electric. When all is said and done, strategy is essentially about gambling on the future. Visions, no less than plans, are only as good as those who make them.

Improving Corporate Governance

The latest management fashions have made the job of leading organizations even more challenging and the presence of good leadership even more critical to corporate success. In general, management books on leadership have not been that helpful as they suggest either that leadership can be readily learned or it is so esoteric and instinctive that only those who are born with it can lead. Books written by those who have actually led, such as Bill Gates, Mark McCormack, and Rupert Murdoch, have done little to help because they rarely connect their ideas with management theory. The general separation of theory from practice is yet further evidence of the relative immaturity of management theory. The leadership issue is being brought to the fore by shareholder activists who are concerned about escalating executive compensation, the closed-door nature of decisions about succession, and the lack of representation of key stakeholder interests in board membership. Several writers, most notably Charles Handy, have argued that shareholder capitalism should be replaced by the kind of stakeholder capitalism that is found in countries like Germany. Within the stakeholder model, corporations are made to become more accountable to all of the groups that they depend upon for their continued wealth (i.e., employees, customers, and the general public). The authors believe that, rather than throw out shareholder capitalism, it should become more contestable so that shareholders are given the authority to change managers who are not doing a good job.

The Future of Work

Writers like Jeremy Rifkin and William Bridges have somewhat gloomily predicted the end of jobs and a future of mass unemployment. Although some aspects of the transition to a knowledge society have been painful, jobs are not so much coming to an end as they are changing. They are different in that many more workers are being contracted by smaller organizations on a temporary basis, and much of the work is conducted in the home. Within larger organizations, the flattened hierarchy offers fewer avenues for vertical advancement. Individuals are, therefore, moving laterally rather than vertically within and between organizations. During the 1980s, the middle manager became the scapegoat of many management gurus—cast as the primary obstacle in the way of organizational transformation. In the mid-1990s, however, there has been a growing realization that they bring an important "mid-level" perspective and strategy translation role to a company's work. There is also considerable debate about whether the new work culture liberates or enslaves the working man or woman. Critics point to the growing gap between the "haves" and "have-nots," the chronic overwork of the "haves," and the lack of loyalty shown by employees to their employers. Management theorists suggest that a new moral compact has to be developed between employers and employees which encompasses incentive-based pay, opportunities to learn, and greater involvement in running the company.

EXTENDING THE REACH OF MANAGEMENT THEORY

The Global Market for Management Theory

The management theory industry has always been primarily a business that is made and sold in America. Almost all of the leading management gurus are American, and most of the demand emanates from North American business. More recently, the industry has spread into Western Europe, the former Soviet bloc, and Asia. Much of the original impetus for the rapid growth in the industry came from the phenomenal success that Japanese companies were achieving in the early 1980s. The Western world, and the United States in particular, became anxious to learn the secrets of lean production, supply-chain management, consensus, and *kaizen* that made Japan so successful. By the mid-1990s, however, the prevailing wisdom suggested that Western companies had learned everything they needed to know about Japanese management, and it was time now for the Japanese to learn from the West. There are signs that a growing number of younger managers in Japan are starting to embrace Western management thinkers so that Western-style assessment procedures are creeping into big Japanese firms and jobs are not as safe as they once were. Japan still has something to teach the West, especially in the areas of cost cutting and managing knowledge, however.

The developing economies of countries of Asia also have management ideas of their own, which will have a powerful effect upon management theory. The "bamboo network" of family businesses created by Chinese businesspeople at home and abroad presents an intriguing alternative model of organization. This model is a loose entrepreneurial network based on trust and led by the head of the family. Although the Chinese have had only limited success outside of Asia, they are beginning to mix Asian and Western ideas to create something new and exciting. Taiwan's leading computer manufacturer, Acer, provides a remarkable illustration of what can be achieved by institutionalizing speed, entrepreneurialism, and networking into a meritocratic system.

Reinventing Government

Political leaders throughout the Western world, most notably Bill Clinton and Tony Blair, have shown a great deal of enthusiasm for applying management theory to the public sector. Because of this enthusiasm, management fashions such as total quality management, reengineering, benchmarking, and customer service have been introduced into all spheres of public administration, generating considerable business for the major consulting firms in the process. The newfound obsession with management theory is being driven by three concerns. The first is a crisis of faith in the public sector and a resurgence of faith in the private sector. Liberals, in particular, have been the most passionate supporters because they view it as a means for salvaging government. The second concern emerges from a general desire to "do more with less." A third concern is rooted in the desire to be seen as being up with the times. Very few gurus have taken an interest in developing theory that can be applied specifically to the public sector. Gurus like Michael Porter and Rosabeth Moss Kanter have taken a high level look at the relationship between public policy and international competitiveness. The onus for translating these and other private sector-based ideas has been placed on public sector administrators with mixed results. The National Health Service in the United Kingdom is an example of an organization that has benefited from the internal market concept that was originated by an American consultant, Alain Enthoven. The BBC, on the other hand, most certainly has not. Those who criticize the application of management theory to the public sector argue that government and management are two entirely different activities. The former is essentially a political activity designed to serve citizens. The latter is an economic activity that serves customers. Moreover, governments have tended to apply management theory wholesale without properly understanding the specific contexts of the organizations that they are seeking to change. They have proven to be just as faddish as their corporate counterparts.

Reinventing the Self

A new breed of management gurus is directing its attention toward improving the individual within the organization rather than the organization itself. The best known of these, Stephen Covey, argues that by developing personal character and trust, organizations will improve because they will be staffed by better people. Other gurus, like Anthony Robbins and Edward de Bono, have also garnered impressive worldwide followings with a similar self-help message. Companies are beginning to show a real interest in "new age" philosophies prompted by a desire to promote spirituality in the workplace. Much of this interest has been expressed by members of the generation who came of age during the 1960s and are now occupying senior positions in business, consultancy, and academia. Recognizing the demoralizing effect that reengineering and downsizing has had upon employee morale, this new breed of leader is attempting to restore harmony by sending their workers on a spiritual quest. This spiritual turn poses two main problems for management theory. First, when management theory explores remote intellectual terrain like this, it seems to lose the little structure and coherence that it had in the first place. Second, these fringe areas tend to rely even more upon marketing as opposed to substance for their legitimacy than the traditional mainstream of management theory.

CHOOSING THE RIGHT WITCH DOCTOR

Management theory has extracted some important lessons that have been learned by a few companies and has disseminated them widely. The continuously experimenting laboratories of companies like Motorola, Merck, and 3M are providing broadly positive results, from which many other companies are benefiting. The management theory industry will continue to thrive and prosper because its clients are still looking for answers. Despite its successes and progress, management theory continues to be plagued by persistent problems. It is still a relatively immature discipline that attracts more than its fair share of charlatans looking to make a quick buck by pouring old wine into new bottles. In the face of frequent disappointment, its audience continues to demand and expect management solutions that are instant and all-encompassing.

The following weaknesses need to be resolved before management theory can join the ranks of the more mature and respected disciplines:

1. The contradictory nature of management theory pulls corporations in conflicting directions. This problem has been further compounded by the tendency on the part of many managers to pay lip service to theories without really understanding them.
2. Management theorists use language that is sloppy, fuzzy, and convoluted. The worth of a good theory should be judged by what it achieves in practice, not on the novelty and elegance of its language.
3. Management theory is insensitive to the wider effects of its work. Most gurus appear to be oblivious to the fact that businesses are social and political communities with their own distinctive mores, power struggles, and social dynamics.
4. Management gurus have predicted a future of chaos and uncertainty that their own work has only made more likely. Because of their enormous influence, much of what they say becomes self-fulfilling prophecy.

In view of these weaknesses, it is crucial that managers should strive to become selective and critical consumers of the products and services offered by the management theory industry. In particular, they should bear in mind this advice when making purchase decisions:

1. Anything that you suspect is bunk almost certainly is.
2. Beware of authors who aggrandize themselves more than their work and who argue almost exclusively by analogy.
3. Be selective. No one management theory will cure all ills. Bear in mind that the cure can sometimes be worse than the disease.
4. Consult the business press to get an informed and critical perspective on new management theories and their proponents.

READING 3

Reflections on the Best-Sellers: A Cautionary Note

Jon L. Pierce and John W. Newstrom, with Larry L. Cummings

This opening section provides our reflections upon management (both the body of knowledge and its practice), as well as upon the wave of management books that have almost become an institutionalized part of the popular press. We hope it will provide some helpful perspectives and point you in some new directions.

Management can be defined as the skillful application of a body of knowledge to a particular organizational situation. This definition suggests to us that management is an art form as well as a science. That is, there is a body of knowledge that has to be applied with the fine touch and instinctive sense of the master artist. Execution of the management role and performance of the managerial functions are more complex than the simple application of a few management concepts. The development of effective management, therefore, requires the development of an in-depth understanding of organizational and management concepts, as well as the capacity to grasp when and how to apply this knowledge.

The organizational arena presents today's manager with a number of challenges. The past few decades have been marked by a rapid growth of knowledge about organizations and management systems. As a consequence of this growth in management information, we strongly believe that it is important for today's manager to engage in *lifelong learning*, by continually remaining a student of management. It is also clear to us that our understanding of organizations and management systems is still in the early stages of development. That is, there remain many unanswered questions that pertain to the effective management of organizations.

Many observers of the perils facing today's organizations have charged that the crises facing American organizations are largely a function of "bad management." Similarly, Tom Peters and Bob Waterman have observed that the growth of our society during the earlier part of this century was so rapid that almost any management approach appeared to work and work well. The real test of effective management systems did not appear until the recent decades, when competitive, economic, political, and social pressures created a form of environmental turbulence that pushed existing managerial tactics beyond their limits. Not only are students of management challenged to learn about effective management principles, but they are also confronted with the need to develop the skills and intuitive sense to apply that management knowledge.

Fortunately, there are many organizations in our society from which they can learn, and there is a wealth of knowledge that has been created that focuses on effective organizational management. There are at least two literatures that provide rich opportunities for regular reading. First, there is the traditional management literature found in management and organization textbooks and academic journals (e.g., *Academy of Management Journal, Administrative Science Quarterly, Harvard Business Review, Managerial Psychology, Research in Organizational Behavior*, and *California Management Review*). Second, this past decade has seen the emergence of a nontraditional management literature written by management practitioners and management consultants who describe their organizational experiences and provide a number of other management themes. Knowledge about effective and ineffective management systems can be gleaned by listening to the management scholar, philosopher, and practitioner.

Since not all that is published in the academic journals or in the popular press meets combined tests of scientific rigor and practicality, it is important that motivated readers immerse themselves in *both* of these literatures. Yet, neither source should be approached and subsequently consumed without engaging in critical thinking.

CRITICAL THINKING AND CAUTIOUS CONSUMPTION

We believe that the ideas promoted in these best-sellers should not be blindly integrated into any organization. Each should be subjected to careful scrutiny in order to identify its inherent strengths and weaknesses; each should be examined within the context of the unique organizational setting in which it may be implemented; and modifications and fine-tuning of the technique may be required in order to tailor it to a specific organizational setting and management philosophy. Finally, the process that is used to implement the management technique may be as important to its success as the technique itself.

This is an era of an information-knowledge explosion. Perhaps consumers of that information need to be reminded of the relevance of the saying *caveat emptor* (let the buyer beware) from the product domain, because there are both good and questionable informational products on the market. Fortunately, advisory services like *Consumer Reports* exist to advise us on the consumption of consumer goods. There is, however, no similar guide for our consumption of information in the pop-management press. Just because something has been a best-seller or widely promoted does not mean that the information contained therein is worthy of direct consumption. It may be a best-seller because it presents an optimistic message, it is enjoyable reading, or because it has been successfully marketed to the public.

The information in all management literature should be approached with caution; it should be examined and questioned. The pop-management literature should not be substituted for more scientific-based knowledge about effective management. In addition, this knowledge should be compared and contrasted with what we know about organizations and management systems from other sources—the opinions of other experts, the academic management literature, and our own prior organizational experiences.

We invite you to question this literature. In the process there are a myriad of questions that should be asked. For example, consider the following: What are the author's credentials, and are they relevant to the book? Has the author remained an objective observer of the reported events? Why did the author write this book? What kind of information is being presented (e.g., opinion, values, facts)? Does this information make sense when it is placed into previously developed theories (e.g., from a historical context)? Could I take this information and apply it to another situation at a different point in time and in a different place, or was it unique to the author's experience? These and similar questions should be part of the information screening process.

INTERVIEW WITH PROFESSOR L. L. CUMMINGS*

As we became increasingly familiar with the best-sellers through our roles as editors, we found ourselves asking a number of questions about this type of literature.

As a part of our reflection upon the currently popular literature, we talked with a distinguished management scholar, organization and management consultant, and educator of MBA and doctoral students, Professor L. L. Cummings. Following are excerpts from that interview.

Question to Professor Cummings   We have witnessed an explosion in the number and type of books that have been written on management and organizations for the trade market. Many of these books have found themselves on the best-sellers list. What, in your opinion, has been the impact of these publications? What is the nature of their contribution?

Answer   Quite frankly, I think these books have made a number of subtle contributions, most of which have not been labeled or identified by either the business press or the academic press. In addition, many of their contributions have been misappropriately or inaccurately labeled.

Permit me to elaborate. I think it is generally true that a number of these very popular "best-seller list" books, as you put it, have been thought to be reasonably accurate translations or interpretations of successful organizational practice. Although this is not the way that these books have been reviewed in the academic press, my interactions with managers, business practitioners, and MBA students reveal that many of these books are viewed as describing organizational structure, practices, and cultures that are thought to contribute to excellence.

On the other hand, when I evaluate the books myself and when I pay careful attention to the reviews by respected, well-trained, balanced academicians, it is my opinion that these books offer very little, if anything, in the way of *generalizable* knowledge about successful organizational practice. As organizational case studies,

---

*At the time of this interview and prior to his death, Larry L. Cummings was the Carlson Professor of Management in the Carlson School of Management at the University of Minnesota. Formerly, he served as the J. L. Kellogg Distinguished Research Professor of Organizational Behavior at Northwestern University and was the Slichter Research Professor, the H. I. Romnes Faculty Fellow, and Director of the Center for the Study of Organizational Performance in the Graduate School of Business, University of Wisconsin, Madison. In addition, he also taught at Columbia University, Indiana University, and the University of British Columbia. Professor Cummings published more than 80 journal articles and authored, coauthored, or edited 16 books. In addition, he was an active member of several professional associations (e.g., Academy of Management, American Psychological Association, American Institute for Decision Sciences). He served as the editor of the *Academy of Management Journal*, a member of the Academy's Board of Governors, and president of the same association. Dr. Cummings served as a consultant for several national and international corporations including Cummings Engine, Dow Chemical, Eli Lilly, Prudential, Samsonite, Touche-Ross, and Moore Business Forms.

they are the most dangerous of the lot, in that the data (information) presented has not been systematically, carefully, and cautiously collected and interpreted. Of course, that criticism is common for case studies. Cases were never meant to be contributions to scientific knowledge. Even the best ones are primarily pedagogical aids.

The reason I describe the cases presented in books like *When Giants Learn to Dance* and *In Search of Excellence* as frequently among the most dangerous is because they are so well done (i.e., in a marketing and journalistic sense), and therefore, they are easily read and so believable. They are likely to influence the naive, those who consume them without critically evaluating their content. They epitomize the glamour and the action orientation, and even the machoism of American management practice; that is, they represent the epitome of competition, control, and order as dominant interpersonal and organizational values.

Rather, I think the contributions of these books, in general, have been to provide an apology, a rationale, or a positioning, if you like, of American management as something that is not *just* on the defensive with regard to other world competitors. Instead, they have highlighted American management as having many good things to offer: a sense of spirit, a sense of identification, a sense of clear caricature. This has served to fill a very important need. In American management thought there has emerged a lack of self-confidence and a lack of belief that what we are doing is proactive, effective, and correct. From this perspective these books have served a useful role in trying to present an upbeat, optimistic characterization.

Question to Professor Cummings   In addition to a large volume of sales, surveys reveal that many of these books have been purchased and presumably read by those who are managing today's organizations. Does this trouble you? More specifically, are there any concerns that you have, given the extreme popularity of these types of books?

Answer   I am of two minds with regard to this question. First, I think that the sales of these books are not an accurate reflection of the degree, the extent, or the carefulness with which they have been read. Nor do I believe that the sales volumes tell us anything about the pervasiveness of their impact. Like many popular items (fads), many of these books have been purchased for desktop dressing. In many cases, the preface, the introduction, and the conclusion (maybe the summary on the dust jacket) have been read such that the essence of the book is picked up and it can become a part of managerial and social conversation.

Obviously, this characterization does not accurately describe everyone in significant positions of management who has purchased these books. There are many managers who make sincere attempts to follow the management literature thoroughly and to evaluate it critically. I think that most of the people with whom I come in contact in management circles, both in training for management and in actual management positions, who have carefully read the books are not deceived by them. They are able to put them in the perspective of representations or characterizations of a fairly dramatic sort. As a consequence, I am not too concerned about the books being overly persuasive in some dangerous, Machiavellian, or subterranean sense.

On the other hand, I do have a concern of a different nature regarding these books. That concern focuses upon the possibility that the experiences they describe will be taken as legitimate bases or legitimate directions for the study of management processes. These books represent discourse by the method of emphasizing the extremes, in particular the extremes of success. I think a much more fruitful approach to studying and developing prescriptions for management thought and management action is to use the *method of differences* rather than the *method of extremes*.

The method of differences would require us to study the conditions that gave rise to success at Chrysler, or McDonald's, or which currently gives rise to success at Merck, or any of the other best-managed companies. However, through this method we would also contrast these companies with firms in the same industries that are not as successful. The method of contrast (differences) is likely to lead to empirical results that are much less dramatic, much less exciting, much less subject to journalistic account (i.e., they're likely to be more boring to read), but it is much more likely to lead to observations that are more generalizable across managerial situations, as well as being generative in terms of ideas for further management research.

Thus, the issue is based on the fundamental method that underlies these characterizations. My concern is not only from a methodological perspective. It also centers on our ethical and professional obligations to make sure that the knowledge we transmit does not lead people to overgeneralize. Rather, it should provide them with information that is diagnostic rather than purely prescriptive.

The method of extremes does not lead to a diagnostic frame of mind. It does not lead to a frame of mind that questions why something happened, under what conditions it happened, or under what conditions it would not happen. The method of differences is much more likely to lead to the discovery of the conditional nature of knowledge and the conditional nature of prescriptions.

Question to Professor Cummings   A CEO or middle manager is about to take a sabbatical and has on his or her agenda the reading of a number of these best-sellers. What advice would you like to offer?

Answer   Let me make the assumption that the sabbatical is for three months. My first advice would be to make an absolute public commitment to spend not more than one month of the sabbatical (i.e., not more than one-third of it) reading these best-sellers. That would be the absolute maximum! Because of the lack of generalizability and validity of much of this information, any more time than this would be poorly spent. A crash course of one month, supplemented by perhaps video and audio tapes, would be sufficient to get the manager up to the place where he or she knows basically what is in these books. At this point the manager would have a working knowledge of the material as well as be capable of carrying on a reasonable conversation about the contents of the books.

Far more important, and worthy of at least two-thirds of the time, would be reading of a different sort. Reading and study of the classics, both the intellectual and the philosophical classics, as well as the spiritual classics and historical classics, would be of significant value.

I think one of the most important disciplines for the study of management, particularly for an experienced manager on sabbatical, is the study of history—the study of the development and decline of nation states and religious empires. The manager should look at history from a strategic perspective (i.e., what things did important nations and leaders take into consideration and what did they fail to take into consideration; what were their points of vulnerability and how could that have been prevented). It seems to me that this kind of knowledge is far more likely to lead to the discovery of useful diagnostics than the knowledge that is likely to be gained from reading the best-seller list.

CONCLUSION

We hope that you have enjoyed reading the views of a management scholar (Professor Cummings) on the role of popular management books. In addition, we hope that the readings contained in the fifth edition of *The Manager's Bookshelf* will stimulate your thinking about effective and ineffective practices of management. We reiterate that there is no single universally applicable practice of management, for management is the skillful application of a body of knowledge to a particular situation. We invite you to continue expanding your understanding of new and developing management concepts. In a friendly sort of way, we challenge you to develop the skills to know when and how to apply this knowledge in the practice of management.

PART TWO
Management Paradigms

Management consultants (specifically, Tom Peters) comment that the management philosophy reflected by the notion "If it ain't broke, don't fix it," needs to be discarded if organizations are going to enter the twenty-first century as viable and competitive social systems. In its place, Peters argues, is the need for the philosophy which espouses "If it ain't broke, fix it anyway"—reasoning that, if something is working in today's highly turbulent environments, it will most likely be short-lived. In order to make this change, managers need to make a major paradigm shift. The two books summarized in this section of *The Manager's Bookshelf* focus on management paradigms and the need for managers to identify theirs, change them as needed, and work with multiple (and sometimes competing) paradigms.

Joel Barker continues his interest in paradigms and the business context with the publication of a new book *Paradigms: The Business of Discovering the Future.* A paradigm is a set of rules and regulations that establishes boundaries and tells people how to behave within the boundaries in order to be successful. Barker discusses innovation and anticipation as the keys to organizational survival in the twenty-first century. An organization's position relative to the dominant paradigms and paradigm shifts within its industry will also play a critical role. He discusses paradigm leaders—those who change the rules by shifting the paradigms—and the forces that are associated with paradigm shifts.

Joel Barker has been a teacher, advertising executive, and served as the director of the Future Studies Department of the Science Museum of Minnesota. In addition to his writing, he is a corporate consultant.

Lee G. Bolman and Terrence E. Deal's book, *Reframing Organizations: Artistry, Choice, and Leadership,* focuses on ways of becoming a more versatile manager and artistic leader. They approach these issues by focusing their attention on structure, human resources, political, and symbolic frames for bringing major leadership and organizational change.

Lee Bolman is a Lecturer on Education at the Harvard Graduate School of Education, and Terrence Deal is Professor of Education at the Peabody College at Vanderbilt University. They also serve as codirectors of the National Center for Educational Leadership.

READING I

Paradigms: The Business of Discovering the Future

Joel A. Barker
Summary prepared by Brian E. Kahlbaugh

Brian Kahlbaugh *is a manager of administration, operations, human resources, and customer relations for a Hertz car rental franchise in Duluth, Minnesota. He graduated with honors from the University of Minnesota, Duluth, with a degree in Business Administration.*

What is impossible to do in your business (field, discipline, department, division, technology, etc.) but, if it could be done, would fundamentally change it (p. 141)?

Joel Barker's quote encourages consideration of three complementary routes to success: creative thought (innovation), concern for the development of quality in ongoing business operations (excellence), and thought with regard to future opportunities and their consequences (anticipation). These three elements—innovation, excellence, and anticipation—are seen as necessary ingredients for organizational systems to move successfully into and through the twenty-first century. *Paradigms: The Business of Discovering the Future* focuses on innovation and anticipation within the key context of paradigms.

Creative thinking involves *innovation*, which is the key to gaining and maintaining a competitive advantage. Innovation is crucial for a system to survive in a constantly changing environment. Managerial attitudes and actions (their paradigms) within a system can either enhance or inhibit the ability of the system to innovate. Paradigms become a major factor affecting innovation and survival, especially when the system is confronted with rapid change.

Anticipation is founded in exploration of changing trends while keeping an eye open for possibilities arising as an outcome of change. Anticipation forces proactive thought, which seeks to prevent problems by staying ahead of them as opposed to responsive thought, which seeks to solve problems after they have arisen. An ability to accurately anticipate the future is as much, or more, artistic in nature as it is scientific. The ability to anticipate a successful direction for the future of a system based on uncertainty and lack of proof is art. The art of good anticipation is based on strategic exploration, which consists of the following elements:

Joel A. Barker, *Paradigms: The Business of Discovering the Future.* New York, NY: Harper-Collins, 1993.

- *Understanding influence* To understand what influences perception.
- *Divergent thinking* To seek more than one answer.
- *Convergent thinking* To assess all the perceived options and information and then focus and prioritize among choices.
- *Mapping* To highlight the routes that will get the system from here to the future.
- *Imaging* To picture in words, drawings, or models the results of your exploration of the future.

Good anticipation provides a system with tools to move into the future and gives the system a greater likelihood of succeeding through accelerating change.

What are paradigms? A *paradigm* can be defined as *"A set of rules and regulations (written or unwritten) that does two things: (1) establishes or defines boundaries, and (2) tells you how to behave inside the boundaries in order to be successful* (p. 32)."

For example, consider the fast-food industry. Employees in a fast-food restaurant must comply with both formal and informal rules. Formal rules may include policies and standards of operation defined by management and laws regarding cleanliness. Informal rules may include unwritten expectations regarding how customers are treated, readiness, food preparation, and how employees should interact with each other. Together, the written and unwritten rules and regulations establish the boundaries for the fast-food restaurant. Fast food will be served by the rules and methods defined. New York Strip steak and lobster served in a quiet, private atmosphere is out of bounds for a fast-food restaurant. If the food preparers, order takers at the front counter and at the drive-up window, and other employees at the restaurant comply with the established rules within the established boundaries, a lot of tasty fast food will be sold, employees will keep their jobs, and the fast-food restaurant will be successful.

A *paradigm shift* is a change to a new paradigm having new rules, boundaries, and behaviors. Consider the paradigm of the cigarette industry. How might trends in the environment, such as recent legal and public health issues and changes in the public's attitudes, affect the prosperous cigarette manufacturing industry in the future? Could a profound paradigm shift be forthcoming?

Paradigms are not exclusive to business organizations. Paradigms exist in all areas of human interaction where the interactions have established boundaries (limits placed on participants within the paradigm) and where the interactions require success-oriented behaviors of the participants within these boundaries. Any particular sport, education, marriage, business organization, or even a whole society may be considered a paradigm. The list of all possible paradigms would be endless.

Successful is a key word in the definition of paradigm. A paradigm's degree of success is measured by its ability to solve increasingly difficult problems. If a paradigm is not able to solve increasingly difficult problems, it will have short-lived success. This suggests that paradigms have an identifiable life span. Paradigms are born all the time, but the length of their life depends on their ongoing problem-solving ability. Paradigm shifts involve the birth of new paradigms and the death (or at least obsolescence) of old paradigms. As established paradigms lose their ability to solve new problems, new paradigms with the ability to solve new sets of problems need to emerge.

The long-term survival of a business is dependent on the business' ability to innovate and its ability to anticipate the future. If these activities are done well the probability increases that the business will be able to avoid or solve future problems.

WHEN DO PARADIGM SHIFTS OCCUR?

During the life span of a system, problems are encountered and solved. As more and more increasingly difficult problems are solved, the system goes through a period of success. The success convinces participants that the rules for "*doing things*" are correct, and a mindset may develop whereby participants no longer are able or allowed to solve new problems in any way other than in the ways that have, historically, proven themselves to be the "*right*" ways! Sooner or later, however, the system encounters problems that it does not solve, perhaps as a result of the established mindset. When this happens participants within the system, and others external to the system who are in some way aware of the problems, observe the unsolved problems. Both frustration and opportunity reveal themselves. The time is now ripe for change. When unsolved problems are not dealt with and start accumulating within a system, a paradigm shift is likely to occur. Someone sees the unsolved problems and goes about forming a new paradigm to take on the unsolved problem set. *The status quo becomes challenged.*

If a system is aware of where it is in this process, it can better anticipate what is ahead, and perhaps even stimulate a search for new paradigms.

WHO ARE THE PARADIGM SHIFTERS?

There are basically four types of paradigm shifters. Three of the four exist outside of, or are new to, an established system. *All* types of paradigm shifters face conflict and resistance to their ideas for change. This occurs as a result of the prevailing mindset in most systems. Because the existing paradigms have performed well and because the rules/boundaries have become so potent inside the system, suggestions for change seem unnecessary and almost insulting. Those who are resistant to suggestions for change proclaim that, "*I have done well for a long time, and I don't need you telling me anything different!*" The problem with this attitude is that it bases itself in past successes as though the ways in which the system has solved problems before are the same ways in which future problems will be solved. These individuals neglect to anticipate changing trends or new paradigms, and they will not allow themselves to acknowledge the new types of problems that will be encountered.

The first type of paradigm shifter is the "green horn." This person knows of a system only through study, not through personal experience. This person has not learned the rules/boundaries of the system through hard knocks as have those who have been working within the system for some time. The mind of the green horn has not been constricted by the established rules of the system and, therefore, is capable of perceiving problems and solutions in a fresh light.

The second type of paradigm shifter is the veteran of one system changing over to a new system. These people have become proficient in one system, and, as a result, they bring with them actual problem-solving experience that may be adapted to solve different sets of problems in the new paradigm. They also bring with them a mind not constricted by the established rules/boundaries and, therefore, can offer ideas and perspectives unique to the new system.

An important element shared by the first two types of paradigm shifters is a combination of naiveté and creativity due to a lack of familiarity with the new system. This can be a powerful resource for a system willing to tap into it.

The third type of paradigm shifter is the "maverick." These people are insiders of a system who see the unsolved problems stacking up, who know the existing rules/boundaries of the system will not provide the necessary solutions, and who challenge the existing system in an attempt to force a paradigm shift from within the system. The unique aspect of mavericks is that they are practitioners of a system but are not shackled by the system's rules/boundaries.

The fourth type involves people in scientific and technical systems. These people have a natural curiosity that motivates them to play around with unsolved problems in an attempt to come up with new solutions.

The four types of paradigm shifters are important resources for systems concerned with longevity. Their value can support both the process of innovation and the process of anticipation.

WHO FOLLOWS THE PARADIGM SHIFTERS?

The group of people who follow someone who has initiated change share important traits. Their primary traits are courage and intuition. To choose to follow someone into uncharted territories takes courage. To choose to follow a new path treaded by someone who has met resistance along the way involves intuition and trust. A new path presents unknown risk. To follow someone into a new system requires a gut feeling that the risk is worth the attempt. These people face high risk, but they also face the potential of high gain if the new paradigm (system) is successful. The followers provide energy and momentum for the new paradigm.

WHAT IS THE PARADIGM EFFECT?

When someone offers us a paradigm-enhancing innovation—one that improves upon what we are already practicing—we see that easily. But when someone offers us a paradigm-shifting innovation, we find ourselves resistant to it, because it just doesn't fit the rules we are so good at. (p. 92)

Opportunity is in the future. Changing trends provide hints about the future, but they do not provide certainty. The future and dynamic change are inevitable. Without a doubt, there will be new paradigms that seek to capitalize on the problems of the future. The rules will change. *The tendency, however, is for practitioners of an established paradigm to resist participating in new paradigms and the opportunities they present.*

Perception is shaped by the established paradigm, which limits the ability to recognize and internalize new rules that are developing with the process of changing trends. An established paradigm has been functioning for a period of time. This leads to a logical belief that things are being done right (and for the time being they are), that the rules, as they are, are sufficient for continued success. We see what has worked and stand by it. It is very difficult to argue with what has worked out well. Because of these shaped perceptions it is also very difficult to acknowledge changing rules and changing trends in the environment. It is easier to acknowledge the success of rules that have previously worked within the established paradigm and, further, to assume that those same rules will continue to be successful. For progress and long-term survival, it becomes necessary to challenge existing perceptions and realize that the future is coming, times will change and the rules will change. To take part in the future requires acceptance of new paradigms. No one stays on top forever. The paradigm effect is a process whereby we are forced to review our own perceptions, shaped by our own paradigm, and begin considering the merits of other perceptions being shaped by newly developing paradigms.

Understanding when paradigms shift, who initiates paradigm shifts, who follows into the new paradigm, and how paradigms and paradigm shifts affect the perceptions of people are key elements in anticipating future trends. These are the elements that help in a proactive approach to change.

The paradigm principles are seven fundamental generalizations about the characteristics and operation of paradigms and are presented as a part of the focus on anticipating your future and increasing your innovative capacity. The *paradigm principles* include:

1. *Paradigms are common*—They exist in all areas of society—some on a small scale and some on a large scale. All paradigms, however, provide the participants with specific understanding and specific problem-solving abilities.

2. *Paradigms are functional*—They provide rules and directions for weaving a route through complex environments. Good paradigms focus our perceptions and our resources on what is important and keep us from straying into areas that are not immediately important. They also combine talents of diverse participants into problem-solving endeavors.

3. *The paradigm effect reverses the commonsense relationship between seeing and believing*—We normally believe something when we see it. The paradigm effect forces us to see something when we believe it. Before we can change our perceptions to acknowledge the value and the inevitability of new paradigms that differ from our own, we must first come to believe in their value and their inevitability. Only then will we come to acknowledge their merit and their potential for opportunity.

4. *There is almost always more than one right answer*—By acknowledging paradigm shifts our perceptions are broadened so that we see our world from a new standpoint. This does not mean either our old perceptions or our new perceptions are the right or wrong perceptions, only that we can now see there are more ways to solve problems.

5. *Paradigms too strongly held can lead to paradigm paralysis, a terminal disease of certainty*—A paradigm achieves power through its ability to solve problems. A very powerful paradigm is one that has been successful. This leads to *paradigm paralysis*—a belief that the existing paradigm is *the* paradigm and any other alternatives are wrong. ("*This* is the way we do things around here!") The result may be that new ideas are quashed or do not even get a chance to be known. This is a dangerous place to be in, especially in times of rapid change, and may lead to obsolescence of the strongly held paradigm.

6. *Paradigm pliancy is the best strategy in turbulent times*—Greater opportunity can be recognized when practitioners of an established paradigm actively promote *paradigm pliancy*—a tolerance of suggested alternative paradigms

for solving new problem sets created by a rapidly changing environment. Practitioners of paradigm pliancy encourage and genuinely consider suggested alternative paradigms.

7. *Human beings can choose to change their paradigms*—People have a demonstrated ability to adapt to change and to survive through seemingly overwhelming obstacles. It oftentimes is an arduous process and would not be possible without our determination to prevail. This determination forces us, as a whole, to *choose* to find new ways of solving problems. Not everyone makes this choice, and not everyone will prevail through rapid change by holding on to existing paradigms. We do, however, have the options of leading, or following, into new paradigms, taking with us our skills and abilities developed in our existing paradigms.

The future is coming. What are we going to do with it, what kind of problems will it present, and what can we do now to ready ourselves? The answers lie in our understanding and use of paradigms.

READING 2

Reframing Organizations: Artistry, Choice, and Leadership

Lee G. Bolman and Terrence E. Deal
Summary prepared by Robert Marx

Robert Marx *is a Professor of Management at the University of Massachusetts at Amherst. He is the coauthor of* Management Live! The Video Book. *Marx was the 1991 recipient of the Bradford Outstanding Educator Award from the Organizational Behavior Teaching Society in recognition of his excellence in teaching.*

THE POWER OF REFRAMING

In this century, our society has evolved from a simple, local lifestyle where people could manage their own affairs to a global, technologically sophisticated world dominated by large, complex organizations. These new organizations have proliferated because they have been enormously successful at producing a wide range of goods and services, including better health care, education, and communication linkages. Yet, for all their successes, there are flaws in these large companies and government organizations.

Indifferent salespersons, meaningless work, contradictory and unethical policies, and shoddy products represent the price paid for creating these unwieldy groups of people that comprise organizations. Despite the best efforts to improve these organizations through new management techniques, the use of consultants, and government interventions, organizations still do more of the same, handling problems the "only way"[1] they could be handled. *Managers and leaders must be able to expand their repertoire of ideas to handle the complex problems of organizations.* They must be able to "reframe" their thinking.

THE FOUR FRAMES

"The truly effective leader will need multiple tools, the skill to use each of them, and the wisdom to match frames to situations."[2]

Based on insights from research and experience working with many organizations and managers, four perspectives or frames have emerged. Each frame views the world from a particular set of values and basic assumptions. They are:

Lee G. Bolman and Terrence E. Deal, *Reframing Organizations: Artistry, Choice, and Leadership*. San Francisco, CA: Jossey-Bass, 1991.

The Structural Frame

Based on rational systems theory, the structural frame emphasizes the rational aspect of organizational life. The organization is viewed as a machine whose parts must be run and maintained efficiently. Organizations create structures to fit their environment and technology. Formal roles, clear rules, and responsibilities are necessary for efficient functioning. When problems arise, reorganizing is the primary method for restoring equilibrium.

The Human Resources Frame

Based on theories of human behavior from the psychological sciences, the human resources frame views the organization as a family. People are the heart of the organization and they have needs and feelings which must be understood and addressed. There must be a good fit between the organization's structure and the needs of its people. That is, people must be able to get the job done and feel good about what they're doing. When problems arise, communication and support are required.

The Political Frame

Based on theories of power, the political frame sees the organization as a jungle where different interest groups compete for scarce resources. Conflict is a part of everyday life in organizations because each interest group has its own agenda. Effective managers must understand how to build power bases and coalitions and manage conflict as productively as possible. When problems arise, power may be concentrated in the wrong places and negotiating may be required.

The Symbolic Frame

Based on anthropological theory, the symbolic frame emphasizes the meaning of organizational activity. It views the organization as a theater, in which stories, rituals, and myths make up a culture which helps to give employees a sense of shared values and mission. The symbolic frame considers the importance of history and tradition in building a strong culture that employees can believe in. Problems may develop when symbols lose their meaning. The culture may be improved by developing meaningful rituals, traditions, and visions.

Taken one by one, each frame offers its own perspective on a problem and each frame provides a set of ideas and techniques that managers can employ in order to enhance organizational efficiency and effectiveness. For example, an executive trying to reduce turnover among middle managers might receive the following suggestions from consultants representing each of the four frames:

"As your firm has grown, managers' responsibilities have probably become blurred and overlapping. When reporting relationships are confused, you get stress and conflict. You need to restructure." (Structural)

"You are probably neglecting your managers' needs for autonomy and for opportunities to participate in important decisions. You need an attitude survey to pinpoint the problems." (Human Resource)

"Your real problem is that you have been ignoring the realities of organizational politics. The union has too much power and top management has too little. No one knows how to deal with conflict. There's turf protection everywhere. You have to bring politics out of the closet and get people to negotiate." (Political)

"Your company has never developed a strong value system, and growth has made the situation worse. Your managers don't find any meaning in their work. You need to revitalize your company's culture." (Symbolic)[3]

Each of these suggestions is based on a different frame and would result in very different courses of action. However, managers who adhere too tightly to one frame that is most consistent with their professional training or personal values are *unnecessarily limiting themselves to a single tool for solving organizational problems* that are complex, changing, and ambiguous.

Some problems in organizations have little to do with rational and quantitative analysis, but are caused by poor interpersonal communication. Other problems are essentially based on a cloudy picture of the organization's mission and values and have little to do with power and influence. All managers must develop self-awareness of their prevailing frames and their blind spots, and they must develop the ability to view complex organizational activities through *each of the four frames* from a multiple perspectives point of view. Managers must be able to think and act in more than one way and to ask new questions that will reveal creative possibilities for effective action.

GETTING ORGANIZED: THE STRUCTURAL FRAME

The structural frame inquires about the best way to structure the organization given the goals that it is pursuing. This frame is based upon the work of Frederick Taylor and a German sociologist, Max Weber. Taylor introduced time and motion studies as a way to determine scientifically the most efficient way for a laborer to complete a task. Weber introduced the concept of bureaucracy as a rational approach to structuring organizations.

McDonald's and Harvard University are both highly successful organizations, yet each has a radically different structure that is designed to fit its circumstances. All organizations, for example, have goals, boundaries, levels of authority, and procedures, yet they differ widely on how these structural characteristics appear.

McDonald's is highly centralized. Most decisions are made at the top and efforts are made to ensure conformity, so that a "Big Mac" tastes the same at McDonald's franchises all over the world.

Harvard is highly decentralized, with each school of the University controlling its own destiny. Unlike the McDonald's employees, who have little discretion about how they carry out their tasks, Harvard faculty have enormous autonomy over what they research and how they run their classes. People therefore expect a predictable product from McDonald's but a unique learning experience from a Harvard professor.

Organizations such as McDonald's, which have highly specific and easily measurable goals such as profitability, growth, and market share, are able to structure themselves tightly through written procedures and detailed checklists. Harvard's teaching and research goals are much less routine and predictable. Producing knowledgeable students and "important research" are rather diffuse goals that require a more decentralized and loosely connected structure.

Organizations change their structure to fit a changing environment. A simple structure that worked with a boss and a small number of employees will likely give way to a machine bureaucracy for routine tasks or a professional bureaucracy for more creative activities. Divisional forms serve specific areas or products within the larger organization while ad hocracy and matrix structures are helpful for adapting to a rapidly changing, turbulent environment.

Groups and teams must grapple with the same kinds of design questions that face the large organization. Likewise, it has been shown that the structure of the group may need to change significantly over the group's life as the group develops and different tasks are required.

When the structural frame is overutilized by the manager, adherence to the rulebook and established procedures may interfere with creative input. Management may be cold and impersonal. Good ideas may not be implemented because of insufficient power and influence. Work may be done without a clear set of values or mission.

When the structural frame is underutilized, the organization may not be designed in a manner that optimizes output. Role confusion and unclear job descriptions may result in repeated conflict. An appropriate emphasis on structure will help the organization cope with these problems.

PEOPLE AND ORGANIZATION: THE HUMAN RESOURCE FRAME

The human resource frame is grounded in psychological theories of human behavior, including the work of Maslow, McGregor, and Argyris. This frame "starts from the premise that people's skills, insights, ideas, energy and commitment are an organization's most critical resource. Organizations, however, can be so alienating, dehumanizing, and frustrating that human talents are wasted and human lines are distorted."[4] This frame assumes that organizations exist to serve human needs, and a good fit between the individual and the organization benefits both. People find meaningful work, and organizations receive people's talents and commitment.

Numerous strategies have been developed to improve human resource management. These activities generally involve listening more closely to the ideas of employees and allowing them a voice in how their work is carried out. These interventions include management training, job enrichment, participative management, survey feedback, organization development consultation, and self-managed work teams.

When managers overuse the human resource frame, they may focus too heavily on resolving problems by open communication and support while overlooking structural flaws that may precipitate such conflict. Overuse of this frame may also fail to give proper acknowledgment of the role of power and authority in dealing with competitive issues. Overuse of the human resources frame may result in an overly optimistic view that all organizational issues can be resolved through consensus and collaborative activities.

Underuse of the human resource frame may be seen in organizations which have not bothered to ask what the needs and aspirations of their workers are. Such organizations may not experience the increased creativity, commitment, and communication from employees who feel that they are heard and supported.

POWER, CONFLICT, AND COALITIONS: THE POLITICAL FRAME

The tragic explosion of the space shuttle Challenger with seven astronauts aboard was in part caused by political forces which created a context for conflict and power plays among individuals and groups.

The procedure had always been clear. Before any space vehicle could be launched, NASA and its contractors had to prove that it was safe to fly. But on the night of January 27, 1986, Morton Thiokol senior managers overruled the no-launch decision by their engineers; the next day seven astronauts were killed and the nation's space program was in a shambles. Technically, the record cold temperature on the launch pad had caused the "O-rings" to fail, thus allowing hot gases to escape. Further investigation revealed that the decision-making process had changed significantly since NASA's early days when decisions were made on the lowest possible level. Clearly the evolution of NASA since the heady days of the Apollo moon landing had changed the structure of the organization so that the people making the important decisions were getting farther and farther away from the people getting their hands dirty.

In addition to these structural problems, the human resource view of NASA showed an organization whose morale had diminished since the days of generous funding and national commitment to push back the frontiers of space. The fit between the organization's needs and the needs of its employees had eroded. The space pioneers of the early years had given way to the shuttle program's "box car in space."[5] But correcting the structural and human resource problems in the space program may not have prevented the tragedy of the space shuttle Challenger.

The political forces in Washington, in NASA, and in Morton Thiokol (the contractor responsible for the O-rings) collectively overruled the advice of technical experts and put the space shuttle in harm's way.

The political frame views organizations as living political arenas that house a complex variety of individual and group interests. Because of competition for scarce resources (time, money, positions), conflict is inevitable in organizations and members of different coalitions must know how to bargain and negotiate for their positions.

In the Challenger case there were many political forces that affected the decision-making process.

NASA ran the space program because a complex coalition of Congress, the White House, the media, and the public supported them. Crista McAuliffe, the teacher-in-space, was aboard the Challenger because having an ordinary citizen as a member of the crew built public support for the program.

The president intended to mention the launch of the Challenger in his State of the Union speech to Congress and to a national TV audience, but Morton Thiokol engineers recommended against the launch for valid scientific reasons. However, corporate executives feared that more delays would put their lucrative government contract in jeopardy. Similarly, NASA managers were aware that NASA's credibility was slipping, deemed the engineering data inconclusive, and recommended the launch.

On the night before the fateful launch, a coalition of managers from NASA and Morton Thiokol brought together by the dwindling space budget combined forces to overrule the scientists, who in the end had made the right recommendation.

The political frame focuses on situations of scarce resources and incompatible preferences and thus the collision of different needs. If a group of graduate students, for example, wants the university to become more democratic and responsive to their needs, while the faculty wishes to tighten controls and standards, the political theorist might emphasize how each group articulates its preferences and mobilizes the power to get what it wants. The structural view assumes that some solutions are better than others and urges rational problem-solving methods to reach a discussion. The human resource approach seeks a "win-win" outcome of this conflict where the needs of both groups are shared and an integrative solution is reached. For the political manager, scarcity and conflict are enduring facts of organizational life, and they are less optimistic than the structural- and human-resource-oriented managers of achieving the "best" or win-win resolutions.

The political frame is focused on the use of power and the tactics of conflict. Power can come from authority, expertise, control of rewards and punishments, alliances and networks, control of agendas, control of meetings and symbols, and personal power. Most managerial jobs are characterized by an imbalance where responsibility seems to be larger than the authority to get things done. As a consequence, other forms of power (e.g., reward) must be enlisted to manage effectively.

Within the political frame, conflict is not necessarily seen as something bad and to be avoided. Therefore, its focus is not always on the resolution of conflict, as is often the case for the human resource and structural frames. The political frame asserts that conflict has benefits, such as encouraging innovative approaches to problem solving, challenging the status quo, and reducing complacency. Because conflict is not going to disappear, the political frame asks how groups and individuals can make the best use of it. To use the political frame effectively, managers must understand the strategy and tactics of conflict. According to the political frame, not only do the authorities have power, but there are many in the organization who have different forms of power. Those who get and use power best see their ideas implemented. The use of power does not need to be destructive. Constructive use of power is necessary to create effective organizations.

Managers who underutilize the political frame may be ignoring an enduring reality of organizational life. The political perspective can be a powerful antidote to the rationality of the structural frame.

Overuse of the political frame can be equally restrictive. The political frame can be cynical and pessimistic, overestimating the inevitability of conflict and understating the potential for rational analysis and interpersonal collaboration.

ORGANIZATIONAL CULTURE AND SYMBOLS: THE SYMBOLIC FRAME

When Martin Luther King spoke to the huge throng that participated in the march on Washington in August 1963, he said to them, "I have a dream." In that memorable speech, Dr. King spoke with conviction and passion about American values. He included many of the most cherished symbols of our country. His speech included "My country 'tis of thee, sweet land of liberty," and other songs and phrases uttered daily in every school in our land. He reminded his listeners of the basic values and principles that our country was founded upon when its first settlers sought refuge from political persecution nearly two centuries earlier.

The symbolic frame emphasizes the symbolic aspect of the human experience. It departs from the rational, linear view of organizations and recognizes the importance of culture, rituals, stories, and metaphors. Just as the earliest tribal rituals may have required a youngster at puberty to kill a lion and be circumcised, large corporations have their modern-day versions of initiation rituals.

In a strong culture, the message to newcomers will be "you are different and not yet one of us." The newcomer (in this example, a woman) may say "I know this place is hostile to women and I expect that to change." In this symbolic interchange, newcomers have a part to play by bringing new ideas and perspectives into the organization. At the same time, old-timers act as a force for cohesion, stability and the wisdom of the past.[6]

The basic assumption of the symbolic frame is that what is important about any event is not what happened, but *what it means to people*. Because organizations are so complex, it is often hard to know what is happening and why it is happening. With such uncertainty and ambiguity, it is difficult to analyze rationally the causes of problems and their solutions. People create symbols to reduce confusion and provide direction in their lives. The core values of McDonald's, the golden arches, and the stories of its founder, Ray Kroc, give direction to franchise holders. The history and rituals of Harvard University offer professors and students a common set of values from which to work.

In Martin Luther King's memorable "I have a dream" speech, he was able to articulate how a set of values based on our country's history could serve as a vision for our future. A more structural Dr. King might have spoken about "I have a plan" while a human resource or political leader would have emphasized feelings and coalition-building. But in that moment, he chose to reach people with his vision. Managers who understand the importance of the symbolic frame appreciate the power of rituals, ceremonies, and stories, and they use them to articulate a set of shared values called *culture*.

The symbolic frame views the organization as theater. For example, the structure of an organization may be seen as more than the structural view, which emphasizes the network of interdependent roles and linkages that are determined by goals, technology and environment. To the symbolic manager, the structure may be more like a stage design and props that make the organization look credible to its audience. For example, because of their elusive goals and underdeveloped technologies, schools have symbols of effectiveness and modern appearance. Certified teachers, American flags, and computers are part of the props. The schools achieve legitimacy by maintaining an appearance "that conforms to the way society thinks they should look."[7]

There are two faces of the symbolic perspective. Symbols can be used to camouflage or distort. The certified teacher may be incompetent. The corporation that states "People come first" may have an abysmal record in dealing with people. Managers who emphasize vision and charisma may be inept at enacting their vision. The symbolic frame is on dangerous ground when symbols are not congruent with reality. On the other hand, *symbols offer order and predictability in an ambiguous and uncertain world.* When the space shuttle Challenger exploded, killing its precious crew, people engaged in rituals to help them deal with their collective loss. In this way the symbolic frame can give meaning and hope to organizational activities that defy explanation in more rational terms.

INTEGRATING FRAMES FOR EFFECTIVE PRACTICE

While each of the frames emphasizes a different slice of organizational life, each one alone serves only as an incomplete map of a complex terrain. Each frame has a unique comparative advantage. For example, the structural frame will be most salient under conditions of stable authority, clear goals, and well-developed technologies. Human resource issues are likely to become prominent in an organization where employee motivation is important but problematic, and when resources are abundant. When goals and values are in conflict, resources are scarce, and the distribution of power is unstable, the political frame is likely to stand out. The symbolic frame is likely to be important under conditions of high ambiguity and inadequate information.

Taken together, the frames remind us that people and organizations try to behave in rational ways, but they are also affected by their needs and biases. They are adaptable but not infinitely so. They often will be dealing with scarce resources, and the importance of power and politics cannot be underestimated. Finally, the symbolic frame reminds us that we attribute meaning to organizational events. It is only in this multiple-perspective mode that we can begin fully to understand organizational activity at the level of complexity that is experienced by managers.

Multiple-perspective managers are able to interpret the same event in many different ways. A simple meeting can, for example, be a formal occasion for making decisions. Besides this structural interpretation, it can serve human resource needs by being an occasion for sharing feelings and building commitment to an idea. Meetings can serve as occasions to gain power and win points, and they can symbolically reaffirm values or transform the culture. Managers who can apply all of these frames and diagnose which perspectives are being used by the meeting's participants are likely to be more effective than those limited to a single perspective.

REFRAMING CHANGE

Modern organizations are being buffeted by powerful external forces that threaten the status quo.

Globalization requires organizations to enter new markets, adapt to new cultures, and reorganize their management structure. New technologies introduce new production and communication strategies. Deregulation in the airline and communications fields has forced these industries to shift from a service emphasis to a marketing emphasis. Demographic shifts have meant a changing workplace which is more diverse and multicultural, resulting in a sense of loss for some members.

The four frames can help managers anticipate the impact of change and act in ways to reduce resistance to change. The four approaches to change may look like this:

1. *Structural*—Change alters existing structural arrangements, causing confusion and ambiguity. Formal patterns and policies need to be realigned.
2. *Human Resource*—Change causes people to feel incompetent and powerless to handle new situations and behaviors. Training and psychological support are necessary when employees feel insecure.
3. *Political*—Change causes conflict and creates winners and losers. Managers must create arenas where issues can be negotiated.
4. *Symbolic*—Change creates loss of meaning and purpose. When attachments to symbols are severed, transition rituals are required and new symbols created.

"A fully effective change requires attention to all four issues: structure, needs, conflict, and loss. Changes in one frame inevitably reverberate through the others and the frame that is ignored is very likely to be the one that distorts or undermines the effort."[8]

REFRAMING LEADERSHIP: LEADERS AS ARCHITECTS, CATALYSTS, ADVOCATES, AND PROPHETS

Many current views of leadership have been based on oversimplified models. Each of the frames offers a different perspective on how leaders might behave when they are effective and ineffective.

Effective leaders are more likely to have the skills to lead from a multiple perspectives framework, and they are more likely to know which frame might be the most appropriate fit for the situation at hand. Effective leaders can develop rational systems but avoid leading too heavily by the rules. They can support and empower people but avoid abdicating their leadership role. Effective leaders are able to build coalitions and advocate for their constituents, but use power fairly and judiciously. They can inspire others by giving meaning to their experience and by communicating a vision, but they can avoid the use of hollow symbols and balance their vision with concrete action.

ARTISTRY, CHOICE, AND LEADERSHIP

The best managers and leaders understand their prevailing frames and know how those frames both benefit and limit their effectiveness. Wise leaders know how to build teams that can provide leadership across all four frames as the situation requires. They will be able to create a balance between core values and elastic strategies. They can be dramatically explicit about their core values and beliefs but apply frames flexibly in pursuit of their mission.

In a world of constant change, leaders of complex organizations will need the ability to see new possibilities and to discover choices, even when options seem severely constrained. The ability to reframe their thinking can give them new power and new skills.

Notes

1. Bolman, Lee G., and Terrence E. Deal, *Reframing Organizations: Artistry, Choice, and Leadership*. San Francisco, CA: Jossey-Bass, 1991. p. 4.
2. Bolman and Deal, p. 12.
3. Bolman and Deal, p. 10.
4. Bolman and Deal, p. 120.
5. Bolman and Deal, p. 184.
6. Bolman and Deal, p. 249.
7. Bolman and Deal, p. 275.
8. Bolman and Deal, p. 402.

PART THREE
Best-Seller "Classics"

Many of those books that have found their way into earlier editions of *The Manager's Bookshelf* as a part of our *mosaic of contemporary views* continue to have a message that many managers reference and still want to hear. As a result, for the fifth edition of *The Manager's Bookshelf* we have included summaries of selected books published in earlier years that continue to be popular among managers today.

While working as partners for McKinsey & Company (a management consulting firm), Thomas J. Peters and Robert H. Waterman Jr. conducted research that led to their book *In Search of Excellence*. The results of their study of management practices in several dozen companies in six industries led to the identification of eight attributes that were practiced consistently and appeared to be related to organizational success. Peters and Waterman's work also sparked an interest in looking at management through a different set of lenses and defined management's role as coach, cheerleader, and facilitator. Subsequently, Peters co-authored *A Passion for Excellence, Thriving on Chaos, Liberation Management*, and *The Tom Peters Seminar*. Waterman wrote *The Renewal Factor* and *What America Does Right*.

Quality, customer service, total quality management, and continuous improvement became organizational buzzwords in the past several years. One of the leaders in developing strategies for building quality into manufacturing processes was the late W. Edwards Deming. During the 1950s, Deming went to Japan to teach statistical control, where his ideas received a very warm reception. The Japanese built on Deming's ideas and moved the responsibility for quality from the ranks of middle management down to the shop floor level. Deming's ideas on quality control soon became an integral feature in Japanese management. Deming has been called by his admirers both the "prophet of quality" and the "man of the century." He certainly demonstrated a powerful force of personality and a singular focus.

Total quality control (TQC) means that responsibility for quality is a part of every employee's job. Deming's *Out of the Crisis* calls for long-term organizational transformation through the implementation of a 14-step plan of action focusing on leadership, constant innovation, and removal of barriers to performance. Interested readers may also wish to examine other books about Deming and his influence in *The World of W. Edwards Deming, The*

Deming Dimension, Thinking About Quality, and *Deming's Road to Continual Improvement*.

Kenneth Blanchard and Spencer Johnson, in the widely read book *The One Minute Manager*, build their prescriptions for effective human resource on two basic principles. First, they suggest that *quality time* with the subordinate is of utmost importance. Second, they adopt Douglas McGregor's notion that employees are basically capable of *self-management*. These two principles provide the basis for their prescriptions on goal setting, praising, and reprimanding as the cornerstones of effective management.

Kenneth Blanchard was a professor of management at the University of Massachusetts, and has been active as a management consultant. With Norman Vincent Peale, Blanchard has also published *The Power of Ethical Management, Gung Ho*, and *Raving Fans*. Spencer Johnson, the holder of a medical doctorate, is interested in stress and has written extensively about medicine and psychology.

A true classic in the management literature is Douglas McGregor's *The Human Side of Enterprise*, first published in 1960. Because of the book's popularity, its timeless theme, and genuine relevance for organizations as they prepare to enter the twenty-first century, there was a twenty-fifth anniversary printing of McGregor's seminal work.

McGregor presents us with two sets of assumptions that managers might hold and that drive two very different approaches to the management of organizations and their employees. Through the presentation of two sets of assumptions—labeled *Theory X* and *Theory Y*—McGregor urges managers to see employees as capable of innovation, creativity, commitment, high levels of sustained effort, and the exercise of self-direction and self-control.

Douglas McGregor received his doctorate at Harvard University. Before his death in 1964, he served on the faculties of Harvard University and the Massachusetts Institute of Technology and was president of Antioch College. McGregor is also the author of *The Professional Manager*.

A contemporary of McGregor's, Abraham Maslow, has sometimes been called the "greatest psychologist since Freud," and a "significant contributor to the humanistic psychology movement." He is well-known to psychology students for his books *Toward a Psychology of Being* and *The Psychology of Science*. However, he is equally well-known to most business students for his highly popularized and defining work on postulating a hierarchy of human needs beginning at the physiological level and proceeding up through safety, social, esteem, and self-actualization levels, and suggesting that any need level, when fully satisfied, can no longer be a powerful motivator. Maslow also published *Eupsychian Management* (which received little acclaim in the 1960s), which has been republished (with additional material from a variety of admirers) as *Maslow on Management*. In this book, Maslow lays out the underlying assumptions for a eupsychian organization. Maslow taught at Brooklyn College and Brandeis University, and while writing his final book, he was an in-depth observer of worker behaviors at the Non-Linear Systems plant in Del Mar, California.

READING 1

In Search of Excellence

Thomas J. Peters and Robert H. Waterman, Jr.

What makes for excellence in the management of a company? Is it the use of sophisticated management techniques such as zero-based budgeting, management by objectives, matrix organization, and sector, group, or portfolio management? Is it greater use of computers to control companies that continue to grow even larger in size and more diverse in activities? Is it a battalion of specialized MBAs, well-versed in the techniques of strategic planning?

Probably not. Although most well-run companies use a fair sampling of all these tools, they do not use them as substitutes for the basics of good management. Indeed, McKinsey & Co., a management consultant concern, has studied management practices at thirty-seven companies that are often used as examples of well-run organizations and has found that they have eight common attributes. None of those attributes depends on "modern" management tools or gimmicks. In fact, none of them requires high technology, and none of them costs a cent to implement. All that is needed is time, energy, and a willingness on the part of management to think rather than to make use of management formulas.

The outstanding performers work hard to keep things simple. They rely on simple organizational structures, simple strategies, simple goals, and simple communications. The eight attributes that characterize their managements are:

- A bias toward action.
- Simple form and lean staff.
- Continued contact with customers.
- Productivity improvement via people.
- Operational autonomy to encourage entrepreneurship.
- Stress on one key business value.
- Emphasis on doing what they know best.
- Simultaneous loose-tight controls.

Although none of these sounds startling or new, most are conspicuously absent in many companies today. Far too many managers have lost sight of the basics—service to customers, low-cost manufacturing, productivity improvement, innovation, and risk-taking. In many cases, they have been seduced by the availability of MBAs, armed with the "latest" in strategic planning techniques. MBAs who specialize in strategy are bright, but they often cannot implement their ideas, and their companies wind up losing the capacity to act. At Standard Brands Inc., for example, Chairman

45

F. Ross Johnson discovered this the hard way when he brought a handful of planning specialists into his consumer products company. "The guys who were bright [the strategic planners] were not the kinds of people who could implement programs," he lamented to *Business Week*. Two years later, he removed the planners.

Another consumer products company followed a similar route, hiring a large band of young MBAs for the staffs of senior vice-presidents. The new people were assigned to build computer models for designing new products. Yet none of the products could be manufactured or brought to market. Complained one line executive: "The models incorporated eighty-three variables in product planning, but we were being killed by just one—cost."

Companies are being stymied not only by their own staffs but often by their structure. McKinsey studied one company where the new product process required 223 separate committees to approve an idea before it could be put into production. Another company was restructured recently into 200 strategic business units—only to discover that it was impossible to implement 200 strategies. And even at General Electric Co., which is usually cited for its ability to structure itself according to its management needs, an executive recently complained: "Things become bureaucratic with astonishing speed. Inevitably when we wire things up, we lose vitality." Emerson Electric Co., with a much simpler structure than GE, consistently beats its huge competitor on costs—manufacturing its products in plants with fewer than 600 employees.

McKinsey's study focused on ten well-managed companies: International Business Machines, Texas Instruments, Hewlett-Packard, 3M, Digital Equipment, Procter & Gamble, Johnson & Johnson, McDonald's, Dana, and Emerson Electric. On the surface, they have nothing in common. There is no universality of product line: Five are in high technology, one is in packaged goods, one makes medical products, one operates fast-food restaurants, and two are relatively mundane manufacturers of mechanical and electrical products. But each is a hands-on operator, not a holding company or a conglomerate. And while not every plan succeeds, in the day-to-day pursuit of their businesses these companies succeed far more often than they fail. And they succeed because of their management's almost instinctive adherence to the eight attributes.

BIAS TOWARD ACTION

In each of these companies, the key instructions are *do it, fix it, try it*. They avoid analyzing and questioning products to death, and they avoid complicated procedures for developing new ideas. Controlled experiments abound in these companies. The attitude of management is to "get some data, do it, then adjust it," rather than to wait for a perfect overall plan. The companies tend to be tinkerers rather than inventors, making small steps of progress rather than conceiving sweeping new concepts. At McDonald's Corp., for example, the objective is to do the little things regularly and well.

Ideas are solicited regularly and tested quickly. Those that work are pushed fast; those that don't are discarded just as quickly. At 3M Co., the management never kills an idea without trying it out; it just goes on the back burner.

These managements avoid long, complicated business plans for new projects. At 3M, for example, new product ideas must be proposed in less than five pages. At Procter & Gamble Co., one-page memos are the rule, but every figure in a P&G memo can be relied on unfailingly.

To ensure that they achieve results, these companies set a few well-defined goals for their managers. At Texas Instruments Inc., for one, a typical goal would be a set date for having a new plant operating or for having a designated percent of a sales force call on customers in a new market. A TI executive explained: "We've experimented a lot, but the bottom line for any senior manager is the maxim that more than two objectives is no objective."

These companies have learned to focus quickly on problems. One method is to appoint a "czar" who has responsibility for one problem across the company. At Digital Equipment Corp. and Hewlett-Packard Co., for example, there are software czars, because customer demand for programming has become the key issue for the future growth of those companies. Du Pont Co., when it discovered it was spending $800 million a year on transportation set up a logistics czar. Other companies have productivity czars or energy czars with the power to override a manufacturing division's autonomy.

Another tool is the task force. But these companies tend to use the task force in an unusual way. Task forces are authorized to fix things, not to generate reports and paper. At Digital Equipment, TI, HP, and 3M, task forces have a short duration, seldom more than ninety days. Says a Digital Equipment executive: "When we've got a big problem here, we grab ten senior guys and stick them in a room for a week. They come up with an answer and implement it." All members are volunteers, and they tend to be senior managers rather than junior people ordered to serve. Management espouses the busy-member theory: "We don't want people on task forces who want to become permanent task force members. We only put people on them who are so busy that their major objective is to get the problem solved and to get back to their main

How 10 Well-Run Companies Performed in 1979				
	Millions of dollars		*Percent*	
	Sales	*Profits*	*Return on sales*	*Return on equity*
IBM	$22,862.8	$3,011.3	14.8%	21.6%
Procter & Gamble	10,080.6	615.7	5.6	19.3
3M	5,440.3	655.2	12.2	24.4
Johnson & Johnson	4,211.6	352.1	6.5	19.6
Texas Instruments	3,224.1	172.9	5.1	19.2
Dana	2,789.0	165.8	6.1	19.3
Emerson Electric	2,749.9	208.8	7.5	21.5
Hewlett-Packard	2,361.0	203.0	8.2	18.1
Digital Equipment	2,031.6	207.5	9.7	19.7
McDonald's	1,937.9	188.6	8.7	22.5
BW composite of 1,200 companies			5.1	16.6

jobs." Every task force at TI is disbanded after its work is done, but within three months the senior operations committee formally reviews and assesses the results. TI demands that the managers who requested and ran the task force justify the time spent on it. If the task force turns out to have been useless, the manager is chided publicly, a painful penalty in TI's peer-conscious culture.

SIMPLE FORM AND LEAN STAFF

Although all ten of these companies are big—the smallest, McDonald's, has sales in excess of $1.9 billion—they are structured along "small is beautiful" lines. Emerson Electric, 3M, J&J, and HP are divided into small entrepreneurial units that—although smaller than economies of scale might suggest—manage to get things done. No HP division, for example, ever employs more than 1,200 people. TI, with ninety product customer centers, keeps each notably autonomous.

Within the units themselves, activities are kept to small, manageable groups. At Dana Corp., small teams work on productivity improvement. At the high-technology companies, small autonomous teams, headed by a product "champion," shepherd ideas through the corporate bureaucracy to ensure that they quickly receive attention from the top.

Staffs are also kept small to avoid bureaucracies. Fewer than 100 people help run Dana, a $3 billion corporation. Digital Equipment and Emerson are also noted for small staffs.

CLOSENESS TO THE CUSTOMER

The well-managed companies are customer driven—not technology driven, not product driven, not strategy driven. Constant contact with the customer provides insights that direct the company. Says one executive: "Where do you start? Not by poring over abstract market research. You start by getting out there with the customer." In a study of two fast-paced industries (scientific instruments and component manufacturing), Eric Von Hippel, associate professor at Massachusetts Institute of Technology, found that 100 percent of the major new product ideas—and eighty percent of the minor new product variations—came directly from customers.

At both IBM and Digital Equipment, top management spends at least 30 days a year conferring with top customers. No manager at IBM holds a staff job for more than three years, except in the legal, finance, and personnel departments. The reason: IBM believes that staff people are out of the mainstream because they do not meet with customers regularly.

Both companies use customer-satisfaction surveys to help determine management's compensation. Another company spends twelve percent of its research and development budget on sending engineers and scientists out to visit customers. One R&D chief spends two months each year with customers. At Lanier Business Products Inc., another fast growing company, the twenty most senior executives make sales calls every month.

Staying close to the customer means sales and service overkill. "Assistants to" at IBM are assigned to senior executives with the sole function of processing customer complaints within 24 hours. At Digital Equipment, J&J, IBM, and 3M, immense effort is expended to field an extraordinarily well-trained sales force. Caterpillar Tractor Co., another company considered to have excellent management, spends much of its managerial talent on efforts to make a reality of its motto, "24-hour parts delivery anywhere in the world."

These companies view the customer as an integral element of their businesses. A bank officer who started his career as a J&J accountant recalls that he was required to make customer calls even though he was in a financial department. The reason: to ensure that he understood the customer's perspective and could handle a proposal with empathy.

PRODUCTIVITY IMPROVEMENT VIA CONSENSUS

One way to get productivity increases is to install new capital equipment. But another method is often overlooked. Productivity can be improved by motivating and stimulating employees. One way to do that is to give them autonomy. At TI, shop floor teams set their own targets for production. In the years since the company has used this approach, executives say, workers have set goals that require them to stretch but that are reasonable and attainable.

The key is to motivate all of the people involved in each process. At 3M, for example, a team that includes technologists, marketers, production people, and financial types is formed early in a new product venture. It is self-sufficient and stays together from the inception to the national introduction. Although 3M is aware that this approach can lead to redundancy, it feels that the team spirit and motivation make it worthwhile.

Almost all of these companies use "corny" but effective methods to reward their workers. Badges, pins, and medals are all part of such recognition programs. Outstanding production teams at TI are invited to describe their successes to the board, as a form of recognition. Significantly, the emphasis is never only on monetary awards.

AUTONOMY TO ENCOURAGE ENTREPRENEURSHIP

A company cannot encourage entrepreneurship if it holds its managers on so tight a leash that they cannot make decisions. Well-managed companies authorize their managers to act like entrepreneurs. Dana, for one, calls this method the "store manager" concept. Plant managers are free to make purchasing decisions and to start productivity programs on their own. As a result, these managers develop unusual programs with results that far exceed those of a division or corporate staff. And the company has a grievance rate that is a fraction of the average reported by the United Auto Workers for all the plants it represents.

The successful companies rarely will force their managers to go against their own judgment. At 3M, TI, IBM, and J&J, decisions on product promotion are not based solely on market potential. An important factor in the decision is the zeal and drive of the volunteer who champions a product. Explains one executive at TI: "In every instance of a new product failure, we had forced someone into championing it involuntarily."

The divisional management is generally responsible for replenishing its new product array. In these well-managed companies, headquarters staff may not cut off funds for divisional products arbitrarily. What is more, the divisions are allowed to reinvest most of their earnings in their own operations. Although this flies in the face of the product-portfolio concept, which dictates that a corporate chief milk mature divisions to feed those with apparently greater growth potential, these companies recognize that entrepreneurs will not be developed in corporations that give the fruits of managers' labor to someone else.

Almost all these companies strive to place new products into separate startup divisions. A manager is more likely to be recognized—and promoted—for pushing a hot new product out of his division to enable it to stand on its own than he is for simply letting his own division get overgrown.

Possibly most important at these companies, entrepreneurs are both encouraged and honored at all staff levels. TI, for one, has created a special group of "listeners"—138 senior technical people called "individual contributors"—to assess new ideas. Junior staff members are particularly encouraged to bring their ideas to one of these individuals for a one-on-one evaluation. Each "contributor" has the authority to approve substantial startup funds ($20,000 to $30,000) for product experimentation. TI's successful Speak'n'Spell device was developed this way.

IBM's Fellows Program serves a similar purpose, although it is intended to permit proven senior performers to explore their ideas rather than to open communications lines for bright comers. Such scientists have at their beck and call thousands of IBM's technical people. The Fellows tend to be highly skilled gadflies, people who can shake things up—almost invariably for the good of the company.

The operating principle at well-managed companies is to do one thing well. At IBM, the all-pervasive value is customer service. At Dana it is productivity improvement. At 3M and HP, it is new product development. At P&G it is product quality. At McDonald's it is customer service—quality, cleanliness, and value.

STRESS ON A KEY BUSINESS VALUE

At all these companies, the values are pursued with an almost religious zeal by the chief executive officers. Rene McPherson, new dean of Stanford University's Graduate School of Business but until recently Dana's CEO, incessantly preached cost reduction and productivity improvement—and the company doubled its productivity in seven years. Almost to the day when Thomas Watson Jr. retired from IBM he wrote memos to the staff on the subject of calling on customers—even stressing the proper dress for the call. TI's ex-chairman Patrick Haggerty made it a point to drop in at a development laboratory on his way home each night when he was in Dallas. And in another company, where competitive position was the prime focus, one division manager wrote 700 memos to his subordinates one year, analyzing competitors.

Such single-minded focus on a value becomes a culture for the company. Nearly every IBM employee has stories about how he or she took great pains to solve a customer's problem. New product themes even dominate 3M and HP lunchroom conversations. Every operational review at HP focuses on new products, with a minimum amount of time devoted to financial results or projections—because President John Young has made it clear that he believes that proper implementation of new-product plans automatically creates the right numbers. In fact, Young makes it a point to start new employees in the new-product process and keep them there for a few years as part of a "socialization" pattern. "I don't care if they do come from the Stanford Business School," he says. "For a few years they get their hands dirty, or we are not interested." At McDonald's the company's values are drummed into employees at Hamburger U., a training program every employee goes through.

As the employees who are steeped in the corporate culture move up the ladder, they become role models for newcomers, and the process continues. It is possibly best exemplified by contrast. American Telephone & Telegraph Co., which recently began to develop a marketing orientation, has been hamstrung in its efforts because of a lack of career telephone executives with marketing successes. When Archie J. McGill was hired from IBM to head AT&T's marketing, some long-term employees balked at his leadership because he "wasn't one of them," and so was not regarded as a model.

Another common pitfall for companies is the sending of mixed signals to line managers. One company has had real problems introducing new products despite top management's constant public stress on innovation—simply because line managers perceived the real emphasis to be on cost-cutting. They viewed top management as accountants who refused to invest or to take risks, and they consistently proposed imitative products. At another company, where the CEO insisted that his major thrust was new products, an analysis of how he spent his time over a three-month period showed that no more than 5 percent of his efforts were directed to new products. His stated emphasis therefore was not credible. Not surprisingly, his employees never picked up the espoused standard.

Too many messages, even when sincerely meant, can cause the same problem. One CEO complained that no matter how hard he tried to raise what he regarded as an unsatisfactory quality level he was unsuccessful. But when McKinsey questioned his subordinates, they said, "Of course he's for quality, but he's for everything else, too. We have a theme a month here." The outstanding companies, in contrast, have one theme and stick to it.

STICKING TO WHAT THEY KNOW BEST

Robert W. Johnson, the former chairman of J&J, put it this way: "Never acquire any business you don't know how to run." Edward G. Harness, CEO at P&G, says, "This company has never left its base." All of the successful companies have been able to define their strengths—marketing, customer contact, new product innovation, low-cost manufacturing—and then build on them. They have resisted the temptation to move into new businesses that look attractive but require corporate skills they do not have.

SIMULTANEOUS LOOSE-TIGHT CONTROLS

While this may sound like a contradiction, it is not. The successful companies control a few variables tightly, but allow flexibility and looseness in others. 3M uses return on sales and number of employees as yardsticks for control. Yet it gives management lots of leeway in day-to-day operations. When McPherson became president of Dana, he threw out all of the company's policy manuals and substituted a one-page philosophy statement and a control system that required divisions to report costs and revenues on a daily basis.

IBM probably has the classic story about flexible controls. After the company suffered well-publicized and costly problems with its System 360 computer several years ago—problems that cost hundreds of millions of dollars to fix—Watson ordered Frank T. Cary, then a vice-president, to incorporate a system of checks and balances in new-product testing. The system made IBM people so cautious that they stopped taking risks. When Cary became president of IBM, one of the first things he did to reverse that attitude was to loosen some of the controls. He recognized that the new system would indeed prevent such an expensive problem from ever happening again, but its rigidity would also keep IBM from ever developing another major system.

By sticking to these eight basics, the successful companies have achieved better-than-average growth. Their managements are able not only to change but also to change quickly. They keep their sights aimed externally at their customers and competitors, and not on their own financial reports.

Excellence in management takes brute perseverance—time, repetition, and simplicity. The tools include plant visits, internal memos, and focused systems. Ignoring these rules may mean that the company slowly loses its vitality, its growth patterns, and its competitiveness.

READING 2

Out of the Crisis

W. Edwards Deming
Summary prepared by William B. Gartner and M. James Naughton

William B. Gartner *is a Professor at Georgetown University.*
M. James Naughton *is the owner of Expert-Knowledge Systems, Inc.*

Deming provides an ambitious objective for his book when he begins by saying:

> The aim of this book is transformation of the style of American management. Transformation of American style of management is not a job of reconstruction, nor is it revision. It requires a whole new structure, from foundation upward. *Mutation* might be the word, except that *mutation* implies unordered spontaneity. Transformation must take place with directed effort.

Few individuals have had as much positive impact on the world economy as Dr. W. Edwards Deming. With the broadcast of the NBC white paper, "If Japan Can, Why Can't We?" on June 24, 1980, Dr. Deming gained national exposure as the man responsible for the managerial theory that has governed Japan's transformation into a nation of world leaders in the production of high quality goods. This transformation did not happen overnight. Since 1950, when Dr. Deming first spoke to Japan's top managers on the improvement of quality, Japanese organizations have pioneered in the adaptation of Dr. Deming's ideas.

As a result of his seminars, Japan has had an annual national competition for quality improvement (the Deming Prize) since 1951. Japan has numerous journals and books devoted to exploring and furthering the implications of Deming's theory. However, it has only been within the last few years that a number of books have been published in the United States on "the Deming Theory of Management." An overview of the ideas that underlie Deming's theory, which cut across all major topical areas in management, will be provided here.

DISEASES AND OBSTACLES

Deming's book is not merely about productivity and quality control; it is a broad vision of the nature of organizations and how organizations should be changed. Deming identifies a set of chronic ailments that can plague any organization and limit its success. These, which he calls "deadly diseases," include an overemphasis on short-term profits, human resource practices that encourage both managers and employees to be

---

W. Edwards Deming, *Out of the Crisis*. Cambridge, MA: MIT Press, 1986.

mobile and not organizationally loyal, merit ratings and review systems that are based on fear of one's supervisor, an absence of a single driving purpose, and management that is based on visible figures alone.

The reason that managers are not as effective as they could be is that they are the prisoners of some structural characteristics and personal assumptions that prevent their success. Among the obstacles that Deming discusses are the insulation of top management from the other employees in the organization, lack of adequate technical knowledge, a long history of total reliance on final inspection as a way of assuring a quality product, the managerial belief that all problems originate within the work force, a reliance on meeting specifications, and the failure to synthesize human operators with computer systems for control.

THE CONCEPT OF VARIABILITY

The basis for Deming's theory is the observation that variability exists everywhere in everything. Only through the study and analysis of variability, using statistics, can a phenomenon be understood well enough to manipulate and change it. In many respects, using statistics is not very radical. Statistics are fundamental to nearly all academic research. But Deming asks that the right kind of statistics (analytical) be applied to our everyday lives as well. And that is the rub. To recognize the pervasiveness of variability and to function so that the sources of this variability can be defined and measured is radical. In Deming's world, the use of statistical thinking is not an academic game; it is a way of life.

The concept of variability is to management theory and practice what the concept of the germ theory of disease was to the development of modern medicine. Medicine had been "successfully" practiced without the knowledge of germs. In a pre-germ theory paradigm, some patients got better, some got worse, and some stayed the same; in each case, some rationale could be used to explain the outcome. With the emergence of germ theory, all medical phenomena took on new meanings. Medical procedures thought to be good practice, such as physicians attending women in birth, turned out to be causes of disease because of the septic condition of the physicians' hands. Instead of rendering improved health care, the physicians' germ-laden hands achieved the opposite result. One can imagine the first proponents of the germ theory telling their colleagues who were still ignorant of the theory to wash their hands between patients. The pioneers must have sounded crazy. In the same vein, managers and academics who do not have a thorough understanding of variability will fail to grasp the radical change in thought that Deming envisions. Deming's propositions may seem as simplistic as "wash your hands!" rather than an entirely new paradigm of profound challenges to present-day managerial thinking and behaviors.

An illustration of variability that is widely cited in the books on Deming's theory is the "red bead experiment." Dr. Deming, at his four-day seminar, asks for 10 volunteers from the attendees. Six of the students become workers, two become inspectors of the workers' production, one becomes the inspector of the inspectors' work, and one becomes the recorder. Dr. Deming mixes together 3000 white beads and 750 red beads in a large box. He instructs the workers to scoop out beads from the box with a beveled paddle that scoops out 50 beads at a time. Each scoop of the paddle is treated

| | | Day | | | |
Name	1	2	3	4	All 4
Neil	3	13	8	9	33
Tace	6	9	8	10	33
Tim	13	12	7	10	42
Mike	11	8	10	15	44
Tony	9	13	8	11	41
Richard	12	11	7	15	45
All 6	54	66	48	70	238
Cum $\bar{x}$	9.0	10.0	9.3	9.92	9.92

$$\bar{x} = \frac{238}{6 \times 4} = 9.92$$

$$\bar{p} = \frac{238}{6 \times 4 \times 50} = .198$$

$$\left.\begin{array}{l} \text{UCL} \\ \text{LCL} \end{array}\right\} = \bar{x} \pm 3\sqrt{\bar{x}(1 - \bar{p})}$$

$$= 9.9 \pm 3\sqrt{9.9 \times .802}$$

$$= \begin{cases} 18 \\ 1 \end{cases}$$

Adapted from Deming, p. 347.

FIGURE 1 Number of defective items by operator, by day.

as a day's production. Only white beads are acceptable. Red beads are defects. After each worker scoops a paddle of beads from the box, the two inspectors count the defects, the inspector of the inspectors inspects the inspectors' count, and the recorder writes down the inspectors' agreed-upon number of defects. Invariably, each worker's scoop contains some red beads. Deming plays the role of the manager by exhorting the workers to produce no defects. When a worker scoops few red beads he may be praised. Scooping many red beads brings criticism and an exhortation to do better, otherwise "we will go out of business." The manager reacts to each scoop of beads as if it had meaning in itself rather than as part of a pattern. Figure 1 shows the number of defective beads each worker produced for four days of work.

Dr. Deming's statistical analysis of the workers' production indicates that the process of producing white beads is in statistical control; that is, the variability of this production system is stable. The near-term prediction about the *pattern*, but not the individual draws, of the system's performance can be made. Near-future draws will yield about an average, over many experiments, of 9.4 red beads. Any one draw may range between one and 18 red beads. In other words, the actual number of red beads scooped by each worker is out of that worker's control. The worker, as Dr. Deming says, "is only delivering the defects." Management, which controls the system, has caused the defects through design of the system. There are a number of insights people draw from this experiment. Walton lists the following:

- Variation is part of any process.
- Planning requires prediction of how things and people will perform. Tests and experiments of past performance can be useful, but not definitive.
- Workers work within a system that—try as they might—is beyond their control. It is the system, not their individual skills, that determines how they perform.
- Only management can change the system.
- Some workers will always be above average, some below.[1]

The red bead experiment illustrates the behavior of systems of stable variability. In Deming's theory, a system is all of the aspects of the organization and environment—employees, managers, equipment, facilities, government, customers, suppliers, shareholders, and so forth—fitted together, with the aim of producing some type of output. Stability implies that the output has regularity to it, so that predictions regarding the output of the system can be made. But many of these systems are inherently unstable. Bringing a system into stability is one of the fundamental managerial activities in the Deming theory.

In Deming's theory, a stable system, that is, a system that shows signs of being in statistical control, behaves in a manner similar to the red bead experiment. In systems, a single datum point is of little use in understanding the causes that influenced the production of that point. It is necessary to withhold judgment about changes in the output of the system until sufficient evidence (additional data points) becomes available to suggest whether or not the system being examined is stable. Statistical theory provides tools to help evaluate the stability of systems. Once a system is stable, its productive capability can be determined; that is, the average output of the system and the spread of variability around that average can be described. This can be used to predict the near-term future behavior of the system.

The inefficiencies inherent in "not knowing what we are doing," that is, in working with systems not in statistical control, might not seem to be that great a competitive penalty if all organizations are similarly out of control. Yet we are beginning to realize that the quality of outputs from organizations that are managed using Deming's theory are many magnitudes beyond what non-Deming organizations have been producing. The differences in quality and productivity can be mind-boggling.

For example, both Scherkenbach[2] and Walton[3] reported that when the Ford Motor Company began using transmissions produced by the Japanese automobile manufacturer, Mazda, Ford found that customers overwhelmingly preferred cars with Mazda transmissions to cars with Ford-manufactured transmissions—because the warranty repairs were ten times lower, and the cars were quieter and shifted more smoothly. When Ford engineers compared their transmissions to the Mazda transmissions, they found that the piece-to-piece variation in the Mazda transmissions was nearly three times less than in the Ford pieces. Both Ford and Mazda conformed to the engineering standards specified by Ford, but Mazda transmissions were far more uniform. More uniform products also cost less to manufacture. With less variability there is less rework and less need for inspection. Only systems in statistical control can begin to reduce variability and thereby improve the quality and quantity of their output. Both authors reported that after Ford began to implement Deming's theory over the last five years, warranty repair frequencies dropped by forty-five percent and "things gone wrong" reports from customers dropped by fifty percent.

FOURTEEN STEPS MANAGEMENT MUST TAKE

The task of transformation of an entire organization to use the Deming theory becomes an enormous burden for management, and Deming frequently suggests that this process is likely to take a minimum of ten years. The framework for transforming an organization is outlined in the fourteen points (pp. 23–24):

1. Create constancy of purpose toward improvement of product and service, aiming to become competitive, to stay in business, and to provide jobs.
2. Adopt the new philosophy. We are in a new economic age. Western management must awaken to the challenge, must learn their responsibilities, and must take on leadership in order to bring about change.
3. Cease dependence on inspection to achieve quality. Eliminate the need for inspection on a mass basis by building quality into the product in the first place.
4. End the practice of awarding business on the basis of the price tag. Instead, minimize total cost. Move toward a single supplier for any one time and develop long-term relationships of loyalty and trust with that supplier.
5. Improve constantly and forever the systems of production and service in order to improve quality and productivity. Thus, one constantly decreases costs.
6. Institute training on the job.
7. Institute leadership. Supervisors should be able to help people to do a better job, and they should use machines and gadgets wisely. Supervision of management and supervision of production workers need to be overhauled.
8. Drive out fear, so that everyone may work effectively for the company.
9. Break down barriers between departments. People in research, design, sales, and production must work as a team. They should foresee production problems and problems that could be encountered when using the product or service.
10. Eliminate slogans, exhortations, and targets that demand zero defects and new levels of productivity. These only create adversarial relationships because the many causes of low quality and low productivity are due to the system, and not the work force.
11. **a.** Eliminate work standards (quotas) on the factory floor. Substitute leadership.
11. **b.** Eliminate management by objectives. Eliminate management by numbers or numerical goals. Substitute leadership.
12. **a.** Remove barriers that rob the hourly worker of his right to pride of workmanship. The responsibility of supervisors must be changed from sheer numbers to quality.
12. **b.** Remove barriers that rob people in management and in engineering of their right to pride of workmanship. This means, inter alia, abolishing the annual or merit rating and management by objectives.

13. Institute a vigorous program of education and self-improvement.
14. Put everybody in the company to work to accomplish the transformation. The transformation is everybody's job.

As mentioned earlier, the fourteen points should not be treated as a list of aphorisms, nor can each of the fourteen points be treated separately without recognizing the interrelationships among them.

CONCLUSIONS

Out of the Crisis is full of examples and ideas, and Deming calls for a radical revision of American management practice. To his credit, Deming constantly recognizes ideas and examples from individuals practicing various aspects of his theory. This constant recognition of other individuals provides a subtle indication that a body of practitioners exists who have had successful experiences applying his fourteen steps and other ideas.

A transformation in American management needs to occur, it can take place, and it has begun already in those firms applying Deming's theory. Deming offers a new paradigm for the practice of management that requires a dramatic rethinking and replacement of old methods by those trained in traditional management techniques. In conclusion, Deming recognizes that "it takes courage to admit that you have been doing something wrong, to admit that you have something to learn, that there is a better way" (Walton, 1986, p. 223).

Notes

1. William B. Gartner and M. James Naughton, "The Deming Theory of Management," *Academy of Management Review*, January 1988, pp. 138–142.
2. William W. Scherkenbach, *The Deming Route to Quality and Productivity: Roadmaps and Roadblocks*, Milwaukee, WI: ASQC, 1986.
3. Mary Walton, *The Deming Management Method*, New York: Dodd, Mead, & Company, 1986.

READING 3

The One Minute Manager

Kenneth Blanchard and Spencer Johnson
Summary prepared by Charles C. Manz

> *Charles C. Manz is a Professor of Management at the University of Massachusetts at Amherst. He holds a doctorate in Organizational Behavior from Pennsylvania State University. His professional publications and presentations concern topics such as self-leadership, vicarious learning, self-managed work groups, leadership, power and control, and group processes. He is the author of the book* The Art of Self-Leadership *and co-author of* The Leadership Wisdom of Jesus.

The most distinguishing characteristic of *The One Minute Manager* by Kenneth Blanchard and Spencer Johnson is its major philosophical theme: Good management does not take a lot of time. This dominant theme seems to be based on two underlying premises: (1) *Quality* of time spent with subordinates (as with one's children) is more important than quantity; and, (2) in the end, people (subordinates) should really be managing themselves.

The book is built around a story that provides an occasion for learning about effective management. The story centers on the quest of "a young man" to find an effective manager. In his search he finds all kinds of managers, but very few that he considers effective. According to the story, the young man finds primarily two kinds of managers. One type is a hard-nosed manager who is concerned with the bottom line (profit) and tends to be directive in style. With this type of manager, the young man believes, the organization tends to win at the expense of the subordinates. The other type of manager is one who is concerned more about the employees than about performance. This "nice" kind of manager seems to allow the employees to win at the expense of the organization. In contrast to these two types of managers, the book suggests, an effective manager (as seen through the eyes of the young man) is one who manages so that both the organization and the people involved benefit (win).

The dilemma that the young man faces is that the few managers who do seem to be effective will not share their secrets. That is only true until he meets the "One Minute Manager." It turns out that this almost legendary manager is not only willing to share the secrets of his effectiveness, but is so available that he is able to meet almost any time the young man wants to meet, except at the time of his weekly two-hour meeting with his subordinates. After an initial meeting with the One Minute

Kenneth Blanchard and Spencer Johnson, *The One Minute Manager*. La Jolla, CA: Blanchard Johnson Publishers, 1981.

59

Manager, the young man is sent off to talk to his subordinates to learn, directly from those affected, the secrets of One Minute Management. Thus the story begins, and in the remaining pages, the wisdom, experience, and management strategies of the One Minute Manager are revealed as the authors communicate, through him and his subordinates, their view on effective management practice.

In addition to general philosophical management advice (e.g., managers can reap good results from their subordinates without expending much time), the book suggests that effective management means that both the organization and its employees win, and that people will do better work when they feel good about themselves; it also offers some specific prescriptions. These prescriptions center around three primary management techniques that have been addressed in the management literature for years: goal setting, positive reinforcement in the form of praise, and verbal reprimand. The authors suggest that applications of each of the techniques can be accomplished in very little time, in fact in as little as one minute (hence the strategies are labeled "one minute goals," "one minute praisings," and "one minute reprimands"). The suggestions made in the book for effective use of each of these strategies will be summarized in the following sections.

ONE MINUTE GOALS

"One minute goals" are said to clarify responsibilities and the nature of performance standards. Without them, the authors suggest, employees will not know what is expected of them, being left instead to grope in the dark for what they ought to be doing. A great deal of research and writing has been done on the importance of goals in reaching a level of performance (c.f., Locke, Shaw, Saari, and Latham, 1981). The advice offered in *The One Minute Manager* regarding effective use of performance goals is quite consistent with the findings of this previous work. Specifically, the authors point out through one of the One Minute Manager's subordinates that effective use of One Minute Goals includes:

- agreement between the manager and subordinate regarding what needs to be done;
- recording of each goal on a single page in no more than 250 words that can be read by almost anyone in less than a minute;
- communication of clear performance standards regarding what is expected of subordinates regarding each goal;
- continuous review of each goal, current performance, and the difference between the two.

These components are presented with a heavy emphasis on having employees use them to manage themselves. This point is driven home as the employee who shares this part of One Minute Management recalls how the One Minute Manager taught him about One Minute Goals. In the recounted story, the One Minute Manager refuses to take credit for having solved a problem of the subordinate, and is in fact irritated by the very idea of getting credit for it. He insists that the subordinate solved his own problem and orders him to go out and start solving his own future problems without taking up the One Minute Manager's time.

ONE MINUTE PRAISING

The next employee encountered by the young man shares with him the secrets of "one minute praising." Again, the ideas presented regarding this technique pretty well parallel research findings on the use of positive reinforcement (c.f., Luthans and Kreitner, 1986). One basic suggestion for this technique is that managers should spend their time trying to catch subordinates doing something *right* rather than doing something wrong. In order to facilitate this, the One Minute Manager monitors new employees closely at first and has them keep detailed records of their progress (which he reviews). When the manager is able to discover something that the employee is doing right, the occasion is set for One Minute Praising (positive reinforcement). The specific components suggested for applying this technique include:

- letting others know that you are going to let them know how they are doing;
- praising positive performance as soon as possible after it has occurred, letting employees know specifically what they did right and how good you feel about it;
- allowing the message that you really feel good about their performance to sink in for a moment, and encouraging them to do the same;
- using a handshake or other form of touch when it is appropriate (more on this later).

Again, these steps are described with a significant self-management flavor. The employee points out that after working for a manager like this for a while you start catching yourself doing things right and using self-praise.

ONE MINUTE REPRIMANDS

The final employee that the young man visits tells him about "One Minute Reprimands." This potentially more somber subject is presented in a quite positive tone. In fact, the employee begins by pointing out that she often praises herself and sometimes asks the One Minute Manager for a praising when she has done something well. But she goes on to explain that when she has done something wrong, the One Minute Manager is quick to respond, letting her know exactly what she has done wrong and how he feels about it. After the reprimand is over, he proceeds to tell her how competent he thinks she really is, essentially praising her as a *person* despite rejecting the undesired *behavior*. Specifically, the book points out that One Minute Reprimands should include:

- letting people know that you will, in a frank manner, communicate to them how they are doing;
- reprimand poor performance as soon as possible, telling people exactly what they did wrong and how you feel about it (followed by a pause allowing the message to sink in);
- reaffirm how valuable you feel the employees are, using touch if appropriate, while making it clear that it is their *performance* that is unacceptable in this situation;
- make sure that when the reprimand episode is over it is over.

OTHER ISSUES AND RELATED MANAGEMENT TECHNIQUES

These three One Minute Management techniques form the primary applied content of the book. Good management does not take a lot of time; it just takes wise application of proven management strategies—One Minute Goals, Praisings, and Reprimands. Beyond this, the book deals with some other issues relevant to these strategies, such as "under what conditions is physical touch appropriate?" The book suggests that the use of appropriate touch can be helpful when you know the person well and wish to help that person succeed. It should be done so that you are giving something to the person such as encouragement or support, not taking something away.

The authors also address the issue of manipulation, suggesting that employees should be informed about, and agree to, the manager's use of One Minute Management. They indicate that the key is to be honest and open in the use of this approach. They also deal briefly with several other issues. For example, the book suggests that it is important to move a subordinate gradually to perform a new desired behavior by reinforcing approximations to the behavior until it is finally successfully performed. The technical term for this is "shaping." A person's behavior is shaped by continuously praising improvements rather than waiting until a person completely performs correctly. If a manager waits until a new employee completely performs correctly, the authors suggest, the employee may well give up long before successful performance is achieved because of the absence of reinforcement along the way.

The authors also suggest substituting the strategies for one another when appropriate. With new employees, for instance, they suggest that dealing with low performance should focus on goal setting and then trying to catch them doing something right rather than using reprimand. Since a new employee's lack of experience likely produces an insufficient confidence level, this makes reprimand inappropriate, while goal setting and praise can be quite effective (so the logic goes). The authors also suggest that if a manager is going to be tough on a person, the manager is better off being tough first and then being supportive, rather than the other way around. Issues such as these are briefly addressed through the primary story and the examples described by its primary characters, as supplemental material to the management philosophy and specific management techniques that have been summarized here.

Eventually, at the end of the story, the young man is hired by the One Minute Manager and over time becomes a seasoned One Minute Manager himself. As he looks back over his experiences, the authors are provided with the occasion to summarize some of the benefits of the management approach they advocate—more results in less time, time to think and plan, less stress and better health, similar benefits experienced by subordinates, and reduced absenteeism and turnover.

THE ONE MINUTE MANAGER IN SUMMARY

Perhaps one bottom-line message of the book is that effective management requires that you care sincerely about people but have definite expectations that are expressed openly about their behavior. Also, one thing that is even more valuable than learning to be a One Minute Manager is having one for a boss, which in the end means you really work for yourself. And finally, as the authors illustrate through the giving attitude of the young man who has now become a One Minute Manager, these management techniques are not a competitive advantage to be hoarded but a gift to be shared with others. This is true because, in the end, the one who shares the gift will be at least as richly rewarded as the one who receives it.

References

Locke, E., K. Shaw, L. Saari, and G. Latham. "Goal Setting and Task Performance 1969–1980." *Psychological Bulletin* 90 (1981), 125–152.

Luthans, F. and T. Davis. "Behavioral Self-management (BSM): The Missing Link in Managerial Effectiveness." *Organizational Dynamics* 8 (1979), 42–60.

Luthans, F. and R. Kreitner. *Organizational Behavior Modification and Beyond.* Glenview, IL: Scott, Foresman and Co., 1986.

Manz, C. C. *The Art of Self-leadership: Strategies for Personal Effectiveness in Your Life and Work.* Englewood Cliffs, NJ: Prentice-Hall, 1983.

Manz, C. C. "Self-leadership: Toward an Expanded Theory of Self-influence Processes in Organizations." *Academy of Management Review* 11 (1986), 585–600.

Manz, C. C. and H. P. Sims, Jr. "Self-management as a Substitute for Leadership: A Social Learning Theory Perspective." *Academy of Management Review* 5 (1980), 361–367.

READING 4

The Human Side of Enterprise

Douglas McGregor
Summary prepared by Gayle Porter

Gayle Porter obtained her doctorate from The Ohio State University in Organizational Behavior and Human Resource Management and is now at Rutgers University—Camden. Articles and ongoing research interests include the effects of dispositional differences in the workplace, group perceptions of efficacy and esteem, and the comparison of influence on employees through reward systems, leadership, and employee development efforts. Her prior experience includes positions as Director of Curriculum Development for a human resource management degree program; consultant on training programs, financial operations, and computer applications; financial manager for an oil and gas production company; and financial specialist for NCR Corporation.

The Human Side of Enterprise was written during an ongoing comparative study of management development programs in several large companies. In McGregor's view, the making of managers has less to do with formal efforts in development than with how the task of management is understood within that organization. This fundamental understanding determines the policies and procedures within which the managers operate, and guides the selection of people identified as having the potential for management positions. During the late 1950s McGregor believed that major industrial advances of the next half century would occur on the human side of enterprise and he was intrigued by the inconsistent assumptions about what makes managers behave as they do. His criticism of the conventional assumptions, which he labels Theory X, is that they limit options. Theory Y provides an alternative set of assumptions that are much needed due to the extent of unrealized human potential in most organizations.

THE THEORETICAL ASSUMPTIONS OF MANAGEMENT

Regardless of the economic success of a firm, few managers are satisfied with their ability to predict and control the behavior of members of the organization. Effective prediction and control are central to the task of management, and there can be no prediction without some underlying theory. Therefore, all managerial decisions and actions rest on a personally held theory, a set of assumptions about behavior. The as-

---

Douglas McGregor, *The Human Side of Enterprise*. New York: McGraw-Hill, 1960.

sumptions management holds about controlling its human resources determine the whole character of the enterprise.

In application, problems occur related to these assumptions. First, managers may not realize that they hold and apply conflicting ideas and that one may cancel out the other. For example, a manager may delegate based on the assumption that employees should have responsibility, but then nullify that action by close monitoring, which indicates the belief that employees can't handle the responsibility. Another problem is failure to view control as selective adaptation, when dealing with human behavior. People adjust to certain natural laws in other fields; e.g., engineers don't dig channels and expect water to run uphill! With humans, however, there is a tendency to try to control in direct violation of human nature. Then, when they fail to achieve the desired results, they look for every other possible cause rather than examine the inappropriate choice of a method to control behavior.

Any influence is based on dependence, so the nature and degree of dependence are critical factors in determining what methods of control will be effective. Conventional organization theory is based on authority as a key premise. It is the central and indispensable means of managerial control and recognizes only upward dependence. In recent decades, workers have become less dependent on a single employer, and society has provided certain safeguards related to unemployment. This limits the upward dependence and, correspondingly, the ability to control by authority alone. In addition, employees have the ability to engage in countermeasures such as slowdowns, lowered standards of performance, or even sabotage to defeat authority they resent.

Organizations are more accurately represented as systems of *inter*dependence. Subordinates depend on managers to help them meet their needs, but the managers also depend on subordinates to achieve their own and the organization's goals. While there is nothing inherently bad or wrong in the use of authority to control, in certain circumstances it fails to bring the desired results. Circumstances change even from hour to hour, and the role of the manager is to select the appropriate means of influence based on the situation at a given point in time. If employees exhibit lazy, indifferent behavior, the causes lie in management methods of organization and control.

Theory X is a term used to represent a set of assumptions. Principles found in traditional management literature could only have derived from assumptions such as the following, which have had a major impact on managerial strategy in organizations:

1. *The average human being has an inherent dislike of work and will avoid it if possible.*
2. *Because of this human characteristic of dislike of work, most people must be coerced, controlled, directed, and threatened with punishment to get them to put forth adequate effort toward the achievement of organizational objectives.*
3. *The average human being prefers to be directed, wishes to avoid responsibility, has relatively little ambition, and wants security above all.*

These assumptions are not without basis, or they would never have persisted as they have. They do explain some observed human behavior, but other observations are not consistent with this view. Theory X assumptions also encourage us to categorize certain behaviors as human nature, when they may actually be symptoms of a condition in which workers have been deprived of an opportunity to satisfy higher-order needs (social and egoistic needs).

A strong tradition exists of viewing employment as an employee's agreement to accept control by others in exchange for rewards that are only of value outside the workplace. For example, wages (except for status differences), vacation, medical benefits, stock purchase plans, and profit sharing are of little value during the actual time on the job. Work is the necessary evil to endure for rewards away from the job. In this conception of human resources we can never discover, let alone utilize, the potentialities of the average human being.

Many efforts to provide more equitable and generous treatment to employees and to provide a safe and pleasant work environment have been designed without any real change in strategy. Very often what is proposed as a new management strategy is nothing more than a different tactic within the old Theory X assumptions. Organizations have progressively made available the means to satisfy lower-order needs for subsistence and safety. As the nature of the dependency relationship changes, management has gradually deprived itself of the opportunity to use control based solely on assumptions of Theory X. A new strategy is needed.

Theory Y assumptions are dynamic, indicate the possibility of human growth and development, and stress the necessity for selective adaptation:

1. *The expenditure of physical and mental effort in work is as natural as play or rest.*
2. *External control and the threat of punishment are not the only means for bringing about effort toward organizational objectives. People will exercise self-direction and self-control in the service of objectives to which they are committed.*
3. *Commitment to objectives is a function of the rewards associated with their achievement* (satisfaction of ego and self-actualization needs can be products of effort directed toward organizational objectives).
4. *The average human being learns, under proper conditions, not only to accept but to seek responsibility.*
5. *The capacity to exercise a relatively high degree of imagination, ingenuity, and creativity in the solution of organizational problems is widely, not narrowly, distributed in the population.*
6. *Under the conditions of modern industrial life, the intellectual potentialities of the average human being are only partially utilized.*

The Theory Y assumptions challenge a number of deeply ingrained managerial habits of thought and action; they lead to a management philosophy of integration and self-control. Theory X assumes that the organization's requirements take precedence over the needs of the individual members, and that the worker must always adjust to needs of the organization as management perceives them. In contrast, principle of *integration* proposes that conditions can be created such that individuals can best achieve their own goals by directing their efforts toward the success of the enterprise. Based on the premise that the assumptions of Theory Y are valid, the next logical question is whether, and to what extent, such conditions can be created. How will employees be convinced that applying their skills, knowledge, and ingenuity in support of the organization is a more attractive alternative than other ways to utilize their capacities?

THEORY Y IN PRACTICE

The essence of applying Theory Y assumptions is guiding the subordinates to develop themselves rather than developing the subordinate by telling them what they need to do. An important consideration is that the subordinates' acceptance of responsibility for self-developing (i.e., self-direction and self-control) has been shown to relate to their commitment to objectives. But the overall aim is to further growth of the individual, and it must be approached as a managerial strategy rather than simply as a personnel technique. Forms and procedures are of little value. Once the concept is provided, managers who welcome the assumptions of Theory Y will create their own processes for implementation; managers with underlying Theory X assumptions cannot create the conditions for integration and self-control no matter what tools are provided.

The development process becomes one of role clarification and mutual agreement regarding the subordinate's job responsibilities. This requires the manager's willingness to accept some risk and allow mistakes as part of the growth process. It also is time-consuming in terms of discussions and allowing opportunity for self-discovery. However, it is not a new set of duties on top of the manager's existing load. It is a different way of fulfilling the existing responsibilities.

One procedure that violates Theory Y assumptions is the typical utilization of performance appraisals. Theory X leads quite naturally into this means of directing individual efforts toward organizational objectives. Through the performance appraisal process, management tells people what to do, monitors their activities, judges how well they have done, and rewards or punishes them accordingly. Since the appraisals are used for administrative purposes (e.g., pay, promotion, retention decisions), this is a demonstration of management's overall control strategy. Any consideration of personal goals is covered by the expectation that rewards of salary and position are enough. If the advancement available through this system is not a desired reward, the individuals are placed in a position of acting against their own objectives and advancing for the benefit of the organization only. The alternative (for example, turning down a promotion) may bring negative outcomes such as lack of future options or being identified as employees with no potential.

The principle of integration requires active and responsible participation of employees in decisions affecting them. One plan that demonstrates Theory Y assumptions is *The Scanlon Plan.* A central feature in this plan is the cost-reduction sharing that provides a meaningful cause-and-effect connection between employee behavior and the reward received. The reward is directly related to the success of the organization and it is distributed frequently. This provides a more effective learning reinforcement than the traditional performance appraisal methods. The second central feature of the Scanlon Plan is effective participation, a formal method through which members contribute brains and ingenuity as well as their physical efforts on the job. This provides a means for social and ego satisfaction, so employees have a stake in the success of the firm beyond the economic rewards. Implementation of the Scanlon Plan is not a program or set of procedures; it must be accepted as a way of life and can vary depending on the circumstances of the particular company. It is entirely consistent with Theory Y assumptions.

Theory X leads to emphasis on tactics of control, whereas Theory Y is more concerned with the nature of the relationship. Eliciting the desired response in a Theory

Y context is a matter of creating an environment or set of conditions to enable self-direction. The day-to-day behavior of an immediate supervisor or manager is perhaps the most critical factor in such an environment. Through sometimes subtle behaviors superiors demonstrate their attitudes and create what is referred to as the psychological "climate" of the relationship.

Management style does not seem to be important. Within many different styles, subordinates may or may not develop confidence in the manager's deeper integrity, based on other behavioral cues. Lack of confidence in the relationship causes anxiety and undesirable reactions from the employees. No ready formula is available to relay integrity. Insincere attempts to apply a technique or style—such as using participation only to manipulate subordinates into believing they have some input to decisions—are usually recognized as a gimmick and soon destroy confidence.

In addition to manager-subordinate relationships, problems connected to Theory X assumptions can be observed in other organizational associations such as staff-line relationships. Upper management may create working roles for staff groups to "police" line managers' activities, giving them an influence that equates psychologically to direct line authority. Top management with Theory X assumptions can delegate and still retain control. The staff function provides an opportunity to monitor indirectly, to set policy for limiting decisions and actions, and to obtain information on everything happening before a problem can occur.

Staff personnel often come from a very specialized education with little preparation for what their role should be in an organization. With full confidence in their objective methods and training to find "the best answer," they often are unprepared for the resistance of line managers who don't share this confidence and don't trust the derived solutions. The staff may conclude that line managers are stupid, are unconcerned with the general welfare of the organization, and care only about their own authority and independence. They essentially adopt the Theory X assumptions and readily accept the opportunity to create a system of measurements for control of the line operations.

To utilize staff groups within the context of Theory Y, managers must emphasize the principle of self-control. As a resource to all parts and levels of the organization, staff reports and data should be supplied to all members who can use such information to control their own job—not subordinates' jobs. If summary data indicate something wrong within the manager's unit of responsibility, the manager would turn to subordinates, not to the staff, for more information. If the subordinates are practicing similar self-control using staff-provided information, they have most likely discovered the same problem and taken action before this inquiry occurs. There is no solution to the problem of staff-line relationships in authoritative terms that can address organizational objectives adequately. However, a manager operating by Theory Y assumptions will apply them similarly to all relationships—upward, downward, and peer level—including the staff-line associations.

THE DEVELOPMENT OF MANAGERIAL TALENT

Leadership is a relationship with four major variables: the characteristics of the leader; the attitudes, needs, and other personal characteristics of the followers; the characteristics of the organization, such as its purpose, structure, and the nature of its task; and the social, economic, and political environment in which the organization operates. Specifying which leader characteristics will result in effective performance depends on the other factors, so it is a complex relationship. Even if researchers were able to determine the universal characteristics of a good relationship between the leader and the other situational factors, there are still many ways to achieve the same thing. For example, mutual confidence seems important in the relationship, but there are a number of ways that confidence can be developed and maintained. Different personal characteristics could achieve the same desired relationship.

Also, because it is so difficult to predict the situational conditions an organization will face, future management needs are unpredictable. The major task, then, is to provide a heterogeneous supply of human resources from which individuals can be selected as appropriate at a future time. This requires attracting recruits from a variety of sources and with a variety of backgrounds, which complicates setting criteria for selection. Also, the management development programs in an organization should involve many people rather than a few with similar qualities and abilities. Finally, management's goal must be to develop the unique capacities of each individual, rather than common objectives for all participants. We must place high value on people in general—seek to enable them to develop to their fullest potential in whatever role they best can fill. Not everyone must pursue the top jobs; outstanding leadership is needed at every level.

Individuals must develop themselves and will do so optimally only in terms of what each of them sees as meaningful and valuable. What might be called a "manufacturing approach" to management development involves designing programs to build managers; this end product becomes a supply of managerial talent to be used as needed. A preferred alternative approach is to "grow talent" under the assumption that people will grow into what they are capable of becoming, if they are provided the right conditions for that growth. There is little relationship (possibly even a negative one) between the formal structure for management development and actual achievement of the organization, because programs and procedures do not *cause* management development.

Learning is fairly straightforward when the individual desires new knowledge or skill. Unfortunately, many development offerings soon become a scheduled assignment for entire categories of people. Learning is limited in these conditions, because the motivation is low. Further, negative attitudes develop toward training in general, which interferes with creating an overall climate conducive to growth. In many cases, managers may have a purpose in sending subordinates to training that is not shared with or understood by that individual. This creates anxiety or confusion, which also interferes with learning. It is best if attendance in training and development programs are the result of joint target-setting, wherein the individual expresses a need and it can be determined that a particular program will benefit both the individual and the organization.

Classroom learning can be valuable to satisfying needs of both parties. However, it can only be effective when there is an organizational climate conducive to growth. Learning is always an active process, whether related to motor skills or acquisition of knowledge; it cannot be injected into the learner, so motivation is critical. Practice and feedback are essential when behavior changes are involved. Classroom methods such as case analysis and role playing provide an opportunity to experiment with decisions and behaviors in a safe environment, to receive immediate feedback, and to go back and try other alternatives. Some applications of classroom learning may be observed directly on the job. In other cases, the application may be more subtle, in the form of increased understanding or challenging one's own preconceptions. Care must be taken so that pressures to evaluate the benefits of classroom learning don't result in application of inappropriate criteria for success while the true value of the experience is overlooked.

Separate attention is given to management groups or teams at various levels. Within Theory X assumptions, direction and control are jeopardized by effective group functioning. On the other hand, a manager who recognizes interdependencies in the organization—one who is less interested in personal power than in creating conditions so human resources will voluntarily achieve organization objectives—will seek to build strong management groups. Creating a managerial team requires unity of purpose among those individuals. If the group is nothing more than several individuals competing for power and recognition, it is not a team. Again, the climate of the relationships and the fundamental understanding of the role of managers in the organization will be critical. One day the hierarchical structure of reporting relationships will disappear from organizational charts and give way to a series of linked groups. This shift in patterns of relationships will be a slow transition, but will signify recognition of employee capacity to collaborate in joint efforts. Then we may begin to discover how seriously management has underestimated the true potential of the organization's human resources.

SUMMARY COMMENTS

Theory X is not an evil set of assumptions, but rather a limiting one. Use of authority to influence has its place, even within the Theory Y assumptions, but it does not work in all circumstances. A number of societal changes suggest why Theory X increasingly may cause problems for organizations needing more innovation and flexibility in their operating philosophy. It is critically important for managers honestly to examine the assumptions that underlie their own behavior toward subordinates. To do so requires first accepting the two possibilities, Theory X and Theory Y, and then examining one's own actions in the context of that comparison. Fully understanding the implications on each side will help identify whether the observed choices of how to influence people are likely to bring about the desired results.

READING 5

Maslow on Management

Abraham H. Maslow

It should be possible to implement an enlightened management policy into an organization, where employees can *self-actualize* (institute their own ideas, make decisions, learn from their mistakes, and grow in their capabilities) while creating *synergy* (attaining beneficial results simultaneously for the individual and the organization). Such a policy (and associated practices) would not necessarily apply to all people, because everyone is at a different level on the motivational hierarchy (from physiological to safety to love to esteem to self-actualization). Nevertheless, the assumptions that would need to be true in order to create an ideal (eupsychian) society can be identified and then explored. They include the following dimensions. People are:

- psychologically healthy;
- not fixated at the safety-need level;
- capable of growth, which occurs through delight and through boredom;
- able to grow to a high level of personal maturity;
- courageous, with the ability to conquer their fears and endure anxiety.

They have:

- the impulse to achieve;
- the capacity to be objective about themselves and about others;
- the capacity to be trusted to some degree;
- a strong will to grow, experiment, select their own friends, carry out their own ideas, and self-actualize;
- the ability to enjoy good teamwork, friendships, group spirit, group harmony, belongingness, and group love;
- the capacity to be improved to some degree;
- the ability to identify with a common objective and contribute to it;
- a conscience and feelings.

Everyone prefers:

- to love and to respect his or her boss;
- to be a prime mover rather than a passive helper;
- to use all their capacities;
- to work rather than being idle;
- to have meaningful work;
- to be justly and fairly appreciated, preferably in public;

Abraham Maslow, *Maslow on Management.* New York, NY: Wiley & Sons, Inc, 1998.

- to feel important, needed, useful, successful, proud, and respected;
- to have responsibility;
- to have personhood, identity, and uniqueness as a person;
- to create rather than destroy;
- to be interested rather than bored;
- to improve things, make things right, and do things better.

Given this portrait of a certain type of individual described by these assumptions, we can conclude the following:

- Authoritarian managers are dysfunctional for them;
- People can benefit by being stretched, strained, and challenged once in a while;
- Everyone should be informed as completely as possible;
- These types of persons will do best at what they have chosen, based on what they like most;
- Everybody needs to be absolutely clear about the organization's goals, directions, and purposes.

In conclusion, *enlightened management is the wave of the future*. It will be seen more and more for a very simple reason that can be stated as a fundamental principle of human behavior: "Treating people well spoils them for being treated badly." In other words, once employees have experienced any aspect of enlightened management, they will never wish to return to an authoritarian environment. Further, as other workers hear about enlightened work organizations, they will either seek to work there or demand that their own workplaces become more enlightened.

PART FOUR

High-Performing Organizations

Most organizations don't want merely to survive; they want to be effective, or even excellent, at what they do. To do so requires a prior definition of success, and this often encourages the managers of an organization to examine the actions of their best competitors for comparative models (benchmarks). The assumption is that if they can identify the organizational characteristics that allow others to succeed, perhaps these attributes can be transplanted (or adapted) to facilitate their own success. There is, therefore, considerable interest across a wide variety of organizations and management groups in what "high-performing organizations" actually do and what the guiding principles are.

The three books in this section concern themselves with issues pertaining to organizational effectiveness. Michael Hammer and James Champy suggest that the high-performing organizations have reengineered themselves by organizing around processes. According to Jay Galbraith and Edward E. Lawler III, competitive pressures have revealed the shortcomings of the functional design, thus creating a need for new organizational designs. James C. Collins and Jerry I. Porras have learned that the truly exceptional and long-lasting companies have not found their essence in visionary leaders and corporate vision. These organizations are more concerned about visionary product concepts, visionary products, and/or visionary market insights.

Michael Hammer and James Champy, authors of *Reengineering the Corporation*, claim that most American companies need to make radical changes if they are to survive long-term. Success, they claim, will require that organizations organize themselves around *processes*, and not around individual tasks or functions. Environmental changes are quickly rendering many organization structures and management principles incapable of the flexibility and responsiveness needed for survival in the turbulent and highly competitive markets of today.

Michael Hammer (Ph.D.) is the president of Hammer and Company, a management education and consulting firm. James Champy is the chairman of CSC Index, a management consulting firm. Both authors have worked with firms as they have undertaken reengineering efforts. Champy is also the author of *Reengineering Management.*

Authors of *Organizing for the Future*, Jay R. Galbraith and Edward E. Lawler III are professors of management and members of the Center for Effective Organizations at the University of Southern California. Observing the shortcomings of the functional unit design revealed by competitive pressures, they offer several suggestions about organizing for the future. Their high-involvement model of organization is seen as an alternative to the slow and inflexible hierarchical organization. In order for the high-involvement model to emerge, management must adopt a new paradigm based on the assumption that *the key to maximizing organizational effectiveness is to maximize the employee's ability to respond directly to changing conditions.* This calls for a new approach to information access, decision-making influence, reward systems, and knowledge (i.e., skills and abilities within the organization).

James C. Collins and Jerry I. Porras, authors of *Built to Last: Successful Habits of Visionary Companies*, are on the faculty at the Stanford University Graduate School of Business. Based upon a six-year research project conducted at Stanford's Business School, *Built to Last* provides insight into the question "What makes the truly exceptional companies different from other companies?" Eighteen truly exceptional and long-lasting companies (e.g., Boeing, Disney, General Electric, 3M, Merck, Motorola, Procter & Gamble, and Philip Morris) that have outperformed the general stock market since the late 1920s were the focus of their research.

Collins and Porras argue that the popular model that attributes organizational high-performance to visionary leadership fails to account for the success of many organizations. For example, the charismatic visionary leader model fails to account for the success of 3M: " . . . neither its current nor past CEOs fit this model. 3M's chief executive officers over the years have been highly competent and effective managers, but from all reports were not the 'larger than life' type of leader commonly associated with . . . charismatic visionaries" (p. 7). Those organizations "built to last" possess characteristics that differentiate them from other organizations. Their findings organize themselves around (a) characteristics of the leadership during the formative years, and (b) characteristics (e.g., a well understood and enduring core ideology) of the organization.

READING I

Reengineering the Corporation

Michael Hammer and James Champy
Summary prepared by Steve Gildersleeve

Steve Gildersleeve is the general manager of Carlson Florist and Greenhouses and the Sylvan Learning Center in Duluth, Minnesota. He has also worked in the Controller's Department for 3M in Austin, Texas, and in Corporate Accounting for The Carlson Companies in Minneapolis, MN. He is actively studying and applying systems thinking principles and methods at Carlson's along with searching for methods to teach it to his coworkers and friends. Another interest is developing a "no-excuses management" system that creates a supportive work environment in addition to focusing employees' efforts on the achievement of daily and long-term business goals.

"Why do we do what we do at all?" This is the key question for organizations to answer as they approach the twenty-first century. No longer will "How can we do what we do faster?" or "How can we do what we do better?" or even, "How can we do what we do at a lower cost?" succeed as questions on which to focus managerial attention. Most American companies have come to a point where radical changes are required in order to survive. The change process required is called business reengineering.

"If I were recreating this company today, given what I know and given current technology, what would it look like?" This question directly expresses the focal point of reengineering.

The basic premise of reengineering is simple, yet, like most simple prescriptions, it can be very difficult to swallow. Success in the marketplace requires that companies become the best in their business at the fundamentals: inventing products and services, manufacturing or providing them, marketing or selling them, and serving customers. To do this, companies must organize around processes, not individual tasks or functions. This dramatic approach may virtually require some to recreate their organizations.

THE REASONS FOR REENGINEERING

The performance of American companies today is suffering for the very same reasons that their performance used to be so strong. *Most businesses are trying to compete in a world that has changed so drastically that their organizational structures and*

Michael Hammer and James Champy, *Reengineering the Corporation*. New York, NY: Harper Business, 1993.

management principles no longer have any hope of adjusting or adapting. It is important to note that these are the same structures and principles that propelled these same American businesses to the forefront in years past.

The historical patriarchs of today's companies are men like Henry Ford and Alfred Sloan and the railroad barons of the nineteenth century. They further developed Adam Smith's eighteenth-century principle of the division of labor by adding the pyramidal organization or bureaucracy, true assembly-line production, decentralized divisions, managing by the numbers, and elaborate centralized planning.

These once crucial managerial techniques certainly had weaknesses, but those were far outweighed by the level of control they allowed and the results they achieved. However, these same techniques are now creating a managerial myopia that is leading businesses toward extinction.

Three forces have been the catalysts for this reversal. They are the three Cs: customers, competition, and change. First, *customers have taken charge.* In the past, customers bought what was offered, whether or not it was what they wanted or needed. They had no choice. Today, customers no longer are a "mass market." Customers demand and receive products and services with the features and prices they want—at least to a degree never known before. This force requires a responsiveness and flexibility previously unknown to the business world.

The second force driving the need for reengineering is *intensifying competition.* In the past, the best price would obtain the customer. Now, niche marketing has created an environment where similar products and services sell for entirely different reasons in different markets. One competitor in almost any part of the world can redefine the playing field for a whole industry virtually overnight through the introduction of new features or a different product that satisfies consumers' needs more effectively. Furthermore, technology has changed the very nature of competition itself, making available all sorts of market data previously unavailable and even eliminating whole segments of industries, such as wholesalers and distributors.

The third force is that *change has become constant.* The pace of change has accelerated, and it relentlessly and continuously alters almost every aspect of every segment of every industry. Life cycles have diminished exponentially. Most importantly, the significant changes will likely come from totally unexpected directions or sources.

These three basic forces have so radically changed the business environment that companies designed to function effectively in the business environment encountered even just a decade in the past or less, not to mention thirty to forty years ago, cannot hope to compete effectively today without totally reinventing their methods of doing business.

Reengineering Defined

Reengineering is the fundamental rethinking and radical redesign of business processes to achieve dramatic improvements in critical, contemporary measures of performance, such as cost, quality, service, and speed. It's the search for new models of organizing work. It's starting over.

There are four key words in the definition. The first is *fundamental*; reengineering asks the most basic questions and ignores what is in favor of what should be. The second key word is *radical*; reengineering is about reinvention, not improvement. The third key word is *dramatic*; improvements in cost, quality, speed, or service are exponential, not incremental. The final key word is *processes*; reengineering focuses on a collection of activities that creates an output that is valuable to a customer rather than on the individual tasks, departments, or structures created by the Adam Smith mindset.

Reengineering is not automation, which just creates more efficient methods of doing the wrong things. It isn't restructuring or downsizing, which only involve doing less with less. Nor is reengineering similar to reorganizing or flattening out an organization. These processes only impose a new organizational structure over the same flawed operational system. Finally, although reengineering shares some of the same ideas as the various modern quality movements, it transcends them by not trying to work within the existing structure. Reengineering looks for continuous incremental improvement. It seeks breakthroughs, not enhancements.

Characteristics of Reengineered Business Processes

Several Jobs Are Combined into One   Formerly distinct and separate tasks are re-united. Frequently the end result is a case worker or case team that accomplishes what used to be spread across many departments and people.

Workers Make Decisions   The creation of a case worker is a form of horizontal compression. This is vertical compression. Decision making becomes part of the work.

The Steps in the Process Are Performed in a Natural Order   They are no longer constrained by the artificiality created by the assembly line mentality.

Processes Have Multiple Versions   Instead of one process that tries to deal with every possible variable, a "triage" step is used to determine which of several versions of the process is most appropriate.

Work Is Performed Where It Makes the Most Sense   Each department might purchase its own supplies, vendors might take over inventory management for their customers, or customers might even become trained repair people for their vendors (e.g., office copiers).

Checks and Controls Are Reduced   Frequently, the cost of "policing" a traditional process outweighs the benefits, or the inherent risk has been greatly exaggerated. Instead of the traditional methods, companies can often enforce the desired behavior by awarding preferred vendor status with the threat of ending the relationship if excesses occur, for example.

Reconciliation Is Minimized   The number of external contact points for a typical process is greatly reduced, along with the number of chances for errors requiring reconciliation.

A Case Manager Provides a Single Point of Contact   Instead of requiring a customer to contact the shipping department to check on a lost order, accounts receivable to adjust an invoice, and sales to place an order, a customer deals with the same person or team who can take care of everything the typical customer needs.

Hybrid Centralized/Decentralized Operations Are Prevalent   Information technology allows organizations to operate as though their units were completely autonomous while still enjoying the advantages of the economies of scale that centralization creates. In addition, everyone in an organization can know the details of events happening anywhere in their organization without the meddling bureaucracy this would normally entail.

Other Changes That Occur in a Reengineered Organization

Work Units Change   The work of a business will no longer be done by representatives of its various functional departments but by a process team that replaces departments.

Jobs Change   The performance of a highly specialized task or set of tasks will be transformed into the performance of a multidimensional role as a member of a team. The once-clear boundaries between engineering and sales, for example, will be blurred. Specialists will become generalists.

People's Roles Change   Traditional companies expect employees to follow the rules and procedures. Reengineered companies expect their employees to use their judgment to find the best solution in each situation.

Job Preparation Changes   Training people to perform a specific set of tasks is replaced with educating people to figure out what their job really is and then letting them do it.

The Focus of Performance Measures and Compensation Shifts   When people are assigned specific tasks and are not responsible for the outcome of the process they're part of, there is no choice but to pay people solely for their time. In a reengineered organization, the results a person generates can be directly measured, and compensation can be tied directly to those results.

Advancement Criteria Change   A person must demonstrate the required abilities for a new position in order for a job change or a promotion to be warranted. Exceptional performance in a current job is no longer an acceptable justification.

Values Change   The belief system a reengineered company reinforces and requires of its people shifts from ideas such as, "No matter what everybody says, the reality is I must keep those above me happy—they pay my salary," to "Customers pay my salary—I need to do whatever makes them happy."

Managers' Roles Change   The traditional company requires managers to be supervisors who design and allocate work. The reengineered company requires managers who act as mentors and coaches.

Executives Change   Their perspective and focus has been primarily a financial one. It changes to ensuring that the organization's performance measurement and compensation systems motivate the team members to define and accomplish their jobs.

Reengineering changes all aspects of a company—because all aspects are interrelated. This fact is represented by the business system diamond. Its four points are business processes, values and beliefs, management and measurement systems, and jobs and structures. If you change one aspect, the others will necessarily adjust, and all four points on the diamond must work together to achieve success.

The Hunt for Reengineering Opportunities

A good way to understand the processes at work in an organization is to give them names that reflect the work that actually gets done from start to finish. For example, product development is more accurately named the concept to prototype process; sales becomes the prospect to order process. Create a process map to illustrate how work flows through a company and to use as a starting point for discussions on reengineering.

Organizations will generally use three criteria to identify the processes to reengineer:

- *Dysfunction*   Which processes are causing the most trouble?
- *Importance*   Which processes have the greatest effect on customers?
- *Feasibility*   Which processes are the best candidates for a successful redesign?

Once a *process* has been selected and a reengineering team formed, they must next reach an accurate understanding of the current process. The best method to accomplish this is to see it from the customer's perspective. Literally becoming a customer, in some cases, or at least working closely with them, is imperative for an accurate understanding.

Benchmarking—identifying excellent industry practices—can also be used, but a team should benchmark the best in the world, not just the best in the industry, to prevent their company from readopting a different version of the industry's current paradigm.

It is important to remember that a team should be studying the old process solely to learn what parts of it are critical for its performance, not because they are considering its redesign.

The Experience of Process Redesign

Teams have used a number of techniques to generate creative redesign ideas. Teams can apply a reengineering principle to the process. An example of a principle: "As few people as possible should be involved in the performance of a process." Use this principle as a goal, and redesign the process in an attempt to achieve it. Another technique is to identify and annihilate assumptions. Find the deeply held beliefs about who can do what or about how things must be done and throw them out or reverse them to observe the effect that would have on the process. A third technique is to survey the current and cutting-edge abilities of information technology and find ways to apply them to the process, seeing what that would allow the company to do.

When asked what lessons they learned during the redesigning phase of the process, team members generally report very similar answers:

1. You don't need to be an expert to redesign a process.
2. Being an outsider helps.
3. You have to discard preconceived notions.
4. It's important to see things through the customer's eyes.
5. Redesign is best done in teams.
6. You don't need to know much about the current process.
7. It's not hard to have great ideas.
8. Redesign can be fun.

Embarking on Reengineering

Two key messages must be articulated and communicated clearly, consistently, and repeatedly for reengineering to be a success. First, *all people involved must understand where their company currently is and why it can't stay like that.* Second, *they must understand what their company needs to become.* The process of reengineering is a selling job that is never really over.

Reengineering Mistakes

Successfully reengineered companies know the rules, follow them, and don't make the common and avoidable mistakes. Some of the most common errors:

Trying to Fix a Process Instead of Changing It   Don't make changes to the existing process and call it reengineering.

Not Focusing on Business Processes   By focusing on processes, most other concerns like empowerment and innovation are addressed. The opposite is not true.

Ignoring Everything Except Process Design   The management systems, organizational structures, and job designs associated with the process also require changes.

Neglecting People's Values and Beliefs   Managers must help their people rise to the challenges of reengineering by fostering and supporting effective beliefs and values.

Settling for Minor Results   Marginal improvements make it more difficult to figure out how things really work. They discourage additional time and capital investments because the original return on investment didn't meet expectations. They also create a company that lacks courage.

Quitting Too Early   Some companies lose their nerve, while others end the effort once they have their first success to display. Both lose the huge benefits that lie further down the road.

Trying to Make Things Happen from the Bottom Up   Any person not at the top of an organization lacks the perspective and the authority to transform a process effectively.

Skimping on the Resources Devoted to Reengineering   Management must assign the best people and give them plenty of time and other resources to accomplish the reengineering efforts. Anything less signals a lack of true commitment that everyone else in the organization will read as an excuse to ignore and impede the efforts.

Dissipating Energy across a Great Many Reengineering Projects   It requires focus and discipline, which can't be achieved if a large number of projects demand attention.

Concentrating Exclusively on Design   Quality ideas are required but are no less important than active and effective follow-through.

Pulling Back When People Resist Reengineering's Changes   Powerful resistance is to be expected and it must be acknowledged and dealt with without losing momentum.

CONCLUSION

People are remarkably resourceful at finding new ways to drop the ball. However, *if reengineering efforts fail, the major cause will always be lack of understanding or commitment at the top of an organization.*

Despite the numerous opportunities for failure, there are many organizations with reengineering sucesses. Organizations that undertake reengineering with understanding, commitment, and strong executive leadership will succeed. The payoffs of successful efforts are spectacular for a company, its employees, and the economy. The time for hesitation is gone; the time for action is now.

READING 2

Organizing for the Future

Jay R. Galbraith and Edward E. Lawler III & Associates
Summary prepared by Gary P. Olson

Gary P. Olson *is the Executive Director of the Center for Alcohol & Drug Treatment, Inc. He received his MBA from the University of Minnesota, Duluth. He has consulted with businesses in the creation of virtual workplaces and employee involvement.*

Businesses do not operate in a vacuum. The business environment has become, like society, increasingly complex and unpredictable. Competitive pressures have increased and what were once considered to be profound competitive advantages have proved short-term or nonexistent. The pace of technological and other changes appears to be increasing. New forms of organization and approaches to management will be needed to enable the business organization to compete effectively in the future.

Traditional organizations were created to achieve stability and predictability. Large corporations offered economies of scale and well-defined career paths for their managers. Shareholders realized good returns on companies whose market value usually exceeded real asset value. Success in a stable environment, however, has not translated into effectiveness in a dynamic, rapidly changing milieu.

In response to competition, strategic initiatives to increase productivity, quality, and customer satisfaction have become commonplace. Instead of creating a sustainable advantage, these initiatives have served mainly to meet basic competitive requirements. Only companies that have been able to implement competitive strategies quicker or better than their competitors have obtained a competitive advantage, and that has often been only temporary.

In the future it is likely that only the *ability of a company to organize effectively and manage change will form the basis for achieving a longer-term advantage*. Companies must acquire and adopt business strategies more quickly than the competition and do a better job implementing these strategies.

DESIGNING ORGANIZATIONS

Organizational design is not only the process of creating a structure, but it also includes alignment of management functions, information systems, human resources, and other elements within that structure. New models attempt to negotiate trade-offs

Jay R. Galbraith and Edward E. Lawler III, *Organizing for the Future*. New York, NY: Jossey-Bass, 1993.

between the benefits of large scale and reduced cycle times and also to resolve conflicts that are inherent in these models.

The design of *new organizational forms is driven by competitive forces including service and product quality, cost, and the need to make rapid adjustments to external market conditions and internal demands.* Also, increased research and development expenditures due to complex product technology require expanded markets just to cover fixed costs. At the same time, technology has contributed to the emergence of new organizational forms. Organizational control methods are changing due to the power of buyers, who demand decision making at the point of buyer–seller contact. Also, buyers expect a functional relationship with the seller where speed of delivery, installation, and service are perceived as product features. The scarcity of highly skilled knowledge workers has required the relocation of work to sites where the workers are located or, alternately, the creation of *"virtual"* worksites using information technology. Several of these forces have resulted in a *power shift away from top-level management control structures and into the workplace.*

Organizational design is, at best, a temporary response to a continuously changing environment. In the future, an increased allocation of resources will be needed to insure the development of knowledgeable, skilled human resources. Speed and flexibility are key advantages of laterally integrated systems. Networking with other organizations enhances organizational learning. A variety of practices and designs can exist within the same organization in order to create a flexible response to change. Top management needs to formulate and articulate a clear vision and strategy.

STRATEGY AND STRUCTURE

Business strategy has always influenced structure. Single-product businesses have used *functional* models, whereas diversified business have tended to use a *divisional* structure. In single-product businesses, management has assumed full operational control. In diversified companies, management control was more strategic, aligning the operation of divisions to reduce duplication and ensure cooperation among divisions.

The emergence of conglomerates, and the creation of holding companies with their portfolios of unrelated businesses, resulted in a third strategy-structure model. In most cases, managers of a *holding* company exert mainly financial control over its diversified holdings. They specify return-on-investment (ROI) targets and acceptable inventory turnover ratios, provide access to capital markets, and so forth. Contrary to widespread belief, little evidence supports the claim that diversification leads to diminished performance. There is evidence that the optimal number of businesses to manage effectively is usually three or four.

New structural models are emerging, driven by competitive forces and the internal adjustments required to successfully respond to them. The *front-end/back-end model* is a hybrid form that separates a front-end unit (organized around customers), from a back-end system or product-oriented area. This hybrid model is often seen in the computer industry, where the customer deals with a single face for a problem-solving system (including software), while the back-end supplies some, but not all, of the hardware to meet the requirements. This model requires some decentralization due to market and product diversity (the front end may be geographically widespread), but strategic and operational control are exercised by the corporation. The front-end and back-end functions also need to be carefully integrated to avoid the conflicts inherent in this model. For example, sourcing arrangements by the front end may conflict with the back-end's desire to be a sole supplier.

Divisionalized forms are moving toward what looks more like the holding company model. This occurs when the need for a coordinated response to market forces exceeds the need for divisional coordination. One of the shortcomings of the traditional divisional form is that divisions must suboptimize in order to adopt a common corporate policy or share a corporate resource. Achieving coordination is expensive and may handicap the division unnecessarily. Decentralization and a move toward divisional autonomy is an outgrowth of this strategic response.

When financial markets, through "sell" recommendations, force up price-earnings ratios of conglomerates (reducing stock prices), the breakup value of the company may exceed the market value. This results in pressure to divest some units or be taken over. Conglomerates will continue to exist, however, and clustering may be a way to deal with the mixed strategies required by both related and unrelated businesses in a portfolio. Where advantage can be achieved (given the cost of managing it), clustering brings together seemingly diverse businesses in a portfolio that share a common market, a common product, or other major factors.

The strategic business unit (SBU) is the building block of structure. An *SBU* is a logical or economic entity with its own set of customers, products, and competitors. Although the divisional profit center is still seen, there is a new focus on the modification of the functional unit, as well as the creation of new models.

Competitive pressures have revealed the shortcomings of the functional unit design. The functional unit, with its own set of rewards and performance measures, tends to create barriers to interfunctional cooperation. Reductions in the number of specialties and hierarchical levels have moved functional performance, particularly of routine activities, closer to the front lines. Still, total quality service and other initiatives require extensive cooperation.

Lateral units are groups that are formally or informally organized across functional boundaries. They are developed around a logical business requirement. Sales functions grouped geographically and engineering organized around similar manufacturing processes would be examples of lateral units. An assembly function may be organized around each component of a complex system. Technology has enabled such units to organize without being tied to a physical location.

Increasingly, management functions need to be diffused into the lateral organization in order to achieve effective integration. Particularly in front-end/back-end structures, the quality of the lateral integrating process is a key to avoiding interfunctional conflicts. Integrated planning and budgeting activities create shared responsibilities for targets, outcomes, and rewards.

Business network units have emerged as an alternative to the autonomous division. One company can assume the role of integrator to a network of efficient single-product or single-service organizations. The integrator must negotiate the interests of the member based on trust and mutual advantage. Business network units are most successful when the integrator performs a dominant functional task such as large scale-buying or intensive research and development.

FLATTER IS SMARTER

The movement toward less hierarchical structures in business is the direct result of competitive pressures that demand greater speed, quality, and productivity. Achieving continuously higher levels of performance demands dramatic changes in the management of internal operations that hierarchical forms cannot produce.

The way organizations acquire, adopt, and implement change will be a critical factor in their ability to adopt new organizational forms and strategy. Organizations "learn" when they alter processes ahead of, or in response to, changes in their environment.

Organizational learning includes innovation, process improvement, and organizational redesign; all of these involve organizational change. Several important conclusions about change stand out:

- Change does not happen without a compelling reason.
- Leadership is crucial to the change process.
- Change in one part of a system creates pressure for change in other parts.
- Change involves conflict.
- Change is not an orderly process.
- Change will be a continual fact of life in the coming decades.

Lateral integration is emerging as an important organizing principle. In hierarchical organizations, integration is achieved within the top-to-bottom structure. An organizational model that is designed to produce stability and predictability cannot adequately respond to multiple products, markets, and customers while simultaneously producing lower cost, achieving high-quality performance, and attracting highly skilled, motivated employees.

The compromises and adjustments of effective lateral design require a continuum of integrating mechanisms. Formalizing the integrating role in management or team structures ensures organizational support of the process. Less formal approaches can co-locate with formal systems within the same organization.

HIGH-INVOLVEMENT ORGANIZATIONS

Up to the present, employee involvement has been limited in its application or undertaken to achieve tactical advantages within the organization. Quality circles, for example, are top-down undertakings that neither transform job design nor permit worker discretion over quality. Companies have also used employee involvement as a tactic to avoid unionization. Even "Japanese-style management" that employs practices like consensus decision making mask the deeper reality of a traditional, control-type practice. The degree of employee autonomy is limited, even though employee suggestions for process improvement are sought and encouraged.

Employee involvement practices exist along a continuum ranging from suggestion systems to the truly high-involvement organization. Intermediate variations like job involvement, job enrichment, or semi-autonomous work teams give employees more control over decisions that directly affect their jobs. High-involvement organizations extend employee participation toward managing the business as a whole.

The four key variables in employee involvement are (1) access to information, (2) the opportunity to influence decision making, (3) participation in rewards, and (4) knowledge. Without knowledge, information cannot be properly interpreted, and the resulting decisions will be flawed. Without accurate and timely information, good decision making is not possible. Without participation tied to rewards, the program has no incentive to succeed.

Working examples of high-involvement models are rare, not because they have proven ineffective, but because they are relatively new and run contrary to the dominant management ideology: control and internal stability. For high-involvement models to emerge, management must adopt a new paradigm based on the assumption that *the key to maximizing organizational effectiveness is to maximize the employee's ability to directly respond to changing conditions.* Currently, many managers verbally support involvement but often fail to see the implications for their own behavior. Managers must be educated and coached to translate theory into practice.

Implementing employee involvement as a means to achieving organizational performance goals is probably the best way to legitimize the effort and ensure full organizational support. Although it is not necessary to use the process of employee involvement to implement a program, unless management is committed to the effort and can experience it firsthand the program will not develop effectively.

Employee involvement, however, is not suited to all organizations. Examples of businesses where employee involvement is unlikely to lead to improved effectiveness are those that involve routine technology and little innovation, where employee attitudes are unrelated to business performance, or where the business operates in an unusually stable environment. *In organizations where it is appropriate, successful employee involvement programs can be expected to increase the speed of decision making, reduce overhead costs, and improve flexibility.* Because management style and organizational design can be sources of competitive advantage, employee participation will be adopted in a number of industries in the near future.

TEAMWORK, PARTNERSHIP, AND LEADERSHIP

If business units are the building blocks of structure, teams and teamwork mechanisms have been the building blocks of performance in many organizations. *What is changing is the way teams are integrated into the organizational structure.* The same competitive forces that are driving organizational redesign are creating an increased interest in teamwork and giving teams more autonomy and power. The use of teams to achieve lateral integration, an important organizing principle discussed earlier, is becoming increasingly evident.

Collaborative networked teams, parallel teams, project teams, and work teams are some of the designs that are used. Teams operate along three dimensions. Teams may be permanent or temporary within a time dimension. They may do the basic work of the organization, as in autonomous work groups, or be dedicated to process improvement, as in the quality circle. A third dimension is the way the team functions within the organization's authority structure. Teams may transcend divisional boundaries or exist within a defined unit and report through existing hierarchical channels.

Human resource management departments were once devoted to the administrative and legal aspects of dealing with employees. Forces such as global competition, the need to manage change, increased knowledge about human resource management, information technology, and the emergence of the knowledge worker have moved human resource managers to the center of the new organizational models. At the same time, these departments must justify their existence by adding value and cutting costs.

Managing change will require new selection, training, appraisal, and reward systems to match new organizational designs, management styles, and work structures. *Human resource functions will contribute to both planning and implementing change.* These departments will not only be involved in the implementation of strategic initiatives, such as employee involvement and teams, but will be integral to planning these strategies and providing expertise about how to organize and conduct the strategizing process.

In addition to the flattening of hierarchical structures, lateral integration, and increased employee involvement, *the importance of leadership has emerged as a critical factor for achieving and maintaining competitive advantage.* Competitive crises may have created a "survival of the fittest" environment from which gifted leaders have emerged. Leadership practices that have been known for decades (setting clear goals, involving people in decision making, motivating through challenge) have reemerged in the search for excellence. It is not enough, however, to assume good leadership will emerge on its own. Leaders can, and must, learn skills and develop attitudes that will help them adapt to the changes that confront the organizations of the future. Their ability to convert missions into reality, align people with direction, develop trust based on integrity, be comfortable with uncertainty, develop self-awareness, and learn from experience will be the keys to future success.

READING 3

Visionary Companies: Why Do They Endure?

Jerry I. Porras and James C. Collins

What is a visionary organization, and what makes it successful over long periods of time? We explored this question in a research project begun in 1988, a point in time in which the concept of visionary organizations had yet to be fully developed. Previously, the focus of management thinking had been on charismatic visionary leadership, and any visionary behavior by an organization was attributed to the visionary leader. We began to wonder how an organization like 3M could be explained using the charismatic visionary leader model, since it seemed that, for 3M, neither its current nor past CEOs fit this model. 3M's chief executive officers over the years have been highly competent and effective managers, but from all reports were not the "larger than life" type of leader commonly associated with the concept of charismatic visionaries. This observation led us to two conclusions. First, our focus should be on the organization and its characteristics, rather than the leader. Second, the type of leadership to be found in 3M-like organizations must be different than the one prescribed by the charismatic visionary leadership model.

METHOD

A survey of 700 CEOs drawn from the two Fortune 500 lists (50 percent sample stratified by industry and size) plus the two *Inc. Magazine* lists of public and private companies (100 CEOs randomly selected from each of these lists) provided the companies we studied. Each CEO was asked to nominate the five companies he/she thought most visionary (using whatever definition of visionary company they personally held). The CEO response rate was approximately 23 percent and was representative of the entire sample. Companies were rank ordered according to frequency of nomination with the top twenty selected for study. This list was reduced to eighteen when we concluded that longevity was a key explanatory factor, thereby eliminating both Compaq (eight years old at the time our research began) and Apple (twelve years old). The remaining companies were all forty-five years old or older (company founding dates ranged from 1945 back to 1812) fitting the criteria for longevity.

The age issue also drove our next methodological decision, which was to study the nominated organizations from their founding date forward rather than over a more

Excerpted, with permission of the publisher, from *Built to Last: Successful Habits of Visionary Companies.* New York, NY: HarperCollins, 1994.

recent period, say the last five or ten years. We wanted to know the principles that guided these organizations and their designs over decades and ultimately over their entire history. We believed that this method had the potential to yield principles that would be more fundamental.

Finally, we selected a comparison group of companies by matching each visionary company with a company founded in approximately the same time period, in the same industry, often a chief competitor of the visionary company, rarely mentioned in the CEO survey as highly visionary, and still alive in 1990.

Since we wished to study these companies over their entire history, our search for information had to be extremely comprehensive. Sources of data included company archival material (provided by the company), published books (over 100 of them, each focused primarily on one company), published and unpublished cases, and magazine and newspaper articles going back to the founding era of each company. A conservative estimate of the number of pages was accomplished using the variables proposed in Porras.[1]

FINDINGS

After our initial analysis of the data, we derived the following general descriptions of a visionary company: Visionary companies are organizations widely admired by their peers, with a history of having made a significant impact on the environments in which they operate, and having been highly successful through multiple cycles of leadership, multiple product cycles, and multiple industry cycles.

Visionary companies are highly respected, well-known and, over the long term, economically very successful. We explored their economic success by creating three mythical stock portfolios and exploring the performance of each. These were: (a) the market as a whole, (b) the set of comparison companies, and (c) the set of visionary companies. We invested one dollar in each portfolio beginning in 1926 and by reinvesting dividends and properly accounting for stock splits, swaps, and so forth, we tracked the investments until 1990. A dollar in the market grows to $415, while a dollar in the comparison company portfolio grows to $955 (more than two times the market performance). A dollar in the visionary company portfolio grows to $6355 (over fifteen times better than the market and six and a half times better than the comparison companies).

Our primary findings can be clustered in two categories: (1) Characteristics of the founding leader or the leader during key formative years of the company, and (2) characteristics of the companies themselves. The findings reported in both of these categories obtained in a preponderance of the visionary companies and not in the comparison companies.

Leader Characteristics

Leaders of visionary companies tended to focus on building the capabilities of their companies to behave in visionary ways rather than on playing a central role in the development of great ideas, strategies, marketing approaches, and so on. We call these leaders "organizational visionaries." In contrast, leaders of comparison companies focused mainly on developing the great product or service, devising innovative marketing and promotions approaches, creating comprehensive strategies, or, in general, being key initiators of activities that already determined the company's success. As a result, the performance of the comparison organizations was heavily predicated on their leaders being the center of decision activity for the organization. We call this type of leader a "product or service visionary."

We came to use a metaphor to describe these two types of visionary leaders; "Organizational visionaries are clock-builders" and product/services visionaries are "time tellers." Clock builders built an "organizational clock," so that the time could be told without their having to be there. Time-tellers, on the other hand, were the only ones who knew how to tell the time, so that whenever people needed to "know the time," they were dependent on the time teller to provide it.

We found that throughout the history of the visionary and comparison companies, the former tended to be led by clock-builders, while the latter by time-tellers. All the comparison companies were founded on a successful product idea, while with only three exceptions, the visionary companies were not founded on a successful product idea. For example, Hewlett-Packard's first products were an automatic urinal flusher, a bowling foul line indicator, a shock machine for weight reduction, and a clock-drive for a telescope. In contrast, Texas Instruments, H-P's comparison, had a very successful first product, a seismographic sensing device used in oil exploration. Hewlett and Packard built a great company that then created great products. Texas Instruments built their company around the great product they started with.

George Westinghouse was a great inventor holding patents for hundreds of products and founding his company on the principle of alternating current electricity. Charles Coffin, founder of General Electric, developed the first industrial research laboratory to invent the great products that made GE successful, even though his company originally had been based on the direct current principle, which initially was a failure. Coffin built a clock: Westinghouse told the time.

Core Ideology and a Drive for Progress

Our analysis of the entire history of the two sets of companies indicated that they possessed two key dimensions—a core ideology (core values plus enduring purpose) and a powerful almost primal drive for progress (change, adaptation, innovation, experimentation). These two dimensions play themselves out in the organization in terms of two sets of processes, the first serves to preserve the core while the second results in stimulating progress. These processes are enacted through a variety of concrete organizational mechanisms. Although both sets of companies possessed many mechanisms in common, we identified six that provided discrimination between the two sets. Visionary companies preserved their core by (a) having a purpose beyond maximization of profits, (b) creating cult-like cultures, and (c) growing their management (especially the CEO and the top-most executives) from within the company. They stimulate progress doing one or more of the following: (a) creating and achieving audacious goals, (b) promoting purposeful evolution, and (c) engaging in continual self-improvement.

Preserve the Core

The core values and enduring purpose were much more well understood (often codified, e.g., Hewlett-Packard Way, Johnson & Johnson Credo, Sony Pioneer Spirit, 3M Manifesto) in the visionary companies than in the comparisons. Core values are those very most fundamental values the organization will continue to hold and behave consistently with even if punished by the environment. Johnson & Johnson's first core value in their credo is, "Our first responsibility is to our customers." Their response to the Tylenol tampering incident demonstrates their commitment to the core value. It included removing the product from all the shelves in the United States, redesigning the bottle's sealing system, and informing the public through a massive information effort that involved approximately 2500 people. All these efforts were estimated to have cost the company $100 million—a pretty significant cost for living a core value. Contrast this to Bristol-Meyers, Squibb who had a somewhat similar event occur with Excedrin a few weeks later. Although the Bristol-Meyers pledge (created in 1987) appears to emphasize a similar core value of commitment to customers, the organization did not behave consistently with it when the "chips were down." This means that this value is not truly a core value of the organization.

Visionary companies preserve and protect their core ideology. As a result, it rarely changes. We found evidence of consistent core values for periods of over 100 years in some cases, and of consistent purpose for over sixty years. Visionary companies tend to think of their purpose as accomplishing an end beyond maximization of profit or shareholder wealth. In seventeen out of eighteen companies, the visionary companies were more ideological driven and less product-maximization driven than the comparison companies. They don't lose sight of their true purpose by letting profit maximization dominate their decision making. Rather, they see profit as a consequence instead of a cause. Disney's purpose is to bring happiness to millions; Merck's is to preserve and improve human life; Marriott's is to make people away from home feel they are among friends and really valued; Hewlett-Packard's is to make a technical contribution; Johnson & Johnson's is to alleviate pain and disease. These companies believe in the words of George Merck II, CEO of Merck, when he said in 1950, "We try never to forget that medicine is for the people. It's not for the profits. The profits follow, and if we remembered that, they have never failed to appear. The better we have remembered it, the larger they have been."

There should be no question that visionary companies are interested in profits, but they believe that if they serve their purpose well, profits will follow, not the other way around.

Core ideology is also preserved by creating strong, cult-like cultures, cultures so tight that if a person doesn't fit, over the longer run, they are "ejected like a virus." Cults are characterized by strong ideologies, extensive indoctrination processes, tightness of fit between the system and the individual, and a sense of elitism among members. Visionary companies hold similar characteristics and do so to a much greater extent than the comparison companies. Disneyland teaches new employees how to frame their job (a role in the show), what language to use (guests rather than tourists, costumes rather than uniforms, on-stage versus off-stage, casting rather than personnel), and generally define the specific behaviors desired from their cast members. Nordstrom has a one-page employee manual that gives substantial autonomy within the context of providing outstanding customer service. Smile contests, most Nordstrom-like contests, phantom shoppers, and sales per hour feedback all result in tight social control of employees and highly consistent behavior.

Core ideology is also preserved in visionary companies by practicing a policy of growing their management from within the corporation. Rarely have visionary companies gone outside the company for a CEO. As of our data collection cut-off date (1992), only two visionary companies had gone outside—Disney, when it hired Michael Eisner, and Phillip Morris, early in the 1900s when it went outside three times for CEOs. In contrast, thirteen comparison companies have brought in outside CEOs at least once in their history. Looked at another way, of the 113 visionary company CEOs for which we have data, only 3.5 percent came from outside. Of the 140 comparison company CEOs, 22.1 percent were outsiders.

In order to preserve the core ideology, a CEO must really have that ideology buried deep in their psyche, put there through countless experiences in which the ideology comes into play and guides behavior. Outsides don't have that fundamental understanding and as a consequence, wind up changing it as they make difficult decisions.

Stimulate Progress

Change and adaptation are fundamental for survival. The comparison companies were much more adept at stimulating progress than they were at knowing and protecting their core ideology. Perhaps this is why they have survived and performed quite well over the decades. The factors that preserve the core and stimulate progress.

Visionary companies stimulate progress in three ways that are not commonly used by the comparisons. First, they set audacious, stretching major goals that coalesce and motivate the organization. Goals that challenge the organization, that aren't easily achievable, excite the imagination, provide substantial innovation and change. We have come to call these "Big Hairy Audacious Goals" (BHAGs) to capture their magnitude and impact. BHAGs can range from "bet the company" types of goals to ones that just are quite audacious (Boeing bet the company on the 707 and 747. Had they failed the company probably wouldn't have survived. IBM bet the company on the 360 computer series, a $5 billion investment that, had it gone sour, may have sunk the company). (In 1991 Wal-Mart set the goal of being a $125 billion company by the year 2000. At the time they set this goal, they were a $30 billion company, and only GM had attained the $125 billion level.)

Purposeful evolution is a second prominent approach to stimulating change used by visionary companies. Just as biological species evolve through variation and selection processes, so do visionary companies "try a lot of stuff and keep what works." By creating policies and strategies that promote experimentation and innovation, then keeping the experiments that are both successful and consistent with the core ideology, a visionary company evolves and adapts. 3M requires technical employees to dedicate 15 percent of their work time to dreaming up new ideas. It requires divisions to generate 30 percent of annual sales from products or services introduced in the previous four years. It provides "Genesis Grants" which are internal venture capital funds of up to $50,000 for researchers to develop prototypes and do market tests.

Visionary companies also stimulate progress by continuous self-improvement. In contrast to the more recent management "fad" of self-improvement, visionary companies have been practicing this concept since their early founding periods, which for some means all the way back to the early 1900s. Johnson & Johnson created their product management structure as a way to keep themselves number one. They believed that if they competed against the best (i.e., themselves) they would always be number one. Motorola cuts off mature product lines while they are still profitable, forcing itself to fill the gap with new products, and have been doing so since they were in the radio business in the late 1920s. David Packard preached continuous improvement beginning in the 1950s.

Never being satisfied and constantly striving for improvement has also played itself out in the ways visionary companies invest for the long term. By analyzing financial statements for the two sets of companies, going all the way back to 1925, we found that for these companies for which data existed that: (a) Visionary companies consistently invested more heavily in new property, plant, and equipment as a percentage of annual sales, than did the comparisons (thirteen out of fifteen cases); (b) Visionary companies plow back a greater percentage of each year's earnings into the company, paying out less in cash dividends to share holders (twelve of fifteen cases with one case being indistinguishable); (c) Visionary companies invest more heavily in R&D as a percentage of sales (eight of eight cases); (d) Broadly, visionary companies invest more aggressively in human capital via extensive recruiting, training, and professional development, as well as in technical know-how, new technologies, and innovative industry practices.

The mechanisms described above differentiate visionary companies from their comparisons. As such, they provide a picture of the key dimensions of highly successful companies.

One final result remains to be described. Visionary companies were more consistently aligned than the comparisons. The mechanisms described above, as well as many other dimensions of the organization's architecture, were highly aligned to deliver consistent messages about desired behavior. Clearly, they are not perfectly aligned systems, but more aligned than their comparisons and, therefore, generating more "organized" behavior from their employees.

In summary, visionary companies possess characteristics that differentiate them from their early competitors. The differences they exhibit appear to have led to significantly different levels of performance over very long time periods. Certainly, more lessons are left to be learned from these companies, but we believe that the results of our study have provided a useful platform for increasing our understanding of what it takes for a company to be truly visionary.

Note

1. Porras, J. I. (1987). *Stream analysis: A powerful new way to diagnose and manage organizational change.* Reading, MA: Addison-Wesley.

PART FIVE

Organizational Vision and Goals

Many of the authors in this book suggest that organizations can benefit by defining their own standard of effectiveness, especially after examining other successful firms. An organization's external environment has a powerful influence on organizational success and needs to be monitored for significant trends and influential forces. In addition, effective executives need to recognize when internal changes are necessary to adapt to the external environment.

The two readings in this section are designed to stimulate thinking about management through a focus on the management and leadership of the internal environment (relative to its external context).

Taken collectively, these two readings suggest that organizations can (and should) proactively *take control of their destinies*. One way of doing this is by articulating an engaging vision that can systematically guide them into the future. In effect, managers are urged to have a master plan that defines their mission, identifies their unique environmental niche, builds on their strengths, and adapts to changing needs. This overall vision is then converted into operational goals.

Burt Nanus, in *Visionary Leadership*, contends that the great leaders—individuals like Abraham Lincoln, Martin Luther King, Jr., and Alfred P. Sloan—are those who were able to develop a unique vision that attracted the commitment of others, inspired people, revitalized organizations, and mobilized the resources that were needed to make their visions a reality. This *vision*, according to Nanus, is the key to leadership, and it serves as the central theme of his work.

Burt Nanus is Professor of Management in the School of Business Administration at the University of Southern California. He is the Director of Research at USC's Leadership Institute and the author or coauthor of several other books focusing on leadership, including *The Leader's Edge* and *Leaders* (with Warren Bennis).

Using a relatively new format (a fictional novel) to convey his thoughts about a process of ongoing improvement, Eliyahu Goldratt's book (*The

Goal) has become a million-seller. The theme of his book is simple and straightforward—use a system of common sense to help people identify their goals and plan how to achieve them. The key to success, he maintains, lies in focusing one's efforts on a single outcome (profits) and identifying and pursuing opportunities to contribute to that goal.

Goldratt, a physicist by training, is an internationally active management consultant. He is also the author of *The Race, It's Not Luck, The Haystack Syndrame*, and *Critical Chain*.

READING 1

Visionary Leadership

Burt Nanus
Summary prepared by Gayle Baugh

Gayle Baugh *is an Assistant Professor of Management at the University of West Florida. She received her doctorate in Management in 1992 from the University of Cincinnati. Her research interests include leadership and team development, organizational attitudes, and gender issues in the workplace. She has published in these areas and presented numerous conference papers at academic meetings. She is a member of the Academy of Management, the American Psychological Association, and the Southern Management Association.*

A good vision, widely shared, can help an organization on its path to excellence and renewal. *Visionary leadership* is the ability to develop and implement an engaging image of what the organization can become, and the ability to set up systems to make that vision a reality. Visionary leadership is less about interactions between leaders and followers (a focal point for many leadership models) and more about interactions between leaders and groups, or leaders and systems.

Although it is easy to talk about great vision, it is much harder to develop and implement it. Practical guidelines are necessary in order to know what steps to take in order to develop and implement a vision for an organization's future. Information from leaders of many sorts, from the private sector and public agencies, and from published literature in the areas of leadership and strategic management, provides a basis for practical instructions for the development of visionary leadership.

DEFINING VISION AND VISIONARY LEADERSHIP

Vision is an engaging picture of what the organization could be like in the future. The vision must, however, be realistic enough to attract the organization's stakeholders, especially employees, to invest time and energy in it. Although vision is not verifiable in any factual sense, it must be based on a realistic assessment of the challenges and opportunities that the organization will face in the future.

Vision is not, however, synonymous with the organization's mission. The *mission* provides the purpose for the business (why it exists), but the vision indicates the direction in which it is moving (what it will become). Vision is also not the same as *objectives*

Burt Nanus, *Visionary Leadership*. San Francisco, CA: Jossey-Bass, 1992.

or *plans*, although both will be necessary in order to pursue the vision. Objectives and plans are much more specific in terms of expected outcomes and how to achieve them than is an organizational vision.

Vision results in several positive outcomes for a business or organization. It attracts commitment and energy. Vision infuses employees' work with meaning, and helps persuade them that their activities are significant to the direction that the organization is taking. Vision also sets standards of excellence, so that progress toward a desirable future can be evaluated. Finally, vision provides a bridge between the present and the future, showing where investment of resources, including time and energy, are most likely to be effective.

An effective vision for an organization has several characteristics. It must

- capitalize on the organization's unique strengths and fit with the organization's current external environment.
- be lofty and inspire followers.
- provide a clear, engaging direction that is easily grasped by followers.
- be challenging in order to command greater performance.

Thus, a vision is not just an endpoint toward which to strive, but instead it provides a clear direction for the organization to take.

Managers can look for several indicators in order to determine if a new vision is necessary. A definite indicator is a sense of uncertainty about purpose or a feeling among employees of being "stalled." Loss of customers or loss of status would suggest the need for a new vision, as would a sense that the organization is somehow out of touch with its surrounding environment. Other indicators include a lack of pride in work or the unwillingness to take risks. Excessive gossip or rumors within the company suggest that workers do not know which direction the company is taking. If managers sense some of these symptoms, then the need for a new vision is apparent.

DEVELOPING THE ORGANIZATIONAL VISION

The first step in developing a vision is to determine exactly what business the organization is in. The definition of the core or *essential business* will influence the future directions available. It is important to determine what the current mission of the organization is and what value it provides to society. In addition, determining the unique position of the organization within its industry is essential in order to create a vision that is consistent with organizational capabilities. Managers need to speculate on what capabilities or strengths will be necessary to succeed in the marketplace of the future.

While these issues involve the organization's position in the external environment, the internal environment must also be addressed. The organization's vision must fit with the *culture*, which is the underlying structure of key beliefs and values that are held in common within the workplace and taught to new members. The vision must capitalize on current operating strengths, whereas weaknesses must be acknowledged in order to avoid stumbling in those areas. An internal assessment of culture, strengths, and weaknesses will provide some clues as to a workable vision for the company.

Organizational vision may be limited in terms of geography and social constraints, depending on the organization in question. The vision may also be limited in terms of its time horizon. The ideal time horizon is that period of time over which major changes can be accomplished, but which is still relevant to the current managerial workforce. One must look beyond that time period, however, in order to measure the success of the vision, because the returns on the investments of resources will probably not be forthcoming until a decade beyond the implementation of the vision.

As a result, the outcome measures for determining success must be contemplated over this longer time horizon. The vision must support the organization's future success, which means that measures of success must be defined. Because there are numerous operational measures of "success," the five or six criteria of success essential to survival must be identified. Then attention can be directed toward the alternative visions (possible futures) that are available to promote success on these essential criteria.

DEVELOPING FUTURE SCENARIOS

Guessing at what will occur in the future is never easy. But in order to develop vision, leaders need not *predict* the future; they need only assess likely future events and how these events would affect the organization. Specific future events can be integrated into *scenarios* that describe sets of possible (and relevant) futures. Flexibility to accommodate the most likely scenarios can then be built into the vision.

Visionary leaders must determine which dimensions of future changes can affect the organization's vision, and what can potentially happen in each of these dimensions. For most organizations, the relevant concerns include changes in the wants and desires of the major market, changes in the desires of the major stakeholders in the organization, and changes in the social, political, economic, and technological environments.

After listing possible changes, some predictions must be made about which are most likely to occur. Then, these probable events must be integrated into scenarios of future states of the world. Usually four to six scenarios are sufficient to accommodate most of the possible states of the future. The scenarios must be internally consistent and must appear to be possible, even likely, to an outside observer. Then the implications of each scenario for the organization in question can be evaluated. The firm must determine how it would position itself to achieve success (as previously defined) under each scenario.

It is easiest to make predictions and develop scenarios when there are multiple perspectives brought to bear on these questions. Thus, *vision is probably best developed by a multidisciplinary team*, wherein speculation is encouraged and synergy is possible. Further, when it comes time to implement the vision, employee commitment to it is much more likely when they have felt involved in the vision from its inception.

Vision is, above all else, innovative. It requires looking at the well-known facts of an organization's situation and putting them together in new and innovative ways. Whereas the process of developing a vision requires some amount of inspiration, insight will most likely occur as a result of deep thinking about the question. Structuring the process of thinking about the future will facilitate visioning.

EVALUATING ALTERNATIVE VISIONS

First, it is helpful to review all of the information about the organization's current situation and anticipated future. A mental map or a schematic model increases the ability to think systematically about the current situation. A schematic can be developed by placing all competitors in the current market on a graph defined by the two key identifying dimensions to which the market responds. Or a mental map can result from listing the distinctive competencies of the business and identifying market niches that use the largest number of them.

Vision, or more appropriately, multiple possible visions, will begin to develop at this point in the process. A series of vision statements should be elaborated, but judgments about practicality or feasibility must be withheld. Once a number of vision statements are generated, the evaluation process will require that the most feasible among them be tested against the qualities of a good vision: consistency with the values and culture of the organization, congruence with its strengths and weaknesses, consistency with possible future scenarios, and the likelihood of success on outcome measures identified earlier.

The most attractive among the vision statements must be evaluated. Alternative visions can be rated according to the degree that they

- Are future-oriented.
- Are based on high principles.
- Clarify purpose and direction.
- Will generate deep commitment.
- Fit with the organization's strengths, weaknesses, and culture.
- Reflect the organization's distinctive competencies.
- Are challenging.

These ratings can be totaled for each vision, providing an indication of how well each vision statement meets the criteria for a good vision. The same process can be used to evaluate the five or six essential criteria for measuring a vision's success and to evaluate its fit with organizational factors. Based on these totals, one vision is likely to emerge as more appropriate than the others.

Two or three alternative visions may emerge that are highly rated in all three areas. These should be examined more closely. Some of the alternative vision statements may be combined, producing a stronger overall vision statement. With some additional experimentation, a vision statement that is focused, exciting, and inspirational can be generated.

The final part of the process is to implement the vision, which is not necessarily straightforward. It is, however, essential if the organization is to move into the future.

IMPLEMENTING THE VISION

Once the vision has been developed and communicated throughout the organization, the remaining task is to make the vision a reality. Although leaders are not generally involved in the day-to-day tasks of accomplishing the work of the organization, there are many things that leaders must do in order to ensure effective implementation of the vision. Three roles are important to the implementation process.

First, the leader must be the *spokesperson* for the vision. The vision must be communicated to others both inside and outside the organization in such a way that it inspires action. Communicating the vision involves networking with major stakeholders in order to ensure that the vision is accepted and that actions congruent with the vision are given the highest priority.

As a spokesperson, the leader must also personify the vision, or "live the dream." Thus, the leader speaks with actions, not just words. How the leader follows through on commitments, what issues and which individuals attract the leader's attention, when and how actions are taken by the leader, and the leader's formal and informal statements are all scrutinized to determine the leader's real desires and commitment to the vision.

The second role the leader takes in the implementation process is as *change agent*. The strongest influence the leader can have as a change agent is through the power to control resources and to direct them to areas crucial to the implementation of the vision. The leader has direct influence on the implementation process through resource allocation, staffing, changing the organizational structure, directing information flows, and changing organizational processes. Indirect influence is exercised through consultation, persuasion, participation, inspiration, and motivation.

The third role the leader takes in the implementation process is as *coach*. For the most part, the leader will not have time to engage in one-on-one coaching, but instead will be involved with work units and groups within the organization. By carefully controlling assignments to groups and tasks, especially the assignment of group leaders, the leader can exert great influence on the implementation process. Further, the design of jobs, the resources and support services made available, the design of the reward system, and the goals and expectations with work units all affect the implementation of the vision. *Leaders must ensure that the vision as implemented is consonant with the vision as communicated.*

RE-VISIONING

The story is not over when the vision is implemented. No vision, no matter how innovative, will be appropriate for an organization for all times. As a result, the leader must look for clues internally and externally that a new vision is needed.

Monitoring the vision internally will ensure that the vision still fits the organization. The leader wants to see that the vision has been adopted by employees at all levels, that influential managers are using their power to enhance implementation, that employees are cooperating in realizing the vision, and that the organization's goals, priorities, structures, and processes are all consistent with the vision.

In addition, *tracking* the vision—gathering information about its effectiveness—through the external environment will ensure that it is appropriate for the current situation. For example, the major stakeholders should all understand and accept the vision, and the organization should be performing well according to the measures of success identified in the visioning process. The situation should be tracked so that if changes occur in the markets or in other facets of the external environment that affect the organization's vision, the organization can adapt to those changes quickly. Competitors, too, should be tracked to ensure that their actions do not endanger achievement of the organization's vision.

The easiest time to make changes is when the organization is running smoothly, not when the company is already under competitive or regulatory pressure. It is important, therefore, to focus on both the internal and external environments to anticipate changes that will affect the organization's vision before they become major threats. Monitoring and tracking the vision will facilitate constant organizational renewal.

Although leadership at the highest levels of the organization has been emphasized, *visionary leaders are needed at all levels within organizations.* If managers at all levels are encouraged to be true leaders, to develop vision for their work units that is consistent with the organization's overall vision, and to imbue their own work units with enthusiasm and energy for pursuing that vision, the organization will thrive. With leaders at all levels seeking to understand the internal and external environment, it is much less likely that important changes in either will pass unnoticed. One of the most important tasks of visionary leaders is to *develop a climate where more visionary leaders are encouraged and developed.*

READING 2

The Goal

Eliyahu M. Goldratt and Jeff Cox
Summary prepared by Michael Roche

> **Michael Roche** *is Vice President and Publisher of The Dryden Press, an imprint of Harcourt Brace. Prior to serving in this position, he was the editor for two editions of* The Manager's Bookshelf.

The Goal by Eliyahu M. Goldratt and Jeff Cox is unlike many business books because the lessons it aims at communicating are in the form of a novel. As a form of communicating ideas, novels tend to be more abstract and more difficult for the reader to understand than the pithy how-to approach taken by most business best-sellers. In spite of this obstacle to critical success, *The Goal* has become a cult classic (over 1,000,000 copies sold) among operation and inventory managers as well as becoming a staple in production and operations management classes. It is appropriate to include this book in a section examining vision and goals, although it profiles a leading character that would not normally be thought of as a leader—generals and political leaders are more commonly thought of as leaders than supply sergeants and campaign managers.

The Goal describes the struggles of Alex Rogo to save his plant. He has just learned that the profitability of his organization is not meeting expectations and that significant downsizing will occur in the near future. Rogo, under the mentoring of Jonah, who acts as a "Platonic" management consultant, begins attacking the problem with his management team, often challenging many of the sacred cows of manufacturing and cost accounting. While Rogo is taking on these challenges, you also witness the deep family problems that Rogo has to deal with. Faced with seemingly insurmountable obstacles, Rogo, with the help of Jonah, begins changing long-held beliefs and procedures that were hindering and not helping the organization meet its goals.

Using analogies and stories, Goldratt illustrates complex theory through easily understood stories. One story that Goldratt uses effectively discusses a situation in which Rogo accompanies his son and his Boy Scout troop on a ten-mile hike through the woods. As they begin their hike, which must be completed before nightfall, Alex notices that the single file line of scouts is stretching out, as the faster marchers outpace the slower ones. In addition Alex recognizes that one scout in particular, Herbie, is causing the greatest bottleneck. Alex first tries to put Herbie first in line, in the hope that the encouragement of the rest of the troop will prod Herbie to march at a faster pace. When this doesn't work, Alex divides the assortment of supplies that Herbie is carrying in his backpack and has portions of the load carried by fellow scouts. This

Eliyahu M. Goldratt and Jeff Cox, *The Goal: A Process of Ongoing Improvement.* New York, NY: North River Press, 1986.

solves the bottleneck problem, and the scout troop completes its hike successfully. Back at the plant, Rogo uses this story to illustrate how bottlenecks slow down a whole process, and by eliminating bottlenecks, the entire process can run more smoothly.

One of the things that rings true in *The Goal* is bottlenecks being given the code name "Herbies"; often, common names are given to processes that have been improved. The manufacturing setting in *The Goal* is not common to all businesses, yet the discipline that Rogo undertakes in analyzing his processes can be applied to any industry or organization.

The field of study that Goldratt has popularized is known as the *theory of constraints*. The theory of constraints is an overall philosophy developed by Goldratt, usually applied to running and improving an organization. Theory of constraints consists of problem solving and management/decision-making tools called thinking processes (TP). Theory of constraints is applied to logically and systematically answer these three questions essential to any process of ongoing improvement:

- "What to change?"
- "To what degree?"
- "How to cause the change?"

More specific uses of the thinking processes can be used to significantly enhance vital management skills, such as the following:

- win-win conflict resolution
- effective communication
- team building skills
- delegation
- empowerment

Theory of constraints recognizes that the output of any system that consists of multiple steps in which the output of one step depends on the output of one or more previous steps will be limited (or constrained) by the least productive steps. In other words, the strength of any chain is dependent upon its weakest link.

Where manufacturing is concerned, theory of constraints postulates that *The Goal* is to make (more) money. It describes three avenues to this goal: increase throughput, reduce inventory, and reduce operating expense. As Goldratt notes, the opportunities to make more money through reductions in inventory and operating expense are limited. The opportunities to make more money by increasing throughput, on the other hand, are unlimited.

More than that, though, theory of constraints challenges us to define a goal and reexamine all of the organization's actions and measurements based on how well or how poorly they serve it. This is done through a set of tools that help us identify and resolve bottlenecks.

The theory and processes discussed in *The Goal* can be applied to a variety of business areas in addition to production, such as distribution, marketing and sales, project management, and strategy, to name only a few.

A word of caution, however, is needed. Some of the practices discussed in *The Goal* may be detrimental to an organization. For instance, Rogo decides to increase production and sell some products at what would be a loss to a European customer. The idea is that these units cover the cost of production and fixed cost and that any money made is contributing to *The Goal* of the firm. In reality, such arrangements can be detrimental, since other domestic customers will discover the arrangement and demand the same price, or worse yet deal with competitors instead of you. As well, *The Goal* seems to single out cost accounting and accountants as the culprit, yet most accountants will admit that they are the first to recognize the limitations of the data they prepare. Just like the box score does not reveal everything that goes on in a baseball game, the limitations of cost accounting should be thought of in those terms.

PART SIX

Motivation

A number of readings contained in the fifth edition of *The Manager's Bookshelf* attempt to focus the manager's attention on the social-psychological side of the organization. Authors, concepts, and suggestions for proactive management call our attention to the importance of recognizing that all organizations have a natural (human) resource that, when appropriately managed, can lead to dramatic performance effects.

Part Six has three readings. In the first, Alfie Kohn, drawing from his book *Punished by Rewards*, discusses the problems associated with the use of incentives. In the second, Aubrey C. Daniels applies concepts from learning theory and organizational behavior modification to present his approach to the management of employee motivation. In the third, Jeffrey Pfeffer advocates several humanistic practices that could contribute to organizational success.

Alfie Kohn argues that it is common to believe that "people will do a better job if they have been promised some sort of incentive." As a result many organizations have a motivational program that attempts to tie compensation to some index of performance. Yet, according to Kohn, it is common to observe rewards *undermining* that which they were intended to enhance. In his article "Why Incentive Plans Cannot Work," Kohn discusses this motivational problem.

Alfie Kohn is the author of four books and is a corporate lecturer. Mr. Kohn has written on competition and incentive plans.

Aubrey C. Daniels, in his book *Bringing Out the Best in People*, discusses the use and effects associated with the application of positive reinforcement as a motivational technique. Daniels, a behavioral psychologist, boldly suggests that managers can forget such fads as reengineering, self-directed work teams, and organizational cultural changes. There is, he argues, a management system that can and has produced short- and long-term results.

According to Daniels, the solution to organizational productivity, for example, can be found in the laws of human behavior. *People engage in those behaviors that get reinforced*. Through the skillful management of organizational reinforcers, you can attain the kinds of individual performance that add up to organizational performance. Thus, Daniels calls for defining reinforcers that work; setting fair performance measurement standards; building effective reinforcers into every area of your organization; and eliminating those management practices that have been shown not to bring out the best in people.

Aubrey C. Daniels (Ph.D.) is the president of Aubrey Daniels & Associates and Precision Learning Systems—two firms that work with companies to find solutions to quality, productivity, education, and morale problems.

People should be viewed as the key route to organizational success, according to Jeffrey Pfeffer. In *The Human Equation*, he suggests giving employees control over their work, providing them with opportunities to use their knowledge, and building cooperative relationships with their managers. In a seven-part model, he points out the value of employment security, selective hiring, self-managed teams, at-risk compensation, extensive training, reduction of status differences, and information sharing. These practices put meaning behind the common cliche that "people are our most important asset."

Pfeffer is a professor of organizational behavior at Stanford's graduate school of business, and an active business consultant. He has written several other books, including *Managing with Power* and *Competitive Advantage through People*.

READING I

Punished by Rewards

Alfie Kohn

It is difficult to overstate the extent to which most managers and the people who advise them believe in the redemptive power of rewards. Certainly, the vast majority of U.S. corporations use some sort of program intended to motivate employees by tying compensation to one index of performance or another. But more striking is the rarely examined belief that people will do a better job if they have been promised some sort of incentive. This assumption and the practices associated with it are pervasive, but a growing collection of evidence supports an opposing view. According to numerous studies in laboratories, workplaces, classrooms, and other settings, rewards typically undermine the very processes they are intended to enhance. The findings suggest that the failure of any given incentive program is due less to a glitch in that program than to the inadequacy of the psychological assumptions that ground all such plans.

TEMPORARY COMPLIANCE

Behaviorist theory, derived from work with laboratory animals, is indirectly responsible for such programs as piece-work pay for factory workers, stock options for top executives, special privileges accorded to Employees of the Month, and commissions for salespeople. Indeed, the livelihood of innumerable consultants has long been based on devising fresh formulas for computing bonuses to wave in front of employees. Money, vacations, banquets, plaques—the list of variations on a single, simple behaviorist model of motivation is limitless. And today even many people who are regarded as forward thinking—those who promote teamwork, participative management, continuous improvement, and the like—urge the use of rewards to institute and maintain these very reforms. What we use bribes to accomplish may have changed, but the reliance on bribes, on behaviorist doctrine, has not.

Moreover, the few articles that appear to criticize incentive plans are invariably limited to details of implementation. Only fine-tune the calculations and delivery of the incentive—or perhaps hire the author as a consultant—and the problem will be solved, we are told. As Herbert H. Meyer, professor emeritus in the psychology department at the College of Social and Behavioral Sciences at the University of South Florida, has written, "Anyone reading the literature on this subject published twenty years ago would find that the articles look almost identical to those published today."

That assessment, which could have been written this morning, was actually offered in 1975. In nearly forty years, the thinking hasn't changed.

Do rewards work? The answer depends on what we mean by "work." Research suggests that, by and large, rewards succeed at securing one thing only: temporary compliance. When it comes to producing lasting change in attitudes and behavior, however, rewards, like punishment, are strikingly ineffective. Once the rewards run out, people revert to their old behaviors. Studies show that offering incentives for losing weight, quitting smoking, using seat belts, or (in the case of children) acting generously is not only less effective than other strategies but often proves worse than doing nothing at all. Incentives, a version of what psychologists call extrinsic motivators, do not alter the attitudes that underlie our behaviors. They do not create an enduring *commitment* to any value or action. Rather, incentives merely—and temporarily—change what we do.

As for productivity, at least two dozen studies over the last three decades have conclusively shown that people who expect to receive a reward for completing a task or for doing that task successfully simply do not perform as well as those who expect no reward at all. These studies examined rewards for children and adults, males and females, and included tasks ranging from memorizing facts to creative problem-solving to designing collages. In general, the more cognitive sophistication and open-ended thinking that was required, the worse people performed when working for a reward. Interestingly enough, the researchers themselves were often taken by surprise. They assumed that rewards would produce better work but discovered otherwise.

The question for managers is whether incentive plans can work when extrinsic motivators more generally do not. Unfortunately, as author G. Douglas Jenkins, Jr., has noted, most organizational studies to date—like the articles published—have tended "to focus on the effects of *variations* in incentive conditions, and not on whether performance-based pay per se raises performance levels."

A number of studies, however, have examined whether or not pay, especially at the executive level, is related to corporate profitability and other measures of organizational performance. Often they have found slight or even *negative* correlations between pay and performance. Typically, the absence of such a relationship is interpreted as evidence of links between compensation and something other than how well people do their jobs. But most of these data could support a different conclusion, one that reverses the causal arrow. Perhaps what these studies reveal is that higher pay does not produce better performance. In other words, the very idea of trying to reward quality may be a fool's errand.

Consider the findings of Jude T. Rich and John A. Larson, formerly of McKinsey & Company. In 1982, using interviews and proxy statements, they examined compensation programs at ninety major U.S. companies to determine whether return to shareholders was better for corporations that had incentive plans for top executives than it was for those companies that had no such plans. They were unable to find any difference.

Four years later, Jenkins tracked down twenty-eight previously published studies that measured the impact of financial incentives on performance. (Some were conducted in the laboratory and some in the field.) His analysis, "Financial Incentives," published in 1986, revealed that sixteen, or 57 percent, of the studies found a positive effect on performance. However, all of the performance measures were quantitative in nature: a good job consisted of producing more of something or doing it faster. Only five of the studies looked at the quality of performance. And none of those five showed any benefits from incentives.

Another analysis took advantage of an unusual situation that affected a group of welders at a Midwestern manufacturing company. At the request of the union, an incentive system that had been in effect for some years was abruptly eliminated. Now, if a financial incentive supplies motivation, its absence should drive down production. And that is exactly what happened, at first. Fortunately, Harold F. Rothe, former personnel manager and corporate staff assistant at the Beloit Corporation, tracked production over a period of months, providing the sort of long-term data rarely collected in this field. After the initial slump, Rothe found that in the absence of incentives the welders' production quickly began to rise and eventually reached a level as high or higher than it had been before.

One of the largest reviews of how intervention programs affect worker productivity, a meta-analysis of some 330 comparisons from ninety-eight studies, was conducted in the mid-1980s by Richard A. Guzzo, associate professor of psychology at the University of Maryland, College Park, and his colleagues at New York University. The raw numbers seemed to suggest a positive relationship between financial incentives and productivity, but because of the huge variations from one study to another, statistical tests indicated that there was no significant effect overall. What's more, financial incentives were virtually unrelated to the number of workers who were absent or who quit their jobs over a period of time. By contrast, training and goal-setting programs had a far greater impact on productivity than did pay-for-performance plans.

WHY REWARDS FAIL

Why do most executives continue to rely on incentive programs? Perhaps it's because few people take the time to examine the connection between incentive programs and problems with workplace productivity and morale. Rewards buy temporary compliance, so it looks like the problems are solved. It's harder to spot the harm they cause over the long term. Moreover, it does not occur to most of us to suspect rewards, given that our own teachers, parents, and managers probably used them. "Do this and you'll get that" is part of the fabric of American life. Finally, by clinging to the belief that motivational problems are due to the particular incentive system in effect at the moment, rather than to the psychological theory behind all incentives, we can remain optimistic that a relatively minor adjustment will repair the damage.

Over the long haul, however, the potential cost to any organization of trying to fine-tune reward-driven compensation systems may be considerable. The fundamental flaws of behaviorism itself doom the prospects of affecting long-term behavior change or performance improvement through the use of rewards. Consider the following six-point framework that examines the true costs of an incentive program.

1. "Pay Is Not a Motivator"   W. Edward Deming's declaration may seem surprising, even absurd. Of course, money buys the things people want and need. Moreover, the less people are paid, the more concerned they are likely to be about financial matters. Indeed, several studies over the last few decades have found that when people are asked to guess what matters to their coworkers—or, in the case of managers, to their subordinates—they assume money heads the list. But put the question directly— "What do you care about?"—and pay typically ranks only fifth or sixth.

Even if people were principally concerned with their salaries, this does not prove that money is motivating. There is no firm basis for the assumption that paying people more will encourage them to do better work or even, in the long run, more work. As Frederick Herzberg, Distinguished Professor of Management at the University of Utah's Graduate School of Management, has argued, just because too little money can irritate and demotivate does not mean that more and more money will bring about increased satisfaction, much less increased motivation. It is plausible to assume that if someone's take-home pay was cut in half, his or her morale would suffer enough to undermine performance. But it doesn't necessarily follow that doubling that person's pay would result in better work.

2. Rewards Punish   Many managers understand that coercion and fear destroy motivation and create defiance, defensiveness, and rage. They realize that punitive management is a contradiction in terms. As Herzberg wrote in HBR some twenty-five years ago ("One More Time: How Do You Motivate Employees?" January–February 1968), a "KITA"—which, he coyly explains, stands for "kick in the pants"—may produce movement but never motivation.

What most executives fail to recognize is that Herzberg's observation is equally true of rewards. Punishment and rewards are two sides of the same coin. Rewards have a punitive effect because they, like out-right punishment, are manipulative. "Do this and you'll get that" is not really very different from "Do this or here's what will happen to you." In the case of incentives, the reward itself may be highly desired; but by making that bonus contingent on certain behaviors, managers manipulate their subordinates, and that experience of being controlled is likely to assume a punitive quality over time.

Further, not receiving a reward one had expected to receive is also indistinguishable from being punished. Whether the incentive is withheld or withdrawn deliberately, or simply not received by someone who had hoped to get it, the effect is identical. And the more desirable the reward, the more demoralizing it is to miss out.

The new school, which exhorts us to catch people doing something right and reward them for it, is not very different from the old school, which advised us to catch people doing something wrong and threaten to punish them if they ever do it again. What is essentially taking place in both approaches is that a lot of people are getting caught. Managers are creating a workplace in which people feel controlled, not an environment conducive to exploration, learning, and progress.

3. Rewards Rupture Relationships   Relationships among employees are often casualties of the scramble for rewards. As leaders of the Total Quality Management movement have emphasized, incentive programs, and the performance appraisal systems that accompany them, reduce the possibilities for cooperation. Peter R. Scholtes, senior management consultant at Joiner Associates Inc., put it starkly, "Everyone is pressuring the system for individual gain. No one is improving the system for collective gain. The system will inevitably crash." Without teamwork, in other words, there can be no quality.

The surest way to destroy cooperation and, therefore, organizational excellence, is to force people to compete for rewards or recognition or to rank them against each other. For each person who wins, there are many others who carry with them the feeling of having lost. And the more these awards are publicized through the use of memos, newsletters, and awards banquets, the more detrimental their impact can be. Furthermore, when employees compete for a limited number of incentives, they will most likely begin to see each other as obstacles to their own success. But the same result can occur with any use of rewards; introducing competition just makes a bad thing worse.

Relationships between supervisors and subordinates can also collapse under the weight of incentives. Of course, the supervisor who punishes is about as welcome to employees as a glimpse of a police car in their rearview mirrors. But even the supervisor who rewards can produce some damaging reactions. For instance, employees may be tempted to conceal any problems they might be having and present themselves as infinitely competent to the manager in control of the money. Rather than ask for help—a prerequisite for optimal performance—they might opt instead for flattery, attempting to convince the manager that they have everything under control. Very few things threaten an organization as much as a hoard of incentive-driven individuals trying to curry favor with the incentive dispenser.

4. Rewards Ignore Reasons   In order to solve problems in the workplace, managers must understand what caused them. Are employees inadequately prepared for the demands of their jobs? Is long-term growth being sacrificed to maximize short-term return? Are workers unable to collaborate effectively? Is the organization so rigidly hierarchical that employees are intimidated about making recommendations and feel powerless and burned out? Each of these situations calls for a different response. But relying on incentives to boost productivity does nothing to address possible underlying problems and bring about meaningful change.

Moreover, managers often use incentive systems as a substitute for giving workers what they need to do a good job. Treating workers well—providing useful feedback, social support, and the room for self-determination—is the essence of good management. On the other hand, dangling a bonus in front of employees and waiting for the results requires much less effort. Indeed, some evidence suggests that productive managerial strategies are less likely to be used in organizations that lean on pay-for-performance plans. In his study of welders' performance, Rothe noted that supervisors tended to "demonstrate relatively less leadership" when incentives were in place. Likewise, author Carla O'Dell reports in *People, Performance, and Pay* that a survey of 1,600 organizations by the American Productivity Center discovered little in the way of active employee involvement in organizations that used small-group incentive plans. As Jone L. Pearce, associate professor at the Graduate School of Management, University of California at Irvine, wrote in "Why Merit Pay Doesn't Work: Implications from Organization Theory," pay for performance actually "impedes the ability of managers to manage."

5. Rewards Discourage Risk-Taking   "People will do precisely what they are asked to do if the reward is significant," enthused Monroe J. Haegele, a proponent of pay-for-performance programs, in "The New Performance Measures." And here is the root of the problem. Whenever people are encouraged to think about what they will get for engaging in a task, they become less inclined to take risks or explore possibilities, to play hunches or to consider incidental stimuli. In a word, the number one casualty of rewards is creativity.

Excellence pulls in one direction; rewards pull in another. Tell people that their income will depend on their productivity or performance rating, and they will focus on the numbers. Sometimes they will manipulate the schedule for completing tasks or even engage in patently unethical and illegal behavior. As Thane S. Pittman, professor and chair of the psychology department at Gettysburg College, and his colleagues point out, when we are motivated by incentives, "features such as predictability and simplicity are desirable, since the primary focus associated with this orientation is to get through the task expediently in order to reach the desired goal." The late Cornell University professor, John Condry, was more succinct: rewards, he said, are the "enemies of exploration."

Consider the findings of organizational psychologist Edwin A. Locke. When Locke paid subjects on a piece-rate basis for their work, he noticed that they tended to choose easier tasks as the payment for success increased. A number of other studies have also found that people working for a reward generally try to minimize challenge. It isn't that human beings are naturally lazy or that it is unwise to give employees a voice in determining the standards to be used. Rather, people tend to lower their sights when they are encouraged to think about what they are going to get for their efforts. "Do this and you'll get that," in other words, focuses attention on the "that" instead of the "this." Emphasizing large bonuses is the last strategy we should use if we care about innovation. Do rewards motivate people? Absolutely. They motivate people to get rewards.

6. Rewards Undermine Interest If our goal is excellence, no artificial incentive can ever match the power of intrinsic motivation. People who do exceptional work may be glad to be paid and even more glad to be well paid, but they do not work to collect a paycheck. They work because they love what they do.

Few will be shocked by the news that extrinsic motivators are a poor substitute for genuine interest in one's job. What is far more surprising is that rewards, like punishment, may actually undermine the intrinsic motivation that results in optimal performance. The more a manager stresses what an employee can earn for good work, the less interested that employee will be in the work itself.

The first studies to establish the effect of rewards on intrinsic motivation were conducted in the early 1970s by Edward Deci, professor and chairman of the psychology department at the University of Rochester. By now, scores of experiments across the country have replicated the finding. As Deci and his colleague Richard Ryan, senior vice president of investment and training manager at Robert W. Baird and Co., Inc., wrote in their 1985 book, *Intrinsic Motivation and Self-Determination in Human Behavior*, "the research has consistently shown that any contingent payment system tends to undermine intrinsic motivation." The basic effect is the same for a variety of rewards and tasks, although extrinsic motivators are particularly destructive when tied to interesting or complicated tasks.

Deci and Ryan argue that receiving a reward for a particular behavior sends a certain message about what we have done and controls, or attempts to control, our future behavior. The more we experience being controlled, the more we will tend to lose interest in what we are doing. If we go to work thinking about the possibility of getting a bonus, we come to feel that our work is not self-directed. Rather, it is the reward that drives our behavior.

Other theorists favor a more simple explanation for the negative effect rewards have on intrinsic motivation: anything presented as a prerequisite for something else—that is, as a means toward another end—comes to be seen as less desirable. The recipient of the reward assumes, "If they have to bribe me to do it, it must be something I wouldn't want to do." In fact, a series of studies, published in 1992 by psychology professor Jonathan L. Freedman and his colleagues at the University of Toronto, confirmed that the larger the incentive we are offered, the more negatively we will view the activity for which the bonus was received. (The activities themselves don't seem to matter; in this study, they ranged from participating in a medical experiment to eating unfamiliar food.) Whatever the reason for the effect, however, any incentive or pay-for-performance system tends to make people less enthusiastic about their work and therefore less likely to approach it with a commitment to excellence.

DANGEROUS ASSUMPTIONS

Outside of psychology departments, few people distinguish between intrinsic and extrinsic motivation. Those who do assume that the two concepts can simply be added together for best effect. Motivation comes in two flavors, the logic goes, and both together must be better than either alone. But studies show that the real world works differently.

Some managers insist that the only problem with incentive programs is that they don't reward the right things. But these managers fail to understand the psychological factors involved and, consequently, the risks of sticking with the status quo.

Contrary to conventional wisdom, the use of rewards is not a response to the extrinsic orientation exhibited by many workers. Rather, incentives help create this focus on financial considerations. When an organization uses a Skinnerian management or compensation system, people are likely to become less interested in their work, requiring extrinsic incentives before expending effort. Then supervisors shake their heads and say, "You see? If you don't offer them a reward, they won't do anything." It is a classic self-fulfilling prophecy. Swarthmore College psychology professor Barry Schwartz has conceded that behavior theory may seem to provide us with a useful way of describing what goes on in U.S. workplaces. However, "It does this not because work is a natural exemplification of behavior theory principles but because behavior theory principles . . . had a significant hand in transforming work into an exemplification of behavior theory principles."

Managers who insist that the job won't get done right without rewards have failed to offer a convincing argument for behavioral manipulation. Promising a reward to someone who appears unmotivated is a bit like offering salt water to someone who is thirsty. Bribes in the workplace simply can't work.

READING 2

Bringing Out the Best in People

Aubrey C. Daniels
Summary prepared by Gayle Porter

Gayle Porter *is an Assistant Professor of Management at Rutgers University, School of Business—Camden. Her research focus is employee development, including aspects of team training, motivational reward systems, and individual differences that inhibit development efforts. Her previous experience includes positions as Director of Curriculum Development for a human resource management degree program; consultant on training programs, financial operations, and computer applications; financial manager for an oil and gas production company; and financial specialist for NCR Corporation.*

Because behavior of people is at the center of every business decision, the science of human behavior offers a great deal to managers. Drawing from a body of knowledge referred to as behavior analysis, *performance management* applies those findings to the workplace. The central idea is *to create the right environment and conditions to bring out the best in people.*

Management is often approached as a matter of personal style, as common sense, or as an "art." In addition, when one company experiences success following the implementation of some new program, other managers too easily accept that intervention as the cause for success, which creates a cycle of fads in management theory. Performance management differs from style approaches and fads because it is precise and data oriented. It offers scientifically based management methods that will solve problems permanently. To understand people, you need only to witness their behavior and observe the consequences of that behavior. From that information, performance management is the means for managers to change behavior.

Managers can influence behavior by doing something before or after the behavior occurs. The actions before behavior are called *antecedents*; these set the stage for a behavior to occur. Effective antecedents are necessary to initiate performance, but are not sufficient to sustain it. Memos, training, policies, mission statements, slogans, posters, and buttons are all antecedents. These antecedents can get people going, but consequences keep people going. *Consequences* alter the probability that behavior will recur—whether the behavior occurs more or less often in the future. No matter

Aubrey C. Daniels, *Bringing Out the Best in People.* New York, NY: McGraw-Hill, 1993.

how strong an antecedent is, it will have a long-lasting effect only if it is consistently paired with a meaningful consequence. *Behavior is a function of its consequences.*

REINFORCEMENT AS THE FOUNDATION OF PERFORMANCE MANAGEMENT

The reality of human behavior is that everything people do relates to what is being reinforced. When experiencing poor outcomes, you have to identify the behaviors causing the outcome, and arrange consequences that will stop these behaviors; identify behaviors that will produce the desirable outcomes and arrange consequences that will positively reinforce them.

There are four types of behavioral consequences. Two are used to increase behavior; these are positive reinforcement and negative reinforcement. Two are used to decrease behavior; these are punishment and extinction. *Extinction* occurs when the performer does something and nothing happens, so the behavior stops. For example, going above and beyond the requirements of the job is not rewarded, so people stop doing it. This is important to understand. Management changes behavior by inaction, as well as by action. *Punishment* is a consequence that causes behavior to stop. We can only define something as punishment by observing the effect on behavior, because positive and negative aspects of a consequence are defined by the person who receives it. Punishment never solves a problem, it only stops a behavior. There is no assurance that a positive or productive behavior will take its place.

Negative reinforcement is the process by which demonstration of a desired behavior serves to avoid a punishment. Reliance on negative reinforcement is still the dominant management style. The result from this approach is that people perform as instructed only to avoid undesirable outcomes of not doing so. We see evidence of this style: when performance shows a sharp rise just before the deadline or goes flat after reaching the goal; when there is no celebration of accomplishment, completion of a project leads only to starting the next one; or when performance drops as soon as a specified requirement is removed. Although managers will agree that it is better to manage with positive reinforcement than with negative, few understand the difference. Negative reinforcement generates just enough behavior to get by. It works, when all we need is compliance or minimum performance. But negative reinforcement requires a continual push that is punishing for both the employees and their management. It is only effective in the short term, it can never sustain high levels of performance.

Positive reinforcement is any consequence that follows a behavior and increases its frequency in the future. It occurs any time there is a favorable change in the environment. Only positive reinforcement generates more behavior than is minimally required, and this *discretionary effort* in the workplace is the only way an organization can maximize performance. Again, whether or not a reinforcer is positive depends on the perception of the performer. If performance is not improving, reinforcement is not occurring, in spite of management intentions to provide rewards.

Because the reinforcement value of anything is highly individualistic, it is important to establish what people want. One direct approach is to ask them, but people may not know or want to tell you. If they are suspicious of your motives, they may say what they think you want to hear. There is also danger that the question itself may set up expectations. A better variation is to try something and then ask people what they did or didn't like about it. When you try to provide positive reinforcers, people find even the attempt itself to be reinforcing; they tend to be forgiving, if you make a mistake in this effort. The best way to determine positive reinforcers (what people want) is to observe. What do people talk about and how do they spend their time when they have a choice?

Positive reinforcement may be work related, peer related, or management related. Work related refers to the task itself. This was the basis of job-enrichment initiatives, and these have failed to show long-term improvement. Other sources of reinforcement are needed along with work related. Peer-related reinforcement is the most effective source of reinforcement at work and the most underutilized. Peers are in a position to observe performance more closely and more often than a supervisor or manager, but employees have never learned that it is their responsibility to give reinforcement to co-workers. Unfortunately, employees are rarely reinforced by management for providing peer reinforcement. Management-related reinforcement is the opportunity for managers to capture and enjoy the benefits of discretionary effort. The manager must realize that responsibility for performance includes responsibility for coordinating reinforcement. Managers do not provide all reinforcement, but they must ensure that reinforcement occurs for the right behavior, at necessary frequency, and from all sources available.

Effective use of reinforcement involves providing it as close in time to the behavior as possible, preferably while the behavior is occurring. Greater frequency of reinforcement strengthens this time connection. *The performer must perceive a clear and contingent relationship between the behavior and the consequence.* Also, everyone who earns reinforcement should receive it, regardless of who else is being reinforced. When there is too little reinforcement to go around, people will compete for it. Competition generates political behaviors and sabotage, which are incompatible with the team-oriented work environment most organizations are trying to promote.

A SCIENTIFIC APPROACH TO LEADERSHIP

No longer is it sufficient to manage strictly by results. Even when things are working, understanding why is important. When circumstances change, that information will be needed to fix new problems. Even inappropriate behaviors may lead to desired results in the short term, and tolerating those behaviors will eventually cause problems. It is critical to know what results you want and what behaviors are required to achieve that result. Don't assume, for example, that zero defects equates to quality-oriented behavior. Both aspects are important, but begin with identification of desired results, and don't initiate process changes without linking them to needed results. To test whether specified behaviors actually lead to the desired results, always evaluate changes in behavior against changes in results. Use actual observation and solid evidence, not intuition.

Pinpointing involves specifying results and the behaviors required to achieve them. Pinpoints are real, tangible results and behaviors, not beliefs, attitudes, or anything else internal, subjective, or abstract. Pinpointing requires precise description of results and behaviors that are observable, measurable (in terms of frequency or duration), and reliable. The reliability aspect means that two or more people observing a behavior or result will come up with the same count or measure. This usually must be refined over a period of time.

Many people find it difficult, at first, to differentiate between results and behavior, but there are cues in common language that help. For example, behaviors are usually expressed in present tense, with verbs ending in "ing." Results tend to be expressed in past tense or describe something you see after people have stopped working.

It is critical to pinpoint in terms of behavior that is under the performer's control. No one has complete control, but the performer should have more control than other people. Correlating changes in behavior with changes in results is a means to check whether they are properly identified.

People have learned to avoid measurement whenever possible, because of the way organizations have used it. Based on measurement, we typically identify poor performers and take a negative action to correct that problem. If measurement instead is used to help people do better, and those improvements are positively reinforced, people will seek out or even create measurement opportunities.

Performance is measurable through either counting or judging. Counting is preferable, because it is objective. Judging is more subjective, but it is useful when counting is not a possibility. To avoid the appearance of arbitrary judgments, establish specific criteria that can be reliably observed by two or more people. *Behaviorally anchored rating scales* (BARS) is one approach. Ranking is not effective, because it sets one employee against another. With established criteria, everyone can be a top performer. Whatever measurement is used, it is important to validate the behavioral measures by comparing against results. If the behavior is good but not the results, you have the wrong pinpoints. Overall, measurement helps to identify small, incremental changes and, thus, provides opportunities to reward improvements. This brings out the best in people.

Performance data does not necessarily tell a person what to do to improve performance. Feedback is information about performance that allows the individual to adjust. It clarifies where current performance is in relation to past performance and against some goal. Learning requires information about how behavior is affecting the environment, so there is no learning without feedback. However, feedback is an antecedent and, as such, will not sustain behavior change. How performers choose to respond to the antecedent depends on the consequences they experience. When people know positive reinforcement is consistently paired with improved performance, a feedback trend may also become a source of reinforcement. *Feedback and positive reinforcement form the most powerful combination of techniques to bring out the best in people.*

The elements discussed here must be applied in a systematic format:

1. Pinpoint
2. Measure
3. Feedback
4. Reinforce
5. Evaluate

Use of pinpointing alone won't induce a lasting change; measurement alone does not solve performance problems; feedback without reinforcement can't sustain improvement. Even reinforcement alone is dangerous, due to the likelihood of reinforcing the wrong behavior at the wrong time. Companies often think this model is too simple for their complex problems, but there are no exceptions to its applicability. The model works on all performance problems and any aspect of business and lends itself to scientific analysis.

WHAT ABOUT OTHER APPROACHES AND EXISTING SYSTEMS?

A number of strategies or techniques have gained popularity in the past few years, although many companies have not been entirely satisfied with outcomes. The principles of performance management offer some explanations for why their good intentions do not always result in higher performance.

- Goal setting has been extremely popular in organizations, in spite of the fact that it consumes a great deal of management time and there is no agreement on how to set goals and document their value to business. Goals may limit performance, because people capable of more will stop when they achieve the goal. Goals are antecedents. The purpose of setting goals should be to increase the opportunities for positive reinforcement, and this will accelerate the rate of improvement. A key aspect in shaping behavior is to break down the task into small steps, supply incremental reinforcers for gradual improvement, and then celebrate achievement of the final goal.
- Quality-improvement programs also emphasize features such as training, policies, and meetings, which are antecedents. Often they are based on implementing dozens of new practices simultaneously, with very little connection between behaviors and results. A quality system may or may not result in improving the product or service. The real test is whether a company can accelerate the rate of improvement in order to outdo competitors. This acceleration effect happens only with precise and effective use of positive reinforcement.
- Teams and employee empowerment are desirable based on both common sense and theory, but there is not consistent evidence of success. The benefits of teamwork have been translated into a need for formal team structures, which takes tremendous effort from both the individual and the organization. One problem is that the process may consume more focus than the results. Another issue is that, too often, people are pushed into forming teams and given empowerment noncontingently. Teams progress at different rates and should be rewarded with empowerment gradually and systematically. In other words, people must earn empowerment. Unfortunately, one of the most important benefits of teams is almost entirely overlooked. The use of teams dramatically increases the opportunities for receiving reinforcement. Every team member is a potential source of reinforcement for other members.
- Downsizing has been used as a primary method to give shareholders a higher return on investment. At best it is a stop-gap measure, used because companies are unable to solve fundamental problems. If management is reinforcing the wrong things, reducing the workforce or putting these people into different jobs will not cause them to suddenly do anything differently. The after-

math of a layoff is often that those left behind feel punished or afraid they will be next. Needed people may decide to leave, possibly joining the competition. The job of management during downsizing is to develop a system of reinforcement—one that ensures the right consequences for progressive behaviors; behaviors that allow the organization to do more with less.

- Recognition ceremonies are removed in time from behaviors and celebrate the accomplishments of a few; those who miss by a close margin are put in the position of losers. The larger the prizes awarded, the more they encourage behaviors to win (lie, cheat, sabotage) rather than to perform. Similar problems exist with the use of suggestion systems. Managers judge whether to implement a new idea based on dollar savings and totally ignore the motivational value of employees seeing their ideas put to use. Someone reinforced for a suggestion worth very little now may submit another one in the future that results in great savings. But without reinforcement, that person will not continue to make suggestions.

- Traditional compensation systems are primarily noncontingent. How hard you work today will not affect your next paycheck. Pay raises are competitive due to finite resources, so any gain is someone else's loss. To alleviate competition many companies have moved toward across-the-board increases, which is demotivating. Benefit plans—even the popular "cafeteria" plans—give as much total benefit to poor performers. Gain sharing is more closely aligned with controllable outcomes than straight profit sharing, but the usual plan is based on some formula to divide the benefit equally among all participants. There is no individual performance contingency. Annual performance appraisals are too far removed in time from performance demonstration. Forced-ranking or forced-distribution systems are demotivating; a company hires the best people possible and then forces them into a system that labels all but a few as average. In most cases, managers do not have enough flexibility to make pay and benefit plans contingent, but performance management offers suggestions on how to bring out the best in people in spite of traditional systems.

PERFORMANCE MANAGEMENT TO REVITALIZE THE WORKPLACE

To executives who understand human behavior, changing business conditions don't present problems, just additional opportunities to exercise their skills. Those who don't understand will not survive, and they put their companies at financial risk. Executives establish the guiding principles and values of the organization, which lead to definition of desired results and the behaviors that will be reinforced to obtain them. Lack of success often results from saying one thing but rewarding another, so the executives must establish clear guidelines. It is also important to define limits of reinforcement that managers and supervisors have at their discretion. Managers and supervisors must be reinforced for their use of reinforcement with employees, rather than for short-term results that may be obtained through unwanted behaviors. Remember that all behavior is choice behavior, and people will engage in a particular behavior in direct proportion to the amount of reinforcement received.

Changes now occur so rapidly that on-the-job training is not practical, and we must do a better job of training people before they enter their jobs. The focus should be on achieving an advanced level of performance, called *fluency*. Repeated practice with feedback and reinforcement leads to fluency. The result is high retention, and people need less concentration and energy to perform, so they are able to stay on task longer and perform even under duress or when distracted.

People should be active participants in recognizing achievement, not just recipients of the company's benevolence. Rather than simply praising their accomplishments, engage them in telling the story of how they achieved their success. This becomes a true celebration for that person and may be an antecedent for other employees to try similar things. Whatever the number of employees in the company, each individual has that many possible sources of positive reinforcement. Imagine being excited to go to work every morning and working for a company where everyone else is, too!

Performance management is built around certain values: honesty, integrity, equality and respect, justice, self-esteem and personal growth, peace of mind, and the golden rule. These are demonstrated through making desired outcomes known to all; assuming that all people can be better than they are now, with support from their environment; and reducing stress by clarifying behavior/reinforcement connections and diminishing threats and punishment. Performance management is a precise scientific approach that works without gimmicks, because the laws of behavior are the same for all people.

READING 3

The Human Equation: Building Profits by Putting People First

Jeffrey Pfeffer
Summary prepared by Kelly Nelson

Kelly Nelson *is the Director of Human Resources for Armco's Mansfield Operations. Since receiving her Bachelor of Business Administration degree from the University of Minnesota, Duluth, Kelly has been involved in the steel industry as both a human resource manager and operations manager. She is currently pursuing an MBA degree and, although thankful for the lessons learned through work and school, learns the most about people-centered management from being a parent to her son, John.*

Management practices define an organization's ability to optimize profits. Although it is possible for organizations to succeed in spite of the fact that their management practices do not fully support their strategic goals, more often misalignment causes a downward spiral that leads to the organization's demise. Instead, optimized profits and long-term viability are realized when practices and goals are fully integrated and an organization's management practices create a system for success.

COMMON SEARCHES FOR SUCCESS

Companies strive for a unique characteristic that will distinguish them from their competitors. Most often, leaders look to their product line to provide their uniqueness. When companies fail to look to their employees to provide a competitive advantage, a downward spiral occurs. Typically, an organization's performance problems are identified by low profits, high costs, reduced customer service, and low stock prices. Leaders then seek to cut costs using hierarchical control (a traditional, top-down management style that provides an employee's immediate supervisor with the responsibility and authority to reward/discipline the employee). Historically, this has been done through layoffs, salary freezes (or reductions), hiring and promotion freezes, reducing (or eliminating) employee training, and the use of part-time or contract labor. Instead of producing the desired result of providing a competitive advantage, more often, the consequences have been decreased motivation and effort, reduced job focus and satisfaction, higher accident rates and turnover. The resultant

Jeffrey Pfeffer, *The Human Equation: Building Profits by Putting People First.* Boston, MA: Harvard Business School, 1998.

turmoil within the organization is actually counter to the desired results. Employees remaining on the worksite are uncertain about the company's future as well as their personal future within the company. All of this happens at a time when the company needs to have employees focused on making the company a success. All of this results simply because leaders viewed employees as a "cost," not as the unique resource needed to make the organization a success.

COMPONENTS OF LONG-TERM SUCCESS

Success is not achieved by viewing employees as a cost item. Instead, success is generated by putting faith in and developing a system that relies on employees. This is started by understanding and relying upon three basic principles:

- People work harder and have increased commitment when they have control over their work.
- People work smarter when they have an opportunity to apply their knowledge and energy to improve operational performance.
- People will be responsible for accomplishing their objectives when they are involved in a cooperative relationship with managers.

Trust in these principles and placing faith in employees is difficult for leaders. It takes a sustained commitment to change the philosophy of what constitutes "successful" leadership. Understanding and believing the principles is not enough to make an organization successful. This must be coupled with high-performance management practices that are aligned with the organization's goals. The seven practices are as follows:

1. *Employment security*   Employees who are freed from the concern of "working themselves out of a job" are freed to put their creativity to work for the company's success—thus helping to assure job security for themselves in the future. Furthermore, employment security not only ensures careful scrutiny about the need to hire additional employees, it also leads to more carefully selecting candidates to fill vacancies. Hiring managers know that they cannot simply lay off employees if they have overestimated their labor need. However, employment security should not be confused with accepting substandard employee performance. Employees who do not meet or exceed expectations need not be "carried" under the name of employment security. Instead, employment security ensures that those employees who are working to support the organization's success will not become the victims of market downturns or increased efficiencies.

2. *Selective hiring*   Organizations that view their employees as assets have an obligation to hire the right people. To do so requires a number of criteria. A large applicant pool is needed. The organization must be clear about what critical skills and attributes are needed and those skills and abilities need to be considered and consistent with the job requirements and the organization's objectives. The applicant screening process should focus on attributes that are difficult (if not impossible) to change through training. Using several rounds of screening builds commitment and illustrates to candidates that the hiring process is taken seriously by the organization. Candidates

also understand the commitment to hiring the right people when senior members of the organization are involved in the hiring process. Finally, it is essential that the hiring process involve post-hire feedback and assessment to ensure the right people are being selected in the hiring process. When deficiencies are detected, it is important they are corrected immediately.

3. *Self-managed teams*   Organizing self-managed work teams offers a number of advantages over traditional supervisor–employee lines of progression. Teams provide *peer-based control* (the power of team members to enforce and encourage certain behaviors) and this is frequently more effective than hierarchical control. Further, this frees managers to concentrate efforts on strategic planning. Further, team-based organizations allow all employees to feel accountable and responsible for the operations and the success of the organization. This, in turn, stimulates initiative and energy. Also, teams permit group problem solving and encourage all employees to build upon the suggestions offered from individuals. This unleashes the creativity of all employees and it provides freedom for all employees to offer suggestions and ideas. Finally, teams provide an opportunity to remove layers of hierarchy, and individuals can perform tasks formerly completed by administrative specialists. This not only eliminates excess personnel, it also puts decision-making responsibility into the hands of employees closest to the relevant information.

4. *High compensation contingent on organizational performance*   The philosophical shift to understanding that employees are assets, not costs, is supported by relatively high employee compensation. This reward system encourages employees to stay with the organization, thereby reducing costs associated with recruiting, hiring, and training new employees. Further, tying compensation to organizational performance provides "at-risk" compensation and helps to ensure that all employees work toward the goals of the organization. Contingent compensation can be provided in a number of ways, such as gain sharing, profit sharing, stock ownership, pay for skills, and individual/team incentives.

5. *Training*   Training not only increases the skill level of employees, it also serves as a reminder to all that the company is making a continual investment in its employees. Knowledge and skills are critical to an organization's success and providing these to employees helps create a competitive edge for the organization. Although return-on-investment analysis for training is difficult, it must be included in high performance management principles and be viewed as an integral part of the organization's future success.

6. *Reduction of status differences*   It is important that all members of an organization understand that they are equally responsible for the firm's future success. This business fundamental is supported by reducing the symbolic and compensatory differences between the layers of the organization. Symbolic items such as reserved parking spots and dress codes for levels of employees serve as an illustration that the organization is not truly committed to the philosophy that all employees are equally needed to ensure success. Large compensation differences between the layers also sabotage this philosophy. It is important to reduce *status differences*—the psychological and

compensatory differences between layers of an organization—and replace those differences with rewards to many. However, opportunities for compensation based on performance do provide avenues by which to reward groups who "go above and beyond the call of duty" to ensure the future success of the organization.

7. *Sharing information* To have information is to have power. Thus, it is an essential part of high-performance management practices to provide power to all members of the organization. Knowledge of items such as financial performance, strategy, and operational measures is essential in order for each employee to work to support the goals of the organization. A second element of sharing information is to ensure that all employees understand the information and its implications. Even employees who have access to the information cannot use it to the organization's benefit if the employees do not understand what the information implies. Therefore, training employees in the use of the information is essential.

ALIGNING BUSINESS STRATEGY WITH MANAGEMENT PRINCIPLES

Organizations embracing high-performance management principles must ensure all seven factors are aligned with the *business strategy* (the future-focused plans of the organization). To do so, the organization must (1) determine the organization's strategy; (2) determine the skills and behaviors that are necessary to implement the strategy; (3) list the organization's management practices; (4) assess external and internal consistency; and (5) make changes to ensure alignment. In order for those changes to occur, management must build trust with all employees and encourage changes. Encouraging changes takes a belief and understanding on the part of management that mistakes will occur. It is part of the growth process and must be viewed as such by all in the organization. Finally, management must ensure that the measurements chosen for success are the correct ones and that incentive systems are in alignment with the measurements.

BARRIERS TO IMPLEMENTATION

As simple as the principles and the steps are, only one-eighth of the managers will take the action needed to support high performance management practices. Why? Because only one-half will see the usefulness; one-half of those will make the changes necessary to implement; one-half of those will give the practices enough time to make a difference in the success of the organization. The information presented throughout the principles, factors, and procedures are not a quick fix to achieving long-term success. Rather, they represent a philosophy that is difficult for many to achieve because they take commitment, patience, and a basic understanding that long-term success is achieved only through the commitment of many. There are a number of reasons for organizations to forego putting people first:

- Many have the desire to "follow the crowd."
- Most career incentives are based on short-term financial gains.

- There is a tendency to overvalue personal, hands-on results.
- Expertise is highly valued.
- Financial management (versus human resource management) is more readily rewarded.
- Measurements are made in straight costs versus return on investments.
- "Tough" management is often regarded highly.
- Management education normally focuses on financial rather than human or organizational factors.
- Financial analyses are viewed more favorably than the ability to manage people.
- Short-term performance is demanded from the market and stakeholders.

Another factor often viewed as a barrier to implementation is organized labor. Labor unions have historically been viewed as an adversary, not an ally. However, the principles supporting high-performance management are in line with the goals of organized labor. Furthermore, soliciting the help of union leadership will help gain the buy-in of all employees at a unionized facility. Gaining this trust and cooperation will result in less time, money, and energy being focused on labor problems. Therefore, all employees' energies can be directed toward improvements and avoiding problems in the future.

WHAT HIGH PERFORMANCE MANAGEMENT ACCOMPLISHES

People-centered management is a philosophy that believes the organization's success will be maximized when employees are treated as partners in the business. The commitment to shift to a people-based strategy is not easy, and although not a new philosophy, it flies in the face of modern management style. However, it provides organizations with a competitive edge for success in the future. High performance provides this edge by being difficult for other firms to imitate. It is difficult to imitate because it involves changing basic views about people, organizations, and sources of success. This is a difficult task, particularly in view of the fact that modern management style rewards financial and/or operational management instead of human resource management. Furthermore, people-centered management provides organizationwide learning, skill development, innovation, customer service, labor productivity, and cost reduction—all factors necessary for long-term survival. However, perhaps most significantly, it provides a *system* for success, a system that is not dependent upon a few strategically placed management personnel. Instead, the system is run by all employees of the organization, and the success is a result of the synergy created.

PART SEVEN

Empowerment and Participation

For several decades there have been a small number of highly visible advocates of participative approaches to the practice of management. During the early 1960s, University of California-Berkeley Management Professor Raymond Miles, for example, built upon the earlier work of many behavioral management theorists as he advanced the human resource model. This model argues that through employee involvement, organizational performance will increase. Increases in performance (accomplishments) are satisfying to employees, and this satisfaction breeds the motivation and commitment for deeper involvement.

In spite of such claims, different participative management approaches (e.g., management by objectives, job enlargement, and job enrichment) are not always widely practiced in American organizations. The classical (hierarchical, Theory X, top-down) approach continues in the practice of management. The Japanese challenge, continued decline of American productivity and product quality, and other forces have caused many U.S. organizations to reexamine, adopt, and integrate participation into their management philosophies and practices.

In Part Seven several themes related to employee involvement and participation are addressed. Each of the readings looks at the *empowerment* of the employee.

James Belasco and Ralph Stayer, authors of the *Flight of the Buffalo*, discuss their views on organizational leadership and the need for a new leadership paradigm in their article "Why Empowerment Doesn't Empower: The Bankruptcy of Current Paradigms." According to Belasco and Stayer, the current command and control paradigm, with its emphasis on placing leaders into roles where they plan, organize, command, coordinate, and control, places responsibility for other people's performance on the shoulders of the leader. *This system guarantees organizational failure.* The authors argue that in high-performance organizations leaders have made it their job to make people responsible for their own performance—reasoning that the best person to be responsible for the job is the person doing the job, because that person is the "expert in that job." This theme is similar to that presented by William Glasser in *The Control Theory Manager.*

James Belasco is a Professor of Management at San Diego State University, and Ralph Stayer is the chief executive officer of Johnsonville Foods in Johnsonville, Wisconsin. Mr. Stayer's management philosophy was presented in an interesting article published in the *Harvard Business Review* (1990, November/December, pp. 66–75, 80, 82).

Through fables, William C. Byham and Jeff Cox focus on ways to improve productivity, quality, and employee satisfaction in *Zapp! The Lightning of Empowerment* and a subsequent book *Heroz.* The authors argue that for organizations to be competitive during the beginning of the twenty-first century, it is essential that the organization's human resources be used in such a way that their energies are focused on ways of making improvements in the organization's quality, output, sales, and customer satisfaction.

Through the empowerment of people, the organization's workforce will take on responsibility, experience a sense of ownership, gain satisfaction from accomplishment, and acquire power over the ways things are done. Through this process they will come to know that they are important to the organization, and the organization will have strong, enthusiastic, dedicated employees working toward improved quality and productivity.

Continuing with his "fable" format in *Heroz*, Byham and co-author Cox again promote empowerment as a viable management tool, resulting in the enhancement of worker satisfaction, motivation, cooperation, and performance. The net effect of empowerment for organizations, according to consultants Byham and Cox, is increased efficiency, productivity, and organizational competitiveness.

Dr. William C. Byham is President and Founder of Development Dimensions International, a human resource training and development company.

John Case calls for a major paradigm change in Readings 4 and 5. Open Book management calls for sharing key financial information with employees—but only after educating them in how to understand, interpret, and apply that information to improve operating decisions. It is a rather simple yet daring empowerment technique that some organizations (notably Springfield Remanufacturing) have used with great success to stimulate employee interest in the successful implementation of their own ideas. Essential to open book management's success, however, is providing employees with a financial stake in the success of the company. John Case has identified the keys to the program's effectiveness after observing several organizations, and these include determining the "critical numbers" to monitor, posting them on "scorecards"; education; empowerment; the possibility of financial gain or loss by employees; and relying on games to create a "fun" atmosphere. John Case is the author of two books, editor/publisher of an open-book newsletter based in Boston, and an editor-at-large at *Inc.* magazine.

READING I

Flight of the Buffalo

James A. Belasco and Ralph C. Stayer

The president shifted nervously in his big chair. His youngish face—belying his 50ish age—was creased with worry. His was a most admired company. Mentioned frequently in business magazines, his stock sold at healthy profit-to-earnings multiples. With his Ivy League training he was a leading spokesperson for American business. Yet now his eruditeness had deserted him.

He rose, strode to the window, and peered out at the bucolic setting. "Not on my watch," he said to the huge oak outside his window. "This can't happen on my watch." After an eternity of shuffling his feet and clasping and unclasping his hands, he whirled and faced me, steel flashing in his eyes. "I've got five years to retirement. What can I do to make these five years count?"

The challenge was daunting. The company, despite its favorable press, was failing badly. It had lost market share in every single phase of its business. It was significantly late in several new product launches. Its cash cow was under attack by the Japanese. Despite its cash hoard and dominant market position, the company was in serious trouble. He saw with crystal clarity the potential danger if the business did not change—radically—now. The unthinkable could happen on his watch—and he did not know what to do. Nothing in his previous experience or training had prepared him to deal with this situation.

This president's problem is all too familiar. Though he sat in the CEO's chair, he was powerless to accomplish the changes he knew had to be made. He saw clearly what had to be done. The management mantra of the 1990s was familiar: teamwork, better quality, improved service, faster time to market. He knew them well. He preached them to anyone who would listen. Yet he was unable to make any of these vital outcomes occur in his organization.

It was not for lack of trying. In the last six years he had instituted programs designed to stimulate quality, customer service, and teamwork. He had slimmed down the organization, reorganized functional groups into product/customer focused units, and reduced the number of management layers. Yet he continued to lose market share, competitors continued to beat him to the market, and he had lost 50 percent of his market value. He just couldn't make his people do what he knew had to be done.

The leader presumably sits at the pinnacle of power. At least that's what we are led to believe. The corner office is the symbol of authority in America. Yet read the business press and feel the pain and anguish of so many executives as they are unable to make people produce the changes they know are essential to their organization's survival.

We know how it feels. We've been there through the long sleepless nights. One CEO said, "It's a cruel joke. I work a whole lifetime to make it to the top. 'Now,' I say to myself, 'I can finally do things the way I want them done.' Only now I discover that I have less ability to do things than in any other position I've ever held. It's a cruel joke." The power vacuum in the corner office is an epidemic. It undermines ability to compete in world markets. It deepens recession and flattens growth. In the long run, it is fatal.

Why does this power vacuum exist at the pinnacle of power? The single biggest reason is the obsolete leadership paradigm that robs leaders of their effectiveness. Under the current paradigm leaders are responsible for the performance of their people. They fix problems—including people problems. They answer questions. They make decisions. They do things to the organization and the people in it.

You've probably read it and heard it a million times. Leaders plan, organize, command, coordinate, and control. That's the current command and control paradigm. It's found in every management textbook, taught in every college classroom and seminar room. You see it practiced in almost every organization. It is "conventional wisdom."

Take vision, for instance. Leaders are responsible for crafting a vision, implementing it, and empowering their people to use it. It is this paradigm of leader responsibility for other people's performance that, given today's circumstances, guarantees organizational failure.

Our experiences in researching high performance organizations, running our own companies, and helping other people run theirs demonstrate that the leader's job is to make people responsible for their own performance. Kotter and Heskett (1992) report a significant relationship between economic performance and culture that emphasizes personal accountability to customers. Leonard-Barton (1992) cites the experience of Chaparrel Steel in managing so that individuals own the responsibility to solve production problems. Osborne and Gaebler (1992) argue that government can be reinvented by making people assume responsibility for their own performance serving their citizen-customers. Much of the work of Lawler (1992) leads in the same direction of self-management; Ouchi (1978) and Walton (1985) have presented a similar argument. There is considerable evidence to support this new approach to leadership. One of the consequences of this revised leadership paradigm is that it significantly alters the behavior of everyone in the organization.

An example will clarify the differences in leadership paradigms. We were visiting the president of a $6 billion company. As we walked with him out of his office one day we passed a groundskeeper raking leaves. She was using a rake that, when it was new, had thirty-one teeth; now it was very old with only five teeth, and wasn't raking up many leaves. We stopped and asked her, "What are you doing?"

"Raking the leaves," she replied.

"Why are you using that rake?" we asked. "You're not picking up many leaves."

"Because that's what they gave me to use," she replied.

"Why didn't you get a better rake?" we asked.

"That's not my job," she said.

As we walked away the president was visibly angry. "We have a backlog big enough to choke a horse," he said, working hard to restrain the level of his voice, "and it's growing every day. We're way behind on two large development projects that are draining us of cash. We're behind in both production lines and bleeding cash there too. This incident is a perfect example of what is wrong. People are constantly complaining because they don't have the right tools, parts, drawings, and God knows what. This just caps it for me. It's a perfect example of the lack of a sense of urgency I talked to you about. How are we ever going to make it if we can't even give someone a decent rake? I've got to find her supervisor and make sure she gets a better rake."

"Are you certain the supervisor is responsible?" we asked.

"Absolutely!" he almost yelled. Gaining his composure, he continued, "His job is to make certain his people have the right tools."

"Are you sure?" we asked.

"Well," he replied hesitantly, "If I'm going to be a hands-on leader—if I'm going to demonstrate a personal sense of urgency—if I'm going to live the vision—I guess I'll lead by example and go and get the rake myself." He turned and headed in the direction of the storeroom.

Who is the only person who can get the right tools? Obviously the person doing the job. Yet, hear the old paradigm at work: "It's the supervisor's responsibility to get the right tools. . . . I'll go and get the rake myself." This man had been working fourteen hours per day, seven days a week, and getting farther and farther behind—all because he had defined his role according to the old paradigm. He could chase rakes all day and not put his development projects back on time or his production lines back on schedule. As long as he sees his role as solving problems, people will bring him problems to solve. They won't be responsible for solving their parts shortage or inappropriate tool problems themselves, because he's there to solve them for them.

THE EVOLUTION OF MANAGEMENT PARADIGMS

A little history puts the absolute necessity of this paradigm shift in perspective. Karl Marx was right: the owners of the tools of production determine economic structure. When Marx looked around in the middle of the nineteenth century he saw that capitalists owned the equipment and machinery, which were the tools of production. Therefore, capitalists, who set up the economic system, wielded the power and made the decisions. This system arose because in the mid-nineteenth century markets were local or national, communication took days or weeks, work was unskilled and manual, workers were uneducated, and stability was the rule.

Capital was the critical scarce resource. People were plentiful, being driven in droves from the farms by the agriculture revolution. The Scottish businessman and early management writer-philosopher Robert Owens wrote in the early 1830s, "A good horse is worth five pounds a day. A good man is worth two pounds." Guess who was treated better, the man or the horse?

Early entrepreneurs accumulated capital and risked it to build factories, buy equipment, and produce goods in advance of payment for those goods. All this required high risk, for which there was great return. Jobs, on the other hand, were rudimentary and mechanical. Factory jobs demanded little of the then typical craftsman skill.

Leadership paradigms emerged that reflected these economic conditions. The best examples were the German army and the French coal mines of the late nineteenth century. Henri Fayol wrote his *Principles of Administration* almost 100 years ago. In that book, based upon his experience running the French coal mines, he outlined the functions of management as planning, organizing, commanding, coordinating, and controlling. Max Weber, studying the German army of approximately the same time, came to very similar conclusions. Our present leadership paradigm methods are based on their model—even though our circumstances are far different from what they were then.

Times changed, however. In the mid-1930s another historian, James Burnham, realized that professional managers effectively controlled corporations, which were the tools of production. In his book *The Managerial Revolution* (1941), he argued that power had passed from the shareholder owners of the major corporations to professional managers. He realized that because professional managers set up the system, they wielded power and made the decisions.

Adolph Berle and Gardener Means came to the same conclusion in their book, *The Modern Corporation and Private Property* (1932). They clearly understood the separation between managers, who effectively ran the corporation, and owners, who had little or nothing to say about the disposition of their "property."

In his recent book, *Short-Term America: The Causes and Cures of our Business Myopia* (1991), Michael Jacobs updates and validates the Berle and Means and Burnham observations. He argues that the short-term myopia that plagues American business is the result of the separation of management from ownership and the ascendancy of management to the seat of power.

This transfer of power occurred because the brainpower capital supplied by professional managers became more important than the financial capital supplied by the shareholders. The critical capital resource needed for survival changed from such tangible physical assets as plant, equipment, and money to the brainpower capital supplied by managers. Capital had been transformed from a physical to an intellectual form. Karl Marx was right again: the owners of the tools of production become the dominant power in the economic landscape. But Marx could not have envisioned the day human brainpower would be more important than tangible assets.

Today circumstances have changed again. The principle tools of production today are not machinery and equipment, but the ideas and talents of the people. Today, the intellectual capital of the scientist, the machinist, and the programmer is the critical resource, so the possessors of the intellectual tools of production—people—will come to exercise effective power. Markets are now global, electronic highways enable instant communication and rapid competitive responses, work involves the creation, transmission, and manipulation of information and knowledge, and workers are highly educated.

Cadavers of Leadership Paradigms: 100 Years and Still Stinking

Unfortunately, leadership practice hasn't caught up with this new reality. The leadership systems currently in use are designed to control relatively uneducated, mostly untrustworthy people in an environment of very slow change. In our free and democratic society, employees park their rights—along with their brains—at the door. Companies today are the last remaining feudal enclave. Too many people in organizations are subjected to authoritarian—and what they believe to be unreasonable—treatment. This is why there is so little effort to excel in authoritarian firms.

Several authors have written about the negative impacts of low trust and commitment, particularly Cook and Wall (1982), Wilkins (1989), and Kotter and Heskett (1992). The current popular management literature is also filled with examples of the negative impact of declining trust and commitment. Recent articles report employees' lack of commitment and loyalty, as well as the fear that cost cutting has gone too far and may be the precipitating cause of corporate disasters ranging from Exxon's string of spills and explosions to IBM's chronic underperformance.

The following anecdote highlights leaders' feudal thinking. A mid-level supervisor in a large, publicly traded company asked her secretary to wash and detail her car. Her instructions were not to do it if they didn't take her credit card because she didn't have enough money in her checking account to cover any cash expenditures. The secretary took the car down during working hours. When the car wash didn't take the credit card, she paid for the wash and detail herself, telling her boss, "Pay me back when you have the money, no problem." The boss was furious and fired the secretary on the spot.

Notice several assumptions. The boss thought nothing of asking the secretary to run a personal errand for her during working hours—or to terminate her at will when she was displeased with the performance. After all, the secretary "worked" for her. Notice the master-slave concept in action. So much of the early thinking about the employment relationship was based upon that concept. The vestiges of that thinking still exist. It didn't even occur to the boss that her request was inappropriate or her termination action likely illegal.

Notice also the boss's assumption that she could take care of her personal business during working hours and use company resources to do so. Hear the assumption, "I'm the boss and I'm in control of these resources to use as I see fit." This is managerial capitalism at its best. Hear how the property rights of the boss take precedence over the civil rights of the employee. Furthermore, the stockholders in this publicly traded company must be exceedingly angry with the boss for breaching her fiduciary responsibility to them—the owners of the resources she so freely uses for her own personal use.

The payoff was the immediate dramatic fall in her department's productivity. She couldn't figure out why, but it is clear to us. The people in the department were withholding their intellectual capital. In many departments in many companies across the world this same soap opera is being played out—to the detriment of everyone.

We both were thoroughly caught up in the old paradigm. We believed it, practiced it, taught it—even wrote about it (Belasco, Price, and Hampton 1978). We spent long sleepless nights wondering why it didn't work. The old paradigm was so logical. It was "proven." We loved being the drivers of things in our organizations. No matter how hard we tried, though, we couldn't make the old planning and control paradigm work. Out of our frustration came the search for a new, more effective model.

THE INTELLECTUAL CAPITALISM PARADIGM

We have all grown up learning to follow authority: parents, teachers, bosses. The first and probably most often reinforced lesson we learn is: "Do as you are told by the person in charge." Now, however, the "person in charge" is the person who formally reports to you. In this topsy-turvy world as a leader you actually work for the people who work for you.

In the past, leaders planned products, budgets, facilities—the concrete financial aspects of the business. The assumption was that people would go along with the plan. Many authors have examined the relationship between strategic planning and its execution. The assumption in all this work has been that it is management's task to craft strategic plans and the worker's task to execute them. That assumption is no longer safe. Leaders must plan for the mind-sets and mentalities of the people if they want the financial plan to work.

Leadership tools have not changed significantly. The focus of their use has changed. The primary purpose of strategic planning is not to plan strategically for the future—although that is an important purpose of the exercise. It is primarily to develop the strategic management mindset in every person in the organization. The purpose is not only to produce a plan; it is to produce a plan that will be owned and understood by the people who have to execute it.

Leaders in the era of intellectual capitalism have a new set of responsibilities. At every level in the organization leaders must (1) transfer ownership for work to those who execute the work, and (2) create an environment for ownership in which each person wants to be responsible for his or her own performance. This can be accomplished by the following acts:

- Paint a clear picture of great performance for the organization and each person.
- Focus individuals on the few factors that create great performance.
- Develop the desire for each person to own—be responsible—for his or her own great performance.
- Align organization systems and structures to send a clear message as to what is necessary for great performance for the individual and the organization.
- Engage individuals—their hearts and minds as well as their hands—in the business of the business.
- Energize people around the focus of the business.

Leaders also must (3) coach the development of individual capability and competence, and (4) learn faster by learning themselves, and by creating the conditions under which every person in the organization is challenged to continually learn faster as well. Let's examine each of these leadership functions in turn.

The Leadership Function: Transfer of Ownership

Early in our leadership careers we became grounded in employee involvement. We read a lot about it, and it sounded good. The human relations movement dominated the academic literature when we were undergraduate students. We used textbooks authored by the classic human relations writers Mayo (1933), Maslow (1943), and McGregor (1960).

We began by holding employee meetings to solicit employee participation. We wanted them to share in a two-way exchange of information and, hopefully, some problem solving as well. It rapidly deteriorated, however, into a bitch session. Employees kept bringing up situations that needed fixing. We made long lists of things to fix and worked hard to fix everything before the next meeting. But this turned out to be a full-time job. We told ourselves, "You have to demonstrate good faith. It will take time. Eventually they'll run out of things to fix and you can get on with solving the plant's real problems." Fixing their problems, after all, was part of our leadership responsibility. Eighteen months later, we were still receiving long lists to fix at every meeting. We ran out of patience before they ran out of lists.

In retrospect, the problem is clear to us. We were owning all the responsibility for fixing the problems. The employees' job was to identify what needed to be fixed; they were dedicated to doing that job well. They worked hard to keep us working hard; and we worked hard solving their problems. The plant continued to flounder. Our "fix them" leadership paradigm was failing.

We graduated from the university too soon. While we were discovering the inappropriateness of the simplistic employee participation notions of the human relations school in the 1960s and 1970s, a whole body of new research emerged to validate our experiential conclusions. Clayton Alderfer (1972) proposed a variation on Maslow's hierarchy. Frederick Herzberg (1959) revealed a different approach to motivation that challenged many of the original human relations assumptions about people's behavior. Many popular management books of the 1980s—including Peters and Waterman's *In Search of Excellence* (1982) and William Ouchi's *Theory Z* (1981)—echoed our experience.

Some time in the early 1980s after we had read "newer" research, we encountered a quality problem in one plant. Vowing to learn from the new data and avoid taking responsibility for the problem, we called a meeting of the employees involved and asked them for their input on fixing the problem. This time, however, we insisted that they had to be responsible for implementing any solution they suggested. The discussion took a very different tack.

The first suggestion was to change the equipment. When we revealed that the cost of such a change would be $1.5 million, they were shocked. Next, they suggested that we talk the customer into taking a lesser quality product. We arranged for a group of them to visit customers and discuss the problem in person. The group returned from the visit with higher quality standards, not lower ones. "Whew!" one member of the group told us. "This is hard work."

As the group struggled with what to do, several members complained. "This is management work," they said. "We are not paid to do this. This is your job. Stop imposing it on us." We were stunned and hurt by the comment. Writers told us that everyone wants to be self-actualized. People really love to be responsible, they wrote. We asked ourselves, "Why is it that our people don't? What are we doing, or not doing, that causes our people to not want to assume responsibility?" We then realized that we had trained them to be dependent upon us. We liked their doing whatever we told them to do. When we wanted them to be flexible, they had no model or training in how to share leadership.

We asked them if they would rather have us make the decision. They mumbled, "Well, no. But it isn't supposed to be so hard." We asked, "Haven't we been making all the decisions? Do you really think it's working out better? What do you need to do to make the decision easier, and to make a better decision? How can we help you make the decision?" The stewing and shuffling of feet convinced us that we were on the right track.

We got a few requests, but it was clear that the people were wrestling with what to do. After what seemed an eternity (but was only four days) the group came back with a plan to redo several of the procedures and learn a new process. The quality problem was solved. Total cost: less than $10,000. The group tried one last time to hand us the problem. "Here it is," they proudly said, "Now go fix it." We said. "Whoa, that wasn't the deal. How are you going to make it work?"

The sheepish grins told us we had successfully transferred the responsibility. "Here's the plan," they said. "We're ready to roll." Without looking at the papers thrust in front of us, we said "Go for it." It took a lot of restraint not to respond to our old leadership instincts and rush in to "help." Their answer was not as good as our own—or so we told ourselves. It took maximum control to keep from reading their proposal and "improving" it. Our restraint paid big dividends. Their execution of their own plan was flawless. The problem was solved and never came back. It was a win-win outcome. Gradually, we learned to transfer responsibility for solving other similar problems to the rightful owner.

We learned that the best person to be responsible for the job is the person doing the job. Because that person is the expert in that job, he or she should be the one to make the decision about how the work can best be done. The job design movement is based on this premise. Recent popular literature reports many successful examples of this approach. Theoretical literature leads to a similar conclusion. In the intellectual capitalism model, people with the knowledge about the immediate responsibilities have the ultimate power.

We resolved to stop providing answers and start asking questions. We learned to ask questions such as the following:

- What do you think?
- Why do you think that will or won't work?
- What else might you do?
- What prevents you from doing that?
- How can you overcome that obstacle?

These questions caused consternation. Because we were no longer providing a specific set of answers, people had to find their own answers. That was difficult for some.

Several employees informed us that there was a drug problem on the second and third shifts. Our first reaction was to order drug testing and hire undercover people to catch the users. Then, remembering our commitment to transferring ownership, we chose another route.

We passed on the information to the Quality of Work Life Pride Team, composed of people from all levels. They found that drug use was indeed a problem. After meeting with people throughout the company, they got together with us and set a goal of a drug-free plant. They announced a treatment program for anyone who needed help. They also promised that people who refused help would be asked to leave.

The program was very successful. The incidence of drug usage now is negligible. The program worked because the right people—fellow workers—owned the problem.

Resolve is never sufficient. Old leadership habits die hard. It takes much practice to rid ourselves of them. Leaders frequently fall back into the problem-solving trap. Our academic background taught us that leaders have powerful tools to institutionalize the transfer of ownership. Systems and structures could be modified to create the ownership environment.

Our focus on systems and structures stems from our academic experience. Much of the original thought in management by Weber, Fayol, and Marx was based on the implication that structure shaped behavior. The entire field of organizational theory is based on the same hypothesis. Much of Peter Drucker's writings are based on the similar premise that organizational attributes, similar to systems and structures, shape behavior. Rensis Likert (1961) and the Michigan study of leadership reflects the same presumption that organizational context controls behavior. Studies of organizational culture reaffirm the dominant place of structures and systems in shaping people's behavior within firms. The close relationship between organizational structure characteristics and organizational performance was demonstrated in at least three empirical studies. We therefore modified several systems and structures.

The Leadership Function: Create the Ownership Environment

A team in our company sold software to government units in one local geographic region. Initially, the first team of employees sold, installed, and supported all the systems because they were the only people in the company. Everyone assumed that pattern would change as soon as the company grew sufficiently. After all, it is standard in our industry to separate selling, installation, and support. There is an assumption that salespeople are not good programmers and good programmers are not good salespeople, and good support people are different from both. That assumption, however, did not prove true.

The team quickly sold out its local market. To grow, it either had to seek out smaller customers within its geographic area, which meant changing its product, or move into new geographic areas. Sensing an opportunity for people to assume increased responsibility, we posed the following question to the group: "What can you do to ensure that each customer receives the best service and at the same time ensure that you personally continue to learn and grow?" Rather than our deciding what to do, we turned the decision over to the people who had to make the decision work.

The people decided to hire new people to both sell to smaller customers in their original geographic area and move into new geographic areas. They set up a rotation system within the teams so that everyone learned all the skills. They set up an internal monitoring system to keep the skills current. They assumed ownership for training and monitoring themselves—and for assuring superior service to their customers. One of the team members offered to start the new team for the smaller customers. Another offered to relocate temporarily to start up a new operation in a new geographic area.

Today there are more than seven hundred people in the company, organized into thirty-seven semi-autonomous teams stretching from Singapore to Moscow. These team members are responsible for hiring, training, and maintaining superior levels of service to customers. The team members themselves have assumed responsibility for delivering great performance to their customers. Getting people to own the responsibility for making crucial strategic decisions is leadership in the intellectual capitalism age.

As the company grew, so did complaints about performance discrepancies among teams. We tried several different tactics to deal with the discrepancies—all to no avail. Eventually we realized this was another opportunity to transfer ownership. At the next all-employee meeting we asked, "How can we assure consistent high performance across all teams? What can we do to be certain that we are all equally proud of the work of each person in the company?"

The employees wrestled with the problem for an entire day. Eventually they decided that each team would meet every week and set individual and team goals. These goals would be validated by customers and would expect measurable, responsible action from each member. The goals would be entered on the e-mail system along with daily progress. Team members agreed to help other team members—in their own team as well as in others—set realistic but challenging goals and then support each other in attaining them.

Today each team member inputs individual and team goals every week, reviews and comments on others' goals, and reports daily progress. There is a lively e-mail exchange about goals and performance among most people in the company. And goal attainment averages more than 99 percent every week. A system of goal planning, designed by the people, helped create the environment wherein the people assumed ownership for their results.

We have an extensive full-cost, real-time cost accounting system that uses "activity based costing." Everyone charges time, expenses, and materials directly to a project, customer, or program. These costs are collected daily and a real-cost, 30-day rolling average is computed for every product for every team. This real-time, full-cost data bank gives teams the opportunity to make such business decisions as pricing and delivery. It enables them to accept responsibility for making profitable bids.

Our decision to use the information system to shape behavior is supported by extensive research. The idea that controlling the information premises in an organization shapes individual behavior was most clearly articulated by Nobel laureate Herbert Simon (1945). Much of Edward Lawler's work leads to the similar conclusion that information is a powerful influencer of behavior in organizations. Much of the financial control literature is also based on the same premise that information is the central ingredient in control. Research in the 1980s demonstrated that access to information is a way of building commitment. The Management of the 1990s Research Program at MIT's Sloan School of Management empirically demonstrated how information technology shapes organizational behavior.

Initially we reviewed and approved each bid. We were concerned that bid prices wouldn't be high enough and they weren't. We found ourselves continually raising bids, and realized that we had to change the situation or else be forever reviewing bids—not exactly the future we had envisioned for ourselves. So we changed another critical system—the reward system.

Again, research offered good guidance in choosing a focus for leadership behavior. The works of Edward Lawler articulate the premise that you get what you pay for. In addition, Luthans and Kreitner (1985) support the linkage between reward (in its broadest sense, not just compensation) and performance.

In the first year, each person was paid a bonus based on a percentage of overall company profit and determined by the executive committee. In the beginning the bonuses were not very large, because start-up costs ate into profits and we needed to conserve cash. This caused considerable discontent. Eventually, after much fruitless discussion, we realized we had yet another opportunity to transfer ownership.

At the next quarterly all-employee meeting we asked, "What is a fair and equitable bonus system? What would make you feel like a winner and still leave a return to our shareholders and enough capital to grow the business? What bonus system would reward people on the basis of their contribution?" As a trigger to the discussion we suggested a 50/50 split of net profits before tax to be allocated on the basis of team performance.

The group took some time to decide. Eventually, the group chose to use the 50/50 split as a framework but added certain provisions. They decided that teams would allocate the bonus among team members, ensuring that everyone received a reward based upon his or her contribution. Eligibility for the bonus pool initially was restricted to individuals who met their weekly individual and team goals 90 percent of the time and received a rating of 8 or better (out of a possible 10) on the monthly customer satisfaction survey. The group has continually raised the standard for admission into the bonus pool. Today it has established 100 percent goal achievement and a perfect score of 10 on the customer survey as the eligibility standards.

Almost immediately bid prices and margins rose, as did the preoccupation with supplying superior products and services to create additional value. Further, after the initial excitement caused by the distribution of big monthly team bonus checks, the focus shifted to the weekly performance management reports. E-mail notes flew back and forth challenging, supporting, and sharing information relevant to attaining individual and team goals.

Over the period of a few months we withdrew from approving bids. The teams now had full responsibility to bid jobs and deliver a superior product. This delighted customers and earned the company a profit. They accepted the ownership for running their business. They had the intellectual capital. They were in control.

While we had been changing so dramatically internally, the market was changing as well. Our technology base changed four times in four years. Our programming language changed several times in the same four years. Our customer base shifted five times. All our leadership efforts directed toward transferring ownership paid off. Despite the external chaos, the people were able to remain focused on delivering great performance for their customers. By shaping the systems and structures we created the ownership environment. Nevertheless, leadership is a one-on-one phenomenon as well.

The Leadership Function: Coaching Personal Competence

Coaching is frequently listed as an important leadership task. One of the first major writers to explore the coaching rather than directing role of a leader was Chris Argyris (1957, 1964). Tom Peters and Nancy Austin (1985) specify five coaching roles: educating, sponsoring, coaching, counseling, and confronting; they then cite numerous examples of successful coaching. Noel Tichy and Mary Anne Devanna (1986) visualize the leader as the coach of the change process. Edgar Schein (1983, 1985) makes the coaching role pivotal as the preferred change process. Stephen Covey (1990) uses coaching as the principal organizational leadership activity.

What does coaching mean? What does a world-class coach do? How does one measure whether one is a world-class coach or not? These are not easy questions, particularly because most of us have been raised in the old command-and-control leadership style: asking questions and not giving answers.

Initially we believed that great coaches helped other people find their own answers. So we concentrated on asking questions. We became experts in the "grunt and pause" methodology. That frustrated many people. It was certainly not a style they had come to expect. They believed we should tell them what to do, not ask them what they thought should be done. It came as a big shock. Many never recovered. Moreover, because we had been providing them with answers, they had difficulty finding their own. We had trained their incapacity.

We missed several significant business opportunities because senior people didn't know what to do. We learned that great coaches did more than ask questions and not give answers. Great coaches had to provide guidance so people could find the "right" answer.

Seeking to provide more guidance, we engaged each person in continuing conversations about identifying and measuring great performance for individual jobs. We still asked questions and worked to not provide answers, but this time we focused conversations on great performance. This improved performance but still left many people feeling insecure and unclear about what constituted great performance. We didn't want to provide the answers. We needed a better set of questions to provide more focus.

One day it finally hit us. The real experts in great performance are customers. Everything begins with delighting customers. That's why every one of our job descriptions begins with the statement, "The things I do to get and keep customers are. . . ."

The situation improved when we modified our focus to the following question: "From the customer's point of view, what is great performance?" The employees finally had a way to receive answers to their questions from true experts in what they had to do. As such, they felt more focused and secure.

There is risk in making people too secure, however. Coaches help people see beyond where they are now. Coaches help people see what they *can be*, which is usually much more than what they are now. The view of the tomorrow that *must be* creates discomfort. Nevertheless, discomfort leads to learning and growth. Hear the discomfort and learning that happened in the following anecdote.

A president worked in a very competitive industry. The firm had had a particularly difficult time in recent years and had averaged less than 1 percent net profit margin on sales over the past three years. Last year it averaged 0.5 percent. The CEO had established the goal for this year as a 0.7 percent return on sales.

We asked him if he was satisfied with this return. "Well," he said, "that's not bad. Competition's tough. We've come back from a very bad period. I think that's all we can achieve."

We asked, "Is that really great performance?"

"Well," he replied hesitantly, "maybe we could be a little better than that. Industry average is about 1.1 percent. We even did 1.2 percent once. So maybe 1.3 percent would be great performance."

"Maybe," we replied. "What do the best locations in your industry make?"

"We have locations in our company that make 2.26 percent, 2.08 percent, and several that make between 1.75 and 2.00 percent. One of our competitors has a location that makes a little better than 3 percent. When I think about it, I guess we can do better than 0.7 percent. Now that I think about it, 1.1 percent would be great performance for this year, and 2 percent plus next year would be fantastic."

"That will bring you closer to the best in your business," we responded, "but is that *great* performance? Is that as much margin as you can make? Look, how much do credits cost?" (Credits are returned merchandise, almost always because of shipping or order packing errors.)

After some time searching through papers he replied, "They run about 4 percent."

"How would your margin look if you eliminated all the credits?" we asked.

After some calculation he responded, "3.1 percent."

"So, if you could have zero credits, you could be the best in your industry, right? Why can't you do that?" we asked.

"I don't know why we can't," he said. "In fact. I'm sure we can. We just never thought about it before. We've assumed that credits were a 'normal' part of business."

Listen to how this CEO's low level of expectation yields a low level of return: "The best we can achieve is 0.7 percent; 1.1 percent is great performance; 2.0 percent is fantastic." Yet achieving zero defects in his packing and shipping departments alone could give multiples of that return. How much more money he could make by improving other areas of his operation remain unknown. Coaching questions helped him raise his expectations so he could become more of what he could be, which was far greater than he ever imagined. When you set the high-jump bar at five feet, your performance is average. When you set that bar at eight feet, you put in a gold-medal-winning performance. Moreover, you'd better be able to clear eight feet, one inch, because that's where the record probably will be next year. As one athlete put it, "They keep raising the bar all the time." As a coach you help people raise their expectations high enough to encourage great performance today and even greater performance tomorrow.

The Leadership Function: Learning

Leaders learn fast and keep on learning. The world changes so quickly that we need to keep learning new things just so we can cope. Success is a valuable teacher, provided it does not lull us into complacency. Whatever put us where we are will not take us where we need to go. Circumstances change; leaders must change also, or be left behind. The skills learned to be a good supervisor will not help anyone be a good president. Continued learning is crucial to continued success.

Most armies are perfectly designed to fight the last war, especially if they were victorious in that war. The English destroyed the French nobility at Agincourt in one of the most lopsided victories ever recorded. The French wore armor that made them slow-moving targets for the English, who had longbows powerful enough to pierce it. While the French were forced to fight on the plain, the English fought safely from the hills.

The French knights liked their armor. It gave them status. They knew about the longbow, but they didn't want to change. The longbow transformed their armor—their source of safety and status—into a shiny coffin. One can imagine them discussing the topic before the battle. It probably went something like this:

> GENERAL: Men, we're fighting the English tomorrow. They'll be tough but we're the finest knights in the world. *We will prevail.*
>
> YOUNG KNIGHT: But Sir, the English have longbows. Their arrows can go right through this tin foil.
>
> GENERAL: Nonsense! My father fought in armor. My grandfather fought in armor. My family has fought in armor for 15 generations.

YOUNG KNIGHT: But, sir, times have changed. . . .

GENERAL: Quiet! Don't say another word. That's an order. I've been fighting like this for thirty years and if I haven't learned anything else, I've learned one thing: *If it ain't broke, don't fix it.*

The general was trapped. He had become a general by fighting a certain way. He couldn't change the ideas that had made him successful all his life.

England went on to develop a great empire; success, with the accompanying complacency, became its biggest enemy. In World War I, the English had the chance to pull the same trick again, this time in reverse. The English invented the tank in 1915. Its armor would have protected them against the German guns. Employed in strength, it would have breached the German lines, ended the war quickly, and saved many lives. But the English generals would have nothing to do with the tank. They had enjoyed unprecedented success for two-hundred years. They loved their heritage. They had lost what had put them there: the will to change and adapt to new circumstances. Without that will, they lost their empire.

Johnsonville Foods experienced the same "success malaise." One of us had become a national hero, lecturing around the world on how Johnsonville "did it." Sales grew, margins rose, and profit sharing bonuses increased. Then it happened. People took a deep breath and started to "tweak." Sales continued to rise but margins didn't; bonuses fell. The final blow came when Johnsonville sausage finished out of the running in a taste test in its local area. That experience awakened members to start learning again.

The mentality of "If it ain't broke, don't fix it" focuses on the present rather than the future. The present becomes the past overnight, and the future becomes the present all too soon. Success is the greatest enemy. We must keep learning new leadership skills, new leadership techniques, new leadership approaches, and new leadership paradigms.

We discovered the only way to change our leadership behavior was to learn how to lead differently. We thought we could just "turn on" the new behavior like you "turn on" a light bulb. If only it were that simple.

We hired a consultant to help us. His conclusion was devastating: "You are the problem," he told us. "You prevent people from really doing their jobs. You dominate meetings. You give your own solutions—sometimes even before the problem is raised. You finish other people's sentences. You state your opinions first. Who's going to argue with you? You cut people off. You change agendas during the meeting, raising issues no one else is prepared to discuss. People leave meetings feeling discouraged rather than energized. You insist on making every decision. No wonder people don't take responsibility. You won't let them."

We were stunned, particularly after we listened to several tape recordings of our meetings. But the consultant was right! We saw that our leadership behavior was counter-productive. So we said, "We'll change."

At the next meeting we tried to remain quiet. That lasted about three minutes. We tried to stop providing answers. That lasted about as long. It was tough being different. It was too easy for us to slip back into old leadership patterns. The staff, as much as they complained about the old us, liked the comfort of knowing what we were going to do. That helped them figure out what they needed to do. We all were trapped in this "death dance" of hating what we were doing but hating more the task of changing it.

To change our leadership behavior took conscious effort. First, we changed our mental picture of the leadership job. We stopped being the decision makers and micromanagers. We stopped deciding production schedules and fixing sales problems. Instead, we insisted that others handle those situations.

We needed new leadership skills to support this new leadership job definition. We inventoried what we needed to learn—and went to work to learn it. We worked on people development skills, such as asking questions rather than giving answers. Moreover, we extracted ourselves out of the decision-making and answer-providing loops. By deliberately scheduling ourselves out of production scheduling meetings and sales reviews, we encouraged people to decide those issues without us. Knowing that if we had the information about daily shortages, supplier problems, and such, we'd ask questions about it, we also stopped collecting detailed data about production and sales performance.

It wasn't easy for us to unlearn old leadership habits. We were afraid we'd have no real function to perform. Consultants and writers can talk glibly about coaching and question asking as the "new" leadership responsibilities. We were afraid that people wouldn't respect us if we didn't have quick, good answers. Asking questions looks impish. We still catch ourselves making decisions, telling people how to solve their problems. After all these years we still keep learning that we need to keep learning.

We don't know how to chart a course there. We just know we have to go. When we decided that we absolutely had to alter our management style we didn't know in detail how it would work. We knew we had to change. "How do we change?" and "What would the final change look like?" were questions to which we didn't have good answers. We knew that if we didn't start we'd never finish. If we waited until we had all the answers we'd be old and gray—and probably out of business.

When the head of Johnsonville Foods first stopped tasting the sausage, he didn't have a clear picture of what would happen next. He didn't know that the people would jump in and ask for production and quality data. He didn't know that they'd seize the opportunity to take more control over their work lives. He knew he had to change his style. His ceasing to taste the sausage was an opportunity for him to learn how to manage in a different way.

We did something when we started changing ourselves and the company that made it easier. We told our customers and people what we were trying to do and what it would mean for them. We told them we didn't know how to go there, but doing something was so important we were going to get started anyway. We said this meant we would probably make many mistakes, but nothing would be irreversible. We would make mistakes together and the minute a mistake became apparent we would fix it together. We gave ourselves and everyone else permission not to be perfect. Customers and the people saw our sense of urgency to improve. They knew it would no longer be business as usual.

Karl Marx had it right: those who hold capital exercise power. Today intellectual capital is the scarce resource, so the holders of that capital exert control. Henri Fayol is also correct. Managers plan, organize, command, coordinate, and control. Only now the managers who perform these functions are the holders of the intellectual capital. Leaders now perform the very different functions of transferring ownership, creating the ownership environment, coaching, and learning.

In this upside-down world, leaders lead and employees manage. Leaders who recognize this phenomenon and change their behavior will accrue power. Those who don't will pass from the scene.

READING 2

Zapp! The Lightning of Empowerment

William C. Byham with Jeff Cox
Summary prepared by Constance Campbell

Constance Campbell *is an Assistant Professor of Management at Georgia Southern University and teaches in the areas of Management and Organizational Behavior. Her research interests include learned helplessness, attribution theory, creativity, and intrinsic motivation. Her research has been published in* Psychological Reports, *the* Journal of Social Behavior and Personality, *and the* Proceedings of the Decision Sciences Institute. *Dr. Campbell received her doctorate from Florida State University. She is active in the Academy of Management, the Southern Management Association, and the Decision Sciences Institute.*

Zapp! The Lightning of Empowerment is aimed at improving quality, productivity, and employee satisfaction. It is a story about *empowerment* (employee feelings of ownership and personal interest in their jobs) written in the form of a fable containing dragons, trolls, Ralpholators, Sapps, Zapps, and (most importantly) Joe Mode's notebook.

Empowerment involves helping employees take ownership of their jobs. When this happens, they are more likely to take personal interest in improving the organization's performance. The book describes realistic and practical ways to empower people and uses the format of a fable to present its message.

The first part of the book "Situation Normal," describes a typical organizational setting in which the workers are apathetic, the managers are antagonistic toward the workers, and productivity is marginal at best. However, one of the supervisors, Joe Mode, decides to try to improve the situation, with the help of one of the employees. "The Zapping of Dept. N" describes how Joe Mode empowers the people in his department. In Part Three, "Super-Charged Zapp," Joe Mode learns about the collective energy that is generated when groups are empowered to work together. Finally, in Part Four, "The Zapped Company," Joe Mode and his friends spread their empowerment ideas to the rest of the company. Contrary to the scenario in many fables, however, the characters in this fable do not ride off into the sunset and live happily ever after. Instead, it becomes clear that empowerment is never a finished process.

William C. Byham & Jeff Cox, *Zapp! The Lightning of Empowerment.* New York, NY: Harmony Books, 1988.

147

Throughout all of the sections, key ideas regarding empowerment are highlighted in part of Joe Mode's notebook. Each of these sections, including Joe Mode's discoveries, is described in more detail next.

PART ONE: SITUATION NORMAL

In Part One, several characters are introduced who work in the Normal Company, a manufacturer of normalators, in Normalburg, USA. For example, Ralph Rosco, an employee in Normal Company, has been working on developing a revolutionary product, a Ralpholator. Ralph is trying to present his idea to his supervisor, Joe Mode, only to be rebuffed with three reasons that the Ralpholator is not a good idea:

1. It is not what Joe is supposed to be working on.
2. It is not the Normal way to do things.
3. If it really were a good idea, R & D would have already developed it.

Actually, Joe did not have time to worry about Ralph's invention, because Joe had enough problems of his own. With too much to do and not enough time to do it, Joe had been berated by his boss, Mary Ellen Krabofski, for not getting enough work done. Mary Ellen instructs Joe, in no uncertain terms, that he needs to crack the whip harder over his people to get more work out of them.

At the end of this trying day, Joe Mode goes back to his office to contemplate the events of the day and to record his thoughts in his notebook, as is his habit. This day he made entries about the problems he encountered in his job, ending with the lament that his employees rarely do more than the bare minimum. They never get excited about their work, and the results of his motivational efforts are short-lived. Joe could see no viable solution to his problems.

This is the state of life in Normal Company early in the fable: workers who are discouraged and supervisors who want to give up. But soon, things begin to change—due, in large part, to the fact that Ralph decides not to give up on his new idea. He continues working on it during all of his spare time and even some of his work time. Finally, Ralph's machine, the Ralpholator, is complete. With no one around to observe, Ralph decides to test his machine, sits down in the chair, flips a few switches, . . . and disappears. Later that same day, Joe Mode goes back to Ralph's work area and stumbles, literally, onto the Ralpholator, accidentally zapping himself to the same place that Ralph had gone, the twelfth dimension.

The twelfth dimension is a place with fog and lightning, dragons and trolls, and fire and ice. As it turns out, as Ralph explains it to Joe, in the twelfth dimension one can see things "that we can't see in the normal world . . . like how people feel, what's going on in their minds, what it's like for them on the inside." With these kinds of visual abilities, Ralph and Joe discover that the people in their department, Dept. N, look pretty dark and dismal.

Joe begins to feel pretty dismal, himself, about the whole picture, until Ralph takes Joe to visit Dept. Z, where the people are glowing and happy. Ralph and Joe watch in amazement as one woman in the department grabs lightning bolts and Zapps the people in the department with them. When they are Zapped, Joe and Ralph are surprised to see that the Zapp not only doesn't hurt, but it actually increases the light in the people in the department. It seems to give them added energy.

Naturally, Ralph and Joe are curious about this lightning, but before they have a chance to figure it out, Mary Ellen Krabofski, who is wandering around looking for Joe in Dept. N, manages to trip over the Ralpholator's extension cord and disconnect it from its power source. To their chagrin, this causes Ralph and Joe to become visible again, and they materialize right in the midst of Dept. Z. Standing there in the department, being very visible now, they are greeted by the woman who was Zapping people with lightning in the twelfth dimension, who asks if she can help them. After some fancy footwork (a.k.a. lying) by Joe, the woman, who is Lucy Storm, supervisor of the department, takes them on a tour of the department. During the tour they note that the workers in Dept. Z are productive and content, even though they are in jobs that do not appear to be very challenging at all.

Before Ralph and Joe can solve this puzzle, the tour of Dept. Z ends, and Ralph and Joe go back to their own department, where they find a stark contrast in attitudes from the place they had just seen. Mary Ellen Krabofski is still there, angry about her stumbling encounter with the Ralpholator, and just waiting to take it out on Joe and Ralph. As it happens, she mainly takes it out on Ralph, giving him a three-day suspension from work. Meanwhile, Joe goes back to his office to pick up his notebook once again. In trying to discern what the Zapp of lightning is that he saw flowing into people in the twelfth dimension, he decides to give the lightning a name, calling it *Zapp*, and describes it as "*a force that energizes people*" (p. 38).

Joe's next step is to try to find out how to Zapp people in his department. Of course, asking Lucy Storm for help might have been the easiest way to do it, but Joe had a rule against asking people for help, so Joe tried all sorts of things to Zapp people: Mr. Nice Guy, Mr. Mean Guy, and even Quality Circles. None of them worked. In fact, in looking over the long list of things that had been tried in his department and others, Joe found that they always worked in Lucy Storm's department, but there wasn't much consistency anywhere else. Joe concludes that Zapp is essential for the success of new ideas and programs, for they work with Zapp and they fail without it.

After his suspension time is over, Ralph comes back to work—not too happy to be there—until Joe convinces him to reassemble the Ralpholator so they can both learn about the Zapps. After reassembling the machine, Ralph disappears into the twelfth dimension. What he notices this time is not a Zapp, but a *Sapp*—a force that drains energy instead of giving it. From the twelfth dimension, Ralph watches Joe Sapp his people when he did not listen to them, when he took their problems away from them to solve them himself, and when he made decisions for them.

After further exploration, Ralph learns that Joe is not the only one Sapping people; others are doing it as well. Ralph tries to explain Sapps to Joe, but Joe does not believe it until he sees it himself. After his own trip into the twelfth dimension to observe Sapps, Joe identifies a list of *what Sapps people*:

- lack of trust
- not being listened to
- not enough feedback to judge one's success/failure
- overly simplified jobs

When Joe and Ralph really think about this list, they realize that Zapp and Sapp are opposite sides of the same coin; that Zapp! gives power and Sapp≠; takes it away. In contrasting Zapp and Sapp, Joe writes in his notebook items that people include:

teams, recognition for ideas, support (approval, coaching, feedback, encouragement), and flexible controls. Joe decides to try to make his department more Zapped than Sapped.

PART TWO: THE ZAPPING OF DEPT. N

Joe's first real effort at Zapping is to gather everyone and tell them that they are henceforth in control of their own jobs, will be making their own decisions, and should act like they own their jobs. Unfortunately, no one really understands what he means. However, they try it, with some deciding to take a break for the day. The abysmal failure of this approach causes Joe to conclude in his notebook that *"It is easy to Sapp. It is hard to Zapp"* (p. 66).

Ralph comes to Joe's rescue again, though, when he calls in constant reports from his newly invented Ralphone in the twelfth dimension, and tells Joe that maintaining people's self-esteem is important. Joe decides to try it. Just like everything else he tries, Joe's first efforts at building self-esteem are clumsy at best, but he learns fairly quickly with practice and with help from Ralph that comments designed to build self-esteem must be sincere. It was an important discovery, learning the importance of people's self-esteem, so Joe wrote it in large letters in his notebook:

First Step of Zapp: Maintain Self-Esteem (p. 70) But there were still other important ideas to learn. The next day, Ralph called on the Ralphone to report that he had discovered that Lucy Storm could Zapp people just by listening to them and then repeating back to the person a short summary of what had been said. Joe decided to try it in Dept. N. As usual, his first effort at listening was not a rousing success, but at least he did keep trying. With practice, he improved.

However, as Ralph and Joe were working on a problem one day, they discovered that merely listening was not enough. In addition to listening, it was important to respond with empathy, showing that the feeling behind the words was noted as well as the message. With that, Joe had discovered the second step of Zapp, which he wrote in large letters in his notebook:

Second Step of Zapp: Listen and Respond with Empathy (p. 78) At this point, things were going well for Joe and Dept. N. Ralph could observe many more Zapps in the department during his times in the twelfth dimension. But then, one day, a huge dragon appeared. It was wiping out computer data, it was breaking important machines, and it was starting small fires all around the department. People in the department picked up a hose to extinguish the blazes started by the dragon, but, before they knew what happened, Joe Mode appeared on the scene, grabbed the fire hose himself, and took over the fight. Meanwhile, the employees, who no longer were in on the fight, went back to their routine or simply watched Joe practicing his heroics. Needless to say, the fires weren't extinguished effectively.

At the end of the day, a very tired and frustrated Joe approaches Ralph for some twelfth dimension help on how to deal with this situation. In answer, Ralph takes Joe to the twelfth dimension, where the dragon is wreaking havoc all around the company . . . until they arrive in Dept. Z, Lucy Storm's department. As you might have guessed, things were different there. Instead of fighting all of the fires herself, Lucy Storm was asking her people to pitch in and fight the fires together. This led Joe to a new realization, which he wrote in his notebook:

Third Step of Zapp: Ask for Help in Solving Problems (Seek Ideas, Suggestions, and Information) (p. 89)   And so, of course, Joe tried it, although he got it only partly right. He enlisted people's help in coming up with some great solutions, but he took the projects away when it came to implementing the solutions. After thinking about it for a while, Joe realized that he had been taking away from people the responsibility for carrying out the plans. With some practice, he began to learn, and in his thinking process he was able to make a key discovery and record it in his notebook:

The Soul of Zapp! Offer Help Without Taking Responsibility (p. 97)   With everyone in Dept. N now getting Zapped on a regular basis, things were going rather smoothly. Except for one thing: Joe Mode was unhappy. He was worried about what people would do now that they were making the decisions. He knew that he would catch the heat from Mary Ellen Krabofski if something went wrong in the department. He began to realize that there still needed to be some control . . . but how? After several crises erupt in the department, Joe realizes that there is an appropriate amount of control to use, involving the proper balance between delegation and checking on how people are doing. He decides to tailor the amount of control to the situation.

Even then, all of the problems in Dept. N are not conquered. Another problem appears. People are enthusiastic in the department, they are Zapped, and they are working on projects. Unfortunately, though, they are working on the *wrong* projects. People are charged, but are not necessarily moving in the right direction. After thinking about it, Joe realizes that his department has no clear goals; people have been given no direction. So Joe decides to work on it. The goals that he developed had three parts:

1. "Key Result Area—The direction we want to go";
2. "Measurement—A way to know we're moving in the right direction";
3. "Goal—Something to tell us if we're there yet."

Once he got started, Joe had each person develop personal goals, which led to the accomplishment of departmental goals, which led to the accomplishment of company goals. This allowed everyone to see where they fit into the big picture. Soon Joe had initiated the use of feedback charts that kept track of progress toward goals. He even had people keeping track of their own feedback charts.

All was not perfect in Normalburg yet. Joe still had a problem with one of his employees, Mrs. Estello, who went on making mistake after mistake day after day, oblivious to the need to improve the quality of her work. When Joe's pleas for improvement fell on deaf ears, he finally realized that he should be more like a coach with her and less like a boss. He would go through the process of explaining why the job was important and how to do it, demonstrating how to do it, and then watching as Mrs. Estello did it to give her feedback on her performance. Finally, he would express confidence in her ability and agree on follow-up actions. After he took these steps, Mrs. Estello began to improve. All the while, Joe was making sure to notice when she did something right.

By this time, people were getting Zapped right and left in Joe Mode's department, and Joe realized one day that the nature of his job had changed dramatically.

Instead of telling people what they should do, his role had become more of a facilitator. He discovered that he provided four things to his department: Direction, as in goals; Knowledge, as in training; Resources, as in facilities; and Support, as in encouragement. After reflecting on this, Joe realized that he was more of a Group Leader than a Supervisor. It was time to move on, time to move to Part Three.

PART THREE: SUPER-CHARGED ZAPP

It was time for Joe to go back to the Ralpholator and see what things looked like now in the twelfth dimension. When he arrived at Ralph's work station, he discovered that Ralph was already in the twelfth, so Joe took off, too, looking for Ralph. He found Ralph, with Lucy Storm, standing outside of the company observing how the company looked from the twelfth dimension. The company looked like a large imposing tower, but their own departments were fluid shapes that were in a process of continual transformation.

After a bit of discussion about this new finding, the three parted and went back to their areas, and time passed. Then one day Joe and Ralph discovered a new business area in Dept. Z, so they went to check on it. Instead of bolts of lightning, they were surprised to see wheels of lightning. The wheels did not just go from the supervisor to the employee, but they were generated by the group and went around the work group. After discussions with Lucy Storm, Joe discovered that the key to generating these wheels of lightning was having people work in *semiautonomous teams*, where small groups of employees managed their own work affairs.

Joe decided to try it in his area. He used some of the same group leader skills with the teams that he had used to Zapp individuals. He provided direction, knowledge, resources, and support. Part of the knowledge he found that he needed to give people was in the form of training in "people skills," such as how to solve conflicts in the group, since they were working in teams instead of alone. Joe also found that he needed to train people in technology at the appropriate time but just before they needed it, not a long time before they needed it. After some initial rough spots, the groups became effective for the department, enZapping each other in the process of their work. Some of the functions the groups served were to deal with absenteeism and performance issues, schedule vacations, and improve quality and productivity.

With these groups working together and being supercharged in Dept. N, the next move was to focus on the total organization.

PART FOUR: THE ZAPPED COMPANY

Things were going quite well in Depts. N and Z. In fact, from outside of the company in the twelfth dimension, their towers in the company castle looked more like starships prepared to fly away on some lofty errand. But, alas, they were being held to the ground by their attachment to the weighty gray castle that was the rest of the Normal Company.

A look inside the company showed a dismal situation. There were managers running around taking responsibility away from workers, Sapping them right and left. Mary Ellen Krabofski was especially busy driving around in the executive fire truck, taking away firehoses from people and putting out fires herself all around the company. A look at the customer service area indicated that the people there didn't seem to know how to service customers, and, furthermore, didn't seem to care.

After observing these scenes and other interactions around the company, Joe Mode, with the help of Ralph, made an interesting discovery. They discovered that the person's direct boss has the most influence over how Zapped an individual is. The next greatest amount of influence is held by the other people who affect the person's job, followed by top management, and then by the organization and its systems. Joe and Lucy had worked on number one, the direct boss part, but there was not much that they could do in their positions about other people, top management, and the organization. Except . . . talk to Mary Ellen Krabofski.

Now, by this time, everyone in Normal Company had noticed the improvements in Depts. Z. and N. So it didn't take long to convince Mary Ellen to let them present their views. Joe and Lucy asked the Zapp teams to prepare a presentation. Their presentations were given with such enthusiasm that Mary Ellen, being a rather intelligent person after all, decided to begin using the first three steps of Zapp herself:

1. Maintain self-esteem.
2. Listen and respond with empathy.
3. Ask for help in solving problems.

After some success with these three steps, she went straight to the soul of Zapp— offer help without taking responsibility. Since Mary Ellen was near the top of the company, she also realized that she needed to develop an environment where all people in the company could practice Zapp. Like Joe, she had to try and fail a few times, but she eventually became much better at Zapping.

As part of enZapping people, she encouraged under-utilized workers to form teams trying to develop new products for the business. She encouraged work teams to select their own members with guidance and assistance from Personnel, rather than having Personnel do the job completely. The customer service department even received training in how to Zapp the customers. Even old Ralph got to develop his Ralpholator for new product markets! In short, the whole place became Zapped, with lightning flowing everywhere.

Time goes by. A few years later, a rookie manager, Dave, shows up at Joe's office and wants to find out from Joe how to Zapp people. Dave reports that he has heard that Zapp is a source of energy that enables employees to seek and obtain continuous improvement in their jobs. In the process of showing Dave around, Joe let Dave know that this is not a "happily ever after" fable, because Zapp is not a destination (i.e., not a finished process) but a continuous journey. Joe suggests to Dave that he can start using Zapp by reading the notebook containing all of the main ideas, by seeking training in how to Zapp people, and by seeking continually to learn, grow, and improve.

READING 3

HeroZ: Empower Yourself, Your Co-workers, Your Company

William C. Byham and Jeff Cox
Summary prepared by Jack P. Hoggatt

> **Jack P. Hoggatt** *is Professor and Chair of the Department of Business Communication at the University of Wisconsin-Eau Claire. Dr. Hoggatt received his Ed.D. from Utah State University. His areas of teaching, writing, and research include: business communication, teamwork, computer applications, information processing, and student empowerment.*

How many talented individuals are dissatisfied with their current job? Because better-paying jobs are scarce for individuals with the skills they possess, they often feel trapped. With bills to pay and families to provide for, they see very few options in their lives. So, they go to work, put in their time, do the minimum that it takes to survive, and then go home to wait for tomorrow so they can do the same thing again. Art Halegiver was just such an individual.

Art (a shaft-turner) along with his two friends, Mac (a head-shaper) and Wendy (a wand-waver), are the main characters in this engaging model. Heroz presents a fable about individuals empowering themselves and the impact this empowerment has on the individuals as well as the organization.

The setting for the fable is Lamron Castle. Lamron Castle is in the business of providing rescue services to the citizens of Lamron from attacking dragons. To accomplish this, knights have to be trained to deal with the dragons as well as armor and equipment produced to facilitate the rescue efforts. The "Magic Arrows" created for the knights to use in the rescue efforts require dozens upon dozens of shaft-turners, head-shapers, and wand-wavers.

Lamron Castle had been in business for a long time and had been doing the same thing the same way the entire time. The employees earned good wages and kept the local economy flourishing. Being the only provider of dragon saving services, Lamron Castle could set their price high enough to keep the treasury full of gold.

Times changed, however! Other castles starting appearing that offered better and faster services. Lamron Castle did not change with the times. Because the competition

William C. Byham & Jeff Cox, *HeroZ: Empower Yourself, Your Co-workers, Your Company*. New York, NY: Harmony Books, 1994.

offered superior services, the gold in the treasury chest of Lamron Castle started to disappear as expenses started to exceed dwindling income. Competition was causing problems never before encountered.

Over the years a gray fog had started changing the castle. More of a fog enveloped the castle each year and made it difficult to do anything quickly. It was so difficult that workers did not even try. They gave up and went along at the speed the fog would allow. Eventually everything was gray in the castle and workers went through the motions with no enthusiasm for what they were doing, assuming that nothing could be done about the fog.

As the gold in the treasury started to dwindle, the king of the castle knew that something had to be done. He called the troops together and gave a motivational speech on how the castle was good but that it had to get even better. The impact was short lived. Within a few days, everything was back to the way it had been before the king gave the speech. The king threatened the dukes that "heads were going to roll" unless improvements were seen in rapid order. He offered no suggestions for how this improvement was to take place.

Three of the employees (Mac, Art, and Wendy) were convinced that Lamron Castle was in trouble. They only had to look out the tower windows to see more dragons, more competing castles, and more of the citizens moving out of the area. They knew the situation was serious; they decided to do their part and "work harder."

After working harder for several days and not seeing any results, they decided that they had to *"Figure out what's important! (And what's not)."* Several days later, they met again and discussed whether they were getting more done. Since they did not know, they decided to ask the boss. The boss told them it was against company policy to share numbers (information) with the workers. They should not worry themselves with such things, they should just keep working really hard, and she would take care of the numbers. Mac, Wendy, and Art left, feeling disgruntled. They felt that not having the numbers was like playing a ballgame and never knowing the score. They decided to keep their own score.

By keeping their own score, they had put themselves in control of their own work and had started to empower themselves. They began to feel better about their jobs, their work area seemed brighter, and the castle seemed in less of a fog. They felt they had been Zapped. *Zapp* is the energizing feeling that comes with greater knowledge, greater skill, and greater control. Individuals who have been Zapped feel like:

- they are in charge of their own work.
- their job belongs to them.
- they are responsible.
- they are capable of improving.
- they know what is important and what is going on.
- they take pride in what they do.

This new empowerment made Art, Wendy, and Mac want to do even better. They decided to set goals. To do this they had to get the individuals using their product involved to determine what really mattered and what goals to set. As a result of meeting with the knights, they decided they needed a breakthrough—a way of doing something that would let them accomplish things they had never accomplished before.

After several failures, they found that little gains can add up to produce big improvements, little goals mark the road to bigger goals, and making a lot of little improvements can be highly effective over time.

Art, Wendy, and Mac's production began to increase, but the increase did not result in more arrows being produced. Their work was only part of what it took to produce an arrow. However, they became aware that

- Every job had an effect on every other job ahead of it and behind it.
- An improvement by one person did not necessarily mean an improvement for the whole Tower. The whole Tower needed to improve, not just one job function.
- All the arrow-makers had to be involved.
- Individual success depended on gaining the support of others.

They quickly realized that in order to attain their goals, the entire castle had to buy into their goals. All the castle employees had to support one another (teamwork) in order to achieve the goals.

After learning the importance of teamwork and experiencing several failures, Art, Wendy, and Mac learned that successful teamwork included being able to (1) maintain or enhance self-esteem; (2) listen and respond with empathy; and (3) ask for help and encourage involvement. As they learned the basics for teamwork, the Zapp bolts occurred more frequently in the tower and the light started to replace more of the fog. Work went more smoothly, and the individuals seemed to get along better. People actually began to look forward to coming to work again. However, more dragons were appearing and only a minimal increase in the number of arrows being produced had occurred.

Other problems remained to be dealt with. The lower levels of the tower were not providing the products needed at the upper levels in a timely fashion. It was time to get the boss involved to assist with getting the flow of arrows to move faster. Wendy approached the boss with her idea of having a meeting and getting everyone involved. The boss did not like her idea; Wendy was frustrated.

Art checked the Wizard's Spell Book and found a page titled "Magic Brew to Enhance Acceptance When Presenting Ideas to Bosses." After some convincing by Art, Wendy studied the page. She learned that you have to *start with a good idea*. This means providing satisfactory answers to the following questions:

1. Which organizational goals or values are supported by my ideas?
2. What are the benefits and costs of my idea?
3. What incentive will the boss have for saying "yes"?
4. What will the boss's objections most likely be?
5. What can I say in response if the boss voices those objections?
6. What are some alternatives if the boss won't buy my idea "as is"?

After preparing to present her idea and contemplating the boss's objections, Wendy returned to the boss to again present her idea. This time Wendy's idea was approved.

As Art, Wendy, and Mac sought to turn the fortunes of the castle around, they encountered additional problems dealing with how to *solve problems and implement solutions.* The Zapp! Wizard's Spell Book provided information on how to do this. The ACTION spell can be cast by completing these steps: (1) *A*ssess the situation and define the problem; (2) determine *C*auses; (3) *T*arget solutions and develop ideas; (4) *I*mplement ideas; and (5) make it an *ON*going process. The footnote to the ACTION spell is critical: Involve others while casting each step of the spell.

By using this spell along with the "Master Spell of Support Plan" they were able to get other workers in Tower Two to join their efforts. Transformation throughout Tower Two was beginning to take place from the empowerment of the original three (Wendy, Art, and Mac). This occurred not only at the lower levels, but at management levels as well. The boss had become a leader in this ongoing process.

The result of this process was that the Magic Arrow Output from Tower Two began to increase. By posting the daily total on the inside and outside of the door, employees saw the result of their effort as they left the tower and as they entered the tower the next day. A chart was also made that showed daily progress toward the goal of 200 arrows a day. Some days were better than others, but the graph steadily inched up toward the goal. Individuals made adjustments to their performance to increase their production. However, the need for individuals to understand how their part of the production affected other parts of production was needed to further increase the total production rate. The concept that "Two heads are better than one, and many heads are better than two" was invoked to move Tower Two closer to its goal. To make this concept work, the InterACTION Spell from the Wizard's Spell Book was needed. Successful implementation of the "Team" concept increased production to the 170–180 arrow range. Here it stalled.

In order to reach the 200-arrow-per-day goal, Mac, Wendy, and Art felt that more employees were needed. However, the King had issued an edict prohibiting hiring more castle workers. An alternative solution had to be found.

The solution turned out to be better employee utilization. Certain employees had time left over after doing their own jobs and could be easily trained to assist in various production efforts. By using the "Master Spell of Support," the employees bought into the idea, and production rose to the 190 arrow mark and then for the first time in the history of Tower Two, 200 arrows were produced in a single day.

Before Tower Two had much time to bask in their accomplishment, the boss informed them that their goals were going to have to be changed. The Duke of Arrows and the Duke of Accounting were alarmed by the increased production costs. The diminished gold reserve would never support the increased production costs. They had doubled the production costs, yet the amount of income received for doing the job remained the same. Why did they need twice as many arrows to do the job?

After a bit of frustration, Art, Wendy, and Mac stepped back and looked at the big picture. They determined that it was time to revisit the goal they had established and see if it fit the overall mission of the castle. As a result, a new goal was set, this time involving quality. If they produced arrows that accomplished their goals 100 percent of the time, they would not need to produce so many arrows to accomplish the same job and therefore they could lower production costs. They decided that they had to determine what the customer values in order to improve quality. They found that only half the arrows that they provided the dragon fighters actually accomplished their purpose. If they could increase this to 100 percent, they would only have to produce half as many arrows as they were now producing.

This involved getting another area of the business involved: research and development. The *team* concept took on new meaning for them. In order to develop the perfect arrow, they had to consult with the wizards, the knights, and the boss; they couldn't do the job in isolation.

A short time after Tower Two had completed the quality improvement stage, Sir Fred was called to do battle with a dragon. Armed with 12 magic arrows, he was confident that he had enough arrows to take care of the dragon. When he got to the scene, there were twelve dragons. He knew he was in trouble, ordinarily because only half the arrows worked. However, armed with the new, improved arrows he had a "Twelve-Dragon" day, which was unheard of prior to this time.

Sir Fred proclaimed that he would only carry arrows made in Tower Two from that time on. This alarmed the King. He set out to determine why Tower Two produced higher-quality arrows than the other three towers of the castle. He was told that Tower Two measured its quality and quantity and worked together to keep improving their product. He was also told that they did this at a cost savings over the other three towers because of fewer mistakes, little waste, and the need for fewer arrows to be shot because of the increased accuracy of the arrows.

Soon the King saw to it that the other towers were involved in the same process as Tower Two, and the King declared that the kingdom was saved—"at least for now." Art, Wendy, and Mac were recognized as the real *HeroZ* of the castle. They were the individuals who had empowered themselves and saved the kingdom by getting people to work together to improve in order to keep the dragons away.

Unlike most fairy tales, in which the participants live happily ever after, this fairy tale recognized that nothing stays the same forever. Today's dragon (crisis) was defeated, but tomorrow brings new dragons (more crises). Competition will become tougher, technology will bring about changes in jobs, employees whose jobs become obsolete because of new inventions will need to be retrained, employees will need to be motivated to move forward after each crisis has passed, new products will need to be developed to remain competitive, periodic restructuring will need to take place, and ways to be more efficient will need to be continually explored.

As in the fairy tale these dragons never die; they keep coming back, and if you do not keep them at bay, they will eventually devour you. Only HeroZ can save you!

READING 4

Open-Book Management
The Coming Business Revolution

John Case
Summary prepared by Connie J. Christenson

Connie J. Christenson *is a Community Development Representative with the Planning Department for St. Louis County, Minnesota, facilitating economic development initiatives. St. Louis County is the largest county east of the Mississippi, covering 7,092 square miles and consisting of more than 97 cities and townships. Ms. Christenson received her MBA from the University of Minnesota, Duluth, along with her undergraduate degree in Business Administration, and has received national certification as an Economic Development Finance Professional.*

Open-book management is an innovative approach to involve employees in the organizations' operations through an understanding of the financials of the company. Employees who know and comprehend more about their company's financial situation can more actively participate in creative problem solving and will ultimately take on more individual responsibility for improving the company's performance in the marketplace. The traditional adversarial relationship with employees and management has hampered the successful growth of many organizations. Open-book management provides a basis for the direct relationship between the employee's personal financial well-being with the success of the organization.

The basic principles of open-book management are timely sharing of crucial financial information with employees; educating employees to understand and apply the information; empowering employees to apply the information to their own work; and offering employees a financial interest in the successful implementation of their ideas. The application of open-book management may not be the same for every company, but a number of suggestions and guidelines are provided for customizing the theory. Business case studies are provided on five companies in various industries that have successfully implemented open-book management. *Open-Book Management* is a practical management guide to teaching employees how to "think and act like owners" to successfully improve the competitiveness of the organization.

John Case, *Open-Book Management.* New York, NY: HarperCollins, 1995.

RUNNING A BUSINESS IN THE NEW ECONOMY

Here is a novel idea whose time has come: businesses run by businesspeople. What is more important is that the "businesspeople" are not just at the white-collar management level but are at functional levels throughout the organization, from the janitor on up. But the only way to have the lowest level employee intelligently contribute to the decision-making process is for that person to have all of the same data and information that upper management utilizes to guide the company in its operations. The basic premise is "When employees understand the economics of business they will feel, think, and act like owners." Open-book management attempts to create companies in which *everybody* understands that they are competing in a marketplace, trying to make money. It brings the control of a business to the individual who makes little decisions every day but who never really understands where they fit into "the big picture."

Open-book management is not a substitute for other effective management strategies like total quality management, reengineering, and so on; it is simply another tool in the bag. Companies still need to have an effective business strategy. They must understand their market and industry, how to efficiently use their resources, and still compete on price and value in order to maintain or grow their market niche.

The business world is rapidly changing, and the marketplace is now more globally competitive given the advances made in technology. Successful smaller, entrepreneurial organizations have emerged to displace the market share formerly held by mega-corporations. The very nature of "work" and the traditional workplace is no longer static. The service sector of the U.S. economy is growing by leaps and bounds. This processing of data and exchanging information Peter Drucker calls "knowledge work."

These dramatic changes in the business world, along with ever-emerging new trends, have significantly affected how companies are managed. To stay competitive companies must develop a clear, sensible plan for the business through a well-defined mission and strategy. However, they must also recognize that nothing gets accomplished unless *people* execute the plans. To effectively execute, *people* must work together productively and creatively toward a common purpose. People must have a *reason* to care about their company and ultimately know how to help it succeed. This is essentially the foundation of open-book management.

Companies must first encourage employees to see themselves as "partners" in the business, and second, employees must be empowered to understand what the business is all about. People cannot be empowered without information (and lots of it!), and then they must understand what they have received. They need a basic understanding of financial statements so they can evaluate and act on all that information. Without information and understanding, standard incentives of profit sharing or stock ownership will be just a hollow benefit. In short, unless they *act* and *think* like owners, they do not *feel* like owners.

To encourage this process of information dissemination companies begin with some basics:

- Every employee in an open-book company sees—and learns to understand—the company's financials, along with all the other numbers that are critical to tracking the business's performance. That is why it is called "open book." People will know if they are making money, how much, and why.

- Employees assume that, whatever else they do, part of their job is to move those numbers in the right direction—reduce waste, increase sales, whatever is considered crucial to success.

- Employees must have a direct *financial* stake in the company's success. If the business is profitable, they get a "cut of the action." If it's not, they don't.

- The things that change in an open-book company are simply the ways of thinking and acting. The basic structure of the corporation may or may not change. People get a chance to act, to take responsibility rather than just doing their job by rote. And they know enough about the company to understand what needs to be done to have a positive effect on the business's bottom line.

IMPLEMENTING OPEN-BOOK MANAGEMENT

First Principle: Information

The starting point for implementing open-book management is to provide up-to-date information to *all* of the employees. The more information you supply, the better off you will be. Business information—primarily financial data—is particularly powerful because it shows people the reasons for doing something. The right information would be the *pivotal operational numbers*. These key numbers or measurements will be different for every company, which has to determine individually what they are. Software programs allow them to play "what-if" with these numbers to figure out the best allocation of resources.

In 1954, noted author Peter Drucker emphasized that employees needed information in order to control, measure, and guide their own performance. However, in 1954, distribution of the required level of financial information would have been too costly and would not have met the timeliness requirement; therefore the accuracy of the data would be questionable. The tremendous technological advances have now made this more practical and financially feasible now making it possible to implement open-book management as recommended by Drucker more than forty years ago.

Second Principle: Business Literacy

To properly act upon the information provided it is essential that everyone has to *understand* the information they get. Many employees or even managers may not have had formal financial schooling; therefore, to improve the skills and ability of everyone to understand the financial statements will require training, training, and more training. This can be accomplished either through classroom instruction, workshops, or even by playing business games like *Biz Wiz* or the *Great Game of Business*. Then reinforce the lessons learned on the shop floor as direct application will make more sense. The paramount guide is to make learning fun and allow learning to occur without adverse consequences for temporary failures.

Third Principle: Empowerment

Workplace participation, participatory management, employee involvement or *empowerment.* Lots of different names, but they are all based on the same theory: Employees should involve themselves in running their corner of the business. They should have a say in the decisions that affect their work area and, when possible, be given the power to solve problems and make changes on their own. The logic behind this is that on-the-job decisions will be made faster and better when the employees directly involved are making them. But empowerment requires accurate information first. According to Rich Teerlink, chief executive officer of Harley-Davidson, "If you empower dummies, you get bad decisions faster." Empowered employees need to know about what the destination is, a map for how to get there, and knowledge of how to gauge their progress toward it. Two conditions must be met to make empowerment work:

- *The operations of the business must be transparent.* Everyone needs to know how their own work affects their unit or department and the company as a whole.
- *Empowered employees must be willing—indeed, should be required—to assume responsibility for their decisions and hence for their numbers.* This is called a system of "no excuses management." If you do not have what you need to meet your goals, it is up to you to make sure you get them.

It will not be easy to instantaneously change the culture of an organization or an individual's work ethic. To get people to begin making decisions and take responsibility, first give them the *power*. Simply start by treating them all like businesspeople. The most important method to get employee buy-in is in *establishing goals*, however:

- People have to understand why the goal is important.
- It is wise to involve as many people as possible in setting the goals.
- The goals must be tracked in public, according to criteria everybody understands. You can use signs, posters, newsletters, or anything that is visible for all.
- People should be able to affect the outcome—but the payout must be fiscally responsible.
- Finally, the goals should be ambitious but attainable.

Three different approaches highlighting employee involvement in goal setting:

- Springfield ReManufacturing Corporation, a pioneer in open-book management, developed the *Great Game of Business* and uses a *huddle system*—meetings structured around a very specific agenda of accountability.
  - The company creates its annual plan (game plan), which could consist of sales forecasts, a capital expenditure budget, projected month-by-month income statements, and so on. Employee participation provides individual ownership to the plan. The annual plan is partly about setting operational goals but also financial ones, because business reality always has to be reflected in numbers.
  - Tracking key numbers lets employees assess their performance as they go along.

- People can schedule their work as dictated by their need to reach the goals.
- Managers give people a say. They explain the options and then listen very carefully to employee opinions.
- Published Image Inc. is a service business in the publishing industry. Individual professionals and creative divisions often are at odds with resource allocation and time lines. To make open-book management more effective for them, they turned the company into a *collection of smaller-but-identical companies based on individual projects.*
  - The project teams act like self-contained businesses with both internal and external customers. Each team has individuals representing all aspects of a project. This relative autonomy encourages initiative among its members.
  - Every department acts like a company within a company. The difference with the project team approach is that each department continues to do its specialized tasks on a number of different projects or customers but would be accountable for its performance as a group.

Fourth Principle: A Stake in Success

Make sure that the people share directly in the company's success—as well as the risk of failure. The carrot or incentive must be financial, preferably hard currency. However, sometimes cash is not possible. In those cases, use those incentives that employees have indicated a preference for, such as more vacation time.

The problem with current methods of profit sharing and use of bonuses as incentives is that they are primarily determined at the discretion of management on how much, when, and if money is to be distributed.

Variable compensation systems are group incentives that include across-the-board bonus plans, profit sharing, stock distribution, and so forth. In theory, variable compensation plans are supposed to achieve just what an open-book management pay system should: tying employees' fortunes to how well the company does by letting everyone share in its success. Then why do they fail? One thought is that they do not have any direct (cause-effect) effect on the individual's behavior.

Another problem area of variable compensation plans is that they are discretionary. Management determines what the payout will be each year. Again, there is no direct relationship to individual performance.

Most formal profit-sharing plans are so filled with federal regulations and "legalese" that they are incomprehensible. No one will read, let alone begin to understand, a three-inch-thick document of small print. People cannot support what they do not understand.

Another pitfall of currently used plans is that the payments are always the same. Rather than tying to performance, people begin to expect it as an *entitlement*, not as a reward for successful performance. However the biggest pitfall is that employees do not have a clue as to whether, or how, what they do day in and day out affects the payout. No one understands how it is figured out.

In using the open-book approach the financial stake may still take the form of profit sharing or bonuses (tied to some target other than profit) or stock ownership.

But under this system, people *know* what they have to do to get it, because they can *see* exactly how the business is doing. The *books are open and shared* with everyone.

In finally making a payout, it is important to determine *how much* is the right amount. The rule of thumb to follow is that employees should receive all your company can afford when allocating bonuses or profit sharing. The more that people have riding on the company's success, the more they will be inclined to think like business-people. Generally, anything less than 5 percent of current salary will not have a meaningful impact on the individual for what he or she perceives he or she has contributed to the financial gains the company has made.

Suggestions for determining how the bonus pool should be divided would be that the more responsibility an employee has for the company's operation, the more that employee's total compensation should be at risk. Alternatively, using a straight percentage of total compensation is also thought of as a very good indicator of one's level of responsibility and importance to the company.

WAYS TO GET STARTED

There is no magic formula to do this, no workbook or prepared template, but a few suggestions are provided to get started in the right direction:

- Begin by teaching employees to think of themselves first as businesspeople.
- Play business games that get people to think about what are the key numbers in their organization.
- Start open-book management, but only with the managers. It may be surprising to find out just how much they actually know about the organization and how their unit fits with the others.
- Teach people about business by distributing *complete* financial statements (not just departmental ones) and have people initial the numbers they are responsible for.
- Create a system of week-to-week accountability for managers. (Again, take baby steps.) When they understand the process well enough to predict how well they performed, they can begin to understand how they can improve that performance level.
- Announce the end of annual raises. This should definitely catch their attention quickly, but management should be prepared for open hostility at first until it gets the chance to discuss the new options like bonuses tied to profit sharing.
- Another way to get their attention is to start distributing information with a "dummy" bonus attached representing what would have been earned if the open-book management system had been in place.
- Make a game out of it, like "XYZ Company Jeopardy" or "Challenge Bowl." In these games, the correct answers to financial statement questions are rewarded with points that can be used for some identified reward.
- Set up an employee stock ownership program (very expensive and time-consuming) and then use that information and success as a first step to open-book management.

- Ask people to show how they make money for the company. Most employees have no understanding of whether they are an asset or a liability to the bottom line.

The essence of open-book management is this: "Treat people like adults." For too long management has treated employees like children by ordering them around, punishing behavior, and assuming they cannot make an intelligent decision on their own. Without employee involvement in decision making through a process like open-book management, Yogi Berra's quote rings true—"If you do what you've always done, you're gonna get what you always got." Companies have died by living that truth.

READING 5

The Open-Book Experience

John Case
Summary prepared by Cheri Stine

Cheri L. Stine is a graduate of the University of Minnesota, Duluth. She earned a bachelor of Business Administration degree with an emphasis in Human Resource Management. Upon her graduation, she moved to the Minneapolis/St. Paul area to pursue a career in Human Resource Management. Since that time, she has enjoyed working in a variety of interesting occupations and industries. She is currently taking a leave of absence from the work force to raise her lovely daughter Kayla Ashley.

Theorists and practitioners churn out many new self-help techniques and tools for business each year. Each of these new ideas has as a goal to make businesses more competitive in one way or another. These new approaches generally entail making some changes to the way in which work is accomplished. However, in order to get holistic and long-lasting improvement, businesses need to change not only the way they *do* business, but also the way they *think about doing* business.

In most companies, top executives are the only individuals who have access to financial information and other information about the company's performance in the marketplace. Formal and informal documents, such as the company's balance sheet, income statement, and annual budget information are considered confidential and kept out of the hands of lower-level managers and their employees. However, understanding this information is very useful and even essential to improving employee and companywide performance.

THE PHILOSOPHY

Due to the lack of long-lasting positive results from the latest management technique or approach, companies are becoming frustrated. As this occurs, they begin to question everything about their improvement efforts, from the methods of implementation to the corporate environment's ability to sustain the changes. It has been theorized that people work best when they feel connected to their company and take ownership in their work. Therefore, open-book management merely takes this existing theory and quantifies it by telling us more about how we can achieve the result of employee ownership and make it last. It begins by making the assumption that people who view themselves as partners in a business will strive to perform at their best. When employ-

---

John Case, *The Open-Book Experience*. Reading, MA: Addison-Wesley, 1998.

ees are performing at their best, the company's performance will be (or has the potential to be) stellar as well. Therefore, the goal of open-book management is to create a working environment or a system in which employees can become partners in the company's success.

THE DILEMMA

The immediate practical dilemma is that most employees do not possess the skills or knowledge necessary to act as partners. To do so, they would need to have knowledge and understanding of certain fundamental aspects of the business that have historically been kept secret. For example, in efforts to make better decisions, empower employees, and gain a "buy-in" attitude within the organization, many companies are beginning to delegate more decision-making power to lower-level managers and their employees. Delegating authority and responsibility for decision making can be very beneficial to a company that has previously made decisions centrally. However, making good business decisions requires access to and understanding of the relevant information. Therefore, employees need to have a general understanding of business fundamentals and also be familiar with the goals and aspirations of their company. Herein lies the solution proposed by the practitioners of open-book management.

THE SOLUTION

To achieve the goal of having business-oriented employees that will work together as a team toward company success, you must do the following:

- Create a transparent company.
- Empower employees.
- Give employees a stake in the company's success.

THE TRANSPARENT COMPANY

Unfortunately, most organizations currently keep their business information under "lock and key" and distribute it only on a need-to-know basis. This arrangement is detrimental to overall company success, because people need to have access to this information in order to do their jobs well and contribute to company goals. In a transparent company, vital business information is shared with and understood by all employees, not just those in charge. To become transparent, a company must do three things:

- Determine its critical numbers.
- Post critical numbers on scoreboards.
- Teach employees what the numbers mean and how they can influence the numbers.

The Critical Numbers

Each company may have many different ways to measure how well they are performing. However, critical numbers are not the numbers that measure success, but rather are the numbers that *determine* success. The numbers that determine success are varied dependent upon the company's goals and aspirations, and will most likely change over the course of time.

Critical numbers are key to a business's survival as they drive the key objectives of the business. They must move in the right direction, or the business could fail to achieve its current goals and objectives. For example, most young or startup businesses can survive for only a short time with low quantities of cash. Therefore, cash flow would be considered a critical number for these and many other businesses. To determine your company's critical numbers, you need to take an in-depth look at the company. This process would include the following:

- Devising a long-term and short-term strategic plan;
- Identifying the performance drivers of the company;
- Identifying this year's opportunities or weaknesses; and
- Creating a cascade of critical numbers.

From this analysis you should be able to determine which numbers are the ones that drive your business and determine its ability to survive.

Post the Critical Numbers on Scorecards

When the critical numbers are identified, they need to be posted on some form of scorecard for all of the employees to see. This means that a display mechanism must be devised that will allow the information to be clearly and publicly presented. For example, many companies have constructed a "thermometer" to register the distance the company or a department has to travel to reach its goal. Other companies have used computer-generated printouts or e-mail to distribute the information to all employees. The medium used to display the information is not important; it should be chosen with each particular organization's structure and environment in mind. What is most important, however, is that all employees are able to view the information. Therefore, placement or distribution of the information is much more important than the manner in which it is displayed.

In addition, different parts of the organization may have critical numbers that are specific to their department alone. Therefore, a scorecard needs to be placed in or near each department, and it should highlight the critical numbers for that individual department or branch office. This will allow the individuals in that department to have access to the information they need without having to sort through a lot of other information to find it.

Teach Employees to Understand and Influence the Numbers

Unfortunately, many people suffer from financial and business illiteracy. Even many small business owners fail to understand the fundamentals of business, and more often than not leave the understanding and tracking of their business's performance to their accountants. As a result, the people that should be benefiting the most from items such as a balance sheet or income statement are not fully utilizing them to track and ultimately improve business performance.

An integral part of open-book management is having access to *and* an understanding of critical numbers. Being given the numbers without the capacity to understand them is like being given an assignment to write a report on a book written in a language that is foreign to you. You would be responsible for completing the work but would not possess the skills to accomplish the task. Therefore, training in the fundamentals of business and company-specific information is necessary for open-book management to be effective.

Although training is necessary, businesses should resist the temptation to jump in and mandate employee attendance in boring classes on accounting or some other business basics. If this is done, employees will likely feel as though they are being asked to take on more work, and hence they will retain little of the information. On the other hand, if the company does the following, they are more likely to meet with less resistance from employees and improve the effectiveness of business training.

1. Ask employees questions about the proposed business training.
   - What would they like to learn and what would they feel would be useful?
   - Where would they best learn the information (e.g., staff meetings, team meetings, brown-bag lunches)?
   - How would they best learn the information (e.g., videos, overheads)?
2. Hold a class or two and solicit feedback from employees.
3. Try to drum up employee enthusiasm and interest using games, quizzes, and contests.
4. Be imaginative in designing the training.
5. Make clear and concise connections between the business training people receive and what they do on the job.
6. Build fun into all aspects of the training.

People learn in different ways. Therefore, the training should attempt to utilize a variety of media. In fact, there are many materials on the market right now that can be used for this purpose. For example, some companies have developed computerized business simulation games, created board games, written textbooks and workbooks, and conducted a multitude of seminars and workshops. The key to successful training is to experiment with different media and solicit feedback on its effectiveness until one that works best is discovered.

EMPOWER EMPLOYEES

Empowering employees means that companies give employees more power and simultaneously make them more accountable for their work. Empowerment involves such things as having the employees set their own goals and determine how they will work to meet the company's standards. Many might mistakenly think that empowerment is all that is needed to encourage employees to do well and manage themselves. However, empowerment needs to be implemented within a structure, or else it could hinder a company's performance rather than improve it. For example, employees in a company, each striving to meet his or her own goals in an uncoordinated fashion, could sabotage one another by striving to meet contradictory goals. This chaotic environment could further deteriorate the company's performance.

One of the primary objectives of creating a transparent company is to improve performance and communication of both employees and the company. In a transparent company, people are able to be more effective in their work efforts and make smarter decisions by having access to the information they need. In addition, a transparent company allows all employees the opportunity to communicate with each other in setting company and employee goals. Therefore, having a transparent company helps to enhance the benefit of empowerment efforts by providing an opportunity to align the goals of individuals and coordinate efforts to reach a company goal of higher levels of performance. To begin the empowerment process in a transparent company, companies must do the following:

- Delegate responsibility for the nagging problems that never seem to get fixed.
- Create suggestion systems that require employees to think about their suggestions.
  1. Quantify the nature of the suggestion.
  2. Provide justification for a suggested change or expenditure.
- Notify employees of the action taken as a result of their suggestion.
- Create task forces (made up of volunteer individuals from different levels in the organization) to deal with various issues and or problems.
- Engage in bottom-up budgeting (and planning).

One of the key trademarks of an open-book company is the utilization of a huddle system for communicating throughout the organization on a regular basis. A huddle system is a series of meetings that take place on regular intervals that are designed to enable employee participation in running the business. In these meetings employees are responsible for gathering and presenting (with explanation) their numbers to other members of the organization. After the meetings, representatives are also responsible for going back to their departments and sharing the meeting contents with co-workers. There are several things to keep in mind about huddles:

- Huddles should follow the rules of conduct for meetings:
  1. Have an agenda.
  2. Have predefined activities.
  3. Set a time limit.
- The primary reason for a huddle is to discuss the numbers.
- People need to take responsibility for the numbers.
- Huddles need to be held on a regular basis.
- Huddles need to involve as many people as possible from the organization.
- It may be necessary to supplement huddles with other meetings.
- Fast and thorough communication about the huddle agenda must be provided to nonattending persons.
- Huddles must be linked to all other open-book management efforts elsewhere in the organization.
- Huddles need to be fun and should generate enthusiasm.

Engaging in huddles and other such activities will help to continuously empower employees and build ownership attitudes throughout the company.

Give Employees a Stake in the Company's Success

If people are expected to work harder and smarter to benefit only the company, the resulting attitude of employees may be one of resentment rather than ownership and cooperation. Therefore, as with all other aspects of the organizational environment, the compensation system should also reflect the open-book philosophy.

Many organizations have set up their compensation systems in such a way that they actually reward employees on a regular basis whether the company can afford it or not. This does not make good business sense, nor does it give employees any incentive to work to improve their performance and overall company performance. An example of such an organization would be one in which annual raises are given to all employees routinely despite good or bad company/employee performance.

In an open-book company, employees are being encouraged to think and act like business partners. Therefore, compensation for these employees should include a bonus component that is linked to the business' performance, as does the compensation of business partners. In open-book companies, designing the compensation system entails consideration of the following:

- Bonuses should be built into the compensation package and agreed upon up front.
- Bonuses should be designed to work as educational tools.
- Bonuses need to be linked to goals and critical numbers.
- Bonuses should provide incentive for improvement of company weaknesses.
- Bonuses can be linked to multiple objectives.
- Bonus payout targets should be high but reachable within reason.
- Bonus pools should be created from funds received from improved performance or movement toward goals.
- Bonuses should be celebrated.
- Bonuses should be evaluated on the following and altered if necessary:
    1. Do employees understand the bonus system?
    2. Do employees view the plan as fair and worthwhile?
    3. Does the plan invoke employee enthusiasm?
    4. Are the critical numbers being moved in the right direction?
    5. Is the plan in need of redesign due to changes in the company?

As many employees as possible should be involved in designing the compensation package. By soliciting employee input, the company should be able to design a compensation package that will be viewed by the employees as fair and more acceptable because they assisted in its construction.

GAMES

Open-book management is a way of running a company that encourages employees to learn how to make better decisions and then to do so in order to improve company performance for the benefit of all. After employees have the knowledge and skills to contribute to overall company goals, games are a way to let them utilize those skills in a real life situation. Essentially, a game is a short-term drive designed to reach a particular goal. In order for games to be effective, they must include a way to publicly track the progress of the company toward achieving the objective and some sort of payoff or reward after the objective is achieved.

Games can be used to do many things, including the following:

- Eliminating business problems;
- Helping employees deal with everyday challenges;
- Building a culture of fun; and
- Teaching open-book management.

Over the past few years, open-book companies have learned many lessons about game playing that could be useful to new adopters of open-book management:

- Keep in mind that employees who will play the games should take part in creating them.
- Tailor the games to those who will be playing them.
- Play the games against the problem, not against other employees.
- Pay out rewards to all employees, not just a few.
- Make the rewards small but meaningful.
- Design the games with good business sense in mind.
- Coordinate games among company departments.
- Integrate games with the rest of open-book management.

THE CHANGE PROCESS

Open-book management is a new way of thinking about business. It deals primarily with the "why," the logic of business, when most other managerial tools and techniques produced in the past fifteen years have dealt with the "how" of business. Through open-book management, companies teach people what the company is all about, how they can track their performance and that of the company, and how to hold their co-workers and themselves accountable for what they say they will do. However, open-book management is not without its obstacles. Some obstacles that are specific to open-book management are

- Open-book management is not just a new way of doing things, it's a new way of thinking.
- Not everyone will respond in a positive way to focusing on the bottom line.
- It is difficult to find a place to start the change process.
- Open-book management has no definite end point.

Although it has its problems, open-book management can be implemented much more easily than many other managerial tools or techniques because it also has some unique characteristics:

- People can easily understand the logic behind open-book management.
- There is something to be gained from open-book management for everyone.
- Because it is a system, it is self-reinforcing and changes people.

Unlike other tools and techniques, open-book management does not involve attempting to change the way in which work is to be done. Instead, open-book management changes the way businesses share and analyze business information that is so crucial to improving company performance. Therefore, it can and should be implemented in concert with many other techniques being used (e.g., quality circles, zero defects, employee empowerment). When implemented along with other improvement techniques, open-book management will reap the greatest rewards.

As more companies adopt the open-book philosophy, more will be learned about how effective this management philosophy is and how it should be implemented. However, implementation is no small feat no matter what the size or nature of the company. Implementation requires the organization and its employees to change old ways of thinking and adopt the new philosophy thoroughly in order for it to be effective. This process can be long and difficult, and companies should not expect drastic improvements to occur overnight. However, if open-book management is implemented properly, the payoff for diligence and hard work will be a well-coordinated and educated workforce that can help forge the way to a successful future for your company.

PART EIGHT
Teams and Teamwork

As organizations attempt to move forward in an increasingly hostile and competitive environment, more and more organizations are experimenting with and hoping to realize synergies associated with teamwork. Many organizations, influenced by the Japanese, have ventured into the use of employee involvement systems with problem-solving teams, such as quality control circles. Other organizations have made radical changes in their technologies, and some have organized around organizational processes by employing self-directed work teams. Butler Manufacturing, for example, has a team assembling an entire grain dryer; and at Hallmark a team of artists, writers, accountants, marketers, and lithographic personnel work together producing next year's Mother's Day cards, while another team works on cards for Father's Day.

Three readings in this section focus their attention on teams. The first, co-authored by Jon Katzenbach and Douglas Smith, is titled *The Wisdom of Teams*. The second reading, also by Katzenbach, focuses on executive-level teams at the top of organizational hierarchies. The third, *Empowered Teams*, was written by Richard S. Wellins, William C. Byham, and Jeanne M. Wilson.

In *The Wisdom of Teams*, Katzenbach and Smith argue that teams are the key to improving organizational performance. From a performance perspective teams are generally superior to individuals performing alone or in groups. As a consequence, they will be the building block of organizations in the future.

In their roles as senior consultants for McKinsey & Company, Katzenbach and Smith have worked on organizational performance practices. Drawing on their study of fifty different teams in thirty companies, the authors differentiate various levels of team performance, discuss where and how teams work best, and comment on how team effectiveness can be enhanced.

In *Teams at the Top*, Katzenbach continues his focus on teams. He focuses on the use of teams at the executive level of the organization, arguing that most organizations need additional leadership capacity. He offers insight into the use and integration of top level individual leadership and team leadership, and points out the value of extending teamwork throughout *all* levels of the company.

Many different approaches have been taken by organizations in their move toward the utilization of teams. Among them, it is common to hear about quality-control circles, quality-of-work life programs, and joint labor–management teams. In *Empowered Teams*, Richard S. Wellins, William C. Byham, and Jeanne M. Wilson focus their attention on *self-directed work teams* (SDWT). SDWTs become empowered over time by taking on responsibilities that were once reserved for supervisors and their managers. SDWTs share management and leadership functions; plan, organize, direct, and control; work on improving their own production processes; set schedules; and hire replacement team members along with assuming the responsibility for a number of other human resource management functions. The authors discuss three basic themes: how teams work, how to prepare for teams, and how to build strong teams once they are in place.

Richard S. Wellins is Senior Vice President of Programs and Marketing for Development Dimensions International (DDI). William C. Byham is the President and chief executive officer of DDI, a consulting firm providing human resource training programs and services. Jeanne M. Wilson is project manager for high-involvement clients at DDI. Wellins and Byham (with George Dixon) have also published *Inside Teams: How Twenty World-Class Organizations Are Winning Through Teamwork*.

READING I

The Wisdom of Teams

Jon R. Katzenbach and Douglas K. Smith
Summary prepared by R. Warren Candy

R. Warren Candy *is a Vice President of Generation for Minnesota Power,
Duluth, Minnesota, and General Manager of the Boswell Energy Center near
Grand Rapids, Minnesota. He is responsible for implementing high-
performance organizational improvements and change within the fast-
changing utility marketplace. His areas of interest include teamwork, team
building, high-performance leadership, and socio-technical systems. He
received his B.S. in Production Engineering from Swinburne College of
Technology in Melbourne, Australia.*

Fundamental change is needed in the way that managers and employees think about,
and implement, performance improvements in the 1990s and beyond. Real teams hold
the key to success. Real teams develop when groups of people work together with mutual support, joint accountability, trust-based relationships, and meaningful purpose
with everyone being expected to think and grow.

WHY ORGANIZATIONS NEED TEAMS

Teams outperform individuals acting alone or in large organizational groupings, especially when performance requires multiple skills, judgments, and experiences. Most
people recognize the capabilities of teams, and most have the common sense to make
teams work.

In exploring the use of teams, it becomes increasingly clear that the potential impact of single teams, as well as the collective impact of many teams, on the performance of large organizations is woefully underexploited. This is true despite the
rapidly growing recognition of the need for what teams have to offer.

Teams are more flexible than larger organizational groupings because they can be
more quickly assembled, deployed, refocused, and disbanded, usually in ways that enhance rather than disrupt more permanent structures and processes. Teams are more
productive than groups that have no clear performance objectives because their members are committed to delivering tangible performance results. Teams and performance are an unbeatable combination.

Most models of the organization of the future (e.g., networked, clustered, nonhierarchical, horizontal) are premised on the ability of *teams to surpass individuals as*

Jon R. Katzenbach & Douglas K. Smith, *The Wisdom of Teams.* Cambridge, MA: Harvard Business
School, 1993.

the primary performance unit in the company. According to these predictions, when management seeks faster, better ways to best match resources to customer opportunity or competitive challenge, the critical building block will be at the team, not the individual, level.

Teams usually do outperform other groups and individuals. They represent one of the best ways to support the broad-based changes necessary for the high-performing organization. Executives who really believe that behaviorally based characteristics (such as quality, innovation, cost effectiveness, and customer service) will help build a sustainable competitive advantage will give their top priority to the development of team performance.

The good news is that there is a discipline to teams that, if rigorously followed, can transform reluctance into team performance. The bad news is that, like all disciplines, the price of success is strict adherence and practice. Very few people lose weight, quit smoking, or learn to play the piano or golf without constant practice and discipline.

KEY LESSONS LEARNED ABOUT TEAMS AND TEAM PERFORMANCE

What do we know about teams? Eight lessons stand out:

- No team arises without a performance challenge that is meaningful to those involved.
- Performance is the crux of the matter for teams, including teams who recommend things, teams who make or do things, and teams who run or manage things.
- Organizational leaders can foster team performance best by building a strong performance ethic, rather than by establishing a team-promoting environment alone.
- Real teams are much more likely to flourish if leaders aim their sights on performance results rather than balance the needs of customers, employees, and shareholders. Clarity of purpose and goals have tremendous power in our ever more change-driven world.
- Most people at all organizational levels understand that job security depends on customer satisfaction and financial performance and are willing to be measured and rewarded accordingly. What is perhaps less appreciated, but equally true, is how the opportunity to meet clearly stated customer and financial needs enriches jobs and leads to performance growth.
- Biases toward individualism exist but need not get in the way of team performance.
- Teams are not opposed to individual performance. Real teams always find ways for individuals to contribute and thereby gain distinction. Indeed, when harnessed to a common team purpose and goal(s), our need to distinguish ourselves as individuals becomes a powerful engine for team performance.
- Discipline, both within the team and across the organization, creates the conditions for team performance. Any group seeking team performance for

itself, like any leader seeking to build strong performance standards across the organization, must focus sharply on performance. For organizational leaders, this entails making clean and consistent demands that reflect the needs of customers, shareholders, and employees, and then holding themselves and the organization relentlessly accountable.

Several well-known phenomena explain why teams perform well. First, they bring together *complementary skills and experiences* that, by definition, exceed those of any individual on the team. This broader mix of skills and know-how enables teams to respond to multifaceted challenges like innovation, quality, and customer service. Second, in jointly developing clear goals and approaches, teams establish *communications that support real-time problem solving and initiative*. Teams are flexible and responsive to changing events and demands. As a result, teams can adjust their approach to new information and challenges with greater speed, accuracy, and effectiveness than can individuals caught in the web of larger organizational connections. Third, teams provide a unique *social dimension* that enhances the economic and administrative aspects of work. Real teams do not develop until the people in them work hard to overcome barriers that stand in the way of collective performance. Finally, *teams have more fun*. This is not a trivial point, because the kind of fun they have is integral to their performance. People on real teams consistently and without prompting emphasize the fun aspects of their work together.

WHAT IS A REAL TEAM AND HOW DOES IT DEVELOP?

A real team is a small number of people with complementary skills who are committed to a common purpose, performance goals, and working approach for which they hold themselves mutually accountable.

The team is a basic unit of performance for most organizations. It melds together the skills, experiences, and insights of several people. It is the natural complement to individual initiative and achievement because it engenders higher levels of commitment to common ends. Increasingly, we find management looking to teams throughout the organization to strengthen performance capabilities. A team is *not* a group of people working together. Unlike teams, working groups rely on the sum of "individual bests" for their performance. They pursue no collective work products requiring joint effort.

New teams evolve in five transition stages from "working group" to "high-performing team." In the early stages of development, performance often suffers before significant gains occur and stabilize.

1. *Working group* This is a group for which there is *no significant incremental performance need* or opportunity that would require it to become a team. The members interact primarily to share information, best practices, or perspectives, and to make decisions to help each individual perform within their area of responsibility. Beyond that, there is no realistic or truly desired "small group" common purpose, incremental performance goals, or joint work-products that call for either a team approach or mutual accountability.

2. *Pseudo-team* This is a group for which there could be a significant, incremental performance need or opportunity, but *it has not focused on collective performance and is not really trying to achieve it.* It has no interest in shaping a common purpose or set of performance goals, even though it may call itself a team. Pseudo-teams are the weakest of all groups in terms of performance impact. They almost always contribute less to company performance needs than working groups because their interactions detract from each member's individual performance, without delivering any joint benefit. In pseudo-teams, the sum of the whole is less than the potential of the individual parts.

3. *Potential team* This is a group for which a significant, incremental performance need exists and *that is trying to improve its performance impact.* Typically, however, it requires more clarity about purpose, goals, or work-products; more discipline in hammering out a common working approach, and collective accountability.

4. *Real team* This is a small number of people with complementary skills who *are equally committed to a common purpose, goal(s), and working approach for which they hold themselves mutually accountable.* Real teams are a basic unit of performance.

5. *High-performance team* This is a group that meets all the conditions of real teams and has *members who are also deeply committed to one another's personal growth and success.* That commitment usually transcends the team. The high-performance team significantly outperforms all other like teams and outperforms all reasonable expectations given its membership.

TEAMS AND TEAM PERFORMANCE

A number of factors characterize "real teams." Some of these factors are intuitively known, while others are less obvious.
Commonsense findings:

- A demanding performance challenge tends to create a team.
- The disciplined application of "team basics" is often overlooked.
- Team performance opportunities exist in all parts of the organization.
- Teams at the top are the most difficult to create.
- Most organizations intrinsically prefer individual over group (team) accountability.

Uncommon findings:

- Companies with strong performance standards seem to spawn more "real teams" than companies that promote teams *per se.*
- High-performance teams are extremely rare.
- Hierarchy and teams go together almost as well as teams and performance.
- Teams naturally integrate performance and learning.
- Teams are the primary unit of performance for more and more organizations.

COMMON APPROACHES TO BUILDING TEAM PERFORMANCE

Teams can be created, developed, and maintained as long as a number of key ingredients are present:

1. *Urgency and direction are established.* Team members must believe the team has an urgent and worthwhile purpose; team members want to know what is expected of them.
2. *Members are selected based on skills and skill potential, not personalities.* The team members must have the complementary skills needed to do their jobs.
3. *Particular attention is paid to first meetings and actions.* Initial impressions are important.
4. *Clear rules of behaviors are established.* All real teams develop rules of conduct to help them achieve their purpose and performance goals.
5. *Immediate, performance-oriented tasks and goals are established.* Most teams trace their advancement to key performance-oriented events that forge them together.
6. *The group is regularly challenged with fresh facts and information.* New information causes a team to redefine and enrich its understanding of the performance challenge.
7. *Time is spent together.* Teams must spend a lot of time together, especially at the beginning.
8. *The power of positive feedback, recognition, and reward are exploited.* Positive reinforcement works as well in a team context as elsewhere.

CONCLUSION

At the heart of the definition of *team* lies a fundamental premise that teams and performance are inextricably connected. Truly committed teams are the most productive performance-improvement technique that management has at its disposal–*provided there are specific results for which the team is collectively responsible and accountable, and provided the performance ethic of the company demands those results*. Within an organization, no single factor is more critical to the generation of effective teams than the clarity and consistency of the company's overall performance standards, or "performance ethic."

Within a team, nothing is more important than each team member's commitment to a common purpose and set of related performance goals for which the group holds itself accountable. Each member must believe the team's purpose is important to the success of the company, and they must collectively keep each other honest in assessing their results relative to that purpose. It is insufficient just to put "the monkey on the back" of each individual member; the *same* monkey must be put on their backs as a whole.

Specific performance goals are an integral part of this process. Transforming broad directives into specific and measurable performance goals is the surest first step for a team trying to shape a common purpose meaningful to its members. Specific goals provide clear and tangible footholds for teams while creating the measurement system for team accountability.

At its core, team accountability is about the sincere promises that we make to ourselves and others. These promises underpin two critical aspects of teams: commitment and trust. By promising to hold ourselves accountable to the team's goals, members each earn the right to express their views about all aspects of the team's effort and to have others' views also receive a fair and constructive hearing.

Real teams are deeply committed to their purpose, to their goals, and to their approach. Team members are very committed to one another, and all understand that the wisdom of teams comes with a focus on collective work products, personal growth, and performance-oriented results. These all come from pursuing demanding performance challenges. When you observe a group of people who are truly committed, accountable for joint results, share a strong team purpose, and have embraced a common problem-solving approach, you know that you are seeing a "real team" in action.

– Evaluation process –
team vs. indiv. (How is this handled?)

READING 2

Teams at the Top

Jon R. Katzenbach
Summary prepared by Gary P. Olson

Gary P. Olson *is the Executive Director of the Center for Alcohol & Drug Treatment, Inc. and a consultant in both the profit and nonprofit business sectors. He received his MBA from the University of Minnesota, Duluth.*

Despite the proven success of individual leadership most organizations need additional *leadership capacity*, particularly during periods of growth and change. Leadership capacity is the amount of leadership time and talent available to a group or organization at a specific point in time. With real teams demonstrating leadership and performance improvements at other levels of the organization, ignoring the potential of a "team at the top" would be short-sighted. Nevertheless, no single mode of senior leadership behavior, including real team behavior, can meet the diverse demands of executive leadership. A balance of real team, individual, and conventional single-leader *working group* modes can. (A working group is any small group collaborating together to accomplish a common purpose or goal.) It recognizes the essential role of individual leadership but also offers the possibility of increased leadership capacity and the chance to exploit genuine real team performance opportunities. The goal of a balanced approach is not to replace individual leadership with a team at the top, but to integrate individual and team modes of working. To accomplish this goal, it is essential to understand the difference between *real team discipline* and *executive discipline* and when the use of each is appropriate. *Executive discipline* is the implied rules executives follow to enforce individual accountability and consequence management. Simply calling a working group at the top a "team" or assigning it tasks that are not legitimate team opportunities can actually undermine performance objectives.

NONTEAMS AT THE TOP

Real team discipline is a small group of people with complementary skills, who are committed to a common purpose, performance goal, and working approach for which they are held accountable as a group. The chief executive officer (CEO), on the other hand, is usually the single leader of a group whose membership is based on position rather than skills and whose purpose and goals are identical to overall corporate purpose and goals. Among the typical leadership group, the doctrine of individual accountability is the preferred and proven working approach. They may call themselves

---

Jon R. Katzenbach, *Teams at the Top: Unleashing the Potential of Both Teams and Individual Leaders.* Cambridge, MA: Harvard Business School, 1998.

a team, but rarely function under real team discipline. Real team efforts do occur in most organizations when unexpected challenges and opportunities arise, but the typical leadership group functions primarily as an efficient and usually effective single-leader working group.

Although the team is a simple, proven performance unit, there are a number of good reasons why "nonteams" persist the top:

- The purpose of the leadership group is too broad to provide adequate focus for a team effort.
- Performance goals at the executive level are complex and often less tangible (financial, market share, strategic).
- Individual accountability is accepted as a cardinal element of successful executive leadership.

Furthermore, the single-leader mode of behavior matches the expectations of the governing board or even the employees of most organizations. Executives are presumed to possess all the skills required for any issue the senior leadership group must face. Executives in the senior leadership group want to be involved in every issue whether they can contribute or not. When job titles alone determine membership, a working group may or may not possess the proper skill mix, a key to real team performance advantages.

The fact is that working groups are often fast and efficient. They can be energized and focused quickly by a single leader who understands the goals and the best working approach of the group. Finally, top executives simply prefer to function as single leaders. This is where they excel, and they are often uncomfortable as collaborators in groups where accountability is shared.

REAL TEAM OPPORTUNITIES

The increasing pace of technological, social, and competitive change has created a need for alternative modes of leadership behavior and the conscious application of team discipline that, in the past, was driven primarily by major events and crises. Governments, labor groups, and others have joined competition in demanding a higher level and more balanced mix of performance goals. Strain on the organization has created a shortage of leadership capacity and though they may operate as a team in a crisis, senior leadership cannot rely on natural instinct to shift into real team behavior modes.

A real team is a powerful unit for both performance and organizational change because it can deliver both individual and *collective work product* such that the total is greater than the sum of its parts. The collective work product (the performance improvement that is the tangible result of a group effort and not achievable by a single member alone), shared accountability, and ability to shift the leadership role creates both higher performance capability and increased leadership capacity. *Although real teams take longer to reach full effectiveness, leadership groups that can shift between their traditional working group and real team modes of behavior can, over time, achieve higher performance results and increased leadership capacity.* A conscious, disciplined pursuit of team performance will complement rather than replace executive leadership performance.

The key is to focus team efforts on targets of opportunity. Team performance is about doing real work, not facilitating discussion or debate. The object is never the "team" itself. *Only a truly collective work product can benefit from the performance improvements real teams offer. Real teams apply their complementary skills jointly to a work product that could not be crafted by any individual member and add those results to those obtained by individuals acting alone.* It is this combination of individual and collective work that enables a real team to achieve extraordinary levels of performance.

Collective work products can be more difficult to identify at the top. The typical focus of the leadership group—vision, values, strategy, policy, and so on—may not translate directly into real team work projects. It is often a problem for the top leadership group to select collective work products that match their skill mix and available time. However, every top leadership group should be able to identify and prioritize at least a small set of collective work products, or team opportunities, that offer the most potential benefit for the company. Here are some examples:

1. Specific resolution of a key strategic issue which requires problem-solving through a leadership group effort;
2. Redesign of a faulty management process undertaken directly by the leadership team rather than outside consultants, task forces, or staff specialists;
3. Organizational restructuring in which the entire leadership group is engaged in intensive problem solving;
4. Entry into a new market where a small group of executives share responsibility and authority for a joint decision for which they are held accountable.

Collective work products represent explicit opportunities for real team behavior and an opportunity for higher-performance results than could be obtained through individual work. Disadvantages include more time, increased risk, and a different set of leadership skills. Opportunities for collective work products are often overlooked or pursued through normal working modes, however, and the performance potential of real team behavior never realized.

THE WISDOM TO KNOW THE DIFFERENCE

Careless use of the term *team* or lack of clarity about what constitutes a team performance opportunity undermines efforts to create teams at any level. Almost any working group is likely to be labeled a team, whether real team discipline is enforced or not. *Team basics*, the five essential ingredients for real team levels of performance (size, goals, skills, working approach, and mutual accountability), are often ignored or not understood. Correspondingly, *many top leadership challenges are simply not team opportunities*, and labeling them as such can lead participants to misdirect their energy toward trying to become more "teamlike" rather than focus on a legitimate collective work product. In any case, the result will be lackluster performance.

There are three main tests of whether a group is functioning as a real team:

- The value of the collective work product,
- The mutual accountability of the members, and
- A leadership role that shifts among the participants.

It takes time to learn when and how to apply the discipline of teams, and too much time can be spent chasing team performance when the efficiency of a nonteam mode is more sensible. If the three tradeoffs between team behavior and other options are clearly recognized, however, leadership groups can make better choices.

Time Trade-off   The learning curve for real teams may result in a short-term decline in performance before it reaches its true performance potential. A senior group can seldom work in a real team mode unless members agree that the collective work product is more important than their individual responsibilities and goals. Further, it is difficult to understand the value of real teams without an experience base, and finding the time to do real work together as a team is very important. Sometimes circumstances are such that time for a group to enter and develop into a real team is simply not available.

Capability Trade-off   Team discipline demands the right mix of skills to accomplish the team's purpose. This often conflicts with the formal position of members within the hierarchy. There can be no compromise on this issue, and the team member's formal position must be a secondary consideration after the skill requirements of the group are met. The common practice of assigning team tasks to existing working groups under the assumption that job titles represent specific skills is more common at the top of organizations than the factory floor. On the other hand, the position or influence of a member may also be critical in resolving a performance issue irrespective of the specific skills required.

Capacity Trade-off   Real teams increase leadership capacity by sharing the leadership role among team members. In the traditional working group, a formal leader almost invariably assumes ultimate authority and responsibility for the group's work product. This does not mean real teams are "leaderless." Nor does it mean that CEOs must abandon their leadership style to function in a real team environment, as long as the executive believes in the advantage of team performance and is willing to play a number of different roles. The CEO can spot team opportunities, monitor team discipline, neutralize political influences to protect the team, set themes, integrate conflicting viewpoints, and monitor the skill mix of the team.

PUTTING IT ALL TOGETHER

Leading an organization through a complex environment, particularly when growth and change is expected, places high demands on leadership capacity. *Team performance is only one approach to meeting this need, but it is one with great potential for immediate results and the most neglected within top leadership groups.*

To reach the performance potential of real teams at any level, you should:

- *Pick your shots.* Not every opportunity is a good team opportunity, nor can a leadership group function in a team mode all the time. Any leadership group can function in a team mode if it picks the right targets and is rigorous in enforcing team discipline.
- *Weigh your options.* Single-leader working group, task forces, unit teams, and other models all have a place. A flexible and balanced approach is best. Master the ability to shift modes and membership configurations.

- *Consider the trade-offs.* Team approaches take more time, but will yield superior results where collective work products are required.
- *Learn new roles.* What worked in the past may blind us to new leadership capacity. Executive leadership discipline can be integrated with team discipline. Changing roles is more important than changing styles.
- *Work together.* Time must be set aside for real work together as a team. Both structured and open-ended meetings should be tried.

READING 3

Empowered Teams

Richard S. Wellins, William C. Byham, and Jeanne M. Wilson
Summary prepared by Cathy Hanson

> **Cathy Hanson** *has an MBA degree from the University of Southern California; she has worked for over seven years in human resources. This experience included assisting with the start-up of two team-based manufacturing plants for Kraft General Foods. Cathy is currently a Personnel Manager in the Kal Kan division of M&M Mars.*

What are self-directed work teams? Why are many of today's organizations moving toward teams? How do organizations implement teams? What are the roles of management, administration, and subordinates in a self-directed work team? These are some of the questions addressed here.

The buzzword in many organizations today is self-directed work teams. Many organizations realize that a distinct business advantage accompanies empowering their employees through teams. For organizations just starting this journey or those who are well on their way, many questions arise, and the search for answers can be overwhelming. Managers need to know how teams work, how to prepare for them, and how to build strong teams once they are in place. The information shared in this book comes from a variety of sources: a national survey, research, review of literature, and experience the authors have gained by working with teams.

HOW TEAMS WORK

A *self-directed work team* (SDWT) is an intact group of employees who are responsible for a whole work process or segment that delivers a product or service to an internal or external customer. Some characteristics that differentiate SDWTs from other teams include the following: SDWTs share management and leadership functions; they plan, control, and improve their work processes; they set their own schedules; and they hire replacements for their team.

Organizations are moving toward teams for a variety of reasons. Many organizations report improved quality of products and service; greater flexibility; reduced operating costs; faster response to technological change; and the ability to attract and retain quality employees.

Self-directed work teams become empowered over time by taking on additional responsibilities that were once reserved for supervisors or managers. There are four

Richard S. Wellins, William C. Byham, and Jeanne M. Wilson, *Empowered Teams*. San Francisco, CA: Jossey-Bass, 1991.

levels of responsibility/authority that over time increase as the teams become more mature and able to handle greater responsibilities. At level one, the teams may take on the responsibility for administering and training fellow team members. At level four, the teams may be conducting performance appraisals, budgeting, and working on product development and modification.

The journey to SDWTs does not happen overnight. Many organizations report that SDWTs take between two and five years to develop, with many bumps along the way.

The term *self-direction* may imply that organizations with teams are organizations without leadership. This idea is simply not true. SDWT organizations share leadership responsibility with the teams. The amount of responsibility teams have varies from organization to organization. Another assumption is that these organizations have fewer people. This idea is not necessarily true; these organizations may have fewer managers and supervisors, but the number of people may remain the same. Managers and supervisors can support the team by becoming trainers, team facilitators, and technical experts.

Redesigning an organization into teams is neither simple nor easy to explain, and there is no such thing as a typical team. Teams vary from organization to organization and sometimes across departments. Several key issues focus on how SDWT's work in redesigned organizations. The following discussion addresses a few of these questions and issues.

Number of People in SDWTs

One of the questions often asked concerns how many people in an organization work in SDWTs. According to the authors' survey, 26 percent of organizations use teams. However, only a small percent of the workforce in these organizations is functioning in teams. Of the companies surveyed, teams were found mostly in manufacturing (80 percent). However, some organizations are organizing their white-collar workforce into teams as well.

Titles

What's in a title? In organizations that are moving toward teams, titles signify the change. Titles such as *employee* and *subordinate* are replaced with *team member* and *associate*. Supervisors' titles also change to *coach, team leader*, and *communicator*.

Size

Team size varies; our survey indicated that the ideal size is from six to twelve people. Size is determined by the work process (with positions and functions fit together logically); research says that it is better to keep teams on the small side.

Multiskilling

Many team organizations embrace *multiskilling* and job rotation. The advantages to the organization of having multiskilled team members and members who rotate jobs include greater flexibility and team members who understand the challenges faced by others on the team. Team members also have a better understanding of the total process and how each job contributes to the whole.

Support

Support functions in the team environment have the philosophy of "we serve the team" and often work with coordinators in the team who take the expertise supplied by the functions back to the team. Teams may also integrate the functions into the work teams.

Committees

Team members may participate on companywide committees. The decisions these committees make, such as choosing training programs and preparing the annual business plans, affect all teams. Usually, one person from each team serves on the companywide team.

Other nontraditional activities in which team members may participate include performance appraisals of fellow team members, interviewing new team members, and addressing performance and discipline issues.

PREPARING FOR TEAMS

Deciding to implement teams is no small task; it requires involvement and commitment at all levels of the organization. Senior management must first work on implementing a new vision. The team concept must fit into the overall organizational structure and overall business objectives.

Three groups make strategic decisions when implementing teams. These include senior management, the steering committee, and the design team. After senior management has determined that the team concept fits into its goals and objectives, they play a key role in initiating the implementation.

Senior management is responsible for articulating the vision, deciding whether teams should be studied further, and providing the steering committee and design team with guidance. Senior management must also assess the long-term business needs and define the role of teams within the overall organization, determine if the organization's vision and values are compatible with the team, and determine the membership and responsibilities of the steering committee.

The *steering committee* is usually composed of upper and middle management, union representatives, team leaders, and in some cases prospective team members. This group takes the vision and direction provided by senior management and oversees the design effort. They often develop a team charter, provide the link between the teams and the organization, and protect the design process from negative influences.

The *design team* may be composed of members of the steering team but will also include supervisors, human resource personnel, union officials, team members, and other functional representatives. This team plans the implementation strategy and acts as the champion of the team concept effort. This group will bring the details to the SDWT plan.

If the design team chooses, it may use the *sociotechnical analysis process*. This process involves four steps:

1. *Technical analysis*: This analysis looks at who works with the organization (customers, suppliers, and so on) and their expectations; it also includes the process and technology that will be used.

2. *Social analysis*: This analysis looks at the roles, responsibilities, and tasks that need to be performed in order to produce the product or provide the service. It is then used to create jobs with meaningful content. This analysis also includes how supervisor and manager roles can be transferred to the team.
3. *Joint optimization*: The information obtained in the technical and social analysis is compiled to optimize both the technical and social systems.
4. *Agreement on process and result measures*: Conclusions are reached within the design team as to what will be measured and how it will be measured. These measures should be implemented at the start of the SDWT process.

SDWTs can be implemented in an organization in the following three ways:

- Create a pilot area where a single SDWT is started and evaluated.
- Phase in teams by developing a plan to roll them out sequentially.
- Engage in total immersion, wherein the organization/plant as a whole implements teams; this is often the approach in new plant startups.

Each approach has advantages and disadvantages associated with it. The approach an organization chooses depends on the organization's needs.

During the implementation of the team concept, supervisors and managers often wonder how their roles will change and whether there will be places for them. Many organizations are changing the roles of supervisors and managers by replacing responsibilities that are transferred to the team with new ones that were formally held by upper management. The supervisors may also take on coaching more teams as the teams absorb some of the supervisors' responsibilities.

Selection

A critical step in the success of SDWTs is selection of team players, or identifying individuals who can work well together. The selection system in team-based organizations often differs from that of a traditional organization in many ways. In a team-based organization, team members often participate in the selection of other team members and support staff. Also, different criteria may be used in a team-based organization. Emphasis on how well the person works with others when solving a problem, technical *aptitude*, and desire to work in a team environment are examples of the criteria applied. Sometime during the selection process the candidate is given a realistic picture of the job and what it's like to work in a team environment. Since the criteria tend to be more extensive than in a traditional system, the selection ratio in a startup operation is often as large as 20 to 1.

When an organization is developing the selection system, the first place to start is by conducting a detailed job analysis. This analysis will give the organization a list of behaviors, skills, and knowledge (dimensions) that an incumbent must possess in order to be successful in that position. (This analysis is also the basis for many human resource systems besides selection, such as performance appraisal and training.)

There are many tools to help organizations select team members. One tool, popular when selecting supervisors and manager's is the *assessment center*. This method consists of three types of simulations:

1. *Problem-solving simulation* An applicant is posed with a problem (production or service related) and asked to gather relevant information and make a decision regarding this problem in a given time period.
2. *Manufacturing simulation* Applicants are given a situation typically found in a manufacturing environment and asked to simulate the situation as if they were in this environment. This activity can provide opportunities to demonstrate teamwork, problem-solving ability, learning ability, and work pace.
3. *Group-discussion simulation* Short case studies are given to small leaderless groups of applicants; they are instructed to a solution by consensus. No roles are assigned in the group.

Another tool used in team selection is *video orientation*. Through a videotape, applicants are given a realistic job preview, showing what the various jobs are like and what it is like to work in the team environment. Ideally, people who would not like to work in this environment self select themselves out of the process. This method also allows an organization to begin building excitement for those who like this environment and to let them know what to expect in the selection process.

The *self-report inventory* requires applicants to answer questions regarding their preferences toward the work environment. These inventories show the applicant's desire to work in a team and the organizational environment that goes along with teams.

Cognitive ability tests can also play a critical role in team selection. These tests assess the applicants ability to learn the technical aspects of the job. *Technical skills tests* are usually conducted in two parts. The first part is a paper-and-pencil test, and the second part is observing the applicant perform technically. These tests assess the applicant's technical skills.

The interviewing technique often used by team organizations differs from traditional interviewing in several ways. The most obvious difference is that team-based organizations often call their interviewing system "targeted interviewing." As the name implies, *targeted interviewing* focuses on gathering facts versus theoretical information about the applicant. The questions in targeted interviewing focus on behavior by asking applicants how they have handled similar situations in the past. The underlying premise is that past behavior predicts future behavior.

When developing the selection system in team-based organizations, a combination of these methods may be used. From the job analysis, dimensions are developed, and each selection method evaluates one or more dimensions. Two different methods may assess the same dimension.

Training

Training the new teams can be quite an undertaking. However, the lack of training is the number one barrier to successful team implementation. Most training can be organized into three categories: job skills, team/interactive skills, and quality action skills. These categories have a multiplicative effect on one another. So, increasing the team skills in one area by even a little can increase the team's effectiveness substantially. When planning training for team members, the focus should be on two areas:

1. The core set of skills that must be provided to all team members: team/interactive skills, quality action training, and job-specific skills. Examples of

team/interactive skills include training on handling conflict and on how to teach job skills to other team members. Examples of quality action training include identifying improvement opportunities and developing and selecting solutions. Job-skills training focuses on the specifics of performing the job.

2. Ongoing training that occurs at the "teachable moment." The teachable moment is the moment when the trainee is most apt to understand, internalize, and apply the learnings. Training is also needed for team leaders as well as for support staff. Team-leader training can focus on such areas as coaching skills to prepare the leaders for their changing role.

Building Strong Teams

Team development can be measured by a comparison of the team with the following key factors of effective teams:

- *Commitment* Team members identify themselves with the team and are committed to team goals over their personal goals.
- *Trust* Team members believe in each other and are willing to uphold their commitments to the team.
- *Purpose* Team members see how they fit into the organization and believe they can make a difference.
- *Communication* Team members communicate among themselves as well as with others outside the team.
- *Involvement* Each team member has a role on the team. The team reaches decisions through consensus.
- *Process orientation* The team has several tools, such as problem-solving and planning techniques, to help them attain their goals.

Teams go through four stages as they develop into self-directed work teams. Each stage can be measured in terms of the key factors.

Stage One: Getting   At this stage the team is not yet a team. Members don't know what to expect and are cautious about buying into the SDWT concept. Key factors at stage one include:

- *Commitment* Members are not yet fully committed to the team. They are cautious and not fully participating within the team.
- *Trust* Members are "feeling each other out." They have a wait-and-see attitude.
- *Purpose* While the team understands its purpose and mission, the mission is not a "living document."
- *Communication* The communication goes from leader to members and back again in the form of questions and answers.
- *Involvement* There are varying degrees of involvement. Assertive members may dominate.
- *Process orientation* The process is new and unfamiliar.

Helping the teams through stage one involves helping them to develop the team's identity and a sense of "teamness." This is usually done by having the team write a charter or mission statement.

Stage Two: Going in Circles   At this stage the "honeymoon" is over, and the team struggles with "who does what?" and tends to pull apart. Managers struggle at this stage with how much responsibility to relinquish to the team. Key factors at stage two include:

- *Commitment* Subgroup commitment exists but not to the team as a whole.
- *Trust* Members trust some and not others.
- *Purpose* Members are developing a purpose but still need guidance from others.
- *Communication* Conflicts may arise as individuals express their concerns.
- *Involvement* Domination by some members.
- *Process orientation* Some awkwardness in the use of a group's "standard" processes.

Helping the team through this stage involves letting the individuals know ahead of time what to expect. Reassurance that the team will work through stage two is important.

Stage Three: Getting on Course   The team at this stage is more goal focused, and team members accept the diversity that is needed within the group to get the job done. The members may at this stage put the team and its members above others in the organization. Key factors at stage three include:

- *Commitment* Team members are committed to getting the job done.
- *Purpose* Focus is on the achievement of team and performance goals.
- *Communication* Communication within the team is focused on tasks; the team begins to develop relationships with support groups.
- *Involvement* Team members are comfortable with their roles in the team.
- *Process orientation* Team members feel comfortable with the process.

Helping the team through stage three involves broadening the team's focus. This can be done by training in interdisciplinary groups, encouraging more customer/ supplier contact, and setting up opportunities for the team to work with other levels within the organization.

Stage Four: Full Speed Ahead   After several years of working together, the team may reach stage four. At this stage the team develops expectations about their "rights," such as being consulted on decisions that affect them. Key factors at stage four include:

- *Commitment* Team members are committed to the team and to the organization.
- *Trust* Members trust each other.
- *Purpose* The team has a clear vision and mission; the team is able to change according to business demands.
- *Communication* Communication is complex and adjusted as needed.
- *Involvement* All individuals are highly involved; previously reluctant members are participating.
- *Process orientation* Team processes have become second nature.

Helping the team stay at this level can be even harder than helping the team through the earlier stages. The teams at this level need to learn more about the business through training. Teams at this stage may be interviewing new team members, hiring, or dealing with performance/disciplinary issues. One of the best ways to help the team stay at this level is to let the team mentor less advanced teams.

Organizations wishing to implement teams should design careful, thoughtful, and well-planned implementations; set realistic goals; provide appropriate training; make teams part of an overall business strategy; and always look back and see where the team has been and recognize the accomplishments they have made.

PART NINE
Leadership

The 1990s was the "decade of the leader." Nationally we seem to be looking for the hero who can turn us around, establish a new direction, and pull us through. Organizations are searching for visionary leaders—people who by the strength of their personalities can bring about a major organizational transformation. We hear calls for charismatic, transformational, and transactional leadership. A myriad of individuals charge that the problems with the American economy, declining organizational productivity, and lost ground in worldwide competitive markets are largely a function of poor management and the lack of good organizational leadership.

After studying dozens of leaders, Noel Tichy and Eli Cohen conclude that "leadership engines" are the key to winning companies' success. These companies develop leaders at all levels who are capable of teaching others the critical abilities that will allow them to succeed. These "teaching leaders" help others make tough decisions, develop good business ideas, instill important values, and generate positive energy in themselves and their associates. Great leaders such as Jack Welch and Roberto Goizueta combined a desire to teach, a willingness to teach, and a teachable point of view to fuel their highly successful leadership engines at General Electric and Coca-Cola, respectively.

Noel Tichy is both a consultant and a professor at the University of Michigan's business school, specializing in leadership and organizational transformation. He previously published *Control Your Destiny or Someone Else Will* (with Stratford Sherman). Eli Cohen is a consultant with Bain & Company.

The second book, summarized in Reading 2, is titled *Fusion Leadership: Unlocking the Subtle Forces that Change People and Organizations*, written by Richard L. Daft and Robert H. Lengel. Richard L. Daft is the Ralph Owen Professor of Management and Director of the Center for Change Leadership in the Owen Graduate School of Management at Vanderbilt University. He has written extensively on organizations and management practices. His co-author is Robert H. Lengel, Associate Dean for Executive Education at the University of Texas at San Antonio.

In this book, Daft and Lengel describe a way of leading that is based on the principles of "fusion," the joining together, as opposed to "fission," the splitting apart or creating a separation. The authors detail the use of shared vision and values as a way that leaders can bring people together in the pursuit of common goals. In the opinion of the authors, fusion leadership represents an approach to leading that taps into the "heart and soul" of followers, as opposed to a leadership technique that engages only the body and mind. The authors position vision, heart, mindfulness, courage, communication, and integrity as the central keys to organizational transformation.

Margaret J. Wheatley, in *Leadership and the New Science: Learning about Organization from an Orderly Universe*, draws from recent advances in physics, chemistry, and biology to challenge conventional thinking about organizations. Her book provides us with a new way to think about organizations en route to the development of new organizational forms. The leader is encouraged, for example, to see chaos in the environment not as something to be feared and avoided, but as an opportunity for system growth; to come to understand relationship and processes that connect elements instead of paying particular attention to specific tasks (elements); and to recognize that the universe has a participative quality to its very nature.

Margaret J. Wheatley, Ph.D., is president of The Berkana Institute and a principal of Kellner-Rogers & Wheatley, Inc. Formerly on the faculty at Brigham Young University, she has consulted for a variety of *Fortune* 500 clients and educational, health care, and nonprofit organizations.

Peter Block, in his book *Stewardship*, argues that the environment confronting organizations today requires the replacement of traditional concepts of leadership and management with new ideas of stewardship. *Stewardship means empowering people to be accountable for their own actions*, rather than being dependent on leaders and managers. Stewardship is predicated on the notion that people in organizations are willing to choose service over self-interest.

In order to move toward the stewardship model, Block notes that the traditional pillars of management (i.e., an emphasis on control, consistency, and predictability) must be replaced, partnership must be created between employees and top management, and a new governance system and structure that integrates managing and doing the work must be created. Consistent with Manz and Sims' (see Part Seven) work on superleadership, and Wellins, Byham, and Wilson's focus on self-directed work teams, stewardship-based organizations stress a major role placed upon *self-management*.

Peter Block is a founding partner of Designed Learning, Inc., a training firm, and the consulting firm of Block Petrella Weisbord, Inc. A consultant to businesses, schools, and governments, he focuses on changing organizations. He is the author of *The Empowered Manager* and *Flawless Consulting*.

A wide array of other books on leadership have appeared. Alternative perspectives can be found in Tichy and Devanna's *The Transformational Leader*; Covey's *The Seven Habits of Highly Effective People* and his follow-up book, *Principle-Centered Leadership*; Jaworski's *Synchronicity: The Inner Path of Leadership*; Bennis' *Managing People Is Like Herding Cats*; Koestenbaum's *Leadership: The Inner Side of Greatness*; and Conger's *Learning to Lead: The Art of Transforming Managers into Leaders* and *The Charismatic Leader*.

READING 1

Training & Development

Noel M. Tichy and Eli Cohen

Since the early 1990s, a number of companies have invested vast amounts of money trying to become learning organizations. Hopefully, they did a good job because to survive in the future, they have to learn one more big lesson: A learning organization isn't enough. They need to become teaching organizations.

The concepts underlying learning organizations are valuable. But to succeed in a highly competitive global marketplace, companies need to be able to change quickly; their people must be able to acquire and assimilate new knowledge and skills rapidly. Though learning is a necessary competency, it's not sufficient to assure marketplace success.

We have looked at winning companies—those that consistently outperform competitors and reward shareholders—and found that they've moved beyond being learning organizations to become teaching organizations. In fact, we believe that when a learning organization comes up against a teaching organization, the teaching organization will win every time. That's because teaching organizations are more agile, come up with better strategies, and are able to implement them more effectively.

Teaching organizations do share with learning organizations the goal that everyone continually acquire new knowledge and skills. But to that they add the more critical goal that everyone pass their learning on to others.

In teaching organizations, leaders see it as their responsibility to teach. They do that because they understand that it's the best, if not only, way to develop throughout a company people who can come up with and carry out smart ideas about the business. Because people in teaching organizations see teaching as critical to the success of their business, they find ways to do it every day. Teaching every day about critical business issues avoids the fuzzy focus that has plagued some learning organization efforts, which have sometimes become a throwback to 1960s- and 1970s-style self-exploration and human relations training.

A teaching organization's insistence that its leaders teach creates better leaders because teaching requires people to develop a mastery of ideas and concepts. In a teaching organization, leaders benefit just by preparing to teach others. Because the teachers are people with hands-on experience within the organization—rather than outside consultants—the people being taught learn relevant, immediately useful concepts and skills.

Teaching organizations are better able to achieve success and maintain it because their constant focus is on developing people to become leaders. An organization's current leaders are creating the next generation of leaders by teaching people about the critical issues facing their business and by teaching them how to anticipate changes and deal with them. Consequently, teaching organizations have a steady supply of talent to keep the momentum going.

THE BEST LEADERS ARE THE BEST TEACHERS

When we set out to write *The Leadership Engine: How Winning Companies Build Leaders at Every Level* (HarperBusiness, 1997), companies around the world were fumbling all over themselves to find the right tools to deal with globalization, technological change, and consumers' rising demands. The many that failed were paying the price. GM, IBM, American Express, Westinghouse, Kodak in the early 1990s, and AT&T and Apple in the latter half of the nineties all said good-bye to their senior leaders and hired new ones. The capital markets were responding to poor corporate results and sending the message to add value or the companies' top leaders would be replaced.

In writing *The Leadership Engine*, we examined some of those failures and compared them with such successes as General Electric, Intel, and Compaq. We concluded that the capital markets were only partly right; leadership was the problem, but the markets were wrong to focus only on top leadership. In the companies we studied, sustained success was a function of leadership throughout. Winning companies win because they have solid leaders not only at the top, but also at all organizational levels.

When we asked why these winning companies had a lot of leaders at all levels, we discovered it was because they deliberately worked at it and had made developing leaders a critical competency. We found that to be true consistently in our research of successful organizations no matter what their size or line of endeavor. Whether they were huge *Fortune* 500 corporations or not-for-profit social agencies, there was one universal characteristic. It was that everyone, including and especially top leaders, were committed teachers. They had developed leadership engines—systems for creating dynamic leaders at all organizational levels. They made themselves into teaching organizations.

Many executives think that they don't have the time to teach because they're too busy dealing with the immediate issues of running a business. But the best leaders we know are, not coincidentally, the best teachers. Larry Bossidy—who transformed AlliedSignal and led it to become the best performing company on the Dow Jones Industrial Average within five years of his arrival in 1991—accomplished his successes largely by being a dedicated teacher. Bossidy didn't transform Allied by replacing senior managers. He diagnosed the company and decided what had to be done. He taught the senior leaders about strategy and spent hundreds of days teaching other people throughout the company. In his first year on the job, Bossidy reached 15,000 AlliedSignal employees personally.

Now, Bossidy is teaching his people how to create a growth mindset and deliver on it. Many people think that AlliedSignal can't be a growth company any longer because many of its businesses are in mature markets. But Bossidy thinks that defeatist attitude carries the seeds of its own fulfillment. So, he is teaching people at Allied to see that growth is possible anywhere and that if they go looking for it, they'll find it.

Other highly effective leaders known for their teaching include Roger Enrico of PepsiCo, Andy Grove of Intel (see *Training & Development*, May 1997) and the late Roberto Goizueta of Coca-Cola. By holding classes and workshops regularly, those leader-teachers serve as role models for everyone in their organizations. Their example emphasizes the importance they place on teaching and encourages others to teach. But even more important than the teaching they do in classrooms is the teaching they do in the course of the daily management of their companies. Bossidy, for example, uses the strategy, budget, and employee-review processes to coach the managers who participate in them. After each meeting, he writes each manager a letter that reviews the meeting and states explicitly what he liked and didn't like about the manager's plans. Bossidy also writes what he expects to happen as a result of the meeting. If a manager doesn't understand or disagrees, he or she gets back to Bossidy immediately.

Similarly, Carlos Cantu, CEO of ServiceMaster says, "Every single person has to come away [from a meeting with him] with something positive." His objective is that the people who are responsible to him feel they gain something from the experience.

NO BLUEPRINT

So, how do you create a teaching organization? What does one look like? The answer is that there is no single blueprint. Teaching organizations require the personal input and dedication of the leaders within them. Therefore, each one is unique in that it's based on the knowledge and experience of its leaders and the realities of its business environment. One premier example is General Electric.

Jack Welch has been lauded as one of the great business minds of the century. Many people saw General Electric as an institution that was *too* successful and too big for it to need change or be changed. But Welch had a very different point of view of GE when he became CEO 17 years ago. Since then, he has creatively destroyed and rebuilt the company. The result is a market value around a quarter of a trillion dollars—the most valuable company on Earth. But, though many people laud Welch's leadership qualities, others miss that he's also a great teacher. He may head a company with annual sales closing in on $100 billion, but he spends 30 percent of his own time teaching and developing others. Equally important, he has made sure that the rest of GE's leaders are also teachers.

The result of Welch's teaching—and the reason GE has achieved marketplace success—is that the company has an abundance of leadership talent. *BusinessWeek* recently ran a list of the 20 executives "most sought after" by search firms looking for CEOs; five were at GE. That's even after several of GE's brightest stars had been plucked away in the '80s and '90s—including Bossidy; John Trani, now of Stanley Works; Glenn Hiner, now of Owens Corning; Harry Stonesifer, now of Boeing; and Norman Blake, now of USF&G.

Welch was involved personally in transforming GE's Crotonville management development center—directing it less toward packaging information and teaching job skills and more toward testing, coaching, and developing leaders. Twice a month, without fail, he goes to Crotonville to teach and interact with new employees and experienced managers. He also teaches constantly through direct feedback and coaching to leaders throughout the company.

Welch also built a system at GE in which leaders teach other leaders. It has the following basic elements.

A Leadership Pipeline   Every professional-level employee at GE has a career map that describes where they are in their career relative to positions they've had and may hold in the future. The map includes an assessment of their skills and the specific skills they'll need for the next positions. It also describes primary job assignment, stretch assignments, and formal development and coaching opportunities through which the skills can be acquired and demonstrated. Such tools, to varying degrees, are commonplace in many companies. The difference at GE is how they're used. Managers at every level look at their staffs' maps and use them as the basis for coaching. Everyone at GE understands that the environment will change and that career maps aren't set in stone. But they do provide a context and starting point to develop technical and leadership ability. They also set expectations for what the company wants each employee to achieve at any given point in his or her career.

A main purpose of the maps, along with GE's other HR processes (more on those later), is to keep the leadership pipeline full—a matter GE takes seriously. Dick Stonesifer, who started at GE as a mechanic and became head of GE's $6 billion appliance business by the time he retired in 1996, says, "One of my most important jobs, and one of the things I evaluated people on, was whether there were four people who could [step in suddenly and] fill someone's position."

He explains: "This wasn't about some type of emergency planning, because you don't need four people to fill a job. The point was that you need bench strength; you need people who are that good to run parts of your business and, eventually, they will take bigger jobs in the company. But if you aren't worried about having people who are that good, you'll never improve your business."

That type of thinking is almost a religion at GE. With Stonesifer, a failure to show your faith usually meant career disaster. He says, "If I had a great manager who didn't have strong candidates that could do his job, I'd make a very explicit deal. I'd say, 'You have six months to find people—from outside or inside—who can perform at a higher level or [you can] develop it in your own people. I'll provide any help you need. But if those people aren't here in six months, I'm going to get rid of you because I can't have you making the numbers but not getting people ready to lead.'"

Coaching Key Leaders   Although GE works hard to develop leaders at every level, the top 500 get special attention. Welch is fanatical that the talents of that distinguished group be upgraded constantly. He demands that whenever one of the 500 positions comes open, several internal and external candidates are examined. That lets him and other senior leaders constantly benchmark GE's talent.

Each of the top 500 leaders regularly receives brutally honest, laser-sharp feedback on their hard-business performance and soft people issues. Welch gives feedback to each of his staff in a two-page handwritten report on his or her performance and attaches last year's note that's annotated to show what has or hasn't been done. He provides more feedback during annual stock-option awards and salary adjustments, which he accompanies with a face-to-face discussion. The discipline of putting his thoughts in writing forces Welch and his staff to focus on the feedback. It also leaves no room for distortion and misinterpretation. That process cascades so that Welch's staff provide the same level of in-depth, personal coaching to their staff, and so on down.

For example, in the early 1990s, Welch began rating managers on a 2-by-2 grid showing their performance relative to quantifiable targets and the extent to which they "lived" GE values. The tool was effective, and now all of GE's 500 officers use it to evaluate and coach their people.

Organizational Structure That Encourages Leadership Development   One of Welch's early activities was to dismantle GE's bureaucracy. In place of 240 profit centers, he created 13 global businesses, each of which now reports to the office of the chairman—Welch and two vice chairmen. Together with other senior executives, these people form the 25-person Corporate Executive Council, which meets four times a year to share experiences and plan for the future. At the sessions, these "best leaders" expand their own abilities by learning from each other. Because they're all working on companywide issues, their thinking about the company and their own businesses is also enhanced. And there's no hierarchy; everyone is expected to contribute.

The CEC structure (think of it as a hub-and-spoke system with the office of the chairman at the center) has been replicated all over the company. GE Appliances has its own business executive council, and GE Capital has set up 27 different businesses—in part to give each unit small-company speed and flexibility and to provide more leadership positions. Though the specific forms may be different, the underlying premise is the same: Bureaucracy stifles people's ability and desire to lead. The CEC-style structure and each business unit encourage people to take the initiative. Several times a year, it lets them stretch their own leadership by thinking more broadly. At these sessions, senior leaders can assess, coach, and teach junior leaders.

HR Systems and Processes   GE's entire HR system is geared to developing leaders and emphasizes the need for leaders to teach other leaders. Selection for a management job early on in one's career is based on demonstrated leadership talents. Once you manage others at GE, you are evaluated on how well you develop them. Your compensation and career opportunities reflect that.

GE also uses several other HR processes to help leaders teach, such as new-manager assimilation. When a leader is about to take a new job, a professional (usually an HR manager) interviews each of the people who will report directly to the new manager. Next, the HR person discusses the findings with the new manager, who then holds several sessions with his or her new staff to talk about the state of the business and to share his or her personal views on business and leadership.

A good example of that is described by Tom Tiller, who worked in GE Appliances for Stonesifer. The new-manager assimilation interviews for Tiller revealed that people, including the top team, had been demoralized by continued plant closings. So, Tiller used assimilation meetings to discuss that issue and teach people what he knew about turning around bad situations. Basically, he says, he found that people like to be winners and be in organizations where positive things happen. So, in the midst of the cutbacks, GE needed to focus on creating new products and getting people excited about the future. At first, his team members doubted that could be done.

But, through the process started in the assimilation meetings, Tiller brought them around to accepting his leadership point of view on how to create positive energy. Nine months later, Appliances had one of the most successful product rollouts in GE's history.

BECOMING A TEACHER

In building a teaching organization, leaders must draw on the unique strengths and talents within their organization. There are, however, certain characteristics that we've found mark all teaching organizations. The most important factor is whether individual leaders are prepared to do it. Specifically, they must

- consider developing leaders a core competitive competency
- develop teachable points of view on how to operate and grow the company, and how to teach others to be leaders
- design and execute methods of teaching on a wide scale, and make sure the teaching goes beyond technical skills to include developing and honing leadership abilities.

Here are those characteristics in more detail.

Developing Leaders As a Core Competency   Most companies view their competitive strengths in terms of the ability to devise smart strategies and efficiently deliver the goods and services that customers want. Teaching organizations also seek winning strategies and brilliant execution, but they view the cause-and-effect equation differently. They start with the premise that people devise the strategies and implement the execution. Then, they focus equally on developing people.

Leaders with that point of view make decisions differently from people using other metrics. That means not only that the choices they make are sometimes different, but also that the way they arrive at those choices is different. Because decision making is an important leadership skill, leaders in a teaching organization teach others by opening up the decision making process so that everyone can see how and why they reached a particular decision.

Debra Dunn, general manager of Hewlett-Packard's video communications division, is an excellent example. Survival in the hotly competitive markets for video broadcast servers, cable modems, and wireless data communication technologies requires that HP's employees exhibit a lot of what we call, "edge." In other words, they must be willing to face reality and make clear, definite decisions about which new products HP will invest in. One reason Dunn has been so successful is that she has never had trouble making those types of decisions. She also knows that for her businesses to be successful, she has to help the people who work for her develop that ability as well. Dunn is deliberate in doing that. "First," she says, "I am very open and honest and direct about whether I see people as having the raw material to develop this edge. Second, I use my decisions as a way to coach, showing people how I understand things at a very detailed level. That includes how I think about the market and about communicating things up and down inside our company."

More than a year ago, Dunn and her staff were reviewing the various businesses they were trying to build. In one business in particular, Dunn felt that HP didn't have a sustainable position and would do better to invest resources other places. She thought that there was a teaching opportunity to help people understand the elements of a viable strategy and to get the management team to internalize why that's necessary and important. So, she held a series of meetings. "The objective was to convey the path I was going down," she says. "At the first meeting, I got up and took out the strategy statement from a year ago and began comparing its assumptions to the current reality. I said, 'Let's revisit this. Here's the strategy we're pursuing. Here are the assumptions we're making. Here's what the market size was. What do you think the market size is now?' [Back then], we felt we had to have a major partner to be successful in this business. So I asked, 'Do we have any reason to think that isn't the case now? Do we have a major partner? Do we see a major partner that we might have?' Next, we walked through every element of the strategy, and I asked, 'What are the options?'"

At the end of the discussion, some people still suggested certain partnerships. But Dunn said, "Guys, I think if we're honest with ourselves, we know enough today to assess, with very high probability, what is the likelihood of partnerships with [those] people, and none look probable. . . . I know that some of you think the right thing to do is to continue spending time on this. But I am deciding that we are not going to; we don't have time and can't afford to go down every theoretical path. We have to apply some intuitive judgment."

Dunn's teaching regarding her decision didn't stop there. She decided to make dealing with the pain of her decision part of her teaching. She says that she found the decision painful because she had invested a lot of personal energy trying to make the business work. "I didn't like the conclusion. But that didn't cause me to deny it or hide from it or pretend that reality is different. I knew this could be a mind-broadening area for part of my team. I went out to lunch, I went out for drinks, I spent time . . . helping them understand the constraints."

Dunn's decision had both supporters and dissenters. But perhaps more important than the decision was that she gave her team first-class lessons on how to be a good leader. One, she was clear and logical, looked reality squarely in the face, and weighed each option against her ultimate goal to invest resources where they were most likely to pay off. Two, she won people over and energized them to pursue the course she'd chosen. She displayed, up-close and first-hand, the leadership quality called edge. She made a tough decision because she felt it was for the good of the company. In a more traditional organization, Dunn might have made her decision differently. If she hadn't been taught and encouraged to have edge, she might not have made the decision at all or might have made it privately to avoid critical questions from her staff. She could have decreed that the division would get out of the business. But in a teaching organization, that would be unthinkable. If an organization places top priority on developing leaders, then its people look for every opportunity to do just that.

Teachable Points of View   A commitment to teaching is an important first step to building a teaching organization. But in addition to wanting to teach, leaders must be able to teach, which means that they must have teachable points of view.

Everyone has points of view, and a wealth of knowledge and experience from which we create assumptions about the world and how it operates. We use such points of view every day to orient ourselves in new situations and make decisions about how to proceed. Leaders generally have pretty good points of view. Otherwise, they wouldn't be able to make smart decisions consistently and take the effective actions that made them leaders in the first place. But in order to pass that knowledge on to others, leaders must be able to articulate their points of view in ways that people can understand. In other words, they have to develop their points of view into *teachable* points of view.

Having a teachable point of view is a sign that person has clear ideas and values. It's also a tool that enables him or her to communicate those ideas and values to others. It isn't enough to have experience; leaders must draw appropriate lessons from their experience and be able to make their tacit knowledge explicit.

We sometimes begin workshops by asking people to think about their own teachable points of view. What are the central ideas driving their business? What are their core values? How do they link them together to direct their own actions and energize other people? Then, we have them stand up and give a three-minute presentation. A few participants are great, but most stumble. Why can't these experienced managers articulate their thoughts? Because the ability to do something, even well, and the ability to articulate how one does it require different skills. For example, a good athlete isn't necessarily a good coach.

Most of us keep our experiences in our hip pockets to use at a later time, but effective leaders keep taking them out and examining them—looking at the lessons they learned and searching for effective ways to express them. Further, they constantly refine their experiences as they accumulate new ones and new information.

Most people have teachable points of view on little things. For example, we frequently hit the save key on our computers, and we can explain why and how that reduces the risk of losing productive work. Effective leaders, however, have teachable points of view on a broad range of less tangible and more complicated topics. They're always coming up with new views because they're always looking to see what can be learned from a situation.

The late Roberto Goizueta of Coca-Cola is a great example of someone who developed teachable points of view and used them—as opposed to using charisma or cheerleading his company to success. When Goizueta became CEO in 1981, he was an underwhelming choice to Coca-Cola veterans and Wall Street. A company built largely on image had just given a 49-year-old, quiet engineer who spoke English with a heavy accent the job of fighting off the threat of a brash and fleet-footed PepsiCo. Goizueta, however, believed that his job was to increase the value of Coca-Cola stock for shareholders, and he was able to teach what was in his head to others. Shortly after becoming CEO, he articulated his point of view on how Coca-Cola would enrich shareholders. He drew on his experience participating in his family's business in Cuba, on the wisdom of his grandfather and Spanish poets, and on his experience leading parts of Coca-Cola's research division. His points of view included how the company would allocate capital and decide on new products—also how to hire, delegate to, and reward talented managers. He taught senior Coca-Cola managers and other employees through speeches, coaching, and actions. Goizueta's teaching allowed him to run the company in a hands-off style. He was notoriously calm because he had groomed talented managers who could run the business day-to-day. When Goizueta died, the final testament to him as a teacher and to the effectiveness of his teachable points of view was the smooth succession of Doug Ivester.

As we outlined in our article in the May 1997 *Training & Development*, leaders need to have teachable points of view in these areas:

- *Ideas*. An enterprise starts with ideas about organizing people, capital, and technology to deliver services or products to customers and value to society.
- *Values*. Many organizations try to launch new strategies without thinking about how the values and behaviors of its workforce need to change—disastrous. Leaders must help people change. That's why when Ameritech, the Chicago-based former Baby Bell, began to enter highly competitive telecommunications markets, it had to abandon its old, plodding corporate values aimed at satisfying regulatory agencies and adopt new ones that prized speed and service.
- *Energy*. In a competitive marketplace, people are constantly buffeted by changes caused by competitors, technology, consumers, and a host of other things. Leaders find ways to turn those changes into positive, energizing events rather than confusing and demoralizing ones.
- *Edge*. Edge is the willingness to make tough decisions. Leaders have clear points of view about how to face reality, incorporate information, and make and communicate decisions.

Institutionalized Methods of Teaching on a Wide Scale   When a company recognizes that developing a lot of leaders is a strategic imperative, then its teaching isn't haphazard or targeted to just a few high-potential players. A company that has chosen to become a teaching organization has formal processes and channels for making sure that teaching takes place throughout.

Because circumstances change quickly in business these days, the company with the fastest and best response is the one that wins. In order to meet the challenges, a company needs all of its people aligned and pulling in the same direction. Everyone must understand and internalize the company's business purpose, operating ideas, and values. Command-and-compliance hierarchies are too slow, and they don't work as well. Welch was able to pull off GE's major culture shift only when he put in place a systematic program to teach new values and operating norms. The original vehicle, Work Out, reached 200,000 people in the first few years. Welch has repeated the pattern of wide-scale programs again and again to advantage, each time learning from the last experience.

The latest incarnation is GE's Six Sigma quality effort. Like Work Out and the Change Acceleration Program that grew out of that, Six Sigma involves teaching GE's ideas and values, such as the importance of having Six Sigma quality (no more than 3.4 defects per million) in all processes. The concept is simple: In the world's current deflationary environment, the cost efficiencies of Six Sigma are a competitive advantage. Further, Six Sigma will aid GE's transition from a product company to a service company by assuring customers about the value of a long-term agreement with GE. Six Sigma training shows how the GE values of boundarylessness, speed, self-confidence, stretch, and simplicity are important. The tight deadlines and high performance expectations of Six Sigma projects encourage people to operate within those norms.

Welch is running Six Sigma with incredible speed and making it the responsibility of tens of thousands of GE leaders to teach others. He has created a stable of black-belt Six Sigma teachers and decreed that anyone wanting to be a senior leader at GE has to be a Six Sigma expert with a proven record of developing Six Sigma knowledge and capabilities in others. The black-belt leaders teach the fundamental Six Sigma goals, rules, and values to hundreds of people, who then design quality projects that engage thousands more. Project teams implement Six Sigma projects, while the black-belt teachers offer coaching and assistance. Though quality-improvement programs have had mixed results at many companies, GE's is going gangbusters. Prudential Securities analysts are projecting a $10 to $12 billion increase in net earnings due to the program over the next five years.

Another leadership example is Bob Knowling, who went from Ameritech to US West in February 1996, as vice president of network operations—which meant he would lead more than 20,000 employees in a company that was up to its eyeballs in trouble.

Knowling describes what he saw when he walked in the door: "The company was experiencing service performance problems. Many customers had to wait more than 24 hours for a repair. New service orders and activation took an unacceptably long time to deliver. . . . My first week on the job, it was apparent that nobody had been accountable for a reengineering effort . . . [and] it was acceptable to miss budgets. Service was in the tank; we were overspending our budgets by $100 million. Yet, people weren't losing their jobs and still got all or some of their bonuses."

Knowling came in with a simple point of view: Hold employees accountable for meeting customers' expectations and for their own commitment to the company. He began teaching people what he meant by "walking the talk." Rather than spend time at Denver headquarters, Knowling told his boss that he was going "to put on fatigues and get out with the troops." After removing some senior people on his team, Knowling spent several hours with the people who worked for them, explaining the firing decision and discussing how they could improve the situation. He brought in people from the outside to help create a new leadership cadre. To get people's attention, he did things in an unorthodox fashion—such as holding phone-call meetings at 6 a.m. to review service performance. His message to the troops: "You're going to serve customers between 8 a.m. and 5 p.m., so the call happens at 6 a.m." When it proved difficult to have the right data at 6 a.m., Knowling relented and moved his conference calls to the lunch hour.

Having literally awakened his top team, Knowling turned his attention to spreading the word throughout the company and doing it quickly. Working with his senior group, he mapped out a program called Focus Customer, which was designed with the twofold purpose to deal with the technical issues of fixing problems and to deal with the emotional issues of fear, distrust, and feelings of chaos. Like most successful wide-scale teaching efforts, Focus Customer was action-based. Knowling and the top team brought together more than 100 of the company's leaders to analyze and understand the most pressing problems. Then, they went back to their departments with a 10-week deadline for taking on a significant project that would engage their people and help solve the identified problems.

The results of Focus Customer include such projects as

- mapping the root causes of repeat customer complaints, and helping people in the field diagnose and deal with the causes
- changing the scheduling process of service operators to reduce overtime and the amount of time a customer is put on hold
- improving the scheduling of repair trucks to reduce dispatches.

Overall, the projects have produced tens of millions of dollars in benefits for the first year of the program, with more projected for next year. Moreover, 100 people felt that they'd reclaimed leadership ground, and acquired a new appreciation of (and practice with) the skills they'd need to keep exercising that leadership. Knowling is now expanding the effort to include more people. His next target is the more than 2,000 supervisors on the front lines. He's starting a program in which they will develop their own points of view on how to manage change and on the most important priorities for their part of the business. Then, they'll teach that to others while launching important projects to get the changes rolling.

We've seen similar processes in other settings. At Royal Dutch/Shell, for example, the committee of managing directors is a small group of people who lead more than 100,000 people spread across 100+ countries. In 1995 and 1996, the committee took the top 50 people in the company through a series of meetings and workshops, in which they challenged the company's direction and developed a new point of view on where it was going. Over the course of the next year, they used that to transform some of Shell's key businesses. Now, in an effort called Focused Results Delivery, Shell is engaging close to 25 percent of its vast workforce by pulling together various business or geographic units to work on what leaders want to teach the employees. They, in turn, put what they learn to use in a real project. The approach gives thousands of Shell employees common goals and ways to achieve them—plus the projects will net hundreds of millions of dollars in such countries as Argentina, Australia, and Brunei.

IT TAKES A TEACHING ORGANIZATION

The learning organization may be a popular model in business circles these days, but becoming a teaching organization is what truly makes a company a winner. Building one requires commitment and determination on the part of a company's leaders. They must be willing to invest not only the resources of the company, but also themselves. They must put in place serious career development mechanisms for people at all levels of the organization, not just at the top. They must build operating structures, create incentives, and instill cultures that encourage teaching. They must also develop broad-scale programs to quickly teach ideas and disseminate new ways of thinking and working.

Most importantly, leaders must be dedicated teachers. They must be willing to open up and share their experiences. They must make the effort to distill from those experiences their own teachable points of view—not only about how to make money in the marketplace, but also about leadership. Last, they must teach. They must use every opportunity to impart their knowledge and understanding, and act as role models for other teachers.

That may sound like a tall order. But for leaders who are dedicated to winning—and who understand that success is the product of having a lot of leaders throughout an organization—it's the smartest way to operate. Building a learning organization may make your company more successful than it is now, but it won't be able to match the number and talent of leaders in a teaching organization.

Warren Bennis notes that the basis of leadership is the ability to change the mindset, the framework, of others. To paraphrase Larry Bossidy: When you want to know how you are doing as a leader, consider how you are doing as a teacher.

READING 2

Fusion Leadership

Richard L. Daft and Robert H. Lengel
Summary prepared by Chris Graves

> **Chris Graves** *is a Financial Consultant in Tucson, Arizona. He has an MBA from Arizona State University and is a certified public accountant. He has worked in accounting as an auditor for Price Waterhouse and as a financial analyst and tax manager for Arizona-based corporations.*

The essential problem with corporate management structures as they exist in most organizations today is that they were not designed with basic human nature in mind. Traditional organizations are not able to harness efficiently the unique skills and abilities of the individual and they are unprepared to adapt quickly to changes in the business environment. The fusion approach views these adaptive abilities as cornerstones for success in today's turbulent business climate.

FUSION IN LEADERSHIP

The fusion approach to organizational leadership, using the metaphor from atomic physics, advocates creating a bond (fusion), not a splitting (fission) or separation between the people that work for and manage the modern corporation. *Fusion leadership* is a style that recognizes one's subtle leadership gifts, potentials, and passions and acts from them to lead organizational change and improvement. The question of how to approach the process of achieving operational success from an organizational management perspective has traditionally been one of division and specialization. This creation of powerful hierarchies, chains of command, and channels of divided departmental communication effectively split the organization into autonomous, functional units.

The fusion approach, in contrast, encourages cross-functional communication and relationships among players in the organization. By doing so it encourages and demands more of the individual in terms of skills and commitment. The advantage of the fusion approach is the unlocking of the human race's most fundamental strengths. Specific human forces deemed essential for the task are mindfulness, vision, heart, communication, courage, and integrity. Organizations must engage these powerful yet subtle characteristics of the individual human spirit at every level and then successfully bond these people and their abilities together into a cohesive team. The synergy

Richard L. Daft & Robert H. Lengel, *Fusion Leadership: Unlocking the Subtle Forces that Change People and Organizations.* San Francisco, CA: Berrett-Koehler, 1998.

created will result in a surge in productivity and efficiency in a new organizational culture that embraces the challenge of new technologies and change.

Meaningful change has to begin with a buy-in from the current leadership. First, formal leaders have to believe in their own individual abilities and be willing to search for untapped capabilities from within; personal fusion is the catalyst. Second, the fusion leader must be open to the potential strengths and desires that everyone in the organization possesses, and believe that the same subtle, nearly forgotten abilities can be nurtured and developed in all. Third, new fusion leaders must be attuned to the pathways of productivity and flow of productive power in the business and be ready to tear down the existing organizational walls and structures that limit the potential of the individual and the entity. Organizational fusion is the ultimate macroeconomic and psychological payoff in nurturing the six subtle forces of human potential.

MINDFULNESS

It is easy to become complacent when thinking and solving problems. Yesterday's business problems have evolved, and the pace and rate of change has accelerated. Business in the global economy has created vast new levels of complexity and has opened up an infinite variety of solutions to the creative thinker. Fusion leaders need to stimulate this desire to think critically in the people around them and encourage

- A beginner's mindset that approaches problems without interference from past experience or pre conceived notions of the way tasks should be accomplished;
- Independent thinking and novel approaches to problems; and
- An appreciation of other people's abilities to generate alternate solutions and to discern the value of the differences.

As a practical illustration, consider Germany's Field Marshal Erwin Rommel, the "Desert Fox" of World War II, in the famous North African campaign. His daring, tactical genius in tank battles over vastly superior British forces was unparalleled. What made these feats even more impressive was that Rommel was trained as an infantry officer and had never commanded a tank division until the war began. He quickly saw the ocean as a metaphor for the vast desert and the new, highly mobile, armored tanks as "destroyers on the sea." Meanwhile, the British were still using their tanks with trench warfare tactics from World War I. Rommel, the inexperienced tank commander, was innovating on the battlefield and became the most feared and highly regarded warrior in the desert.

VISION

A shared vision has become even more important as complexity and speed in business increases. Workers at every level in the organization can focus on a leader's vision for the future. The vision creates a sense of purpose, a positive feeling of shared goals, and an environment of mutual support. An organizational vision or objective that is bigger than any individual can imagine doing alone can give everyone a higher sense of purpose. Walt Disney's legacy and the forward-looking vision he crafted for himself, Disney Company employees, and the world is an example of how the imagination and ingenuity of one extraordinary individual fueled generations of fusion leaders whose unique abilities created some of our culture's greatest works.

HEART

Discussion of heart brings to mind emotions. Finding and developing an emotional balance in an organization is vitally necessary and adds another dimension to the satisfaction people desire in their lives. It is success in the effort to bring out the best in the hearts and minds of employees that creates fusion environments. The masculine element of the heart can be defined as the strong, competitive desire to win that is easily identified in contemporary business culture today. The feminine side, the subtle, emotional, and intuitive aspect of organizational life is often overlooked, forgotten, or ignored as unimportant in the frenetic pace of life today. Have you ever run the numbers on a project and had the results come up green on all counts, but a "gut check" told you the project just did not make sense in the final analysis? The qualitative (feminine) aspects of a complex decision are often strategically much more important in the long view.

COMMUNICATION

Few people practice the fine art of listening today. Many jobs focus on technical proficiency and problem solving without emphasis on the interpretation of interpersonal communication. Everyone in an organization wants to be heard and understood. Fusion leaders recognize that ideas and information flowing across functional lines, both up and down the conventional organizational chart is critical if quality decision making is the objective. Effective leaders listen and seek understanding before moving forward to a solution. Good leaders also participate in open, spontaneous discussions to get an assessment of a situation.

Supervisors can make tremendous progress along communication lines when they get out of their offices and talk to the people doing the technical work. A leader visiting third-shift employees on the job site at midnight, asking questions, listening to responses, and absorbing the attitudes and feelings of the "troops" will begin to unlock and learn about the inner organization. Leaders who show emotion and humor in after-hour visits will often find their experiences canonized and the stories passed quickly and informally among employees. People are searching for a connection and communication outside their functional work-world. Stories about real events are much more meaningful and memorable than a memo or an e-mail to the staff.

COURAGE

Courage, one of the greatest of human virtues, requires us to overcome our fears. The source of most fear is risk. The risk of failure, rejection, or even loss of life can bring tremendous pressure to bear on an individual in organizational or personal life. Examples abound of businesses that do not deal with risk constructively. Government bureaucracies lie on one end of the spectrum; there, employment practices virtually guarantee a job regardless of performance level. What force in basic human nature would motivate the employee to risk anything in an attempt to improve or adapt to a changing environment? On the other side is the harsh, unforgiving organization that demands performance, but makes it clear that it is a "one-mistake world." Basic human survival instinct will propel the individual away from courageous, risk-taking behavior and ensure that meaningful change never occurs in that environment.

Creating an environment that fosters courage and calculated risk taking is absolutely required by today's fast-paced, competitive business climate. Fusion leaders realize that courageous behavior in the organization is a necessity for profitability and survival. They encourage opposing viewpoints, embrace nonconformity, and treat honest failures as part of a normal progression in leadership and growth.

INTEGRITY

A leader with integrity sets the tone for the organization and makes it easy for others to become involved in the process of change and continuous improvement. A person with integrity generally demonstrates a high level of emotional stability and generates positive feelings and relationships based on trust with colleagues. A secure, confident fusion leader delegates authority freely, giving junior managers responsibility and the authority to match it. At times, the fusion leader must be a servant leader, giving others what they need to succeed and to develop confidence. It often means giving up the hammer of authority that has traditionally served as the principle motivator in the workplace. The objective is to bring out the leadership qualities in people in all levels of the organization.

THE NEED FOR ORGANIZATIONAL FUSION

The world around us is changing constantly. The primary challenge for managers and free thinkers is to adapt and overcome the forces that limit their potential for success. Fusion leadership provides a new set of tools and practical guidelines for applications that are more congruent with human nature. Fusion leadership requires looking inward to find answers to better manage the challenges of the modern business environment, and it has the potential to expand the freedom and sense of purpose to jobs and lives. *Organizational fusion* releases subtle forces in a large group in order to build relationships, connections, community, and a positive culture and value system.

READING 3

Leadership and the New Science

Learning about Organization from an Orderly Universe

Margaret J. Wheatley
Summary prepared by Scott L. Newstrom

Scott L. Newstrom *is a graduate of Grinnell College, Iowa, where he majored in English. He has done research at the Newberry Library in Chicago, and at Oxford University, and was a recipient of a 1993 National Endowment for the Humanities Grant. He is currently pursuing a doctoral degree at Harvard University.*

Discoveries and hypotheses in the "new science"—advances in physics, chemistry, and biology that challenge the foundations of our world view—can provide startling examples for basic issues that trouble organizations. Whether taken directly as transferrable lessons or simply metaphors for comparison, *images from these new sciences challenge our conventional perspectives on organizational structure, involvement, and planning.* A technical guide to the research from quantum physics, self-organizing systems, and chaos theory is not necessary to appreciate the stimulative aspects of their insights.

There should be a simpler way to lead organizations. Too often it appears that, through layers of complexity, things seem beyond our control; yet there is a more fundamental reality to life in organizations, and to life in general. We are all familiar with the confusion that can trouble us before proceeding to intellectual clarity; the physicists Niels Bohr and Werner Heisenberg faced precisely this type of confusion, even despair, until they began to formulate some of the basic principles undergirding quantum theory. If we are willing to acknowledge this type of confusion in our own organizational conundrums, we may likewise attain a new vision of order beneath the surface of disorder.

Part of our problem arises from the fact that we live and work in systems designed from images of a Newtonian universe: ordered, predictable, causally related, and in

Margaret J. Wheatley, *Leadership and the New Science: Learning about Organization from an Orderly Universe.* San Francisco, CA: Berrett-Koehler, 1992.

215

general quite rationally designed. With such a model for how things function, we too easily believe that greater control and planning will lead to more manageable results. Likewise, we imagine that if only we had more information and more methods to control its impact, we could introduce more design into our organizations. Yet since one of the primary conclusions of contemporary science is that the physical universe does not function on a mathematically coherent model, perhaps we should heed the lessons from this field of inquiry and seek more flexible models of leadership. *By recognizing the sources of a deeper organizational order, we can stimulate coherence, adaptation, simplification, and freedom without fearing the disorder normally associated with these concepts.*

ORDER WITHIN CHAOS

It seems that we are fixated on structures in our world; note how often we utilize the highly ordered terminology of sports or even the military in organizations: "campaigns," "triumphs," "battles," and so forth. Similarly, we find such structures in the rigid chains of command that impede interdepartmental communication. It appears that we are living in an organizational world influenced by the science of three centuries past, a science that conceived the world as highly mechanical and orderly. God's role was that of a watchmaker father who set the mechanisms ticking and then left them to follow their own logical outcomes. Machines eventually wear down and stop, and from this knowledge the concept of entropy arose. As you may recall from high school physics, *entropy* is the natural tendency for systems to expend energy and produce increasing disorder. If our model of an organizational machine displays a similar tendency, there should be an understandable fear of leaving the machine alone; it needs to be regularly monitored, tweaked, updated, and controlled. Yet new conceptions of entropy have attempted to answer the following question: If entropy is the rule, how does life ever flourish? The answer is in the fact that dissipation does not necessarily lead to the demise of a system. In fact, *dissipative structures*—which dissipate their energy to recreate themselves into new forms—can show that disorder can be itself a source of order; growth is more often found in disequilibrium, not in balance. When a system's environment becomes more complex, it generates new information that provokes the system into response. Usually, the system can refigure itself with a higher level of complexity, incorporating the environmental changes in its new order. Thinking analogically in organizations, we should recognize that order exists within disorder and disorder within order; we should not confuse control with order, but rather *see the chaotic environments as opportunities for greater growth within a system.*

FROM OBJECTS TO RELATIONSHIPS

One of the primary distinctions between a Newtonian physics and a quantum physics is the perception of how objects relate to each other, or rather, how they do not relate. In classical physics, objects tend to be seen as discreet entities, with occasional contacts governed by rational rules. Organizations tend to be similarly Newtonian-conceived as machines, with divisions of parts that can at best be reconfigured but essentially exist in distinct realms. This is a world based on images of boundaries, which understandably provides a sense of solidity, structure, and safety, as well as identity. Discoveries on the subatomic level forced physicists to conceive of new formulations of how entities interact. The fundamental recognition is that *relationships* are far more essential than we imagine; to many quantum physicists, relationships are *all* there is to reality. What is more important than analyzing individual particles is observing general patterns of behavior and interactions. We need to apply this same insight to organizations: No one exists independent of their relationships with others. Rather than being preoccupied with accumulating facts, we ought to focus on issues of effectiveness of organizational realities. In a similar vein, we should stop emphasizing tasks and instead encourage process. *Look beyond fragments to the whole, and by working with what you know, attempt to nurture relationships throughout organizations.*

INVISIBLE FIELDS THAT SHAPE BEHAVIOR

One way that the new science has conceptualized the centrality of relationships has been through the emphasis on *fields*: invisible, nonmaterial connections that form the basic structure of the universe. Whereas previous models of space emphasized the emptiness in the distance between objects—from the cosmic to the microscopic level—current thought attempts to demonstrate the ways these fields influence events. Perhaps the most familiar example of a field is the magnetic field, whose effects can be observed in the patterns iron filings will make on a magnet. Fields are nonmaterial, yet they are considered real. In a world of fields, potentials for action exist in all places. We are already familiar with this type of relationship when we speak of "quality" or "vision" within an organization: something we cannot see, something we cannot even pinpoint from whence it originates, but something whose effects we can observe everywhere. We should think of organizational vision as a field that needs to permeate our group, rather than a linear command from on high. Such a field must reach all parts of the organization, and involve everyone. *Fields develop when all of us are filling space with the messages that are important to us.* Perhaps the most human field is the need for meaning itself; even without knowing the specific outlines of an event, we still seek the meaning inherent within. A leader who can spread the sense of organizational meaning to all those who participate is a leader who will be cherished. In fact, the best field a leader can create is one that gives people the capacity for self-reflection and self-reference.

OBSERVATION AND PARTICIPATION

The universe has a participative quality to it that often appears quite enigmatic, even mystical. An instance of this is the fact that electrons behave in different ways depending on the way they are observed. When they are observed as if they were particles, they behave as particles; when observed as if they were waves, they behave as waves. Which aspect of the electron comes forth is largely determined by *what* is measured. It is perhaps too common to mention "self-fulling prophecies" or the notion that "people perform according to expectations," yet we need to be reminded of these truths. Likewise, we must recall that our observations are inherently limited, and limiting; as in physics, we tend to see what we expect to see. How can this be turned into a strength for organizations? One method is through broad dissemination of information: The more we can share the same observations, the more viewpoints and insights we will have in the end. In this manner, we avoid limiting our interpretation to a select group of people who, unknowingly, too narrowly filter the information. Used in such a way, information can be a source of order (think about the form of the word itself: *in-formation*). Though it can be a disturbing proposition, *we should seek out more information that is ambiguous, difficult, and not even immediately valuable, and then proceed to share it with participants in our organization.* Members of the organization will, understandably, appreciate the sense of ownership created by being involved in decisions, by participating in considerations. This is yet another way to strengthen the field of relationships within organizations; those who will have to implement the decisions are involved in creating the decisions themselves. In such a process, a person's role cannot be described without acknowledging the network of relationships surrounding them.

SELF-ORGANIZING SYSTEMS

As noted previously in the discussion of entropy, disequilibrium can actually produce greater complexity within a system. One of the ways in which a system can successfully counter entropy is by continuously importing free energy (from the environment) and exporting entropy. There are often, in fact, feedback loops within systems that can create their own disequilibrium: a piece of information is repeatedly fed back into the system until it magnifies itself to such a degree that it necessitates change. The spiral pattern, which so often occurs in nature and art, may illustrate a fundamental experience of change that leads to (temporary) dissipation followed by further reordering. In such structures, resiliency is more useful than rigid stability. Contrary to what we would expect, openness to environmental information can, over time, spawn a firmer sense of identity. That is, an organization that reacts to information from outside of its structure will have to identify its essential qualities that provide coherence. As exchange follows between environment and system, the system may develop greater resilience to the demands of the environment. *Core competencies provide a system of self-reference that allow the organization to maintain autonomy while encountering external fluctuations,* just as self-organizing systems in nature continue to reproduce themselves. The organization is *autopoietee*—that is, self-organizing, or self-creating. The next time the environment demands a response, there is a strong reference point for how to engage the challenge.

CONCLUSION

If there is a self-evident conclusion to draw from all of these lessons, it should be the fact that they are related to each other. The movement toward participative organizations encourages greater distribution of information; such distribution can create feedback loops that amplify core qualities within organizations; such amplification produces a greater sense of organizational identity; yet this identity is nurtured in a context that offers a great deal of autonomy without rigid hierarchies; in turn, this autonomy strengthens the invisible fields of interconnectedness with which we desire to permeate our organizations; becoming aware of this interconnectedness leads us to offer greater participation; and so forth. Examples of emergent discoveries in science provide an excellent alternative to standard organizational models; in the end, *we must admit that chaos is a necessary stage within systems and trust that the self-reference of an organization can clarify inherent values*, which will continue to evolve and demonstrate order, however intangible it may feel.

READING 4

Stewardship

Peter Block
Summary prepared by Robert C. Ford

> **Robert C. Ford** *is a Professor and Associate Dean of the College of Business Administration at the University of Central Florida. Bob holds a Ph.D. in Management from Arizona State University. In addition to publishing texts in principles of management and organizational theory, he has authored, or co-authored, a number of articles on applied managerial practices, human resources management, and social responsibility in both applied and academic journals. He is an active member of the Academy of Management, serving as chairperson for the Management Education and Development Division, the Management History Division, and Placement. In addition, he has served as President of the Southern Management Association and is Chairperson of the Accreditation Commission for Programs in Hospitality Administration.*

We live in a world of change. Organizations, like people, are confronting the economic impact of those changes, and this has led to a major reassessment of how organizations are governed, led, and structured. The modern organization promises little and asks a lot of its members. Gone is the security and implied social contract of earlier days when an employee could expect that he or she would be rewarded with loyalty, job security, and an ever-increasing salary as the payment for organizational commitment, hard work, and enthusiastic support for the organizational mission and goals. The new social contract guarantees nothing as organizations are forced to quickly adapt to the changing forces in the market place and a new emphasis on customer responsiveness.

In this new environment, the dominant managerial style must change from the traditional concept of leadership to the new ideas of stewardship. Traditionally, leadership meant that managers are somehow responsible for their subordinates who look to the leader for guidance, direction, reward, evaluation, and protection. A manager and an organization committed to stewardship operate in a very different way. *Stewardship is predicated on the idea that people in communities and in organizations are willing to choose service over self-interest.* They are prepared to take responsibility for the larger community without needing to control it. *Stewardship* means empowering people to be accountable for their own actions rather than asking them to be dependent upon the managers. This is the essence of how a free and democratic people gov-

Peter Block, *Stewardship*. San Francisco, CA: Berrett-Koehler, 1993.

ern themselves and take stewardship for their own lives within that society. It is the antitheses of the managerial practices typically found in most organizations.

THE TRADITIONAL PILLARS OF MANAGEMENT

Choosing stewardship means renouncing three pillars of the traditional organization's managerial practices. These are control, consistency, and predictability. *Control* is achieved through the classic reliance on lines of authority. Top management makes all the important decisions, sets the overall organizational mission, defines its vision, and structures the reward system to encourage everyone to go along and punishes those who do not. People at lower levels are responsible for executing those decisions and implementing the vision. Organizations want *consistency* to ensure they have standardized ways of dealing with policies and people. The need for consistency leads to the creation of staff support people who develop training strategies to make sure everyone does what they do in the same way, oversee the consistent execution of policies and procedures, and audit the results. Organizations seek *predictability* to ensure that events are going to come out the way they want them to come out. Managers set goals and measure progress toward those goals. They do not like or want surprises and therefore design mechanisms to eliminate surprises.

These three pillars of traditional management practice lead to a patriarchal system where leaders are viewed as parents of the organization and the rest of the members are children looking for structure, guidance, direction, praise, and an appropriate allowance (salary) for performing what the leaders want. The problem with reliance on control, consistency, and predictability is that ownership and responsibility for solving the modern challenges of cost reduction, customer satisfaction, and employee commitment are vested in the patriarch and not in the members. If the organization needs a strong sense of ownership, commitment, and responsibility for customer satisfaction from the employees on the firing line, this traditional approach to managing will not work.

CREATING PARTNERSHIPS

Partnerships must be created between employees and top managers in the stewardship-based organization. Each partner has the responsibility for helping the larger community or organization succeed in the face of a dynamic and changing market place. In effect, both have a stewardship role to play whereby they individually take on the responsibility for the organization's success. Partnership changes the balance of power between the top managers and the core employees—those who actually meet the customers, make the product, and deliver the service.

A partnership has four requirements. The first is that *the parties have to define for themselves their own purpose within the organization.* Historically, the organization's top management defines the organizational purpose and sends it down the hierarchy to lower-level employees. A partnership requires dialogue between the partners to give every organizational level and unit the opportunity to define the purpose that makes sense for it. If the departments have no participation in the definition of that purpose then it becomes merely an echo of top management thinking and beliefs rather than providing the necessary ownership that each unit has to have. *Partnership means that everyone at every level is responsible for defining the vision and values for their unit.* Partnership is defined through dialogue, and everyone, including customers, suppliers, and other stakeholders, needs to be a part of the discussion.

The second requirement for a true partnership is *to give everyone the right to say no.* When organizations take away the right to say no, they take away the individual's sovereignty and sense of personal responsibility for the ultimate outcome of a decision. Although the leadership of every community and every organization has the ultimate authority to say yes or no, this should not detract from individuals' rights to say no for themselves. Like a voter in a democratic government, partnership doesn't mean you always get what you want, but it does mean that you never lose your voice in the ultimate outcome.

The third cornerstone of partnership is *joint accountability by the partners.* Each person has an individual responsibility for both the organizational outcomes and their own current situation. Managers are no longer responsible for the morale or career of their subordinates. Partners are not caretakers of each other. Partnership offers individual organizational members freedom but the price of that freedom is personal accountability for results. The fourth requirement for partnership is *absolute honesty* between the partners.

No organizational partnership can ever be a true fifty-fifty relationship. Organizations, like entire social communities, will always continue to have bosses and leaders. The partnership should be as close to this split in responsibility as possible to move toward a stewardship-based organization. Practicing stewardship and partnership is not inconsistent with being a boss. *Stewardship is the willingness to hold power without using reward, punishment, and direct command to get the necessary things done.* Instead, stewardship relies on empowered employees who can and do take the responsibility for themselves and their unit's success.

Stewardship is a difficult thing for most employees to accept. It requires them to choose adventure and freedom over safety and job security. Organizations, especially bureaucratic organizations, have traditionally been safe. Indeed, bureaucracy is patriarchy in the extreme because it provides the ultimate in caution, risk aversion, predictability, and exercising control over others. When employees join such organizations, they collude with the principles of the traditional managerial system and acknowledge the organization's right to control their behavior. Employees accept the dependency relationship as a condition of the job. In return for giving up their individual freedom, however, they then feel entitled to a sense of job safety and security. Empowering employees takes away this entitlement. If the organization gives its people freedom instead of security and safety, it must also have the right to require accountability for the use of that freedom. *Although empowerment means that every person has the right and responsibility to define for themselves what kind of organization they work in, it also creates an obligation for employees to commit themselves and become emotionally involved with the organization.* In effect, if the organization empowers its employees, it must also teach them that the only reliable leadership for monitoring costs, ensuring quality, and providing real service is themselves. Indeed, it is even a responsibility of the employees to teach those above them the concepts of empowerment, stewardship, and service.

DEVELOPING A GOVERNANCE STRATEGY FOR STEWARDSHIP

The concepts of empowerment, stewardship, and service require eliminating the traditional distinctions between managers and workers. Traditional managerial practices created a managerial class separate from those who do the work. Managers were responsible for planning the work and workers were responsible for doing it the way management planned. This leads to two major problems. First, it is expensive, and second, it creates an organizational class system that gets in the way of producing the service, quality, and flexibility the customers and the organization need in a volatile marketplace. If we need an employee who is able and willing to respond correctly to the customers' needs, make the product correctly the first time, and discover new efficiencies in production, then having a class-based organization where one group is responsible for planning, organizing, and controlling the work while the other is responsible only for producing the product or delivering the service is doomed to fail. Real stewardship requires a governance system and structure that completely integrates managing the work with doing the work. Six points capture this idea.

- The organization must affirm the spirit of stewardship. Everyone wants to do something that matters and is important and for which they have responsibility.
- The members of the organization, both core employees and top managers, must confront and successfully resolve the power struggle between a patriarchy form of organization and a partnership forum. Our collective organizational experiences and traditional managerial theory lead everyone to believe that control, consistency, and predictability are essential for organizational success. Partnership substitutes a balancing of power and accountability throughout the organization.
- Each person takes responsibility for creating the organization's culture, delivering outcomes to the customer, and ensuring the quality of their own organizational experience.
- The management of work and the doing of work must be integrated. Otherwise, there is a class system in the organization that leads to patriarchy.
- Organizations cannot legislate partnership, stewardship, and service. One can't order someone to care about their job, themselves, the customer, or the organization. Developing a sense of stewardship is a gradual reeducation process for both employees and management.
- Most existing organizational practices, policies, and procedures, are designed to reinforce and maintain the traditional concepts of control, predictability, and consistency. These must all be carefully reviewed, rethought, and redesigned if they are to lead to partnership instead of patriarchy.

Once the strategy has been set to move toward an organization driven by stewardship, partnership, and service, the next step is to understand the impact this will have on existing organizational governance and authority relationships. Stewardship creates a governance system that dramatically rearranges social and power relationships between the organizational leadership and the core employees. Such a governance system should rest on the following principles:

- Decision-making authority and responsibility must be maximized for those closest to the work. Core employees need to have the training, ability, and freedom to act for the customer.
- Everyone must do work that translates into value in the marketplace, and everyone should do some of the core work of the organization some of the time. No one should think of themselves as above the work done by those who are the primary deliverers of the organization's value to the customer. Even top managers should serve the customer now and then to reinforce the value of the core work of the organization as well as ensuring that they too stay close to the customer.
- Measurements should be developed by those who are going to be measured. The organization should eliminate any measures that have nothing to do with what the person being measured is responsible for.
- Consistency across the organization should be sacrificed in favor of developing local solutions to local problems. One organizational policy or procedure does not fit all organizational situations or departments. Those who know the local problems should develop the local answers.
- Service is the key to everyone's job. Whether this is service to a customer, service to a co-worker, or service to the entire organization, everyone is accountable and stewards to those they serve.
- Minimize staff management. Redefine the role of staff to be a service to the core employees rather than an extension of top management's effort to maintain control, consistency, and predictability. In essence, staff should be valued for what they add to the core employees' output. If the people directly responsible for producing the product or delivering the service do not want the product staff offers because it yields no value to them, or the core people can get the product better somewhere else, then they should be able to do so. This redefines the relationship between the traditional line and the staff support groups as staff must now prove its worth to the line or line will ignore them.
- End secrecy, and give truthful information to anyone who needs and wants it. This creates literacy in the business across the entire organization. Only when people have the necessary and accurate information they need to completely assess the impact of their decisions are they truly empowered.
- Demand commitment to the organization as a whole as the price for individual empowerment and freedom. If one is to be a free partner in an empowered organization, the price is making a commitment to delivering results.
- Redistribute the rewards across the organization. By eliminating the class system through this system of organizational governance, there should be a concomitant elimination of differentials in both the amount of organizational rewards and the reward system among the levels in the organization. The very high salaries of very senior executives in comparison with the core employees must be eliminated. Further, the evaluations system needs to be reworked to ensure that the same premises about employee loyalty, commitment, and individual effort are built into the evaluations for both top

management and core workers. Finally, the reward system must also recognize contributions to a group and collective effort. Individual rewards promote self-interest and work against partnership and stewardship.

THE STEWARDSHIP CONTRACT

This system of governance is implemented through the *stewardship contract*. This becomes the new social contract governing the relationships and behaviors of people inside the organization. Each unit creates a stewardship contract to define and limit what is to be controlled, the boundaries and limitations of the partnership, and the relationship between employees and the organizations. The contract has five key elements:

- The core mission of each organizational unit and its key customers.
- Financial accountability and the results expected. Every boss has the right to define the required outcomes, and the contract spells them out clearly in a way that holds people accountable without controlling them.
- A basic structure that fits the tasks and mission of the organization. It includes what the organization cannot permit as well as what it does allow.
- The basic governance strategy.
- What specifically needs to be done to make stewardship work.

The stewardship contract defines and details the ground rules for employees to participate in the new governance structure. It makes each employee responsible for the institution's well-being and asks them to be clear about their mission, know completely the customers they serve, and the product that they make or produce. Further, it clearly defines the results that are required, the constraints within which they must live, and the changes that will be made toward greater empowerment, partnership, and service. If people cannot commit to the contract, then the time to find out is at the start of creating the empowered organizations that are committed to stewardship.

TRADITIONAL VERSUS PARTNERSHIP ORGANIZATIONS

Organizations that practice stewardship are different from the traditional organizational focus on control, consistency, and predictability. They promote different values, beliefs, and managerial practices. Consequently, they are different in the way they are structured, the roles defined from their managers and their staff groups, and their reward system. Traditional organizations tend to be functional in structure. This makes it relatively easy to supervise people doing like jobs and to structure career paths for functionally trained and oriented people. Accountants can easily see accounting opportunities in a functionally structured organization. *The marketplace demands a customer-focused structure.* Successful organizations in today's highly competitive environment do not switch customers from one function to another until the customer's problem is solved or the service is provided. Further, these organizations are flattened to ensure that the organization is more flexibly responsive to the needs of a rapidly changing marketplace. These two trends put new challenges on core employees who must know more about the product to respond to a broad range of customer needs and about the organization in order to identify how these needs can be best served. Employees must be empowered to respond with service.

Bosses also need to change the way they manage. As the employee at the core level takes on new responsibilities, the boss becomes more of a banker and broker and less of a traditional leader. As a banker, the boss is responsible for securing funds for the unit, communicating the results of the unit to others throughout the organization, and ascertaining the financial requirements that will assure the continuing effective operation of the unit. As a broker, the boss maintains liaisons with other parts of the organization that have services the unit needs or require the services of the unit the boss manages. The boss adds value to the unit by ensuring that the unit has the resources it needs from others, communicates the output value to other parts of the organization, and seeks to ensure the continuing availability of resources the unit needs to continue its role. Beyond that, it is the unit membership's responsibility to articulate the purpose and mission, define the measures of performance, and ensure that the primary product or service that unit produces meets the market test. This is a very different role for the traditional manager because the supervisory roles of training, teaching, and overseeing are now placed in new organizational locations.

The role of staff also changes in the organization that seeks to empower its employees by adopting the concepts of stewardship. The individual operating unit now has the right to use or not use the services that staff offers. If staff cannot defend the value these services add, then the core employees can choose not to use them. This means that staff now has the same market test applied to them that production units have always had. This changes the alignment of staff from being a service to top management to being a service for the core employees. As long as top management was the primary client for staff, they rightfully defined their role as policing, auditing, and acting as the corporate conscience. *The stewardship alternative requires staff to operate as authentic service units.* They must add capability to the core units or they will cease to have function. If the core does not want or need the training programs, expert advice, or other staff policing, inspection, and caretaking type functions that they have traditionally provided in organizations, then the core units can choose not to pay for them. Staff soon learn by their ability to gain billings from the operating departments who and what adds value.

The stewardship-based organization stresses self-control as a substitute for bosses and staff oversight. This means that the financial practices have to change to support this idea. Presenting its financial data in a format that promotes self-management, self-auditing, and self-control. This also means that the traditional human resource management practices have to be rethought in order to promote the organization's commitment to partnership, service, and stewardship. Most traditional human resource policies and practices reinforce the traditional patriarchal system of management in how it hires, fires, pays, promotes, and trains employees. Human resources, like financial reporting staff and other staff support operations, should redefine who its customers are.

Finally, the compensation system needs to be redesigned in order to eliminate the class systems now in place in most organizations. Traditional compensation systems are predicated on the idea that organizations can buy the individual behavior they require, and they communicate the message that the customer for employees is the boss and not the marketplace. The stewardship-based organization seeks to use performance criteria that are linked to the market results of the unit, shares the wealth more equitably across the organization, and ends secrecy about who got what and why. The evaluation of all employees is predicated on trust and self-control and not on the basis that only core employees have to add value while the overhead is a naturally occurring outcome and efficient organizational cost. Thus, *partnership organizations design pay systems that value interdependence, teamwork, and success in the creation of products, customer satisfaction, and other factors that really matter.* There is a price for this new type of organizational governance. The old pay and performance systems disappear. The old promise that employee pay should keep up with inflation, that employees are not responsible for the bad results of the organization, and that rank does not necessarily have its pay and privileges are all at risk in this new organizational orientation.

Stewardship has to be accepted on faith as a governing principle for organizational membership. There is little proof, no handy "how-to" books on implementation, and no guarantee that it will succeed at all levels and in all organizations. Yet, the logic of instituting a governance system inside the organization that is congruent with the larger society's democratic principles and practices and that has proven to be a successful way to govern social relationships is compelling. Just as Eastern European countries have concluded that autocratic and patriarchal regimes are ineffective and inappropriate for managing the affairs of entire economic systems, so, too, are the traditional organizational practices that rely on control, consistency, and predictability inappropriate for managing the modern organization. It is inconsistent to have a patriarchal organization management system in a free society. The principle of stewardship, of being individually responsible for the greater community and for ourselves within that community, is the underlying concept that makes democracy work.

PART TEN
Managing Diversity

Awide range of biases (such as racism and sexism) are still entrenched in our society and—too frequently—exhibited in its organizations. Despite powerful federal and state laws and potent corporate policy statements, both public and private organizations still have a limited number of female upper-level managers. The discrimination is not limited just to women. There are a number of different groups within our society who find themselves singled out and subjected to discriminatory treatment.

Several interesting books and reports have been written on the changing demographics in the United States and the implications for businesses and organizations. The popular press reminds us almost daily that diversity in the workplace will become increasingly common as we manage in the twenty-first century. As a consequence of these dramatic demographic trends and the need for constructive response, Part Ten highlights the issues of gender diversity and its management in the workplace.

Pat Barrentine, in *When the Canary Stops Singing*, applies the miner's canary as a warning of danger to the world of work. She warns that the traditional practices have created a toxic environment for many women, and their dissatisfaction is a harbinger of danger to others and a call for action. This book, a collection of essays by fifteen authors, suggests that the use of feminine ways of relating to others (through the use of love, nurture, and compassion) can enrich the workplace for all employees. Managers are urged to get in touch with their feelings, truly listen to others, seek to establish spiritual havens for workers, and strive toward balance in their thinking and behaviors. Barrentine is the owner of an information packaging and communications company and former editor of *World Business Academy Perspectives*.

In *America's Competitive Secret*, Judy Rosener reminds readers that the glass ceiling still exists, preventing many capable women from rising to appropriate positions of responsibility in organizations. Breaking the glass ceiling is both a social and economic imperative, and only when this is done will companies achieve the overall success of which they are capable. Rosener points out that male and female managers are different, and female top managers often exhibit unique capacities to cope with ambiguity, share power with others, and empower subordinates.

Judy Rosener is a professor in the graduate school of management at the University of California, Irvine. She is the author of "Ways Women Lead" (*Harvard Business Review*) and co-author of *Workforce America: Managing Employee Diversity as a Vital Resource.*

When the Canary Stops Singing: Women's Perspectives on Transforming Business

Edited by Pat Barrentine
Summary prepared by Scott L. Newstrom

> **Scott L. Newstrom** *is a graduate of Grinnell College, Iowa, where he majored in English. He has done research at the Newberry Library in Chicago, and at Oxford University, and was a recipient of a 1993 National Endowment for the Humanities Grant. He is currently pursuing a doctoral degree at Harvard University.*

Early coal miners would guard against potential air poisoning by keeping canaries in the mining shafts with them, because these birds are more sensitive to changes in air quality than people are. Acting as a natural indicator of toxic gases, the canary would warn the miners of impending danger by stopping its singing. Analogously, *many women are currently leaving high levels of corporations to work elsewhere because of the similarly "toxic," stifling, and oppressive business environments they encounter.* Their dissatisfaction with existing corporate structures can serve as a warning to others that corporate structures must be transformed in multiple ways. In particular, feminine notions of *relating to others and the world can enrich and renew American businesses today.* As a consequence, it is desirable to explore the various responses women have and the different values they bring to business today, both of which can lead to constructive change.

The word *feminine* does not imply qualities or emotions that are unique to women, although they may be more prevalent in women than in men. Rather, *feminine* is applied as psychoanalyst Carl Jung defined the term, emphasizing the characteristics of compassion, loving, and nurturing, which can be found in men as well as women. Thus the application of feminine ideas and methods to the workplace does not exclude businessmen. Both men and women can benefit from business environments that encourage and utilize both feminine and masculine qualities. However, masculine structures have been present for so long that an integration and evaluation of feminine structures is necessary and will produce a positive impact upon business.

Pat Barrentine, *When the Canary Stops Singing.* San Francisco, CA: Berrett-Koehler, 1993.

Today's world is marked by accelerating change, and, therefore, the older ways of doing business can become dysfunctional as time progresses. But organizational renewal through a transformation in business practices can produce valuable results. As business becomes an increasingly powerful and prevalent institution throughout the world, it also needs to take responsibility beyond its traditional economic concerns. Business should be a provider of moral and ethical support at work as well as a major catalyst for change in the world. In addition to simply providing employment, business needs to look at how it affects individuals, communities, entire cultures, and nations. This transition will be difficult yet necessary if we are to triumph over the problems facing business and the world today. By valuing integrity rather than simply money, *business can begin to adopt a new tradition of taking responsibility for the whole of the world and its people.*

ALTERNATIVE MODELS

If women are harbingers of a toxic environment that calls for change in business, what kinds of change do they recommend? One major change involves examining existing organizational hierarchies. While hierarchies provide a structural solidity for organizing business, they also can become ineffective as a result of their slow rate of change. Hierarchical business architecture is rooted in a *dominator* model of social organization. Like a hierarchy, the dominator model has a vertical structure in which power means power over people. While a dominator model is not uniquely masculine, historically it emerges as a male's power to control others. Dominator models, in old societies, functioned through fear that was backed by force. A system of vertical ranking can lead to domination and conquest. The modern, hierarchical workplace is based on a ranking, vertical system like a dominator model.

In contrast to a dominator model, a *partnership* model is decidedly nonhierarchical. This model of social organization is more supportive and productive than a dominator model. Our economy, as well as our society, would benefit from redesigning the workplace to be more similar to a partnership model. By compartmentalizing responsibilities and capabilities in a narrowly defined, pyramid-like organizational structure, hierarchies encourage workers to ignore the larger problems of a business and instead focus on their specified assignment. By limiting the scope of their job, hierarchies discourage creativity. Since partnership models encourage thinking about the business as a whole and communicating with others, creativity finds a nurturing environment. A diagram of a partnership model of business would look more like a flat circle than a pyramid. Because of the lack of ranking in this newer model, workers relate to each other as equals rather than as subordinates to superiors.

Another diagram of a partnership model could look like a web of relationships, as opposed to a generally more linear hierarchy. It is appropriate that such a model should be espoused by women, since the theory of female moral development articulated in Carol Gilligan's *In a Different Voice* asserts that women tend to focus on their responsibilities within existing webs of relationships. People can learn the values of interdependence from women business leaders who utilize these kinds of organizational webs in structuring their corporations. While converting from a hierarchical business structure to a web or circle structure may involve extensive transformations in the way people think about business, a more difficult transformation is involved in the creation of *community*. As employees work through changes in the workplace environment, a sense of community as true partnership can significantly reduce the fear and confusion surrounding these changes.

STAGES IN COMMUNITY DEVELOPMENT

Sometimes managers may believe that their business has aspects of a community, when in reality this is simply a *pseudo-community* that projects the surface elements yet lacks the content of true communal spirit. When superficial kindness and respect disintegrate and reveal the hollowness of the pseudo-community, organizations often find themselves in a *chaos* mode, where individual differences prevail. Crisis management takes place here, for without such management little would be accomplished. Many organizations seem to be permanently lodged in this mode, never reaching the important *emptying* stage, in which individuals develop a critical self-awareness. This differs from the chaos mode in that rather than simply being aware of diversity and differences in others, workers recognize their own weaknesses and strengths. The final stage is a true *community* mode, in which people feel comfortable about straightforwardly expressing their ideas on both an interpersonal and group level.

Before community acquires form and structure, it first requires an attitude or feeling. While business tends to ignore this, *getting and staying in touch with feelings is crucial for all human development*. Drives toward consciousness and love are essential, which is why some employees become frustrated at work when they lack a deep, communal, loving connection with colleagues. When employees can feel communal love at work (not in a sexual or amorous way but in a caring, supportive sense) they can achieve more. Because of the connections they create and feel with others, they also become conscious of the responsibilities of business leadership that extend beyond the office into the world. Community, love, and consciousness all have roots in a social organizational model of partnership rather than in domination. Partnership emphasizes collaboration rather than cooperation, and affirms the value of differences rather than enforcing conformity and similarity.

THE ORGANIC METAPHOR

Another model that helps to portray interdependence of life and business is an organic metaphor. For example, when conducting a job search, a person can help their own search by creating a tree-like chart that connects everyone they know. Main branches indicate groups of people (such as friends, colleagues, family), and smaller branches and leaves become more specific as they decrease in size. By charting their acquaintances this way, they can graphically recognize the numerous sources they have for job information and opportunities. Such a "tree" also reminds them of the way relationships grow from one another, rather than sprouting completely independently.

An organic metaphor can apply to businesses as well, for an organization can be viewed as a garden and management as similar to gardening. Life in organizations requires planting of ideas and values, attention, and sensitive nurturing, similar to how gardeners care for a garden. Weeding out destructive forces from organizations is also necessary in order to allow favored concepts and people to flourish. As a final parallel, organizations eventually enjoy the fruits of their harvest, whether through new products, increased employee productivity, improved workplace morale, or anything that they have taken the time to plant and nurture. This reflects the biblical invocation "As you sow, so shall you reap." Like gardens, organizations that lack carefully planned nurturing can become dysfunctional and sterile. A gardener/manager must also confront the lack of resources and support and the differences that always exist between an ideal plan and the reality of the workplace situation. *Organizational gardening* can be another organic metaphor for a business paradigm.

WHOLE-PERSON DEVELOPMENT

Gardening teaches that there is a direct relationship between the amount of attention given to a plant and the success of the plant's development. This is analogous to how people flourish in organizations. Business needs to recognize that its employees can only reach their greatest potential through whole-person development. Among other things, this means being able to feel love in their work and appreciate community as discussed previously. Developing a person also includes an awareness that people are all part of a larger whole (i.e., they live in an interconnected world). Love, community, and wholeness all can find expression through creativity in the workplace. One way to overcome the apathy and self-doubt that often pervade the workplace is through generating the passion that is the primary source of employee creativity. This personal passion stems from the ability to value uniqueness in oneself as well as in others, and to accept the creative tension that arises from the mixture of one's masculine and feminine qualities. Too often the workplace unconsciously stifles creativity, but organizations need to learn that every worker has huge creative potential that can benefit both the individual and the community. Individuals must also remember that the greatest creativity is inspired by limitations, which encourage creative methods and ideas to surpass these limitations. Finally, creativity grows when personal concerns can be integrated in the workplace, rather than being ignored or even repressed.

Developing a whole person also requires developing vision, both in the individual and in the corporation. By creating new visionary realities people can begin to achieve new possibilities. Too often workers accept their surroundings as they are rather than imagine and work toward what they can be. Tolerating one's own unhappiness unfortunately can lead to a forced resignation rather than inspiring work toward change. The vision that is needed to overcome problematic circumstances is in many senses a spiritual vision. Increasingly, people are looking for greater fulfillment through their work by uniting the spiritual and logical aspects of their lives. This is important, because spiritual poverty at the workplace can leave employees as diminished as physical poverty does. When employees lack spiritual authenticity at work, they may experience grief and even despair. This can drain employees of energy that could be exerted on more valuable projects. Sometimes such a spiritual emergency may require temporary relief, such as having an outside consultant come in and examine what ails the business. In order to build community, people at this stage may need to go through the process of self-reflection involved in emptying so that community can be formed with spirituality.

Spiritual crises could be averted if organizations were to set up *spiritual havens* for employees. As people feel the need to develop themselves wholly and fully, business could provide a program of support and education for them during periods of transition. Although programs would vary from business to business, all should include flexibility, solitude, safety, and simplicity. This may mean providing leaves of absence for those who need time for spiritual development, or discussion groups that could provide a dialogue for those who desire to share their experiences. People seek meaning and purpose at work, and providing spiritual havens could encourage employees when they need to turn inward. Because spiritual support is usually absent in today's workplace, a radical shift in values would be required.

Getting in touch with your spiritual side could also include the practical aspect of recognizing the importance of personal intuition. There are times when people need to make a choice based on something beyond their logical capabilities. Intuition gives them this type of insight for important decisions and is actually a skill that can be practiced and improved. One way to improve is through a process of relaxation and meditation called *grounding*. Basically, an individual must relax alone and visualize a grounding cord attached to the base of the spine, where one's intuition will be centered. By using this technique consistently and slowly, trained persons soon will be able to visualize such a grounding cord in stressful situations, which will allow them to check their intuition for the particular situation. If used properly, this relationship with the subconscious can become a useful tool for creative leadership. Proper use includes assessing and questioning the ethical dimensions of intuition, such as confirming that others will not be hurt by personal decisions, making sure that actions are not manipulating others for personal gain, and checking one's intuition against common sense.

Learning to use intuition means learning to listen to the subconscious. Employees also need to relearn to listen to their colleagues. Since every business must operate through communication, listening and understanding are critical to enabling communication. Yet too often co-workers engage in *automatic listening*, where they do not actually attempt to hear what someone has to say, but rather only affirm their own unexamined assumptions. Within seconds of beginning a conversation, some people react as they always do to a certain person or idea. Automatic listening acts as a filter, only allowing people to hear what they already believe. In a sense, during every conversation each party is "voting" whether they agree with the other's ideas or not. An organization that wishes to maximize its abilities must learn to recognize the automatic listening that is too often present in communication.

Managers need to acknowledge that all of these goals—listening, interdependence, intuition, and so on—can be better understood not as goals to be completed ("We now have community in our workplace") but rather as processes ("We are creating community"). Much like the garden that needs continued effort, contemplation, and nurturing, all of these goals are ongoing developments that require energy, thought, and time. Thinking of them as ongoing processes also encourages flexibility in planning; unexpected events do not prevent the goals from being met, they merely add to the development of the process in which the organization is engaging.

As organizations become involved in these progressing processes, they also need to be aware of the values that are created and perpetuated through business. The search for meaning and purpose finds its expression through these values. As business's influence becomes more pervasive in the global marketplace, managers need to scrutinize and transform traditional ways of thinking. The challenge is to support those values (e.g., ecological balance, social responsibility, economic transformation, political participation, global spirituality, and world peace without armed conflict) that will both promote business development as well as improve life—not just for those involved in the business but for people everywhere.

CONCLUSION

Essentially, what is most critical to emphasize is *the importance of balance*, from the local level (workplace) to the global level (world market). Like the strength that arises from the equal and complementary status of *yin* and *yang* in Chinese philosophy, individuals, businesses, and nations can all benefit from a balance in all aspects of life. Feminine traits have historically been overshadowed by masculine traits, and there is a need for a more balanced (yet dynamic) equilibrium. In particular, *managers should work toward balance between short- and long-term thinking, local and global perspectives, the individual and the community, action and contemplation, listening and speaking, rationality and spirituality*. Similarities and diversity need to coexist as well. It is time to listen to others, to listen to oneself, and to challenge the imbalances existing today.

READING 2

America's Competitive Secret

Utilizing Women as a Management Strategy

Judy B. Rosener
Summary prepared by Kristina A. Bourne

Kristina A. Bourne *is currently pursuing an MBA and a Women's Studies Certificate at the University of Massachusetts in Amherst. She received a Bachelor of Business Administration degree with a concentration in marketing and a Bachelor of Arts with a concentration in French and economics from the University of Minnesota, Duluth. Originally from Fargo, North Dakota, she traveled to more than 20 countries while living in France and Germany.*

In an increasingly turbulent global market, America's competitive secret lies in leveraging the leadership skills and abilities of professional women, leading to more innovative, productive, and profitable organizations. Women represent an untapped economic resource with their unique management style. *American organizations must see the link between capitalizing on the underutilized talents of women and improving their bottom-line results.*

THE ONE-BEST-MODEL

Traditionally, in a rapidly changing environment, organizations try to satisfy their longing for certainty with the *one-best-model* mindset, meaning they reward the command-and-control leadership style. The command-and-control leadership style stresses hierarchical lines of authority, the amassing of power and information, a win-lose decision process, and the value of sameness. Organizations try to find a quick fix to complex problems and so they buy into the latest restructuring trend or management theory, believing that there is one best way to operate. Conversely, women tend to use an interactive leadership style, which emphasizes consensus building, comfort with ambiguity, and the sharing of power and information. These are attributes that work best in fast-changing, service-oriented, and entrepreneurial organizations.

Judy B. Rosener, *America's Competitive Secret: Utilizing Women as a Management Strategy*. New York, NY: Oxford University Press, 1995.

✳ *Women have not been seen as potential leaders because their style of leadership differs from the one-best-model (male) command-and-control style.*

Difference as Deficiency

The one-best-model mentality sees difference as deficiency, deviance, or dysfunction. Therefore, if the best standard of quality is male, then being female means being less than that. The one-best-model mindset exhibits itself when reference is made about the "woman doctor" or their "black accountant." Such phrases assume that all professionals are white and male. Women feel the subtle marginalization on both personal and organizational levels.

Devaluation on a Personal Level   The experience of being devalued on a personal level takes many forms. As a woman gets dressed for work she has to make complicated choices that a man does not. If her skirt is short, she may be viewed as unprofessional. If her blouse has a v-neck, she may be accused of being sexy. If her suit is tailored, she may be seen as too masculine for a female.

Devaluation on an Organizational Level   The difference-as-deficiency mindset is deep-seated in organizational policies and practices such as titles and promotions, task assignments, and reward systems. For example, in most large organizations, women rarely make it to vice president, and those few that do are usually in staff rather than line positions, lacking substantial budgetary and decision-making authority. Furthermore, the woman who does make it to a high-level executive position may find herself the only woman in a sea of men, frequently seen as the "token" female executive. Her behavior and performance is easily scrutinized, and as the token woman she is asked to represent all women.

THE UNDERUTILIZATION OF WOMEN

Underutilization is defined as the organization's failure to use their female employees' existing or potential skills and talents primarily because they are women. Quantitative measures can be used to analyze this occurrence, such as unemployment and underemployment rates (part-time work or work in a field outside one's specialty), underrepresentation percentages, occupational segregation figures (the unequal distribution of men and women across occupations), and the relative pay of men and women. Examples include the following:

- *Unemployment:* In the sales industry 8.2 percent of women are unemployed versus 4.8 percent of men.
- *Underemployment:* In 1992, 17.5 percent of all workers were part-time; of that 17.5 percent, women represented 66 percent.
- *Underrepresentation:* In 1994, only 6.2 percent of the seats on boards of directors for *Fortune* 500 and Service 500 companies were women.
- *Occupational segregation:* Female-dominated occupations are nursing, education, social work, secretarial work; male-dominated occupations are engineering, medicine, and forestry.
- *Pay inequity:* For example, female lawyers earn 75 cents for every dollar their male counterparts make.

SEXUAL STATIC

Gender differences give rise to a phenomenon called *sexual static*, which causes interference with messages being communicated between men and women. The sources of sexual static, aside from office romance and sexual harassment, are role confusion, garbled communication, and culture clash.

Role Confusion   The socialization of boys and girls begins at birth. In an experiment in which nurses were handed male newborns wrapped in pink blankets and female newborns wrapped in blue blankets, they were more careful with the boys, who were assumed to be girls. The expectations of boys and girls is prevalent in everyday experience. Nurses are women, doctors are men. Flight attendants are women, pilots are men. Teachers are women, principals are men. It makes sense that as men and women enter the workforce they experience *sex role spill-over*, in which men are expected to take control and women are expected to provide support.

Garbled Communication   Men's and women's styles of communication differ. Men tend to talk about what they *do*, showing status and independence, and women tend to talk about how they *feel*, creating relationships and interaction. Men express themselves in few words, whereas women tend to think while they speak. Men are more apt to speak declaratively, as in "I want the report by Friday"; whereas women are more likely to speak in open-ended sentences, as in "Will the report be done by Friday?" Because of these differences, men and women get frustrated and confused trying to communicate with each other.

Culture Clash   Women and men often develop different cultural characteristics (different systems of shared meaning). For example, many women read romances, whereas many men read westerns.

These three factors cause sexual static because they challenge male values and behaviors, the dominant group of the one-best-model. In order for the dominant group to be more inclusive, men from above, not women from below, must remove the *glass ceiling* (the invisible barrier women face when moving up the corporate ladder). If a pane of glass is hit from below, those under it will get cut and bloody. When sexual static is minimized, men will feel more comfortable working with women.

HOW MEN FEEL WORKING WITH WOMEN

If sexual static is to be reduced, it is important to understand how men feel about working with women, because it is men who have the power to bring about change. In a telephone survey, executive men were asked about their working relationships with women (e.g., supervising, collaborating with, competing with, working for). Their responses included three major issues: loss of power and control, loss of male identity and self-esteem, and discomfort from sexual static.

HOW WOMEN REACT TO DISCRIMINATION

Women generally react to gender discrimination in their work environment in the following ways:

1. *Denial*: "Token" women may deny that gender bias exists because they fear diminishing their status, or they may truly have never experienced discrimination.
2. *Collusion*: Women may fear being ostracized, so they tend to cooperate with the system as a survival strategy.
3. *Acceptance*: Some women accept a slower advancement rate, conforming to the male belief that women cannot compete equally with men because they cannot balance careers and family.
4. *Challenge*: Women who have a continual headache from bumping their heads so many times on the glass ceiling will challenge the status quo by questioning organizational policies and practices, meeting informally with other women to provide support, developing a formal group to discuss issues, and joining statewide and national professional organizations that address gender issues.
5. *Flight*: Other women, whose challenges are not recognized or listened to, may move to smaller, more inclusive organizations or decide to start a business of their own.
6. *Legal action*: Women also take gender bias issues to court, as did Ann Hopkins of Price Waterhouse, a large public accounting firm, when she was passed over for promotion because she was thought to be "too aggressive," a reason rarely used against men.

CHANGING ORGANIZATIONS

Executives have noticed a higher turnover and absenteeism rate for women than for men and difficulty in recruiting and retaining women, but they see these gender issues as a human resource issue. *To fully utilize the talents of women, organizations need to think about female underutilization as a bottom-line rather than social equity issue and as an overall organizational change opportunity rather than only a human resource issue.* When women are valued they will likely have higher morale and higher productivity.

Organizations will go through the following cycle of change as they move to fully utilizing women:

1. *Assessing needs* by finding out how employees feel about their work environment through surveys, executive interviews and focus groups and using these assessments as feedback to executives, leading to forums and dialogue sessions where topics freely emerge from the discussions.
2. *Increasing gender awareness* through in-depth analysis of biases and stereotypes through role playing, videos, case studies, and skill development.
3. *Developing strategies* by overhauling policies and practices requiring an organizational commitment to developing a change strategy and management accountability, as well as support groups, task forces, and networks.
4. *Measuring and monitoring progress* by looking at pre- and post-intervention recruitment, turnover, and absenteeism, along with estimating the costs and benefits of change efforts.

WHAT IT ALL MEANS

The differences women bring to the workplace with their interactive leadership style are particularly effective in today's organizations, yet women's talents remain undervalued and underutilized. The organizations that leverage women's leadership abilities will likely see the added value in their bottom line.

PART ELEVEN

Organizational Change and Renewal

Aphilosopher once noted that a person never steps into the same river twice, for the flowing current is always changing. Contemporary organizations have their own "river"—a turbulent environment around them. Consequently, managers of today's organizations are being called on to integrate their operations with a rapidly changing external environment. To do this, they must often adapt their organization's internal structure, processes, and strategies to meet these environmental challenges. The ability to manage change is far different from the ability to manage and cope with the ongoing and routine side of the organization.

Experts frequently advise American managers to invest in research and development (R & D) to keep their product mix current. Some companies (e.g., 3M Corporation) derive as much as 25 percent of their revenues from products introduced in the past five years. Nevertheless, many critics charge that one of the reasons for the decline in the competitiveness of U.S. industry revolves around its failure to innovate at sufficiently high levels. Clearly, organizations need to manage change, stimulate renewal, and seek to convert themselves into continuously learning organizations.

Tom Peters is a prolific author, dynamic speaker, and highly sought consultant. He has written or coauthored *In Search of Excellence, A Passion for Excellence, Thriving on Chaos, Liberation Management*, and *The Pursuit of WOW!* A man who thrives on being provocative, Peters suggests that not just change, but a total transformation of business is underway, marked by revolution, disorganization, entrepreneurizing of jobs, independent mindsets, virtual organizations, leveraging of knowledge, the encouragement of curiosity, and competitive improvements on a firm's existing products. He bravely urges firms to be willing to abandon everything they are now doing and to reinvent themselves.

Albert Dunlap achieved fame (at least widespread notoriety) in the past decade by his spectacular success in revitalizing Scott Paper. Through his unrelenting "slash and burn" efforts to restructure and pare the organization down to its bare essentials, the stock price soared and shareholders rejoiced.

Critics were many, and labeled him a "Rambo in pinstripes" and "Chainsaw Al." He later became chief executive officer at Sunbeam corporation, where his tactics failed to produce lasting gains and he left the organization soon thereafter. Dunlap tells his rationale for his focus on cost cutting in *Mean Business*.

Dave Ulrich is a professor and co-director of the Human Resource Executive Education program at the School of Business, University of Michigan. He has been honored by *Business Week* as the top educator in human resources (HR), he consults with dozens of very large firms, and has also authored *The Boundaryless Organization, Organizational Capability*, and *Delivering Results*.

Ulrich issues a challenge to HR professionals: They must shift their focus from a process orientation (what they do) to a results orientation (what they deliver) if they are to help organizations face challenges such as profit pressures, technology, globalization, and change. He urges HR professionals to make a transition to becoming strategic partners, employee champions, administrative experts, and change agents. By doing so, he argues, they can help create organizations that change, learn, and act faster than their competitors.

READING 1

The Tom Peters Seminar

Tom Peters
Summary prepared by Jane Giacobbe-Miller

Jane Giacobbe-Miller is an Associate Professor of Management at the University of Massachusetts at Amherst. She received a doctorate from Cornell University. She conducts research in team-based management, labor mobility, and organizational justice. She teaches in the fields of human resource management, labor relations, and employment law. She has also consulted for organizations regarding the implementation of teams, empowerment programs, and Total Quality Management initiatives.

The rapidly changing world and its associated challenges to the ways in which business is conducted should cause all managers to reexamine their previously held beliefs about management. Preservation of the U.S. position in the world economy will come from innovation and the creation/dissemination of knowledge. The emergence of Third-World countries as ready sources of low-paid labor will continue to erode the manufacturing base in the United States. Organizational assets will no longer be valued primarily (if at all) on equipment, machinery, or facilities. Increasingly, "human imagination" will become the primary organizational asset.

"Beyond empowerment," "beyond TQM," "beyond continuous improvement"—the future look and feel of organizations is well "beyond" the button-down corporate world as we know it. The concept of corporations with headquarters, with an established and permanent workforce, with hierarchical structures and systems to support them are revolutionized in the new, innovative, knowledge-based economy. The organizational transformation is well underway, and it is marked by nine major phenomena.

1. NOT CHANGE ... REVOLUTION

In order to prepare for the knowledge-based economy, managers must be prepared to *abandon everything*. Change, continuous improvement, and incremental steps toward implementation of a strategic plan need to be scrapped. Today's emerging economy requires unbounded thinking and quick reactions to customer needs. We are in a period of rapid acceleration, pedal to the metal. The organization that stays in the slow

Tom Peters, *The Tom Peters Seminar*. New York, NY: Random House, 1994.

lane will be run down by the competition. The U.S. organization that thrives, or even survives, will do so by selling its knowledge, its creativity, its magic. Physical products will be of declining importance, particularly if their production is routine, requiring little skill. How does the manager begin the dismantling of the old organization? It begins with . . .

2. DISORGANIZATION

The old, formal, bureaucratic organization has got to go. Up the chain of command, down the chain of command. How many ideas get buried, lost, diluted, or become obsolete by the time they clear all of the hurdles? The new, rapid-response organization has few, if any, layers. Small-scale units, even within large enterprises, are called for in the new, knowledge- and innovation-based economy. Modeled after the "Mom and Pop" corner store, these small-scale units are close to the customer and close to the edge. Their survival is dependent on the goodwill of a handful of customers. Their relationships with their customers are close, intimate, seamless as they work together at all stages of product development and delivery. *Beyond decentralization, what is called for is a new federalism where power is vested in the periphery and shared only sparingly with the center.* The concerns of the center are to support the periphery with information and paperwork.

Titeflex, a company in Springfield, Massachusetts, embodies the new concept of small companies within larger ones. Business-development teams were created out of a larger workforce of 500 employees. Beyond contemporary notions of empowerment, these teams deal directly with customers, generate sales, and engage in capital spending. Without bureaucracies and layers, the teams can respond creatively, and quickly, to the needs of their customers. All of this requires nerves of steel, as managers abandon strategies and relinquish control to the small business unit. Beyond business-development teams, organizations should empower employees more deeply and more meaningfully than ever before.

3. ENTREPRENEURIZING EVERY JOB

How can average employees tap the limits of their imagination when they are told to think no further than their job description? Most employees can do far more than they are currently trusted to do. In their private lives they make mortgage decisions worth hundreds of thousands of dollars. Employees make decisions about cars, insurance, major household purchases and often even run businesses on the side! Yet they are frequently not trusted to make financial decisions at work or even to exercise sound judgments about what they need to make their jobs more efficient or effective. *Employees should be given complete ownership over their jobs.* Employees acquire ownership by having (a) complete knowledge obtained through cross-training in all relevant skills; (b) personal budgets to be expended as they deem necessary to better serve the customer; (c) mechanisms and processes for quality assurance; (d) access to internal and external expertise; (e) their own customers, to whom their service is limited only by their imagination; (f) an unlimited travel budget; and (g) the authority to make final decisions. Period. Beyond entrepreneurship, employees must have . . .

4. THE MINDSET OF AN INDEPENDENT CONTRACTOR

The emerging jobs of today, the good jobs of tomorrow, are lacking in definition. They defy description. They are the products of joint ventures between organizations and customers. The incumbents of these jobs must learn to live and flourish with ambiguity. The only performance appraisal will come in the form of endorsements from customers. Established processes and procedures will be abandoned, to be replaced by blank pages and blank checks, "whatever it takes," constrained only by law, ethics, and the imagination. Career paths within organizations will disappear. Job security comes from investing in oneself, building one's portfolio, increasing the investment in one's human capital. The casual approach to continued learning, attendance at the occasional seminar or two-day training sessions, will no longer be enough to ensure marketability. Introductory courses and passing familiarity will give way to true mastery of cutting-edge research. *Mastery of the ability to acquire knowledge, not just knowledge itself, will be paramount.* Navigating the informational highway at breakneck speed will be a prerequisite to success.

Employees' futures will be secured by their skills inventory, their personal resume, and their network of business contacts. Everything that is done today should be done not only for the business, but also for personal growth and development. Outcomes that can be displayed, identified by customers, and provide testimony to the unique abilities of the employee will replace the references of today. The résumé should tell a story of continuous personal improvement. Taking these steps now will prepare employees for the new, boundaryless organization.

5. ORGANIZATIONS CREATED BY ROLODEXES

Imagine an organization without a headquarters, where employees have laptop computers instead of desks. Imagine a continuous cycle of creating loosely woven organizations in response to specific customer needs and then disassembling them when the job is complete. The temporary "organization" encompasses a collection of the best talent for the particular project, who may never be reassembled in precisely this way again. Imagine projects that are not done vertically, from inception of an idea to completion of a product. Rather, projects are done horizontally, as specialists are called upon to tackle the problem from all perspectives, at all stages, simultaneously. Anything that can be done vertically can be done faster and cheaper horizontally, by a network of specialists. Pedal to the metal.

The new virtual organization will be without boundaries. It will be edgeless, with fluid forms and shifting configurations. The concept of employees will be replaced by independent contractors, who *sign on* for a project and then *move on* when the project is complete. Mutual trust will hold it all together.

But what do organizations do? What is the role of management? *The most important thing management can do in the new organization is to facilitate the acquisition and dissemination of knowledge.*

6. LEVERAGING OF KNOWLEDGE

The organization that learns to leverage knowledge will be most likely to survive, perhaps even thrive, in the new economy. Yet, leveraging knowledge requires organizations to persuade individuals to change old habits. The hierarchial organization rewarded those who possessed information. Information was power. Information was security. In order to leverage knowledge, the new organization must change the basis for power. *The most powerful person in the new organization will be the one who not only acquires knowledge, but shares it freely throughout the organization.* The recognition and reward structure must be changed to support the desired outcome. Those who hoard information will find themselves out of a job.

McKinsey & Co. may serve as an example of the possibilities. The company has established thirty "practice centers" that serve as storehouses of corporate knowledge in specialty areas. The goal is to use electronic network capabilities to share the collective knowledge of the organization with each consultant. Consultants may direct questions to any of the practice centers. Consultant-specialists provide rapid responses using state-of-the-art company practices. This allows general consultants or consultants from different specialties to draw on the best practices the company has in its repertoire. But how does one expand the repertoire of practices, the breadth of company knowledge? Besides encouraging employees to become entrepreneurs and independent contractors, their imaginations must be nurtured.

7. THE CURIOUS CORPORATION

Most companies today are dull, lethargic, stiff, barely breathing. To create a curious corporation, the organization should hire lively, curious people. These are people with gaps in their résumé who have done extraordinary, or extraordinarily weird, things. These unlikely applicants in today's corporate world will show a propensity to follow the road least traveled, if there is any sense of a road or direction at all. Once hired, the organization should foster their creativity. Have contests for the most unusual, the most wacky idea. Banish the idea that "looking busy" is important. Allow for people to explore the depths of their imaginations by letting them do what works for them, whether it's a dart game, working at night and sleeping in the day, or taking extended sabbaticals and vacations. Some of the most creative ideas happen when people are at leisure.

Encourage curiosity by teaching the art of brainstorming and problem solving. Allow employees to clutter their desks and their minds with uncontrolled thinking. Alter the physical environment so that everyone can be self-expressive. Allow for ample open space for sharing of ideas, information or simply building a comfort level so that idea sharing will come easily. Make the workplace comfortable, one that is conducive to dreaming.

Think beyond the one-dimensional measure of excellence. Rather than determining success by the profit margin, stockholder dividends, or customer satisfaction, measure success by the answer to the following question: *Would you want your son or daughter to work here?*

Unleashing creative energies, establishing loose networks of knowledge and information specialists, competition for the craziest idea—where is it all heading? Our nation's corporations have worked so hard to get control, to embrace the concept of continuous improvement, to record what we do so that our processes and outcomes are dependable. All of that was important in the past, but continuous improvement isn't enough. We have to move beyond TQM.

8. BEYOND TQM AND TGW TO TGR AND WOW!

After the quality coup of the 1980s, most U.S. products that survived can today pass the quality test. They have mastered the ability to detect and correct the TGW (things gone wrong). But quality is not enough to ensure a leading position in today's product markets. Flawless products are not a rarity, in domestic or global markets. In order to be a stand-out today, products must pass the "Wow!" test. They have to capture the imagination, rise above the mundane, dazzle the customer. They have to shift their focus to TGR (things gone right).

It all begins with the premise that anything, *anything*, can be made special. Take as an example the cab driver who, besides taking the most direct route and delivering the passenger safely, offers snacks, newspapers, and a choice of music. Then there's the example of the "counterfeit mailbag." In reality, it's an imitation, old-fashioned mail bag. But it's promoted as a national treasure, as the bag that carried the "ideas and feelings" of an entire nation.

Innovation and success brings with it the risk—no, the *promise*—that the product will be copied. Once innovation meets with success, continuous improvement to old ideas will not be enough. The competition will be focusing on ways to improve the idea, too. The companies who flourish in the new product markets will offer a continuous wave of new, vastly different products.

What are the sources of these new ideas? Some will come through collaboration with customers. But if a company listens only to its current customers it limits its own imagination to theirs. If the organization has done what was suggested earlier—hiring curious people and transforming employees into entrepreneurs—the successful organization will have to go beyond meeting its customer's needs in new and creative ways. It will also have to set its people free to *create* customer needs (invention is the mother of necessity).

Before you reach the conclusion that wild and wacky products and symbiotic relationships with the customer is enough, don't forget the importance of process. *Customers are influenced at least as much by the process as they are by the outcomes.* How they are sold a product or treated by the designer will be at least as important as their satisfaction with the product itself. Beyond the "Wow" will be the "Woo."

9. PERPETUAL REVOLUTION

The biggest handicap in today's corporation is conservative thinking, cautious behavior. Ironically, companies should be more afraid of doing nothing, or doing something insignificant, than of doing something that fails. Fear of failure creates paralysis, and paralysis will cause death in the new economy.

To break out of the mold of conservative, "small steps" thinking, *companies must abandon everything.* They must continuously and completely reinvent their products, their standards, their reward structures, and senior management behavior. There should be a continuous turnover of old ideas (an idea is "old" as soon as it reaches the market), or turnover of people if they can't break away from old-pattern thinking.

The new economy is not for the weak of heart. Forget courage. What's needed is well beyond courage. The new economy requires us all to throw caution to the wind.

READING 2

Mean Business: How I Save Bad Companies and Make Good Companies Great

Albert J. Dunlap
Summary prepared by Chris Edwardson

Chris Edwardson *is Program Manager for Forest Products at the University of Minnesota, Duluth's Natural Resources Research Institute, where since 1985, he has managed research and development activities. His team has assisted several hundred lake state companies in process and product development or improvement. He has a masters degree in Wood Science and Technology from the University of Maine and has an MBA from the University of Minnesota, Duluth.*

The verb "to Dunlap" means someone is focusing on what that person does best and eliminating what is not the best. The most basic goal of a business is "being the best." This can be achieved in any organization by following Dunlap's simple four-part "shock treatment" program: (1) get the right management; (2) pinch pennies; (3) improve the balance sheet by focusing the business; and (4) get a real strategy for success.

FOUR SIMPLE RULES

Rule 1: Get the Right Management Team

Companies cannot fix themselves totally from within; there are too many conflicts. Hard decisions that shake the business to its core will not be made by an executive who was part of the culture, but they can be made by managers who are driven to do what is right for the company regardless of the consequences. A new executive must have an inner circle, a mature team that knows the chief executive officer (CEO) and knows one another. This small inner circle forms the management or operating committee with each member playing an equal role in major decisions.

Albert Dunlap, *Mean Business: How I Save Bad Companies and Make Good Companies Great*. New York, NY: Simon and Schuster, 1996.

251

Dunlap's approach to leadership is a seven-point plan:

- *Develop an inner circle.* Build a team, once, of mature individuals who work and fight hard, who know how far to push each other and when to stop. If possible, bring in people who have been with you before and who respond to you, without being "Yes!" men or women. You want people who will challenge you and your ideas to stimulate you and the company. The individuals who are part of the inner circle make up the management or operating committee. Each member plays an equal role in major decisions, even outside their area of expertise.

- *Compress very difficult objectives in time, resources, and achievement.* With the right team in place, you are ready to make things happen. By compressing objectives in time, cutting back on resources, and demanding achievement and assuming your managers will meet or exceed these demands, you force them to always stay sharp. For example, Dunlap notes, at Scott Paper when they decided to do something, they would announce it, set a schedule, and paint themselves into a corner (as with completing Scott's restructuring in eight months). While many thought this would be impossible, the discipline imposed by the schedule forced the company to act.

- *Develop fast opinions about the competency of the managers and staff.* To move quickly in hiring and firing requires you to develop fast opinions about manager and staff competency. Dunlap tests people by asking the same question in different ways on different days, looking for conviction. A mistake of timid executives is to keep the people who created the problem. Existing managers will not change suddenly, and you cannot fix what you were hired for with those individuals.

- *Remember that business is simple; don't overintellectualize it.* I believe that business is simple and there are a few simple things that you have to do: (1) set major, attainable goals that make a difference; (2) hold those responsible for achieving the goals accountable; and (3) focus on a few major goals—don't set too many or you will fail through the diffusion of your effort. Managers and employees complicate business because, rather than solve problems, they put energy into the reasons why something cannot be done. Opportunity is missed if too much time is spent studying something.

- *Keep your staff small.* With a small staff, everyone is part of the team; they work together and are more accountable. Large staffs will pass responsibility to someone else and spend too much time in meetings on discussions, getting nothing accomplished.

- *Never rely on large meetings for important decisions.* Decisions, other than to have another meeting, rarely get made when a large group of people meets. By contrast, in companies Dunlap has run, his very small staff could always decide. A small group does not have the posturing and one-upmanship seen in larger groups.

- *Create opportunities to develop your people.* After "rightsizing" a business, there is great opportunity for the right people. Offer stock options deep into management, not only at the highest levels. Scott, for example, created 62 millionaires. Look for the good people buried within the bureaucracy, the good ones who can show you things that can be done.

Lesson: Magnify your own abilities by surrounding yourself with great people.

Rule 2: Pinch Pennies

Cost must be vigorously attacked. Corporate infrastructure must be sized according to need, not future potential. Find a way to quickly move to and maintain a good cost position through regular budget review, cost control analysis, and rebidding of materials, supplies, and services. Your success in cutting costs is measured not just by what you do, but by how you do it. Never cut hourly production workers until you have dealt with headquarter staff positions. At Scott, Dunlap reduced staff by 71 percent, managers by 50 percent, and the workforce by 20 percent. They also sold headquarters for $39 million and saved $6 million a year in costs.

Purchasing is an area that can be strategically used to save money, because everything that costs money is negotiable. More money can be made by buying right than can be made by selling right. Every one of Dunlap's purchasing departments has used these principles, which saved Scott $100 million:

- Leverage volume to the greatest extent possible.
- Narrow down the number of suppliers to a handful.
- Encourage more than one vendor to bid on requirements.
- Practice brinkmanship. Be sure vendors know that they do not have an exclusive option on your business.
- Challenge and support purchasing to reduce costs.
- Use the expertise and resources of vendors to help reduce costs.

A common denominator strategy can be a useful tool. This involves determining the minimum number of changes required to make everything reach the same specification. For example, using the same cardboard weight in all (similar) cartons reduces the number of different items that need to be purchased. Similarly, define the best practices in your industry and in your operations, and apply them across the board.

Outsourcing can be a powerful tool to cut costs. It allows you to be more focused on those things that deal with the success of the business. What you do in house should be those things that give you a competitive advantage. Payroll, for example, does not help you sell an additional product; therefore it is an ideal candidate for outsourcing. Other areas outsourced at Scott included most human resource work, management information services, pension administration, and parts of the shipping function. Finally, no temps are allowed; either a job needs doing with a full-time staffer or it does not.

The "Rule of 55" can be applied to eliminate the excess baggage that is not producing profits or adding value. Typically, 50 percent of a company's products produce only 5 percent of its revenues and profits; and 50 percent of a company's suppliers provide only 5 percent of the services and products the company buys. Eliminate whatever you can so you can focus on things that make money.

Executives should not spend shareholder money on luxuries for themselves. No houses, boats, multiple secretaries, or extravagant corporate jets should be authorized. Allowing these perks cheats the shareholder. Other perks that can go at most companies are cars (except for salespeople), subscriptions, trade associations, and charitable donations (individuals should give).

Use people outside of their defined function. Everyone on the team needs to contribute to the overall effort. For example, Dunlap expects the general counsel to have a broad overview of corporate issues, as well as interpret the law.

It is important to review old business and legal relationships to keep them from getting stale. You cannot be political and do this. Complacency costs the company.

Lesson: Cost is always your enemy.

Rule 3: Know What Business You're In

You should always be asking yourself two questions: "What business are we in?" and "What business should we be in?" Once this is defined, it is possible to determine what assets can be sold, with funds deployed into the correct part of the business. In general, conglomerates, companies with dissimilar businesses, do not work because they spread capital and management skills over too many businesses. With no focus on a single business, none of them do very well. Bigger is not necessarily better, and selling non–core assets will improve any balance sheet. Of course, executives and boards fear being criticized for becoming smaller. But it is better to have a great $3 billion company than a mediocre $7 billion company. Bigger is only better when you are growing in the same line of business.

Lesson: Focus like a laser.

Rule 4: Get a Real Strategy

Dunlap's first three rules are the building blocks of an overall strategy; Rule 4 is a strategy that tells the rest of the company your vision of the future and how to reach it. Focus on areas where you have a competitive advantage or plan to get one. A plan that capitalizes on your strengths will differentiate you from the competition. A strategy looks at short- and long-term results; your vision must be short- and long-sighted, because without short-term results you will never survive into the long-term. A detailed one-year plan is needed in the context of a longer term (three year) plan. Review action plans regularly to assess changes in conditions that necessitate changes in direction. It is easy for most companies to lay out a strategy, but they fail in implementation because they lack the discipline to follow through with the plan and make changes if it is not working. Corporate culture has a lot to do with failed implementation. You must allow people to make mistakes, because innovation implies risk. A manager who is right seven out of ten times is much more valuable than one who is right ten out of ten times. A degree of open debate is desirable, but at some point there must be a process for closure, for making the decision, and moving forward; that's where questioning ends and implementation begins.

Lesson: Envision the future and plan a route to it.

DUNLAPPING THE CORPORATION

Look Under "M" for Marketing

Marketing at Scott was virtually nonexistent. The company had forgotten that it was a consumer products company, not an industrial paper producer. Staff thought of everything in tons, no one knew Scott's margin, and there was an insane preferential attitude toward private labels over its own brands. We changed all of that through repositioning products and adding and eliminating products. Consistency in quality in all markets was part of our "Scott the World Over" strategy. Scott had great success, achieving sales growth of 25 percent on products it continued producing and tissue margins of 20 percent in less than two years.

The marketing lessons from Scott Paper were (1) define the problem; (2) define alternative solutions; (3) evaluate the possible solutions; (4) lock and load on the best solution and execute it; (5) develop a team willing to work with you and the organization; encourage a winning attitude, strong self-esteem, and the courage to take risks; (6) establish stretch goals; (7) hold staff fully accountable for the goals; and (8) establish an effective monitoring and control system so you know what is happening and can respond quickly to problems.

Lesson: Don't be afraid to replace the way things were with the way they should be.

Fire All the Consultants

Consultants are a crutch. They tell you what you want to hear. Consultants are an unwarranted source of credibility. And they cost lots of money. Remember Rule 2? Don't rely on a consultant to write your ten-year plan; goals and objectives must be your own. If these folks were so clever they could predict the future I'd hire them. Scott had spent $30 million on consultants in one year before Dunlap arrived, and he fired most of them. One consultant had been used to generate a compensation system for the company that no one in the organization could understand or explain to Dunlap.

It is okay to develop a long-term relationship with one multifaceted consultant, but no more than one. Hiring a consultant only works when they are given a specific timetable and a targeted outcome. The consultant you do find should report to the CEO because that is who will push forward the consultant's recommendations. Consultants do not implement, but business leaders do.

Lesson: But if you absolutely must work with one, here's what to do.

Real Jobs, Real Cuts

In restructuring, jobs will be lost. Dunlap notes, "I am not heartless, I do not enjoy putting people out of work. But I won't do it piecemeal—that's a fraud. I recognize that if I don't do it now I will have to do it sometime in the future. I also remember that those who remain have a more secure future than before. The cuts have to be permanent. Firing people and then hiring then as temps or contract workers does nothing to reduce costs. I will err on the side of too much because you can always add back."

Job cuts require communication with everyone involved, especially the unions. Make it clear to the people on the floor that the first cuts will be management and bureaucracy. The proportion of cuts in these areas should be greater than those in union staff. Dunlap's position with unions is simple: "Don't hurt me and I won't hurt you." At Scott, managers explained to the unions why things had to change. They brought in reports, talked through cost structure, presented benchmarks, let the unions know what the competition was doing, and where Scott's margins were. Scott wanted the unions to be part of the solution. And it worked. They were able to make the cuts and never were faced with a strike.

Lesson: Communicate, communicate, communicate.

The Best Bargain Is an Expensive CEO

The CEO who has a competitive compensation package with an opportunity for a big stock equity payoff is a bargain. This is tying compensation directly to results; the executive does not get more than the cash side of the package if stock price does not go up and options cannot be exercised. However, the deal must still be shareholder-friendly and justifiable. Unlike many executives, Dunlap cares about the shareholders; it is their company, and they take the risks: "If I do a poor job, they lose. If executive compensation is aligned with shareholder gains, who can complain? I walked away from Scott with $100 million, but I was worth it because I created $6.5 billion in value. The company was worth $2.9 billion when I arrived and more than $9 billion when we sold it."

Incentive programs based on performance are an important motivation tool. Both restricted stock grants and stock options can be used but should only be awarded when the executive *and* the company are meeting its goals.

Lesson: Tie executive pay to shareholder value.

Whose Company Is It, Anyhow?

Your shareholders are not a bunch of rich people on Wall Street; they are everyday people who have invested their pensions and 401(K) plans in our company. If that invested money does poorly, they will be penalized. That is why the shareholder, not the customer, is the number-one responsibility of the company. The attitude of shareholder value first should be reflected in all corporate decisions. Shareholders own the company, and that means employees, including executives, work for the shareholders.

Lesson: The people who invest in a company own it—not the employees, not the suppliers, and not the community.

Boards of Directors, God Forgive Them

The main role of the board is to hire and fire the CEO and to determine CEO compensation. Boards can have the greatest impact on a company by holding the CEO to a very high standard. The board should be certain the company is properly run from a fiduciary, legal, and moral perspective. Approval (or disapproval) of overall strategy, acquisitions, and major capital expenditures are the purview of the board, but *not* involvement in running the business.

Director's loyalty and allegiance should be with the shareholder. And to help focus this, Dunlap insists that board compensation should take the form of equity in the organization. Any director who is not willing to be paid 100 percent in stock does not believe in the company.

Lesson: Boards of directors perform best when they are aligned with shareholders.

Feed a Company, Starve a Culture

In a dying corporation, the culture will be a part of the problem. How employees and executives act, how they deal with problems, the type of leadership they provide, and how they are compensated are all a matter of culture. Part of Dunlap's strategy is to paint such a bleak picture of the status quo that it is obvious to everyone that the old culture did not work.

An important aspect of a corporate culture needs to be value creation. Great corporations want to use assets profitably to create value. The business is run with a takeover mentality; they make cuts, they innovate, they make tough decisions, and they are focused on company success.

Corporate culture reflects the way things are. If you want change, the culture needs to be changed, and leadership (executives) set cultural expectations and limits. Change starts at the top. A new culture must be established with people of a different mindset who will operate in a different and better way. Scott's culture was too congenial, and decisions took too much time because it was a consensus organization. Dunlap's preference is a culture where you can walk down the hall, get a decision made, and move on with business. At Scott, he set up a culture of change, accountability, and profitability. A great culture should be nourished, sustained, and grown; a bad culture cannot just be put in remission, but it must be killed.

Lesson: Seek out and free the good people. Give them the opportunity to flourish from within.

Impressing the Analysts

The debate over the appropriateness of a proactive investor relations strategy notwithstanding, Dunlap believes that one of his roles as CEO is to communicate with the financial community. Investor relations convey management's intent and belief about the future. Without this communication investors cannot make informed decisions about the company's securities. Being proactive sends a signal that the CEO is concerned about shareholder value. And you should share both the good and bad news.

Lesson: Every business has a message to sell.

Now There's a Bright Idea

Dunlap took over Sunbeam Corporation in July 1996 and applied the four simple rules that he used at Scott and at other companies he has run. The only similarity between Sunbeam and Scott was a lousy management team. So here's how he applied his rules:

"1. *Get the right management team.* For this turnaround, I brought together twenty-five people who had previously worked for me. I demanded the same from them as before and worked them just as hard.

2. *Pinch pennies.* In seven months we reduced annual cost by $225 million. Factories were cut from twenty-six to eight worldwide and warehouses were cut from sixty-one to eighteen. We cut half the workforce of 12,000 through asset sales and layoffs. Of course, we started with headquarters staff, trimming it by 60 percent and consolidating six locations to one. By negotiating, we lowered our audit fee by 50 percent and our insurance by 80 percent. Our greatest cut, in my opinion, and the most controversial was cutting to 1,500 our 12,000 stockkeeping units. We cut to the core of our product lines and began developing new products.

3. *Know what business you are in.* At Sunbeam, we defined our core, determined the categories that should surround this core and would become the new Sunbeam. We decided our core was electric appliances and appliance-related businesses. This is an important step because it allows you to focus on the products that relate to the business and you can sell off the rest.

4. *Get a real strategy.* A vision of the future has been key to every turnaround I have done. And it starts with a clearly defined strategy. At Sunbeam strategy is built around our core businesses, and we will grow through expansion of these businesses by differentiating products, entering new geographic markets, and introducing new products.

Our brightest move in the Sunbeam restructuring was to offer every employee stock options. This changes employees from renters to owners, and it creates stewardship, because if you own something you take better care of it.

We fixed Sunbeam, 'an absolute basket case,' in seven months. Long-term restructuring plans do not work."

Lesson: Everything you've read so far about restructuring works. This chapter proves it—again.

Fighting Words

To avoid being Dunlapped, work as if Dunlap were taking over tomorrow. Be a maverick, do the right things, differentiate yourself, state your views, and write memos so your ideas are out in the open. Don't be afraid of change, embrace it. Don't be a "Yes" person, learn how to listen and contribute to discussion. *But, once a final decision is made, it is time to stop talking and start implementing.*

Take pride in the work you do and where you work, but never lose sight of making money—it's why you are in business.

Lesson: If everybody in the corporation was doing this, they'd never get Dunlapped in the first place.

READING 3

Human Resource Champions

Dave Ulrich
Summary prepared by Stephen Rubenfeld

> **Stephen Rubenfeld** is a Professor of Human Resource Management in the
> School of Business and Economics at the University of Minnesota, Duluth. He
> received his doctorate from the University of Wisconsin, Madison, and was
> previously on the faculty of Texas Tech University. His professional
> publications and presentations have covered a wide range of human resource
> and labor relations topics, including job search behaviors, human resource
> policies and practices, job security, and staffing challenges. He has served as a
> consultant for a number of private and public sector organizations and is a
> member of the Society for Human Resource Management, the Academy of
> Management, and the Industrial Relations Research Association.

The employment relationship—the melding of the organization and its human resources—long has been the focus of efforts to enhance organizational success. Over
the years, human resource professionals and line managers were able to make impressive gains by improving control systems, rearranging work activities, and finding other
ways to contain costs and enhance quality. As the twenty-first century becomes a reality, it is becoming apparent that the traditional ways of managing and the pursuit of
incremental improvements are insufficient to provide the competitive capabilities
needed to ensure organizational survival.

*The changing face and pace of competition requires an intensified effort by man-
agers and human resource professionals to work together as champions of organizational success.* But this partnership cannot succeed without a redefinition of the
human resource (HR) function *and* a shift away from many of the assumptions that
are the basis for "traditional" employment relationships. The ways of yesterday cannot be the ways of tomorrow.

COMPETITIVE CHALLENGES

Organizations must become more capable of success. They must develop the capacity
to recognize forces that may carry with them both threat and opportunity. They must
respond in ways that ensure success and survival. Human resource professionals can
play an essential role in helping managers respond to these major environmental challenges:

Dave Ulrich, *Human Resource Champions: The Next Agenda for Adding Value and Delivering Results.*
Boston, MA: Harvard Business School Press, 1997.

259

1. *Globalization*: Developing competencies, skills, and perspectives that will enable the organization to function effectively in a world without economic boundaries.
2. *Value chain for business competitiveness and HR services*: Enhancing responsiveness to the customer and ensure that this customer orientation is embedded in the organizational culture.
3. *Profitability through cost and growth*: Controlling costs *and* increasing revenues as essential elements of long term financial success.
4. *Capability focus*: Staffing the organization, not just on the basis of the work to be done, but with consideration of the competencies needed.
5. *Change, change, and change some more*: Making the organization more flexible and ensuring that employees have both the capability and willingness to change.
6. *Technology*: Dealing with rapid innovations with an eye to how and where the work is accomplished, and the effects on employees.
7. *Attracting, retaining, and measuring competence and intellectual capital*: Acquiring and developing managers with needed talents and developing leaders who are team-focused and committed to sharing information.
8. *Transformation, not turnaround*: Seeking long-term solutions to underlying problems and not just resolving short term crises.

Organizational leaders must chart the course and create the capabilities that will guide organizations through this complex maze of challenges and opportunities. Beyond this general rallying cry, the specific implications of these business challenges for the HR professional are more difficult to characterize. Obviously, HR policies and practices must be crafted to help the organization meet these challenges and enhance its competitiveness. But beyond this, the HR function and HR professionals, as partners in the enterprise, must be champions of competitiveness. They must focus on HR processes and outcomes, and ultimately, the *value* created through HR activities.

HUMAN RESOURCE ROLES

Rather than highlighting traditional HR practices (e.g., selection, training, compensation), understanding HR's essential role in organizational competitiveness is better served by thinking about four critical outcomes, or *deliverables*: strategy execution, administrative efficiency, employee contributions, and capacity for change. Ultimately, it is these deliverables that define the specific roles that HR, and all business partners, must play in moving the organization forward. Energies must be dedicated to all four domains, and these roles must successfully coexist, within HR as well as between HR and the rest of the management team.

Becoming a Strategic Partner   HR professionals, as strategic partners, should be active participants in the development of organizational strategies. They also must be key players in the implementation of these strategies and must redefine HR policies and practices to support these ends. The critical HR deliverable, and thus the standard of HR success, is executing strategies and contributing to the accomplishment of business objectives.

There are a number of potential pitfalls to avoid if HR is to be an effective strategic partner. First, it is essential that strategies actually guide decision making. In fact, most strategic plans are created and then ignored (strategic plans on the shelf are referred to as "SPOTS"). HR professionals must constantly push to ensure that strategy is considered *before* operational decisions are made. Second, HR must simultaneously serve multiple stakeholders and not focus its attention solely on employees. In this sense, HR must avoid a purely internal focus and redirect its efforts to the value chain. Third, HR plans must be aligned and (ideally) fully integrated with business plans. They cannot be viewed as add-ons; they cannot be independent of other planning. Fourth, HR must avoid the temptation of quick fixes. For example, benchmarking without consideration of context often leads to the adoption of a best practice that does not work in its adoptive setting. Another seductive option is to go with in-vogue, faddish solutions—"Frau-fraus." It is important to recognize that not all popular ideas are good ideas, and not all good ideas work in all settings. Fifth, solving problems without first developing the necessary competencies is a first-class ticket to disaster. HR must stimulate an organizational focus on capabilities, and provide the mechanisms to build these competencies.

As organizations move from strategies to actions, HR can add to its credibility as a strategic partner by guiding a comprehensive *organizational diagnosis* (assessment), which must precede the design of targeted implementation strategies. An audit of organizational systems and processes and a plan for their improvement can be defined and championed by HR.

Developing Administrative Expertise   HR professionals are called upon to deliver administrative efficiency in two ways: helping the organization reengineer its business processes and delivering HR services efficiently.

As HR policies are modified and improved to yield cost savings and higher quality services, the limits of such incremental improvements become apparent. The next step must be to reexamine the basic ways in which HR provides services, and thus value, to the organization. There are three concepts that shed light on how to enhance value creation in this manner:

- Avoid the "centralization versus decentralization" debate. Rather than focusing on *who* should perform specific HR activities, consider the interests of the end user—the internal *and* external customers. Recast the debate to how the function can best be delivered to enhance the quality of service.
- Place creation paramount as HR designs and delivers services. Moreover, it must be recognized that value is defined by the users, not the providers of the service. Depending on the role and context, HR may serve most appropriately as a broker of services, a service center, or a center of expertise.
- Process rather than function should guide value creation. From this perspective, hierarchical power is less important than developing mechanisms to ensure the flow of services to those who need them. This horizontal focus requires teamwork and a customer orientation.

HR's administrative expertise should be used to ensure that processes are conceptualized, designed, communicated, and implemented appropriately. If points of resistance are overcome, this can and should result in substantial efficiencies and value creation.

Serving as an Employee Champion   If HR managers are successful managers of employee contributions, the primary benefits to the organization will be increased employee commitment and competence. Employees whose needs are considered and who are put in a position to succeed are more likely to pursue success.

With competitive forces mandating greater efficiencies, demands on employees are increasing. Raising the performance bar results both in higher-faster-better work expectations and greater psychological pressures. This perceived speed-up and expansion of responsibilities is occurring in tandem with diminished employment security, uncertainty in career progression, and the modification of reward systems. The effects are in the predictable direction, though unevenly distributed among the workforce. For many, the employment relationship becomes more of an equity-driven transaction. With this, employee contributions and commitment may diminish as they see the fairness balance shifting.

HR professionals cannot alter the competitive forces that create these employment pressures, but HR may be able to mitigate their effects. With the perspective of the employee champion, HR professionals may be able to minimize dysfunctional consequences and even create a work environment that is viewed positively. Among the possible HR responses to these increasing demands on employees are the following:

1. *Reducing demands* on employees by setting priorities, focusing and integrating objectives, and reengineering work. Other strategies may include streamlining, simplifying, and automating to reduce workloads.
2. *Increasing resources* to provide the tools and capacity to meet work expectations. This may include the use of process improvements, collaboration, teamwork, rewards, and communication.

As employee champions, HR professionals are focused on facilitating employee contributions and creating a supportive environment. Although not in a literal sense serving as an employee advocate, HR must ensure that the employees' voices are heard in decision-making processes and that resources are made available that will make it possible for employees to meet these new demands.

HR as a Change Agent   Change is inevitable, but it is not always effectively channeled. The HR challenge is to ensure that the organization and its employees adapt, learn, and respond appropriately to change. The desired responses can be in the form of initiatives (modified procedures, new programs), process changes (new ways to get work done), and cultural changes (fundamental shifts in how the organization sees itself and in the ways that it does business).

An organization's capability to change is often overestimated, and the results of change frequently do not meet expectations. Among the long list of possible explanations for disappointing results are

- having a short term perspective,
- lacking leadership to guide change,
- taking action that is not tied to strategies,

- fear of the unknown, and
- inbred inflexibility.

Being an effective agent of change requires HR to undertake thorough organizational analyses and to develop comprehensive action plans to stimulate, guide, and monitor change. HR must also be vigilant that change efforts are not derailed. Obviously, HR's credibility in this regard will be enhanced if it has demonstrated effective and successful changes to the HR function itself.

IMPLICATIONS

Meeting the challenges of competitiveness requires a complex and organizationally specific set of reactions. *HR must have a commitment to growth and developing a culture that supports and sustains it, and at the same time, a commitment to controlling costs. HR must become a champion of organizational success, with an unwavering emphasis on deliverables.* The hallmark of a successful HR function will be the creation of value. Expending efforts on doing what you do but doing it better may yield incremental benefit but will not necessarily create lasting value. For this reason, it almost certainly will be insufficient to achieve true competitiveness.

The reality is that all business partners, including HR professionals, must play the four multiple roles:

Business Partner = Strategic Partner + Administrative Expert
+ Employee Champion + Change Agent

Each of these roles is essential, and although individuals may differentially contribute in each of these domains, the HR function must represent a cohesive team effort to ensure that all of these roles are present in decision making and program implementation. It is true that the relationships among roles may create stresses. Can a strategic partner simultaneously be an employee champion? Can a change agent also function as an administrative expert? The answer is yes, it is feasible, and yes, it is necessary. Organizations must achieve balance and serve practical ends. Roles cannot be pitted against one another.

SUMMARY

HR professionals must focus their efforts on helping the organization become and remain competitive. They must play a variety of roles, offer support and assistance, but ultimately, they must deliver the goods. HR must provide the deliverables: It must add value. Simultaneously, HR must ensure that its own house remains in order. It must develop a strategic perspective and develop the needed capabilities. It must conceptualize a clear mission for the HR function, and it must perform its traditional activities well and with an eye to the needs of its customer.

PART TWELVE

Organizational Learning and Knowledge-Driven Organizations

Organizational buzzwords come and go, but one that may have lasting merit deals with "organizational learning." Corporations (and individuals) spend millions of dollars annually on education, training, and development, but they do not always reap the true benefits that they could. Why? Among the reasons are that some individuals are reluctant to change even when they know they should; some knowledge is held possessively within those trained and consequently not shared with others; and formal mechanisms have not been established that allow for storage and exchange of information within an organization.

Peter M. Senge is the Director of the Systems Thinking and Organizational Learning Program at MIT's Sloan School of Management. His book *The Fifth Discipline: The Art and Practice of the Learning Organization* emphasizes the importance of organizations developing the capacity to engage in effective learning. Senge identifies and discusses a set of disabilities that are fatal to organizations, especially those operating in rapidly changing environments. The fifth discipline—systems thinking—is presented as the cornerstone for the learning organization. Personal mastery, mental models, shared vision, and team learning are presented as the core disciplines and the focus for building the learning organization.

Chris Argyris follows up those thoughts with his book *Overcoming Organizational Defenses*, which portrays ways of overcoming the defenses that tend to slow down change and inhibit the organization's ability to significantly improve performance. Shifting from established tradition, which focuses on morale, loyalty, and satisfaction as the foundation for the achievement of organizational excellence, Argyris argues that a more realistic base for excellence may come from an emphasis placed upon learning, competence, and justice. He alerts managers to the dangers of defensive reasoning and argues that they must learn to engage in double-loop learning. Chris Argyris is the

James Bryant Conant Professor on the Business and Education faculties at Harvard University.

Thomas H. Davenport and Laurence Prusak, in *Working Knowledge*, extend the concept of organizational learning to an exploration of how companies can convert corporate wisdom into market value. They identify four sequential types of work (accessing, generating, embedding, and transferring) and explore the key skills underlying each. They also explore the human characteristics such as experience, intuition, values, and beliefs that make the task of managing knowledge challenging. Davenport is a professor of information management at the University of Texas in Austin; Prusak is a managing principal of the IBM Consulting Group in Boston.

The idea of benchmarking has been added to the manager's vocabulary in recent years. *Benchmarking* is the process of monitoring and learning the methods, practices, and performance measures of one's best competitors (or other successful organizations) so as to create exceptional performance. As portrayed by Gregory Watson in *Strategic Benchmarking*, it is a tool for identifying and upgrading customer satisfaction. Watson discusses four types of benchmarking (internal, competitive, functional, and generic) as ways to gain a (short-term) competitive advantage over one's competitors. Watson is the Vice President of Quality for the Office Document Products Division of the Xerox Corporation and the author of three other books on benchmarking.

READING 1

The Fifth Discipline

Peter Senge
Summary prepared by Dorothy Marcic

> **Dorothy Marcic** *is the president of DM Systems, Ltd. A former Fullbright Scholar and teacher at the Czechoslovak Management Center and the University of Economics in Prague, she has consulted for a variety of organizations, in addition to the U.S. Department of State and the Czech Ministry of Finance.*

Learning disabilities can be fatal to organizations, causing them to have an average life span of only 40 years—half a human being's life. *Organizations need to be learners, and often they are not.* Somehow some survive, but never live up to their potential. What happens if what we term "excellence" is really no more than mediocrity? Only those firms that become learners will succeed in the increasingly turbulent, competitive global market.

LEARNING DISABILITIES

There are seven learning disabilities common to organizations.

Identification with One's Position   American workers are trained to see themselves as what they do, not who they are. Therefore, if laid off, they find it difficult, if not impossible, to find work doing something else. Worse for the organization, though, is the limited thinking this attitude creates. By claiming an identity related to the job, workers are cut off from seeing how their responsibility connects to other jobs. For example, one American car had three assembly blots on one component. The similar Japanese make had only one bolt. Why? Because the Detroit manufacturer had three engineers for that component, while a similar Japanese manufacturer had only one.

External Enemies   This belief is a result of the previously stated disability. External enemies refers to people focusing blame on anything but themselves or their unit. Fault is regularly blamed on factors like the economy, the weather, or the government. Marketing blames manufacturing, and manufacturing blames engineering. Such external fault-finding keeps the organization from seeing what the real problems are and prevents them from tackling the real issues head-on.

The Illusion of Taking Charge   Being proactive is seen as good management—doing something about "those problems." All too often, though, being proactive is a disguise for reactiveness against that awful enemy out there.

Peter Senge, *The Fifth Discipline.* New York, NY: Doubleday, 1990.

The Fixation on Events Much attention in organizations is paid to events—last month's sales, the new product, who just got hired, and so on. Our society, too, is geared toward short-term thinking, which in turn stifles the type of generative learning that permits a look at the real threats—the slowly declining processes of quality, service, or design.

The Parable of the Boiled Frog An experiment was once conducted by placing a frog in boiling water. Immediately the frog, sensing danger in the extreme heat, jumped out to safety. However, placing the frog in cool water and slowly turning up the heat resulted in the frog getting groggier and groggier and finally boiling to death. Why? Because the frog's survival mechanisms are programmed to look for sudden changes in the environment, not to gradual changes. Similarly, during the 1960s, the U.S. auto industry saw no threat by Japan, which had only 4 percent of the market. Not until the 1980s when Japan had over 21 percent of the market did the Big Three begin to look at their core assumptions. Now with Japan holding about 30 percent share of the market, it is not certain if this frog (U.S. automakers) is capable of jumping out of the boiling water. Looking at gradual processes requires slowing down our frenetic pace and watching for the subtle cues.

The Delusion of Learning from Experience Learning from experience is powerful. This is how we learn to walk and talk. However, we now live in a time when direct consequences of actions may take months or years to appear. Decisions in R & D may take up to a decade to bear fruit, and their actual consequences may be influenced by manufacturing and marketing along the way. Organizations often choose to deal with these complexities by breaking themselves up into smaller and smaller components, further reducing their ability to see problems in their entirety.

The Myth of the Management Team Most large organizations have a group of bright, experienced leaders who are supposed to know all the answers. They were trained to believe there are answers to all problems and they should find them. People are rarely rewarded for bringing up difficult issues or for looking at parts of a problem that make it harder to grasp. Most teams end up operating below the lowest IQ of any member. What results are "skilled incompetents"—people who know all too well how to keep *from* learning.

SYSTEMS THINKING

There are five disciplines required for a learning organization: personal mastery, mental models, shared vision, team learning, and systems thinking. The fifth one, systems thinking, is the most important. Without systems thinking, the other disciplines do not have the same effect.

The Laws of the Fifth Discipline

Today's Problems Result from Yesterday's Solutions A carpet merchant kept pushing down a bump in the rug, only to have it reappear elsewhere, until he lifted a corner and out slithered a snake. Sometimes fixing one part of the system only brings difficulties to other parts of the system. For example, solving an internal inventory problem may lead to angry customers who now get late shipments.

Push Hard and the System Pushes Back Even Harder   Systems theory calls this compensating feedback, which is a common way of reducing the effects of an intervention. Some cities, for example, built low-cost housing and set up jobs programs, only to have more poor people than ever. Why? Because many moved to the cities from neighboring areas so that they, too, could take advantage of the low-cost housing and job opportunities.

Behavior Gets Better Before it Gets Worse   Some decisions actually look good in the short term, but produce *compensating feedback* and crisis in the end. The really effective decisions often produce difficulties in the short run but create more health in the long term. This is why behaviors such as building a power base or working hard just to please the boss come back to haunt you.

The Best Way Out Is to Go Back In   We often choose familiar solutions, ones that feel comfortable and not scary. But the effective ways often mean going straight into what we are afraid of facing. What does *not* work is pushing harder on the same old solutions (also called the "what we need here is a bigger hammer" syndrome).

The Cure Can Be Worse Than the Disease   The result of applying nonsystematic solutions to problems is the need for more and more of the same. It can become addictive. Someone begins mild drinking to alleviate work tension. The individual feels better and then takes on more work, creating more tension and a need for more alcohol, and the person finally becomes an alcoholic. Sometimes these types of solutions only result in shifting the burden. The government enters the scene by providing more welfare and leaves the host system weaker and less able to solve its own problems. This ultimately necessitates still more aid from the government. Companies can try to shift their burdens to consultants, but then become more and more dependent on them to solve their problems.

Faster Is Slower   Every system, whether ecological or organizational, has an optimal rate of growth. Faster and faster is not always better. (After all, the tortoise finally did win the race.) Complex human systems require new ways of thinking. Quickly jumping in and fixing what *looks* bad usually provides solutions for a problem's symptoms and not for the problem itself.

Cause and Effect Are Not Always Related Closely in Time and Space   *Effects* here mean the symptoms we see, such as drug abuse and unemployment, whereas *causes* mean the interactions of the underlying system which bring about these conditions. We often assume cause is near to effect. If there is a sales problem, then incentives for the sales force should fix it, or if there is inadequate housing, then build more houses. Unfortunately, this does not often work, for the real causes lie elsewhere.

Tiny Changes May Produce Big Results; Areas of Greatest Leverage Are Frequently the Least Obvious   System science teaches that the most obvious solutions usually do not work. While simple solutions frequently make short-run improvements, they commonly contribute to long-term deteriorations. The *non*obvious and *well-focused* solutions are more likely to provide leverage and bring positive change. For example, ships have a tiny trim tab on one edge of the rudder that has great influence on the movement of that ship, so small changes in the trim tab bring big shifts in the ship's course. However, there are no simple rules for applying leverage to organizations. It requires looking for the structure of what is going on rather than merely seeing the events.

You Can Have Your Cake and Eat It Too—But Not At the Same Time   Sometimes the most difficult problems come from "snapshot" rather than "process" thinking. For example, it was previously believed by American manufacturers that quality and low cost could not be achieved simultaneously. One had to be chosen over the other. What was missed, however, was the notion that improving quality may also mean eliminating waste and unnecessary time (both adding costs), which in the end would mean lower costs. Real leverage comes when it can be seen that seemingly opposing needs can be met over time.

Cutting the Elephant in Half Does Not Create Two Elephants   Some problems can be solved by looking at parts of the organization, whereas others require holistic thinking. What is needed is an understanding of the boundaries for each problem. Unfortunately, most organizations are designed to prevent people from seeing systemic problems, either by creating rigid structures or by leaving problems behind for others to clean up.

There Is No Blame   Systems thinking teaches that there are not outside causes to problems; instead, you and your "enemy" are part of the same system. Any cure requires understanding how that is seen.

THE OTHER DISCIPLINES

Personal Mastery

Organizations can learn only when the individuals involved learn. This requires personal mastery, which is the discipline of personal learning and growth, where people are continually expanding their ability to create the kind of life they want. From their quest comes the spirit of the learning organization.

Personal mastery involves seeing one's life as a creative work, being able to clarify what is really important, and learning to see current reality more clearly. The difference between what's important, what we want, and where we are now produces a "creative tension." Personal mastery means being able to generate and maintain creative tension.

Those who have high personal mastery have a vision which is more like a calling, and they are in a continual learning mode. They never really "arrive." Filled with more commitment, they take initiative and greater responsibility in their work.

Previously, organizations supported an employee's development only if it would help the organization, which fits in with the traditional "contract" between employee and organization ("an honest day's pay in exchange for an honest day's work"). The new, and coming, way is to see it rather as a "covenant," which comes from a shared vision of goals, ideas, and management processes.

Working toward personal mastery requires living with emotional tension, not letting our goals get eroded. As Somerset Maugham said, "Only mediocre people are always at their best." One of the worst blocks to achieving personal mastery is the common belief that we cannot have what we want. Being committed to the truth is a powerful weapon against this, for it does not allow us to deceive ourselves. Another means of seeking personal mastery is to integrate our reason and intuition. We live in a society which values reason and devalues intuition. However, using both together is very powerful and may be one of the fundamental contributions to systems thinking.

Mental Models

Mental models are internal images of how the world works, and they can range from simple generalizations (people are lazy) to complex theories (assumptions about why my co-workers interact they way they do). For example, for decades the Detroit automakers believed people bought cars mainly for styling, not for quality or reliability. These beliefs, which were really unconscious assumptions, worked well for many years, but ran into trouble when competition from Japan began. It took a long time for Detroit even to begin to see the mistakes in their beliefs. One company that managed to change its mental model through incubating a business worldview was Shell.

Traditional hierarchical organizations have the dogma of organizing, managing, and controlling. In the new learning organization, though, the revised "dogma" will be values, vision, and mental models.

Hanover Insurance began changes in 1969 designed to overcome the "basic diseases of the hierarchy." Three values espoused were

1. *openness*—seen as an antidote to the dysfunctional interactions in face-to-face meetings.
2. *merit*, or making decisions based on the good of the organization—seen as the antidote to decision-making by organizational politics.
3. *localness*—the antidote to doing the dirty stuff the boss does not want to do.

Chris Argyris and colleagues developed "action science" as a means for reflecting on the reasoning underlying our actions. This helps people change the defensive routines which lead them to skilled incompetence. Similarly, John Beckett created a course on the historical survey of main philosophies of thought, East and West, as a sort of "sandpaper on the brain." These ideas exposed managers to their own assumptions and mental models, and provided other ways to view the world.

Shared Vision

A shared vision is not an idea. Rather it is a force in people's hearts, a sense of purpose which provides energy and focus for learning. Visions are often exhilarating. Shared vision is important because it may be the beginning step to get people who mistrusted each other to start working together. Abraham Maslow studied high-performing teams and found that they had shared vision. Shared visions can mobilize courage so naturally that people don't even know the extent of their strength. When John Kennedy created the shared vision in 1961 of putting a man on the moon by the end of the decade, only 15 percent of the technology had been created. Yet it led to numerous acts of daring and courage.

Learning organizations are not achievable without shared vision. Without that incredible pull toward the deeply felt goal, the forces of *status quo* will overwhelm the pursuit. As Robert Fritz once said, "In the presence of greatness, pettiness disappears." Conversely, in the absence of a great vision, pettiness is supreme.

Strategic planning often does not involve building a shared vision, but rather announcing the vision of top management, asking people, at best, to enroll, and, at worst, to comply. What Senge talks of is gaining commitment from people. This is done by taking a personal vision and building it into a shared vision. In the traditional hierarchical organization, compliance is one of the desired outcomes. For learning organizations, commitment must be the key goal. Shared vision, though, is not possible without personal mastery, which is needed to foster continued commitment to a lofty goal.

Team Learning

Bill Russell of the Boston Celtics wrote about being on a team of specialists whose performance depended on one another's individual excellence and how well they worked together. Sometimes that created a feeling of magic. He is talking about *alignment*, where a group functions as a whole unit, rather than as individuals working at cross purposes. When a team is aligned, its energies are focused and harmonized. They do not need to sacrifice their own interests. Instead, alignment occurs when the shared vision becomes an extension of the personal vision. Alignment is a necessary condition to empower others and ultimately empower the team.

Never before today has there been greater need for mastering team learning, which requires mastering both dialogue and discussion. *Dialogue* involves a creative and free search of complex and even subtle issues, whereas *discussion* implies different views being presented and defended. Both skills are useful, but most teams cannot tell the difference between the two. The purpose of dialogue is to increase individual understanding. Here, assumptions are suspended and participants regard one another as on the same level. Discussion, on the other hand, comes from the same root word as *percussion* and *concussion* and involves a sort of verbal ping-pong game whose object is winning. Although this is a useful technique, it must be balanced with dialogue. A continued emphasis on winning is not compatible with the search for truth and coherence.

One of the major blocks to healthy dialogue and discussion is what Chris Argyris calls *defensive routines*. These are habitual styles of interacting that protect us from threat or embarrassment. These include the avoidance of conflict (smoothing over) and the feeling that one has to appear competent and to know the answers at all times.

Team learning, like any other skill, requires practice. Musicians and athletes understand this principle. Work teams need to learn that lesson as well.

OTHER ISSUES

Organizational politics is a perversion of truth, yet most people are so accustomed to it, they do not even notice it anymore. A learning organization is not possible in such an environment. In order to move past the politics, one thing needed is openness—both speaking openly and honestly about the real and important issues and being willing to challenge one's own way of thinking.

Localness, too, is essential to the learning organization, for decisions need to be pushed down the organizational hierarchy in order to unleash people's commitment. This gives them the freedom to act.

One thing lacking in many organizations is time to reflect and think. If someone is sitting quietly, we assume they are not busy and we feel free to interrupt. Many managers, however, are too busy to "just think." This should not be blamed on the tumultuous environment of many crises. Research suggests that, even when given ample time, managers still do not devote any of it to adequate reflection. Therefore, habits need to be changed, as well as how we structure our days.

READING 2

Overcoming Organizational Defenses

Chris Argyris
Summary prepared by Jean A. Grube

Jean A. Grube *is a Lecturer in Management at the University of Wisconsin, Madison, where she received her doctorate. Her current research interests include organizational commitment, stress and coping behaviors, and organizational change.*

Managers have long focused on morale, satisfaction, and loyalty as foundations for the achievement of organizational excellence. A more realistic base for excellence may come from organizational members' *learning* (how to detect and correct organizational errors), *competence* (solving problems such that they remain solved and increase the members' ability to solve future problems), and *justice* (promoting values about organizational health that are applicable to all organizational members). These are the underpinnings for *Overcoming Organizational Defenses.*

Although the concept of organizational defenses is not a new one, approaches to understanding how and why such defenses develop have historically focused primarily on *first-order errors*—those caused by "not knowing." This book is directed at understanding how organizational defenses develop from *second-order errors*—those errors that humans actively design and produce.

We need to examine managerial activities that belie sound management practice (puzzles) and how they result from defensive reasoning. It is important to understand how and why defensive reasoning develops in organizational members, and which activities are used to routinize defensiveness and ensure its survival in organizations. Interestingly, the usual help procedures (e.g., consulting practices and organizational surveys) actually compound the problem. Specific advice for dealing with organizational defensiveness (Model II) is needed. New mindsets about management are needed if Model II theories-in-use are to survive in organizations. Organizational defenses and their potential contribution to the "ethical pollution" in organizations must be examined continually.

PUZZLES

The actions of modern management are characterized by *puzzles* that depict weaknesses of modern management behavior. Individuals engage in activities that produce and proliferate errors, even when the results run counter to what they say they want

Chris Argyris, *Overcoming Organizational Defenses.* Needham, MA: Allyn & Bacon, 1990.

and to what they believe reflects sound management. If organizational players are free to choose activities and elect to choose those that are contrary to good management, then defensive reasoning must be taking place.

According to Argyris, *defensive reasoning* occurs when individuals (1) hold premises whose validity is questionable yet they think it is not; (2) make inferences that do not necessarily follow from the premises yet they think they do; and (3) reach conclusions that they believe they have tested carefully yet they have not because the way they have been framed makes them untestable. Defensive reasoning is caused by programs in individuals' heads that are skillfully deployed to deal with errors that are embarrassing or threatening. Utilization of these mental managerial programs results in the creation of organizational defense routines, and activities used to protect the defensive routines emerge as a self-sealing device.

To understand how and why organizational members develop these programs, one must consider the issue of skilled incompetence.

HUMAN THEORIES OF CONTROL: SKILLED INCOMPETENCE

Skilled incompetence has its origins in the fact that human beings seek to be in control of their actions because they feel good when they are able to produce intended results. When faced with situations that could lead to lack of control (i.e., embarrassing or threatening conditions), people look for guidelines to direct their actions. Two programs that exist in the minds of individuals serve as guidelines. The first program, *espoused theories of action*, is comprised of the beliefs and values people hold about how to manage their lives. The second program, *theories-in-use*, contains rules people use to manage their beliefs.

Most people follow a *Model I* theory-in-use which directs them to achieve unilateral control, to win, and to suppress negative feelings. Such theories-in-use are learned at an early age and are supported by such social virtues as caring, helping, and respecting others. Model I action strategies include selling, persuading, and face-saving. Some of these strategies are counterproductive. For example, people tell "little white lies" to salvage another person's pride (face-saving). This requires people to (1) bypass the errors others make, and act as if they are not making errors because one can only save another's face by not revealing what is happening; (2) make the bypass undiscussable, because errors cannot be bypassed successfully if others discuss it; and (3) make the undiscussability of the undiscussable also undiscussable. Consequently, important thoughts and feelings are not communicated honestly and fully by organizational members. This pattern leads to misunderstandings and distortions, making it unlikely that managers or others will be able to detect and correct errors. Ironically, Model I strategies require great skill at doing counterproductive things (e.g., it is difficult to change the mind of an individual without upsetting him or her) and hence are illustrated by the term *skilled incompetence*.

Although such strategies are counterproductive, they are repeated because they have become automatic, spontaneous, and taken for granted by organizational members. Furthermore, such actions are supported by a society that sees giving approval, offering praise, and deferring to others as virtues. Skilled incompetence becomes even more counterproductive when routinized in organizations.

ORGANIZATIONAL DEFENSIVE ROUTINES

Because most individuals' actions are guided by Model I theories-in-use, these activities become organizational norms. Subsequently, *organizational defensive routines* (actions or policies that are established to protect individuals or segments of the organization from experiencing embarrassment or threat) develop. Managers and other organizational members construct the framework for these defensive routines in accordance with Model I: (1) messages are crafted that contain inconsistencies, and yet, individuals act as if the messages are not inconsistent; (2) the inconsistencies of the message are made undiscussable; (3) the undiscussability of the undiscussable is also made undiscussable.

Defenses present a "double bind" for many organizational members. They recognize that organizational performance will suffer if they are not able to discuss errors. However, they find it difficult to change defensive routines because "opening this can of worms" invokes more defensive routines, thus worsening the situation. So they continue to massage the truth, which serves to reinforce and proliferate defenses. The actions becoming self-fulfilling and self-sealing.

How do individuals live with this double bind? Many do not, which may be the most fundamental cause of burnout and turnover in upper-level management. Others rely on "fancy footwork" in order to live with their inconsistencies.

FANCY FOOTWORK AND MALAISE

To deal with the double bind, some organizational members use *fancy footwork* (actions that permit them to ignore inconsistencies in their actions, deny that inconsistencies exist, or place the blame on other people). Eventually, a sense of malaise develops in which members recognize that fancy footwork permeates the organization but feel helpless to change it. There are three symptoms associated with *organizational malaise*. First, members seek and find fault with the organization but do not accept responsibility for correcting its failures. Second, individuals begin to accentuate and magnify negative aspects of the organization. In fact, they find pleasure in doing so because it helps them to justify their own distancing and helplessness behaviors. Finally, people espouse values that everyone knows cannot be implemented. Because they are never implemented, they eventually lose credibility.

The result of skilled incompetence, organizational defensive routines, fancy footwork, and malaise is an *organizational defensive pattern (ODP)*. ODP is generic to all human organization and, unfortunately, traditional techniques are ineffective in reducing its effects.

SOUND ADVICE: IT COMPOUNDS THE PROBLEM

If executives who want to deal with ODP followed the advice of the "best and the brightest," they would find themselves in trouble for a variety of reasons. Management consultants, for instance, rarely deal with ODP. When they do, the advice is too abstract to be of help. The vast majority of leadership books focus on "espoused theories" and, therefore, offer little in the way of correcting the actual behaviors that are guided by theory-in-use. Similarly, problems occur when solutions are sought through organizational surveys, because respondents reply based on their espoused theories of action.

Another problem with advice is that it can reinforce errors and organizational defensive routines. For example, management literature advises that feedback be obtained in a manner that allows subordinates not to worry about negative consequences of being honest. However, the very act of using a third "trusted" party reinforces that subordinates cannot be honest with their supervisors in situations that may be threatening or cause embarrassment. Actions like these further justify defensive routines.

For advice to be implementable or enactable, it must possess certain characteristics. First, it must show *causality* (engaging in this behavior will produce these results). Second, advice must be *concrete* (this is exactly what must be done). Finally, the advice must *make explicit the values* that govern the suggested actions (this action is suggested so that I can monitor the outcome of my decision). Conventional advice does not meet these criteria.

REDUCING THE ORGANIZATIONAL DEFENSE PATTERN

If traditional techniques are ineffective, what should managers do to reduce ODP? The answer lies in double-loop learning.

Model I theory-in-use is characterized as a *single-loop model* because it focuses on the presenting problem (symptom) and does not direct attention to the cause. Consequently, it is only a matter of time before the problem resurfaces. To correct ODP, the initial values that governed the actions that led to errors must be changed. This is termed *double-loop learning*. To sustain double-loop learning, an organization's managers must develop a culture that rewards individuals who learn how to divorce themselves from Model I actions that contribute to ODP. In essence, a new theory-in-use model (*Model II*) must be taught.

To learn new actions for handling situations that are embarrassing or threatening, organizational members must first see how they presently deal with problems under such conditions. Next, the individuals must be shown how these actions are counterproductive. Third, individuals are taught how to use Model II as a theory-in-use and are encouraged to practice this step. Finally, these three steps are repeated for each new problem that arises.

The values governing Model II theory-in-use are valid information, informed choice, and responsibility for evaluating the quality of choice implementation. The actions that flow from Model II are those that invite inquiry into one's stated position and minimize face-saving behaviors. Model II assumes that productive reasoning is occurring; individuals make clear to others what premises and inferences they are using, they develop conclusions that others can test, and they actively look for inconsistencies in their own logic and invite others to do the same. This necessarily means that members must openly deal with organizational defensive routines, fancy footwork, and malaise. Otherwise, Model II theory-in-use cannot survive.

MAKING THE NEW THEORY OF MANAGING HUMAN PERFORMANCE COME TRUE

There are other compelling reasons why Model II theory-in-use must become a reality in organizations. Over the past twenty years, a new theory of managing human performance has evolved. It focuses on employee energy and intiative that can be tapped through the experience of psychological success. It emphasizes the need for commitment and involvement over more traditional values of unilateral control, dependency, and submissiveness. However, some suggest that this new management approach will bring with it new contradictions and dilemmas. Furthermore, some learning through trial and error will naturally occur as managers shift away from a more traditional view of managing employees. This implies that embarrassing and threatening situations will occur which invites ODP to develop. Unless a Model II theory-in-use is utilized, it is difficult to envision how nontraditional management practices can survive.

GETTING FROM HERE TO THERE

How can managers move organizational members from Model I to Model II? Several modes can facilitate the transition. Although there are variations, all modes have features in common. An organizational member writes a case that depicts a particular problem and how he or she responded. Guided by professionals, other participants review the case and offer insights into how the actions contributed to ODP and what corrective actions are available. A six-step procedure can help individuals overcome organizational defenses:

1. Diagnose the problem.
2. Connect the diagnosis to the actual behavior of participants.
3. Show participants how their behavior creates organizational defenses.
4. Help them change their behavior.
5. Change the defensive routine that reinforced the old behavior.
6. Develop new organizational norms and culture that reinforce the new behavior.

UPPING THE ANTE

Some managers are able to ignore or deny the existence of ODP because the building of, and negative consequences associated with, these defenses is an insidious process. Additionally, managers introduce activities that attempt to minimize the likelihood of embarrassment or threat. One such activity is to objectify methods for monitoring actions of the organization in order to minimize the effects of the human element. However, since humans have to implement the systems, such "correcting" methods ultimately fail. Another strategy is to create greater tolerance for embarrassment and threat in organizational members through the development of involvement and internal commitment (the nontraditional management practice). The assumption is that individuals who are more involved and committed will show more initiative for detecting and correcting errors. The problem with such an approach is that it is difficult to use as a foundation for a major organizational strategy, and it does not take into account the ingenious ways that members seek to protect themselves when they encounter situations of threat or embarrassment.

For new management practices to be successful, a new mindset is necessary. There are four activities that will promote the mindset needed to foster new management approaches. First, members must stop taking for granted what is taken for granted (i.e., they must learn to examine more carefully what they assume is obvious). Second, members must make learning as sacred as they make other activities or policies (e.g., such as the policy of face-saving). Third, members must evaluate how they contribute to ODP and accept individual responsibility for reducing defenses in the organization. Finally, members must come to understand that productive reasoning is as critical for human problems as it is for those technical in nature.

ETHICS AND THE ORGANIZATIONAL DEFENSES PATTERN

Many have cited openness and trust as critical to ethical behavior in organizations. By engaging in cover-up behaviors, organizational members may unknowingly be contributing to the "ethical pollution" in organizations. The solution lies within each manager as each must learn to manage and accept responsibility for his or her own actions and help the organization develop rewards for this self-responsible behavior.

READING 3

Strategic Benchmarking

Gregory H. Watson
Summary prepared by David A. Wyrick

Dave Wyrick is an Associate Professor in and Assistant Department Head of the Department of Industrial Engineering at the University of Minnesota, Duluth, where he teaches courses in ethics and law for engineers, engineering management, production management, and capstone design. He received his doctorate in Engineering Management from the University of Missouri, Rolla, in 1989. He also has an M.S. in Engineering Management from the University of Alaska, Anchorage, and a B.S. and M.S. in Mechanical Engineering from the University of Wyoming. He worked for Atlantic Richfield Company in Texas and Alaska in various engineering assignments and also worked with IBM-Rochester as a project management engineer on ISO 9001 preparations. A registered professional engineer, Dr. Wyrick is active in numerous professional societies, including ASEE, ASEM, ASME, ASQC, IIE, NSPE, SME, and TIMS.

What should companies do to compete successfully? The successful company will have higher quality, introduce new technology earlier, and have costs lower than its competitors. To rate its performance, the company needs to "benchmark," that is, to continuously compare and measure its business processes against business leaders anywhere in the world in order to gain information that will help the organization take action to improve its performance.

The term *benchmarking* is relatively new. As a tool for quality improvement, it first became widely publicized in 1989 after Xerox won the Malcolm Baldrige National Quality Award. Several books and numerous articles and reports have addressed the various aspects of benchmarking, but *Strategic Benchmarking* is the first book to address how it can and should be used as an integral part of a company's strategic planning process.

INTRODUCING BENCHMARKING

As a quality process, benchmarking is rapidly being adopted. It is similar to competitive analysis techniques managers have used in the past, and the personal visibility arising from being part of a benchmarking team can be a good career move. Also, many people are comfortable with it because it does *not* have an acronym (such as TQM, SPC, and DOE).

Gregory H. Watson, *Strategic Benchmarking: How to Rate Your Company's Performance Against the World's Best*. New York, NY: Wiley, 1993.

Benchmarking is a measurement process and results in comparative performance measures. Just as importantly, benchmarking identifies and describes process enablers, the practices that lead to exceptional performance.

The basic process of benchmarking follows the Plan-Do-Check-Act (PDCA) cycle. The first step is to answer two fundamental questions: (1) What should we benchmark? and (2) whom should we benchmark? The second step is to conduct secondary and primary research; secondary research includes public or disclosed information, and primary information is gathered through direct contact with the company. The third step is to analyze the data to determine the magnitude of the *gaps* between the companies and to identify the process enablers that facilitated the performance improvements at the leading companies. The final step is to adapt, improve, and implement the appropriate enablers at the home company in order to improve its performance and quality.

The concept of benchmarking dates back almost a century to Frederick W. Taylor, who encouraged comparison of work processes. Today, benchmarking is viewed as a five-generation evolutionary process, beginning with (1) *reverse engineering*, and moving through (2) *competitive benchmarking*, (3) *process benchmarking*, (4) *strategic benchmarking*, up to (5) *global benchmarking*.

Benchmarking is important because it helps identify the level of customer satisfaction. Customers tend to be satisfied with innovative features even if the engineering is lackluster; for items that are offered by several companies, however, customer satisfaction is directly related to the degree of engineering excellence. Customers expect items with basic performance characteristics (such as UL registration for electrical appliances) to perform well, so even outstanding engineering performance is recognized only when the item fails. Product and process design must continually improve because the innovative item is soon imitated and improved, as was the case of the coffee cup holder originally introduced in the Ford *Taurus*.

While companies must be careful about sharing information regarding specific product design and trade secrets, the sharing of information on processes can be mutually beneficial. Benchmarking is not a form of industrial espionage, because it is conducted in an open manner. To ensure that the needs of the participants are met, the Strategic Planning Institute of the American Productivity & Quality Center has developed a *Benchmarking Code of Conduct*.

Senior managers should understand that benchmarking topics and potential partners for benchmarking studies are strategic choices. The benchmarking studies should augment other information when considering company plans. Certain intellectual property must be protected, and employees must understand the criteria for disclosure to other companies. Management should use benchmarking information to establish reasonable goals and to develop the change implementation strategies to achieve those goals.

LINKING STRATEGIC PLANNING WITH BENCHMARKING

Strategy can be called the persistence of a vision. The vision and strategic goals are set by the corporate management team. Middle management teams are responsible for developing the strategy to achieve those goals. The subsequent actions are implemented by operational teams.

Understanding the strategic intent is important. Does the company have the commitment to global leadership over its arch rival? The company must do environmental scanning to guard against latent competitors—companies who are currently not competitors but who have the technology to be, such as Canon becoming a competitor of Xerox.

Companies should understand and develop their five or six core competencies. These provide potential access to a wide variety of markets, make a significant contribution to the perceived customer benefit of the product, and should be difficult for competitors to imitate. Similarly, companies have key business process capabilities that provide them with certain advantages.

Benchmarking becomes strategic when it is used to develop a better understanding of strategic business issues and may include long-term alliances with benchmarking partners. These issues may include building core competencies, targeting a specific shift in strategy, developing a new line of business, or creating an organization more capable of learning and responding to change. Strategic benchmarking should propel companies toward *world class* competition, where they are widely recognized as leading performers.

UNDERSTANDING THE ESSENTIALS OF PROCESS BENCHMARKING

The appropriate acquisition and application of quality methods, combined with the pursuit of business knowledge, sets the foundation for successful benchmarking. An organization must continuously apply and develop key quality and decision tools to analyze both qualitative and quantitative practices. Benchmarking is an advanced quality practice; as such, it is *not* a tool to be used by companies just beginning the implementation of a quality culture.

The degree to which an organization should benchmark is determined by its level of quality maturity, of which there are four levels. In the inspection level, the focus is on quality assurance; teams should concentrate on process improvement rather than benchmarking. In the control level, the focus shifts toward problem prevention as all employees become aware of and begin to regularly use the quality tools, and ISO 9000 may be used as a tool for documenting processes; appropriate benchmarking may be in an industry-specific study or one of the company's key business practices. The third level of quality maturity is partnership, and the focus shifts to improving key processes; "internal customers" may expand to include other business units within the corporation and companies in the supply chain. Benchmarking at this level should move to the strategic level. The fourth level is called maturity; teams work in all areas of operation and all people consider quality issues in all aspects of the business system to insure customer satisfaction; benchmarking is a standard practice.

The benchmarking process is to identify the gap in performance for a given process, to identify the process enablers that allow that gap to exist, to learn from the analysis, and to modify and adapt those process enablers to improve one's own process.

The four basic principles of benchmarking are reciprocity, analogy, measurement, and validity. Reciprocity means that the companies participating in the exercise insure a win-win situation from the start. The processes to be benchmarked should be comparative or analogous. To facilitate analysis, hard data are needed to measure, monitor, and verify process performance. Data also must be valid, timely, and accurate to make sure management is indeed done by fact.

Benchmarking presents significant room for observing another company's proprietary information or intellectual property. Federal anti-trust laws impede intercompany cooperation and hamper American competitiveness and productivity, but must be obeyed. A Code of Conduct is available to industry to provide an accepted standard of behavior. The nine principles of the Code cover the following:

- Legality (all laws must be obeyed).
- Exchange (be open and honest, and do not take any information the partner does not want to release).
- Confidentiality (do not reveal data to nonparticipants).
- Use (only use the information to improve one's own processes).
- First-party contact (initiate benchmarking inquiries through proper channels).
- Third-party contact (do not release partners' names to a third party).
- Preparation (first do a self-analysis on processes, strengths, and weaknesses before contacting potential partners).
- Completion (make sure that results can be given to management and partners in a timely manner).
- Understanding and action (information to share, protocol, and guidelines should be agreed on from the start).

When preparing for a benchmarking study, several questions need to be addressed. What processes should be benchmarked? Who should be the benchmarking partner(s)? How does our own company perform this process? How do they perform this process? Because benchmarking is expensive and time consuming, care should be taken to insure the study addresses a key business process, the business practices used to perform that process, and their impact on critical success factors. Operational definitions are important in preparing the planned study. To understand one's own processes, typical measures include a first-pass yield (effectiveness), value-to-cost ratio (process economy), and cycle time (process efficiency); these metrics and process maps indicate how a process functions. The same measures and process mapping will assess how the partner performs the analogous process.

The process for benchmarking is to first plan the study by identifying the strategic intent, core competencies, key business processes, and critical success factors; the particular process to be benchmarked is documented and characterized; requirements for selecting a benchmarking partner are defined; preliminary questionnaires are prepared and tested (testing is a critical activity). The second step in the process is to collect the necessary data by applying quality tools, performing secondary research in the literature, and conducting the primary research of interviews, mailed questionnaires, or on-site observation of the partner's processes and practices; the data are then sorted and organized. The third step of the process consists of data analysis, data presentation, root cause analysis, results projection, and enabler identification (including evaluating the nature of the process enablers to determine their adaptability to the company culture). The fourth step is to drive selected improvements into the organization as a result of the benchmarking study (some improvements will be obvious from the self-inspection); management may set parity goals (to meet the partner's performance level) or stretch goals (to improve upon the partner's performance level). At the end of the benchmarking process, management should provide a proper celebration and recognition for the benchmarking team.

APPLYING BENCHMARKING RESULTS FOR MAXIMUM UTILITY

Organizations need to evolve from a control-based management system to a learning-based management system. Benchmarking will facilitate this transition. It involves the networking of knowledgable companies and companies with needs or issues to resolve.

Dewey's learning theory cycle is similar to the Deming-Shewhart PDCA continuous improvement cycle. Dewey's Phase 1 is discovering new insights (plan a course of action); Phase 2 is inventing new possibilities (do a test); Phase 3 is producing the action (check to study the results); and Phase 4 is observing the consequences (act on the process based on the trial results). For an organization, learning must be targeted to better understand the customers' needs and expectations.

Organizations do not change quickly, especially if they have done well in the past. Corporate learning can be improved by communicating; program managers for Merck record their best and worst project development experiences in a "Book of Knowledge."

Corporate learning can occur in four basic types of benchmarking studies: internal, competitive, functional, and generic:

- *Internal benchmarking* targets partners within the same corporation and is the easiest to conduct.
- *Competitive benchmarking* evaluates competitors' products for performance, manufacturability, technology, operability, safety, and support.
- *Functional benchmarking* focuses on a particular operating activity or function; evaluation criteria should be established to provide assessments based on facts and data.
- *Generic benchmarking* does not involve an aspect of competitive advantage, but may be of interest in a given industry (such as training and education approaches for the electronics industry). External studies may be competitive or noncompetitive, and noncompetitive studies may be either functional or generic.

DOING AN INTERNAL BENCHMARKING STUDY

Internal benchmarking is an approach to process benchmarking in which organizations learn from other operating units, divisions, or companies within the corporation. These often yield the most detailed information about process improvement potential because intercompany barriers are not present.

In 1986, Hewlett-Packard (H-P) chief executive officer John Young set a stretch goal of cutting development times in half by 1994. Corporate engineering spearheaded the effort by conducting a study within H-P to find the practices that contributed to success in terms of time to market. A companywide productivity network in each of the firm's fifty-six R&D centers conducted best-practice analyses on recently completed projects; because of their autonomy, the project analyses were far from uniform. Corporate Engineering analyzed the reports to identify the common causes of schedule slippage. The most frequent cause of scheduling delays was changing of specifications; moving products to market quickly could be improved by a common measure of time-based performance and a better focus on customer requirements.

Today, H-P provides personnel with software, instructions, and staff consultants on how to use the time-to-market measure. To systematically focus on customer requirements, H-P has adopted Quality Function Deployment; there is no need to change a design specification if it is responsive to the customers' needs. Time to market has been reduced dramatically, from four and a half years for the DeskWriter jet printer to twenty-two months. This project has reduced cycle time and order turnaround in other areas as well.

CONDUCTING A COMPETITIVE BENCHMARKING STUDY

Competitive benchmarking studies target specific designs, process capabilities, or administrative methods used by a company's direct competitors. These studies are frequently conducted by a third party to report information that has been approved by the contributing company, among other reasons. It is much more difficult to share information one-on-one with a competitor because of potential concerns over antitrust violation and unfair trading practices.

In 1978, Ford recalled more U.S. models than it produced and lost $1.5 billion in 1980. The decision to develop the *Taurus* line was an opportunity for Ford to turn their fortunes around. Lew Veraldi was appointed the "heavyweight project manager" for Team Taurus; he could make things happen without seeking numerous approvals. He assembled a team to stay on the project from start to finish rather than a traditional "throw it over the wall" approach. The team first drew up a list of features that would seem important to the customer, and invited comments from many stakeholders, including auto body repair specialists; this took two years and resulted in 400 features to consider.

Taurus was intended to be "best in class" in each feature. To determine what was best, Team Taurus purchased fifty automobiles that catered to the middle-market car buyer; most of the cars were either U.S.-produced or foreign cars made for the American market. Each car was measured for its performance on the 400 selected features. This gave Ford the data to design a world-class car.

The *Taurus* was introduced in 1986, became *Motor Trend*'s car of the year, and helped restore Ford to financial health, surpassing General Motors in earnings for the first time in decades. The production car incorporated 77 percent of the 400 features benchmarked. The aerodynamic styling of the *Taurus*, employee participation, and quality initiatives also helped *Taurus* become a success. The experience taught Ford that competitive benchmarking can provide perspective and guidance on critical design and development issues and that the process is as important as the product.

PERFORMING A FUNCTIONAL BENCHMARKING STUDY

Functional benchmarking investigates the performance of a particular function within an industrywide application. This type of study offers a good opportunity to develop breakthrough results in terms of identifying and understanding process enablers. External consultants usually facilitate this type of study because of the need for logistical coordination and the need for "blinded" results.

Following the problems with the firm's "X" and "J" cars of the early 1980s, General Motors Corporate Quality & Reliability Department (Q&R) began working with Sandy Company consultants and 150 GM managers to study GM's larger quality issues, and to pinpoint matters of product quality, dependability, reliability, and performance that failed to match the expectations of customers. To achieve buy-in from defensive divisional managers, Q&R needed to be process-oriented and deal with quality issues from a strategic standpoint.

The study group identified ninety-two companies that were known for quality; this list was trimmed to twenty, of which eleven agreed to participate. The study was conducted unlike most benchmarking exercises. GM developed hypotheses on ten factors as distinguishing quality-competent companies and contributing to their success. GM teams visited the eleven host companies in the summer of 1983, spending three to five days at each site. A workshop consolidated the findings into a 136-page final report; the scores for each company conformed fairly well to the hypotheses. The report was useful to the team members and the host companies, but it was poorly received by GM management. Implementation did not occur, in part because of a massive reorganization of the company, although many of the people who helped conduct the study for GM have created change in daily activities outside the boundaries of official corporate programs.

DEVELOPING A GENERIC BENCHMARKING STUDY

Generic benchmarking represents the broadest application of data collection to industry partners; it is confined only by the ability to develop an analogous process and understand how it translates across industries. This innovative approach can result in changed paradigms and reengineering of business processes.

A 1981 study revealed that Japanese producers held approximately a one-month inventory, compared to Xerox's 3.2 months of inventory, costing roughly $33 million per month. The order-picking operations at Xerox were typically small-sized orders. Xerox decided to benchmark generically high-quality order-picking operators. Trade journals, professional associations, and management consultants specializing in material handling were researched. One article in *Modern Materials Handling* described L.L. Bean's mail-order operation.

The Xerox team arranged a site visit and prepared a questionnaire. They gathered data on the process, the information system, workers, equipment, and scheduling. Upon analysis, L.L. Bean's productivity was roughly three times that of Xerox. The Xerox team discovered the process enablers and adapted and incorporated them in their warehouse operations. This study has become a classic story of benchmarking at Xerox.

EXPANDING BENCHMARKING FOR BROADER APPLICATIONS

Benchmarking is the search for *best practices* that will lead to superior performance. It can be used in the service industry as well as in manufacturing. The International Facilities Management Association has organized a focus group to provide baseline information to its members on a number of operational parameters. Because associations cut across industry lines and include a diverse membership, they are natural repositories and potential clearinghouses for information on generic business functions.

Because of the rapid rise in health-care costs, providers have begun to examine their internal operations. The Health-Care Forum is an international not-for-profit association of health-care individuals and organizations. It began a study on how hospitals admit patients, with assistance from the International Benchmarking Clearinghouse of the American Productivity and Quality Center. In March 1992, twenty-eight participating hospitals began benchmarking their admitting process for elective acute-care patients. The study is to identify best-practice candidates, determine measurements of the admitting processes, and identify the process enablers, inhibitors, and improvements to guide future action. Each hospital was evaluated for opportunities for improvement. A second phase of this study will go beyond the health-care industry to analogous practices in airlines, hotels, rental-car agencies, and insurance companies.

CREATING A BENCHMARKING CAPABILITY

Benchmarking is a process. Like any process, it can be benchmarked—Hewlett-Packard did it in 1989, beginning with Xerox's process.

Pitfalls to avoid in benchmarking efforts are lack of management commitment (or worse, management disbelief), failure to learn from others' mistakes and failures, not factoring customer expectations into the study, lack of participation by the process owners, penalizing managers or employees for the current gap in performance observed during benchmarking, studying companies with a poor cultural fit, and too much informality in the method of benchmarking.

To help ensure that benchmarking succeeds, the Benchmarking Code of Conduct should be followed, management needs to be committed to the effort, the process cannot be rushed, team approaches are critical, and the study needs to be supportive of the company's strategy and vision.

Benefits of benchmarking include better understanding the needs of the customer and the dynamics of the industry, learning from the successes and failures of others, and providing a sense of urgency for continuously learning and improving.

Senior management must ensure that benchmarking teams focus on strategic objectives and have sufficient resources to succeed. They must also review plans and progress and act accordingly. If an outside consultant is needed to conduct a study, management should allow the team to learn how to conduct the study so that learning takes place. Benchmarking can be likened to a heart transplant; it represents significant change and must be handled carefully.

Benchmarking studies are valid for a point in time. They are perishable and time-sensitive. Benchmarking must be continually updated for those key business practices that affect the competitiveness of the organization.

The recipe for successful benchmarking requires three basic ingredients: a supportive management team with a real problem that needs to be solved; access to prospective benchmarking partners who have previously solved this problem; and a knowledgable benchmarking team with the ability to use basic quality tools and research methods to investigate process problems to their root cause. Add a dash of perseverance and a bunch of patience.

READING 4

Working Knowledge

How Organizations Manage What They Know

Thomas H. Davenport and Laurence Prusak
Summary prepared by Michael D. Kull

> **Michael D. Kull** *is a Doctoral Fellow in the School of Business and Public Management at the George Washington University in Washington, D.C., where he teaches graduate courses in knowledge management, organization, and innovation. His research and consulting work explores knowledge strategy and organizational intelligence. He is the author of several articles related to knowledge management and strategic innovation.*

> *"The great end of knowledge is not knowledge but action."*
> —THOMAS HENRY HUXLEY

> *"In the end, the location of the new economy is not in the technology, be it the microchip or the global telecommunications network. It is in the human mind."*
> —ALAN WEBBER, EDITOR, *FAST COMPANY*

> *"If HP knew what HP knows, we would be three times as profitable."*
> —LEW PLATT, CHIEF EXECUTIVE OFFICER OF HEWLETT-PACKARD

WHAT DO WE MEAN BY KNOWLEDGE MANAGEMENT?

The idea that people in organizations are effective because of their ability to seek, use, and value knowledge is not new. What is new is the movement in management thinking from an implicit to an explicit awareness that *knowledge is a strategic corporate asset*. Unlike traditional assets of land, labor, and capital that decrease with use, knowledge assets grow when shared. It is an insight that accords with what academic and business strategists refer to as a competency-based or resource-based theory of

Thomas H. Davenport & Laurence Prusak, *Working Knowledge*. New York, NY: Harvard Business School, 1998.

the firm. This view holds that companies differentiate themselves on the basis of what they know and how well they create new knowledge. In a deep sense, knowledge actually *is* the organization. Therefore, gaining a knowledge advantage means that a firm can outperform the competition by leveraging its knowledge to improve performance at all levels of the organization. *Knowledge management is the recognition that what matters most to managers today is an understanding of what is known in their organizations and how they can use that knowledge most effectively.*

A WORKING DEFINITION OF KNOWLEDGE

Understanding basic differences among data, information, and knowledge is essential to doing knowledge work. *Data* is a set of discrete facts about an event. For example, when a customer buys gas at a gas station, the transaction (price of gas, time of visit, number of gallons, and so on) can be recorded as data. The data do not tell us why the customer went to the gas station in the first place, or whether that customer is likely to return. *Information* adds meaning to data, literally "gives shape to" or provides a context for why the receivers of data should change their perceptions. It not only shapes data in an organized way, but also shapes the understanding of the people who receive it. Information may be data that has been contextualized, categorized, calculated, corrected, condensed, and may be presented through many different mediums. Information is data that makes a difference. *Knowledge* is a fluid mix of experience, values, shared context, and expert insight that provides a framework for evaluating and incorporating new experiences and information. It derives from individual minds, but it can be embedded in documents, technology, and organizational processes. Knowledge is deeper and richer than information and is sometimes divided into explicit and tacit knowledge: Whereas explicit knowledge can often be written down or codified, tacit knowledge such as human expertise is often too complex to be codified, which is why knowledge management is not simply a variation of information management or data management.

KNOWLEDGE FOR ACTION

The reason why knowledge is more valuable than information or data is that it is more closely linked to action. Knowledge is evaluated by the decisions that are made based on it, and is revised based on the outcomes of those decisions. Better knowledge can lead to measurable efficiencies in product development and marketing, for example. So whereas information and data may be evaluated on its accuracy and completeness, knowledge is evaluated on its relevance in decision making.

KNOWLEDGE MARKETS

Because knowledge is often embedded deep in the organization and can be extremely difficult to find and control, the key to effective knowledge management is to create and nurture *knowledge markets*. Like markets for goods and services, a company's knowledge market allows "buyers" and "sellers" of knowledge to negotiate a mutually satisfactory "price" for the exchange. People often gather informally in hallways to converse about organizational issues. Some managers assume that such socializing is a waste of time, not understanding that in a knowledge-based economy, dialogue is the real work.

KNOWLEDGE MARKET CHARACTERISTICS

Three kinds of players are involved in a knowledge market:

- *Knowledge buyers*: People who seek ideas and insights to solve their problems;
- *Knowledge sellers*: People who hold process knowledge (how things are done) or are experts on a particular subject; and
- *Knowledge brokers*: People who connect buyers and sellers; people who are not domain experts themselves but who know where to find the right people in the organization.

In a knowledge market, these players exchange knowledge for "currency" that takes one of three forms:

1. Reciprocity
2. Repute
3. Altruism

A knowledge seller will devote the time and effort needed to share knowledge if the seller expects to be a buyer of knowledge at some point in the future. *Reciprocity* depends mostly upon the seller's self-interest and builds up one's own "favor bank." *Repute* can be valuable to a seller if he or she wishes to build a reputation as an individual with demonstrable skills and competencies. In consulting firms, for example, repute is often tied directly to bonuses. *Altruism* is the motivation for people who genuinely like helping others. Mentoring is based in part on altruism. For currency to flow, knowledge markets must be established on trust. Trust must be visible, ubiquitous, and start at the top.

To make knowledge markets work, companies must take a systematic approach to encouraging the three core processes of knowledge management: knowledge generation, knowledge codification, and knowledge transfer.

Knowledge Generation

Organizations create new knowledge markets in several ways. The common factor for all these efforts is adequate time and space devoted to knowledge generation:

- *Acquisition*: The most direct method for getting new knowledge into an organization is to buy it, either by purchasing firms with complementary competencies or hiring good people.
- *Rental*: Outsourcing and hiring consultants are examples of renting knowledge. Although temporary arrangements, some knowledge is likely to stay with the firm when the rented knowledge source leaves.
- *Dedicated resources*: Resources dedicated specifically to knowledge generation, such as in-house research and development (R&D), are accomplished

by separating R&D from other internal pressures. It is a risky investment that takes time to recoup but ensures that most of the knowledge will remain with the firm.

- *Fusion*: In contrast to the R&D approach, this methods brings together people with different skills, ideas, and values from across the company to work together.
- *Adaptation*: Firms that survive through adaptation to their business environment are constantly creating new knowledge; learning is continuous and mandatory.
- *Networks*: Informal and formal communities of practice share expertise and solve problems. Allowing people to network is indispensable to knowledge generation.

Knowledge Codification

The purpose of codifying knowledge is to put an organization's existing knowledge into a useful format and make it easy to access. For managers, the main goal of knowledge codification is to explicate knowledge without losing its distinctive qualities as knowledge. Often much of the knowledge that has the greatest value to an organization is the most difficult to codify. To capture tacit knowledge, the value of *narratives* should not be overlooked. Human beings learn best from stories, and a good story is often the most effective way to convey meaningful knowledge.

Knowledge may also be embedded in a company's products and services, processes and technology. *Embedded knowledge* has some independence: A technology or process expert can exit an organization and leave behind his knowledge. In practice, it is difficult to find the line where embedded knowledge ends and where tacit knowledge begins. However, codified knowledge is extremely useful as it lends stability to an organization and provides new employees a basis from which to learn.

The four basic principles for knowledge codification are as follows:

1. Managers must decide what business goals the codified knowledge will serve. (For example, marketing divisions may want to codify knowledge about customer relationships.)
2. Managers must be able to identify knowledge existing in various forms appropriate to reaching their business goals.
3. Managers must evaluate knowledge for usefulness and relevance.
4. Managers must identify an appropriate medium for codification and distribution.

KNOWLEDGE MAPS

To help members of an organization track down the expertise they need, the organization can create and utilize a *knowledge map*. A knowledge map can be a visual representation of knowledge, a "Yellow Pages" of expertise, or a document database. Organizational surveys and interviews help managers assemble maps by capturing employee expertise and their social and informational networks—where they go when they need answers to questions. These private maps can be strung together to create a larger, public map.

An example of a knowledge map developed out of an effort by Microsoft's information systems group to map the knowledge of their systems developers in order to better assign employees to tasks and teams. The project is known as SPUD, for Skills Planning *und* (and) Development. The SPUD project consists of five stages of mapping:

1. Developing a structure of knowledge competency types and levels;
2. Defining the knowledge required for particular jobs;
3. Rating the performance of individual employees in those jobs, using the knowledge competencies;
4. Implementing the knowledge competencies in an online system; and
5. Linking the knowledge model to training programs.

Knowledge Transfer

Knowledge transfer is the transmission, absorption, and use of knowledge. The best way for managers to transfer knowledge from the heads of people to the heads of other people is to get them to talk to one another. Studies have shown that managers get two-thirds of their information and knowledge from face-to-face meetings or phone conversations, and only one-third comes from documents. There is no shortage of bright ideas in organizations, but the people that have them are often isolated or too busy for in-depth conversation.

People transfer knowledge every day, such as when a new sales representative asks a more seasoned sales rep about the needs of a particular client or when an engineer asks a colleague if he or she has ever dealt with a particular problem. Although examples abound of successful knowledge transfer, employees tend to go to the most convenient source rather than the best source in the company. *As the size of an organization grows, there is both a greater likelihood that needed knowledge exists somewhere in the organization and a correspondingly lower likelihood that it is easy to find.*

To encourage spontaneous knowledge transfer and disseminate it broadly, organizations should develop strategies for knowledge transfer. The following three suggestions are designed to encourage face-to-face dialogue—the richest form of knowledge transfer.

- *Assignees*: Sematech found, in attempting to transfer knowledge to its member firms, that the knowledge represented in its documents, document databases, intranet, and other sources were less effective channels than bringing in assignees for face-to-face mentoring.
- *"Water coolers"*: When IBM needed to reinvent itself in the 1980s, a memo was circulated telling employees to stay away from the water coolers and get back to work. When a business is struggling, people naturally gather to talk through problems and share possible solutions. Many Japanese firms have established "talk rooms" where researchers are expected to have a cup of tea and discuss work. Although unstructured, this strategy harnesses the serendipity that leads to innovation.
- *Knowledge fairs*: Regular meetings and fairs at 3M give researchers time and space to share ideas. Forums where professionals can meet to exchange knowledge, such as in-house conferences and retreats, have helped make 3M an exemplar of innovation.

Corporate culture can encourage or inhibit knowledge transfer. The "frictions" that erode the free flow of knowledge include a lack of trust, cultural conflict, lack of time, narrow perspectives of work, incentives to horde knowledge, intolerance for mistakes, and a belief in a knowledge hierarchy (the people at the top know the most). These obstacles can be overcome through education, building trust, job rotation, flexibility, performance appraisals that reward knowledge sharing and learning, and encouraging nonhierarchical interaction and collaboration.

Technologies for Knowledge Management

There is no single tool or "right" technology for knowledge management. Yet a principal reason knowledge management is important today is because of the new tools and technologies that have emerged to enable knowledge generation, codification, and transfer. Dozens of information technologies can be cited as knowledge management tools. The most visible today are *Web-based intranet* applications and *Lotus Notes.* Notes excels at database management and group work management. The Web is ideal for publishing material across multiple system platforms, for multimedia, and for linking knowledge through hypertext. These capabilities will soon be available as integrated packages to install across technical, functional, and business lines.

For both Web- and Notes-based applications, the primary purpose is to allow users to search and retrieve documents from a *knowledge repository*. However, other applications are useful for doing knowledge work, such as an *expert locator*, designed to find people instead of documents. For decision support, *case-based reasoning* (CBR) involves extracting knowledge from narratives of cases, and scripts are then developed to lead users through problem solutions. Unlike expert systems, which require rules to be well structured, CBR can reflect the fluid thinking that was needed to resolve an issue in the first place. *Constraint-based systems* are useful for narrow problem domains by modeling the constraints that govern complex decisions. *Neural nets* and *artificial intelligence* represent the future of knowledge technology, and these are intended to replicate some of the higher cognitive functions. GrapeVINE, used at HP, Andersen Consulting, and Ford, searches external databases for knowledge relevant to the organization. Some knowledge tools for facilitating communication are as simple as e-mail, desktop videoconferencing, or just the telephone. Individual tools can be integrated into enterprise-wide solutions.

Technology alone will not ensure the success of knowledge management and is even less helpful when it comes to knowledge creation. What is most important is that technology is used to expand access and ease the problem of getting the right knowledge to the right person at the right time.

Knowledge Management

Knowledge management is the capture, distribution, and utilization of knowledge. Knowledge management initiatives are composed of projects. These can be divided into three broad types:

- *Creating knowledge repositories*: These "stores" of knowledge are built to capture external knowledge (such as competitive intelligence), structured internal knowledge (such as research reports and design specifications), and informal internal knowledge (such as discussion databases and "lessons learned" databases).

* *Improving knowledge access*: These types of projects focus on connecting via technology the possessors and prospective users of knowledge.
* *Enhancing the knowledge environment*: Some projects attempt to establish a culture and climate conducive to knowledge management, including measuring the value of knowledge capital and improving its value.

Knowledge management is a set of practices in evolution. Successful projects result in growth of knowledge content and usage of repositories, an integration of local knowledge projects with larger organizational initiatives, and some indirect evidence of financial return. In studies of 31 different knowledge management projects in more than 20 companies, the following success factors were identified:

* *Knowledge-oriented culture*: A positive view of creating and sharing knowledge;
* *Technical and organizational infrastructure*: Having appropriate tools and roles;
* *Senior management support*: Executives who set the tone and provide resources;
* *A link to economics or industry value*: Some measurable benefit or value;
* *A process perspective*: A sense of how organizational learning occurs;
* *Clarity of vision and language*: Clear definitions of knowledge and mission;
* *Rewards and incentives*: Motivational approaches to encourage knowledge work;
* *Some degree of structure*: A purposeful balance between structure and fluidity; and
* *Multiple channels*: Several ways to reinforce interaction and knowledge transfer.

GETTING STARTED IN KNOWLEDGE MANAGEMENT

Knowledge management projects are going on in every organization, though they may not be recognized as such. Knowledge management represents a shift in perspective that coexists well with initiatives in business strategy, process improvement, customer relations, human resource management, information systems management, and so on. Leveraging existing management efforts in quality, best practices, reengineering, technology strategy, intellectual capital, and organizational learning is a pragmatic way to build understanding and support. A wise approach suggests the following:

* Begin first with high-value knowledge.
* Start with a focused pilot project; let demand drive new initiatives.
* Work along multiple fronts at once, such as technology, process, and culture.
* Do not put off the most difficult hurdles until it is too late.
* Get help throughout the organization as quickly as possible.

Managing knowledge should be the job of everyone in the company. Whether a dedicated executive is necessary to integrate a company's culture and technology, such as a chief knowledge officer, or whether knowledge management should be decentralized throughout the organization depends on many business factors. Although the motivation to share knowledge comes from the individual employee, often the commitment and initiative must come from the top in order to design a knowledge infrastructure, standardize codification methods, create new roles and positions, lead a knowledge strategy, and allocate organizational resources.

Knowledge management is not rocket science. (In fact, an executive at the Jet Propulsion Laboratory once said that even rocket science is not that hard anymore.) It is sound management principles and good sense presented in a way that is philosophically robust. Though pitfalls exist, knowledge management suggests a future of progressive business practice that embraces new technologies. But before embarking on new programs, managers should remember that just as people should not take action without thinking about what objectives are desired, *knowledge management initiatives should always serve the larger goals of the organization.*

PART THIRTEEN
Ethics and Management

Almost daily, newspaper and television reports appear that document unethical activities engaged in by organizations, their managers, and their employees. Simultaneously, the past several years have seen an increase in the number of schools of business that have introduced ethics courses into their curricula. A large number of organizations are discussing ethical behavior, developing codes of conduct or codes of ethics, and making statements about the core values of their organizations.

Earlier books (e.g., Kenneth Blanchard and Norman Vincent Peale's *The Power of Ethical Management*, Edward Freeman and Daniel Gilbert's *Corporate Strategy and the Search for Ethics*) explored the ethical dilemmas that managers face, the core principles that guide ethical decision making, and the need for linking corporate strategy and ethical reasoning. However, there still seemed to be questions about which values ethical leaders should hold, and how those values could be conveyed to their employees. Two widely read books address the need for managers to be ethical and credible.

James M. Kouzes and Barry Z. Posner surveyed 15,000 managers, analyzed 400 case studies, and interviewed 40 managers prior to writing *Credibility*, their second major book on leadership. (Their earlier work was *The Leadership Challenge*.) They discovered that employees want their ideal leaders to be honest, forward-looking, inspiring, competent, and supportive. Most-admired leaders were highly principled, held clear and strong values, were optimistic and hopeful, and demonstrated their belief in the self-worth of others. Kouzes and Posner urge readers to strengthen their credibility through a continuous internal dialogue, staying in touch with their constituents, developing others' capacities, affirming shared values, and sustaining employee hopes. Kouzes is president of TPG/Learning Systems, and Barry Posner is professor of organizational behavior at Santa Clara University. The newest book by Kouzes and Posner is *Encouraging the Heart*.

In *Defining Moments*, Joseph Badaracco contends that managers often face a cumulative series of situations that force them to choose between a conflict over what is right and what is right. At these times, they must translate their personal values into calculated action. To do this, they must resolve conflicting feelings, explore their deeply rooted values, and couple shrewdness and expediency with imagination and boldness to implement the "right" actions. This requires managers to identify their points of view, view truth as an emerging process, play to win, and move from vision to reality.

Joseph Badaracco is the John Shad Professor of Business Ethics at the Harvard Business School. Prior to writing this book, he wrote *The Knowledge Link* and *Loading the Dice*, and co-authored *Leadership and the Quest for Integrity*.

READING I

Credibility

James M. Kouzes and Barry Z. Posner
Summary prepared by Gregory R. Fox

Gregory R. Fox *is the Vice Chancellor for Finance and Operations at the University of Minnesota, Duluth. He earned his master's degree at the University of Washington, and received a Bush Mid-Career Leadership Fellowship. He has developed instructional support materials for the Newstrom and Bittel book* Supervision: Managing for Results.

Leadership is many things—a series of actions, an encounter between people, an intangible, a performing art. Leadership does not, and cannot, exist independently, for it is a *reciprocal relationship* between those who choose to lead and those who decide to follow. There have been dramatic changes in the nature of the relationship between leader and subordinate (employer–employee) during the past decade. Most significant has been an increased awareness of the leader's need to serve others, to build seamless partnerships with others, and to build a community of individuals and teams at work. Wise leaders have become servers, supporters, partners, and providers, building their relationships on mutual obligations, commitments, and collaboration. This changing leader–follower relationship increasingly creates *servant leaders* who value the role of serving, and giving to, those with whom they work.

KEY LEADERSHIP CHARACTERISTICS

In a survey, 15,000 managers were asked to identify their seven most admired leadership characteristics from a set of twenty qualities. The results of the survey, subsequent case studies, and in-depth interviews were remarkably consistent. The most desirable characteristics (those selected by more than half of the respondents) identified for leaders were honest, forward-looking, inspiring, and competent. *Honesty appears to be essential to leadership*, with 87 percent of the respondents selecting that characteristic.

Results also suggest that *competence* (being capable, effective, challenging, and encouraging), while still widely cherished as a leader characteristic, *is valued somewhat less today than in the past*. This could be seen as a cause for concern if companies start being led by visionary and inspirational individuals who do not have the complex skills needed to implement their visions. In contrast to the decline in valuing competence, the leader quality that has increased most in value during the last ten years is

James M. Kouzes & Barry Z. Posner, *Credibility*. San Francisco, CA: Jossey-Bass, 1993.

supportiveness. This characteristic originally ranked eleventh and now ranks sixth overall as an admired leadership attribute. This change reflects a strong societal trend toward empowerment, and indicates that people are searching for more understanding and encouragement from their leaders.

The qualities of honesty (trustworthiness), inspiration (dynamism), and competence (expertise) in combination are often referred to as source credibility. *Credibility is believed to be the primary foundation of future global leadership*, although it has often been overlooked in the past.

Studies done by Lou Harris, The Opinion Research Corporation, and others suggest that there is a significant gap between the value that constituents place on credibility and the likeliness it will occur in their place of work. The recent savings and loan and Wall Street scandals and religious fraud have led to a sense of betrayal and public disillusionment. Fueling this disillusionment have been recent reports of chief executive officer compensation at up to 150 times the level of the average worker in manufacturing and service industries. When employees believe that management does not "walk their talk," a *credibility gap*—a strong sense of cynicism—occurs, which weakens the bond that is required for effective leadership.

Earning credibility is done one-to-one, a little at a time, through personal contact with constituents. Managers are encouraged to "Do what you say you will do"—and then substitute "we" for "you" in that motto to build a bond with those they are serving. Three critical elements for strengthening leader credibility are clarity, unity, and intensity. *Clarification* of values, visions, and aims helps others understand the guiding principles. *Unity* is the degree to which people understand, agree on, and support the clarified values and directions. *Intensity* is the strength of commitment to deeply held aims and aspirations.

When leaders demonstrate credibility through clarity, unity, and intensity, workers tend to feel enthusiastically motivated, challenged and inspired, capable and powerful, as well as respected, valued, and proud. The predictable employee outcomes of these feelings include pride in belonging, strong team spirit, congruence of personal and organizational values, organizational commitment, and sense of ownership. Credible leadership stimulates employees to contribute their time and talents toward a common purpose.

THE SIX DISCIPLINES

Leaders earn credibility, respect, and loyalty when they demonstrate that they believe in the self-worth of others. Leaders must appreciate others, affirm others, and develop others. They must demonstrate these behaviors persistently and tenaciously. Through the study of leaders and leadership, six disciplines that underlie credibility emerge. They are as follows (see additional details in Table 1):

- Discovering yourself (clarifying your values)
- Appreciating constituents (talking and listening to them)
- Affirming shared values (striving for consensus and community)
- Developing constituents' capacity (constantly educating)
- Serving a purpose (becoming servant leaders)
- Sustaining hope (maintaining energy and optimism)

TABLE 1   The Six Leadership Disciplines

Discovering Yourself *Leaders should*	*Developing Capacity* *Leaders should*
Keep a journal	Stop making decisions
Discover their life themes	Stop talking at staff meetings
Assess their values	Set up coaching opportunities
Audit their ability to succeed	Invite people to assume responsibility
Seek mastery experiences	Give everyone a customer
Ask for support or help	Have an open house
Evaluate the five "Ps" of	Share the big picture
personal mission:	Enrich people's jobs
• Proficiency	Let constituents be the teachers
• Product	Use modeling to develop competencies
• People	
• Place	
• Purpose	

Appreciating Constituents and Their Diversity *Leaders should*	*Serving a Purpose* *Leaders should*
Be accessible, even at home	Manage by storytelling
Listen everywhere and listen well	Create heroes
Learn your constituents' stories	Speak with confidence
Step outside your cultural experience	Reduce fear
Keep in touch with your constituents	Ask questions
Become an employee for a day	Hold yourself accountable
Be the first to take a risk	Keep score
Know what bugs your constituents	Conduct a personal audit
Practice small wins	Conduct an organization audit
	Get everyone to champion values

Affirming Shared Values *Leaders should*	*Sustaining Hope* *Leaders should*
Get together to start drafting your group's credo	Exercise
Make sure there is an agreement around values	Write your vision for the future
Conduct a values survey	Set goals and make a plan
Connect values with reasons	Choose flexible optimism
Structure cooperative goals	Suffer first
Make sure everyone knows the business	Nurture optimism and passion
Be an enthusiastic spokesperson for shared values	Go visiting
Say "yes" frequently	Dispute your negative beliefs
Go slow to go fast	Reclarify your values
Establish a sunset statute for your credo	

Self-discovery

A review of those individuals who are identified as the most admired leaders reveals that they are people who are highly principled, with strong beliefs. Their individual values clarify what they will or will not do, directly contributing to their credibility as a leader. In addition, strong personal values assist in resolving conflicts and serve to motivate others.

Those interested in leadership are encouraged to write their own personal leadership philosophy and then evaluate what has been written. This assessment is aimed at identifying the values that are expressed in this credo. Exercises like this make it possible for those interested in the study of leadership to assess what values are most evident in effective leaders.

Another important characteristic associated with self-discovery is developing confidence and self-efficacy. This requires identifying the skills, knowledge, and abilities that are necessary to represent the values you claim with moral force. Effective leaders identify the skills necessary for their job. They acquire competence (mastery) in each of these areas and then expand the skills they have to be more effective in a wide variety of circumstances. They observe successful role models, seek social support from others, and manage the stresses in their lives. Then they seek to exhibit optimal performance, or *flow*, through goal setting, becoming immersed in their roles, avoiding distraction through intense attention to the present, and learning to enjoy their current activities.

Appreciating Constituents

Effective leaders recognize that organizations (and individuals) are enriched through diversity. They seek to create cultures where each person values and affirms others, relationships are collaborative, co-workers develop a sense of shared history, and the whole person (work and family elements) is recognized. These leaders keep their minds open, appreciate the uniqueness in others, solicit and use feedback from others, trust others, and stimulate constructive controversy.

Affirming Shared Values

Leaders seek a common core of understanding—an identification of shared values and consensus around paradigms. They struggle to identify common ground, they advocate cooperative community of purpose, and they foster consensus around key issues. They create drafts of underlying creeds, and demonstrate flexibility as revisions are sought and made.

Developing Capacity

Credible leaders believe in the abilities of others to grow and develop. They empower others through distributed leadership; they provide educational opportunities for building others' knowledge and skill; they encourage a sense of ownership in employees; and they inspire confidence in employee abilities to act responsibly and capably. They invite employees to accept mutual responsibility for results, and share information and feedback that allows others to grow.

Serving a Purpose

Leaders must have a strong sense of faith in what they are doing, and why. They recognize their servant leader role and set examples that others can follow. They are visibly "out front" demonstrating their priorities, staying in touch with their constituents, and making an impression on others through storytelling, "utilizing the teachable moment" when others are particularly susceptible to learning, and standing up for their beliefs. Perhaps most importantly, they create enduring organizational systems and structures that reinforce and support their values long after the leader has departed.

Sustaining Hope

People struggle. People get discouraged. People lose hope. These are moments when credible leaders need to be proactive, demonstrating that it is possible to regain internal control over external events. Leaders can inspire others to take initiative courageously, to balance hope and work for reasonable results, and to enjoy themselves along the path. And leaders are encouraged to demonstrate the acceptability of being caring, loving, and compassionate in the workplace so as to inspire others to do so, too.

CONCLUSION

Currently, the work world is experiencing a fundamental restructuring. There are no guarantees that a perfectly executed leadership plan will result in a satisfying, successful worklife. Credible leaders, those most in touch with their constituents, feel the pain most strongly. Leaders seeking to establish their credibility are urged to develop understanding and learn to love the struggle. But a caveat is in order: *Excessive emphasis on any one of the six disciplines can damage a leader's credibility.*

Leaders can strengthen their credibility by engaging in a dialogue about the fundamental tension between freedom and constraint. In nearly every workplace, more freedom is becoming commonplace; at the same time, institutions will continue to have some sharp constraints. The dialogue will focus on questions of how many, how much, and what type.

The success of leaders should be measured by whether or not they left their organization a better place than when they found it. To respond to the organizational struggle, credible leaders need to be optimistic, hopeful, and inspiring. They need to discover their own selves, appreciate the diversity of others, and recognize that renewing credibility is a continuous struggle. They need to take risks, accept the associated pain and excitement, and revel in the exhilaration of becoming continual learners about what it means to be leaders. In short, they need to be credible—to themselves and to others.

READING 2

The Discipline of Building Character

Joseph L. Badaracco, Jr.

We have all experienced, at one time or another, situations in which our professional responsibilities unexpectedly come into conflict with our deepest values. A budget crisis forces us to dismiss a loyal, hardworking employee. Our daughter has a piano recital on the same afternoon that our biggest client is scheduled to visit our office. At these times, we are caught in a conflict between right and right. And no matter which option we choose, we feel like we've come up short.

Managers respond to these situations in a variety of ways: some impulsively "go with their gut"; others talk it over with their friends, colleagues, or families; still others think back to what a mentor would do in similar circumstances. In every case, regardless of what path is chosen, these decisions taken cumulatively over many years form the very basis of an individual's character. For that reason, I call them *defining moments*.

What is the difference between a tough ethical decision and a defining moment? An ethical decision typically involves choosing between two options: one we know to be right and another we know to be wrong. A defining moment, however, challenges us in a deeper way by asking us to choose between two or more ideals in which we deeply believe. Such challenges rarely have a "correct" response. Rather, they are situations created by circumstance that ask us to step forward and, in the words of the American philosopher John Dewey, "form, reveal, and test" ourselves. We form our character in defining moments because we commit to irreversible courses of action that shape our personal and professional identities. We reveal something new about us to ourselves and others because defining moments uncover something that had been hidden or crystallize something that had been only partially known. And we test ourselves because we discover whether we will live up to our personal ideals or only pay them lip service.

As I have interviewed and studied business leaders, I have found that the ones who are most satisfied with the way they resolve their defining moments possess skills that are left off most job descriptions. Specifically, they are able to take time out from the chain of managerial tasks that consumes their time and undertake a process of probing self-inquiry—a process that is more often carried out on the run rather than in quiet seclusion. They are able to dig below the busy surface of their daily lives and refocus on their core values and principles. Once uncovered, those values and principles renew their sense of purpose at work and act as a springboard for shrewd, pragmatic, politically astute action. By repeating this process again and again throughout their work lives, these executives are able to craft an authentic and strong identity based on their own, rather than on someone else's, understanding of what is right. And in this way, they begin to make the transition from being a manager to becoming a leader.

But how can an executive trained in the practical, extroverted art of management learn to engage in such an intuitive, personal process of introspection? In this article, I will describe a series of down-to-earth questions that will help managers take time out from the hustle and bustle of the workplace. These practical, thought-provoking questions are designed to transform values and beliefs into calculated action. They have been drawn from well-known classic and contemporary philosophers but remain profound and flexible enough to embrace a wide range of contemporary right-versus-right decisions. By taking time out to engage in this process of self-inquiry, managers will by no means be conducting a fruitless exercise in escapism; rather, they will be getting a better handle on their most elusive, challenging, and essential business problems.

In today's workplace, three kinds of defining moments are particularly common. The first type is largely an issue of personal identity. It raises the question, Who am I? The second type is organizational as well as personal: both the character of groups within an organization and the character of an individual manager are at stake. It raises the question, Who are we? The third type of defining moment is the most complex and involves defining a company's role in society. It raises the question, Who is the company? By learning to identify each of these three defining moments, managers will learn to navigate right-versus-right decisions with grace and strength.

WHO AM I?
DEFINING MOMENTS FOR INDIVIDUALS

The most basic type of defining moment demands that managers resolve an urgent issue of personal identity that has serious implications for their careers. Two "rights" present themselves, each one representing a plausible and usually attractive life choice. And therein lies the problem: there is no one right answer; right is set against right.

Conflicting Feelings   When caught in this bind, managers can begin by taking a step back and looking at the conflict not as a problem but as a natural tension between two valid perspectives. To flesh out this tension, we can ask, *What feelings and intuitions are coming into conflict in this situation?* As Aristotle discussed in his classic work *Ethics*, people's feelings can actually help them make sense of an issue, understand its basic dimensions, and indicate what the stakes really are. In other words, our feelings and intuitions are both a form of intelligence and a source of insight.

Consider, for example, the case of a young analyst—we will call him Steve Lewis—who worked for a well-known investment bank in Manhattan.[1] Early one morning, Lewis, an African-American, found a message on his desk asking if he could fly to St. Louis in two days to help with a presentation to an important prospective client. The message came as a surprise to him. Lewis's company had a clear policy against including analysts in presentations or client meetings. Lewis, in fact, knew little about the subject of the St. Louis meeting, which concerned a specialized area of municipal finance. He was especially surprised to learn that he had been selected over more senior people in the public finance group.

Lewis immediately walked down the hall into the office of his friend and mentor, also an African-American, and asked him if he knew about the situation. His friend, a partner at the company, replied, "Let me tell you what's happening, Steve. Look at you and me. What do we have in common? Did you know that the new state treasurer of Missouri is also black? I hate for you to be introduced to this side of the business so soon, but the state treasurer wants to see at least one black professional at the meeting or else the company has no chance of being named a manager for this deal."

What if at this point Lewis were to step back and reframe the situation in terms of his feelings and intuitions? On the one hand, Lewis believed firmly that in order to maintain his self-respect, he had to earn his advancement at the company—and elsewhere in life. He was not satisfied to move up the ladder of success based on affirmative action programs or being a "token" member of the company. For that reason, he had always wanted to demonstrate through his work that he deserved his position. On the other hand, as a former athlete, Lewis had always prided himself on being a team player and did not believe in letting his teammates down. By examining his feelings and intuitions about the situation, Lewis learned that the issue at hand was more complex than whether or not to go to the presentation. It involved a conflict between two of his most deeply held beliefs.

Deeply Rooted Values   By framing defining moments in terms of our feelings and intuitions, we can remove the conflict from its business context and bring it to a more personal, and manageable, level. Then we can consider a second question to help resolve the conflict: *Which of the responsibilities and values that are in conflict are most deeply rooted in my life and in the communities I care about?* Tracing the roots of our values means understanding their origins and evolution over time. It involves an effort to understand which values and commitments really mean the most to us.

Let's apply that approach to the case of Steve Lewis. On the one hand, he had no doubt that he wanted to become a partner at a major investment bank and that he wanted to earn that position based on merit. Since his sophomore year of college, Lewis had been drawn to the idea of a career on Wall Street, and he had worked hard and purposefully to make that idea a reality. When he accepted his current job, he had finally set foot on the path he had dreamed of, and neither the long hours nor the detailed "grunt" work that was the lot of first-year analysts gave him misgivings about his choice. He believed he was pursuing his own values by seeking a successful career at a Wall Street investment bank. It was the kind of life he wanted to live and the kind of work he enjoyed doing.

---

1. The names in the accounts of Steve Lewis and Peter Adario have been changed to protect the privacy of the principals involved.

On the other hand, when Lewis considered his African-American background, he thought about what his parents had taught him. One episode from the early 1960s stood out in particular. His parents made a reservation at a restaurant that reputedly did not serve blacks. When they arrived, the hostess told them there had been a mistake. The reservation was lost, and they could not be seated. The restaurant was half empty. Lewis's parents turned around and left. When they got home, his mother made a new reservation under her maiden name. (His father had been a popular local athlete, whose name was widely recognized.) The restaurant suspected nothing. When they returned an hour later, the hostess, though hardly overjoyed, proceeded to seat them.

Lewis was still moved by the memory of what his parents had done, even as he sat in his office on Wall Street many years later. With his parents' example in mind, Lewis could begin to sense what seemed to be the best answer to his present dilemma. He would look at the situation as his parents' son. He would view it as an African-American, not as just another young investment banker. Lewis decided that he could not go to the meeting as the "token black." To do so would repudiate his parents' example. He decided, in effect, that his race was a vital part of his moral identity, one with a deeper and stronger relation to his core self than the professional role he had recently assumed.

Shrewdness and Expediency   Introspection of the kind Steve Lewis engaged in can easily become divorced from real-world demands. We have all seen managers who unthinkingly throw themselves into a deeply felt personal cause and suffer serious personal and career setbacks. As the Renaissance philosopher Niccolò Machiavelli and other ethical pragmatists remind us, idealism untempered by realism often does little to improve the world. Hence, the next critical question becomes, *What combination of shrewdness and expediency, coupled with imagination and boldness, will help me implement my personal understanding of what is right?* This is, of course, a different question altogether from What should I do? It acknowledges that the business

A Guide to Defining Moments		
For Individuals	*For Managers of Work Groups*	*For Company Executives*
Who am I?	*Who are we?*	*Who is the company?*
1. What feelings and intuitions are coming into conflict in this situation?	1. What are the other strong, persuasive interpretations of the ethics of this situation?	1. Have I done all I can to secure my position and the strength of my organization?
2. Which of the values that are in conflict are most deeply rooted in my life?	2. What point of view is most likely to win a contest of interpretations inside my organization and influence the thinking of other people?	2. Have I thought creatively and boldly about my organization's role in society and its relationship to stockholders?
3. What combination of expediency and shrewdness, coupled with imagination and boldness, will help me implement my personal understanding of what is right?	3. Have I orchestrated a process that can make manifest the values I care about in my organization?	3. What combination of shrewdness, creativity, and tenacity will help me transform my vision into a reality?

world is a bottom-line, rough-and-tumble arena where introspection alone won't get the job done. The process of looking inward must culminate in concrete action characterized by tenacity, persuasiveness, shrewdness, and self-confidence.

How did Lewis combine idealism with realism? He decided that he would join the presentation team, but he also gambled that he could do so on terms that were at least acceptable to him. He told the partner in charge, Bruce Anderson, that he felt honored to be asked to participate but added that he wanted to play a role in the presentation. He said he was willing to spend every minute of the next 30 hours in preparation. When Anderson asked why, Lewis said only that he wanted to earn his place on the team. Anderson reluctantly agreed. There was, it turned out, a minor element of the presentation that required the application of some basic analytical techniques with which Lewis was familiar. Lewis worked hard on the presentation, but when he stood up during the meeting for the 12 minutes allotted him, he had a terrible headache and wished he had refused Anderson's offer. His single day of cramming was no substitute for the weeks his colleagues had invested in the project. Nevertheless, his portion of the presentation went well, and he received praise from his colleagues for the work he had done.

On balance, Lewis had soundly defined the dilemma he faced and had taken an active role in solving it—he did not attend the meeting as a showpiece. At the same time, he may have strengthened his career prospects. He felt he had passed a minor test, a rite of passage at his company, and had demonstrated not only that he was willing to do what it took to get the job done but also that he would not be treated as a token member of the group. The white analysts and associates who were passed over probably grumbled a bit; but Lewis suspected that, if they had been dealt his hand, they would have played their cards as he did.

WHO ARE WE? DEFINING MOMENTS FOR WORK GROUPS

As managers move up in an organization, defining moments become more difficult to resolve. In addition to looking at the situation as a conflict between two personal beliefs, managers must add another dimension: the values of their work group and their responsibilities to the people they manage. How, for example, should a manager respond to an employee who repeatedly shows up for work with the smell of alcohol on his breath? How should a manager respond to one employee who has made sexually suggestive remarks to another? In this type of defining moment, the problem and its resolution unfold not only as a personal drama within one's self but also as a drama among a group of people who work together. The issue becomes public and is important enough to define a group's future and shape its values.

Points of View   Many managers suffer from a kind of ethical myopia, believing that their entire group views a situation through the same lens that they do. This way of thinking rarely succeeds in bringing people together to accomplish common goals. Differences in upbringing, religion, ethnicity, and education make it difficult for any two people to view a situation similarly—let alone an entire group of people. The ethical challenge for a manager is not to impose his or her understanding of what is right on the group but to understand how other members view the dilemma. The manager must ask, *What are the other strong, persuasive interpretations of the ethics of this situation?*

A classic example of this kind of problem involved a 35-year-old manager, Peter Adario. Adario headed the marketing department of Sayer Microworld, a distributor of computer products. He was married and had three children. He had spent most of his career as a successful salesman and branch manager, and he eagerly accepted his present position because of its varied challenges. Three senior managers reporting to Adario supervised the other 50 employees in the marketing department, and Adario in turn reported to one of four vice presidents at corporate headquarters.

Adario had recently hired an account manager, Kathryn McNeil, who was a single mother. Although she was highly qualified and competent, McNeil was having a hard time keeping up with her work because of the time she needed to spend with her son. The pace at work was demanding: the company was in the middle of finishing a merger, and 60-hour work weeks had become the norm. McNeil was also having difficulty getting along with her supervisor, Lisa Walters, a midlevel manager in the department who reported to Adario. Walters was an ambitious, hard-driving woman who was excelling in Sayer Microworld's fast-paced environment. She was irritated by McNeil's chronic lateness and unpredictable work schedule. Adario had not paid much attention to Walters' concerns until the morning he found a handwritten note from her on top of his pile of unfinished paperwork. It was her second note to him in as many weeks. Both notes complained about McNeil's hours and requested that she be fired.

For Adario, who was himself a father and sympathetic to McNeil's plight, the situation was clearly a defining moment, pitting his belief that his employees needed time with their families against his duty to the department's bottom line. Adario decided to set up a meeting. He was confident that if he sat down with the two women the issue could somehow be resolved. Shortly before the meeting was to begin, however, Adario was stunned to learn that Walters had gone over his head and discussed the issue with one of the company's senior executives. The two then had gone to McNeil's office and had fired her. A colleague later told him that McNeil had been given four hours to pack her things and leave the premises.

Where Adario saw right versus right, Walters saw right versus wrong. She believed that the basic ethical issue was McNeil's irresponsibility in not pulling her weight and Adario's lack of action on the issue. McNeil's customer account was crucial, and it was falling behind schedule during a period of near-crisis at the company. Walters also believed that it was unfair for one member of the badly overburdened team to receive special treatment. In retrospect, Adario could see that he and Walters looked at the same facts about McNeil and reached very different conclusions. Had he recognized earlier that his view was just one interpretation among many, he might have realized that he was engaged in a difficult contest of interpretations.

Influencing Behavior   Identifying competing interpretations, of course, is only part of the battle. Managers also need to take a hard look at the organization in which they work and make a realistic assessment of whose interpretation will win out in the end. A number of factors can determine which interpretation will prevail: company culture, group norms, corporate goals and company policy, and the inevitable political jockeying and battling inside organizations. In the words of the American philosopher William James, "The final victorious way of looking at things will be the most completely impressive to the normal run of minds." Therefore, managers need to ask themselves, *What point of view is most likely to win the contest of interpretations and influence the thinking and behavior of other people?*

Peter Adario would have benefited from mulling over this question. If he had done so, he might have seen the issue in terms of a larger work-family issue within the company. For Adario and McNeil, the demands of work and family meant constant fatigue, a sense of being pulled in a thousand directions, and the frustration of never catching up on all they had to do. To the other employees at Sayer Microworld, most of whom were young and not yet parents, the work-family conflict meant that they sometimes had to work longer hours because other employees had families to attend to. Given the heavy workloads they were carrying, these single employees had little sympathy for Adario's family-oriented values.

Truth as Process   Planning ahead is at the heart of managerial work. One needs to learn to spot problems before they blow up into crises. The same is true for defining moments in groups. They should be seen as part of a larger process that, like any other, needs to be managed. Effective managers put into place the conditions for the successful resolution of defining moments long before those moments actually present themselves. For in the words of William James, "The truth of an idea is not a stagnant property inherent in it. Truth happens to an idea. It becomes true, is made true by events. Its verity is in fact an event, a process." Managers can start creating the conditions for a particular interpretation to prevail by asking, *Have I orchestrated a process that can make my interpretation win in my group?*

Adario missed subtle signals that a process opposed to his own had been under way for some time. Recall that Walters had sent Adario two notes, each suggesting that McNeil be replaced. What were those notes actually about? Were they tentative announcements of Walters's plans or tests of Adario's authority? And what did Walters make of Adario's failure to respond? She apparently interpreted his reaction—or lack thereof—as an indication that he would not stand in the way of firing McNeil. Walters may even have thought that Adario wanted McNeil fired but was unwilling to do it himself. In short, Adario's defining moment had gone badly because Walters presented a compelling story to the company's top management; she thereby preempted Adario and filled the vacuum that he had created through his inaction.

Instead of waiting for the issue of work versus family to arise and take the group by surprise, Adario could have anticipated the problem and taken a proactive approach to defining a work culture that valued both family and work. Adario had ample opportunity to prevent the final turn of events from occurring. He could have promoted McNeil to others inside the company. In particular, he needed to emphasize the skills and experience, especially in account management, that she brought to the company. He also could have created opportunities for people to get to know McNeil personally, even to meet her son, so that they would understand and appreciate what she was accomplishing.

Playing to Win   One of the hallmarks of a defining moment is that there is a lot at stake for all the players in the drama. More often than not, the players will put their own interests first. In this type of business setting, neither the most well-meaning intentions nor the best-designed process will get the job done. Managers must be ready to roll up their sleeves and dive into the organizational fray, putting to use appropriate and effective tactics that will make their vision a reality. They need to reflect on the question, *Am I just playing along or am I playing to win?*

At Sayer Microworld, the contest of interpretations between Walters and Adario was clearly part of a larger power struggle. If Walters didn't have her eye on Adario's job before McNeil was fired, she probably did afterward: top management seemed to like her take-charge style. Whereas Adario was lobbing underhand softball pitches, Walters was playing hardball. At Sayer Microworld, do-the-right-thing idealism without organizational savvy was the sure path to obscurity. Adario's heart was in the right place when he hired McNeil. He believed she could do the job, he admired her courage, and he wanted to create a workplace in which she could flourish. But his praiseworthy intentions needed to be backed by a knack for maneuvering, shrewdness, and political savvy. Instead, Walters seized the moment. She timed her moves carefully and found a powerful ally in the senior manager who helped her carry out her plan.

Although Adario stumbled, it is worth noting that this defining moment taught him a great deal. In following up on McNeil's firing, Adario learned through the grapevine that many other employees shared his view of the work-family dilemma, and he began acting with more confidence than he had before. He told his boss that he disagreed with the decision to fire McNeil and objected strongly to the way the decision had been made. He then told Walters that her behavior would be noted in the next performance review he put in her file. Neither Walters nor the vice president said very much in response, and the issue never came up again. Adario had staked his claim, albeit belatedly. He had learned, in the words of Machiavelli, that "a man who has no position in society cannot even get a dog to bark at him."

WHO IS THE COMPANY?
DEFINING MOMENTS FOR EXECUTIVES

Redefining the direction of one's own life and the direction of one's work group requires a thoughtful blend of personal introspection and calculated action. But the men and women charged with running entire companies sometimes face an even more complex type of defining moment. They are asked to make manifest their understanding of what is right on a large stage—one that can include labor unions, the media, shareholders, and many other company stakeholders. Consider the complexity of the dilemma faced by a CEO who has just received a report of package tampering in one of the company's over-the-counter medications. Or consider the position of an executive who needs to formulate a response to reports in the media that women and children are being treated unfairly in the company's foreign plant. These types of decisions force top-level managers to commit not just themselves or their work groups but their entire company to an irreversible course of action.

Personal and Organizational Strength   In the face of such overwhelming decisions, executives typically call meetings, start negotiations, and hire consultants and lawyers. Although these steps can be helpful, they can prove disappointing unless executives have taken the time, and the necessary steps, to carve out a powerful position for themselves in the debate. From a position of strength, leaders can bring forth their vision of what is right in a situation; from a position of weakness, leaders' actions are hollow and desperate. Also, before CEOs can step forth onto society's broad stage with a personal vision, they must make sure that their actions will not jeopardize the well-being of their companies, the jobs of employees, and the net income of shareholders. That means asking, *Have I done all I can to secure my position and the strength and stability of my organization?*

In 1988, Eduoard Sakiz, CEO of Roussel Uclaf, a French pharmaceutical company, faced a defining moment of this magnitude. Sakiz had to decide whether to market the new drug RU-486, which later came to be known as the French abortion pill. Early tests had shown that the drug was 90% to 95% effective in inducing miscarriages during the first five weeks of a woman's pregnancy. As he considered whether to introduce the drug, Sakiz found himself embroiled in a major international controversy. Antiabortion groups were outraged that the drug was even under consideration. Pro-choice groups believed the drug represented a major step forward in the battle to secure a woman's right to an abortion. Shareholders of Roussel Uclaf's parent company, Hoechst, were for the most part opposed to RU-486's introduction because there had been serious threats of a major boycott against Hoechst if the drug were introduced. To the French government, also a part owner of Roussel Uclaf, RU-486 meant a step forward in its attempts to cut back on back-alley abortions.

There is little doubt that at one level, the decision Sakiz faced was a personal defining moment. He was a physician with a long-standing commitment to RU-486. Earlier in his career while working as a medical researcher, Sakiz had helped develop the chemical compound that the drug was based on. He believed strongly that the drug could help thousands of women, particularly those in poor countries, avoid injury or death from botched abortions. Because he doubted that the drug would make it to market if he were not running the company, Sakiz knew he would have to secure his own position.

At another level, Sakiz had a responsibility to protect the jobs and security of his employees. He understood this to mean taking whatever steps he could to avoid painful boycotts and the risk of violence against the company. His decision was complicated by the fact that some employees were passionately committed to RU-486, whereas others opposed the drug on ethical grounds or feared that the protests and boycotts would harm Roussel Uclaf and its other products.

How could Sakiz protect his own interests and those of his employees and still introduce the drug? Whatever path he chose, he could see that he would have to assume a low public profile. It would be foolish to play the courageous lion and charge forth pronouncing the moral necessity of RU-486. There were simply too many opponents for that approach to work. It could cost him his job and drag the company through a lengthy, painful process of dangerous turmoil.

The Role of the Organization in Society   What makes this third type of defining moment so difficult is that executives are asked to form, reveal, and test not only themselves and their work groups but also their entire company and its role in society. That requires forging a plan of action that functions at three levels: the individual, the work group, and society at large. In which areas do we want to lead? In which areas do we want to follow? How should we interact with the government? With shareholders? Leaders must ask themselves, *Have I thought creatively, boldly, and imaginatively about my organization's role in society and its relationship to its stakeholders?*

What role did Sakiz want Roussel Uclaf to play? He certainly did not want to take the easy way out. Sakiz could have pleased his boss in Germany and avoided years of controversy and boycotts by withdrawing entirely from the market for contraceptives and other reproductive drugs. (Nearly all U.S. drug companies have adopted that approach.) Sakiz could have defined Roussel Uclaf's social role in standard terms—as the property of its shareholders—and argued that RU-486 had to be shelved because boycotts against Roussel Uclaf and Hoechst were likely to cost far more than the drug would earn.

Instead, Sakiz wanted to define Roussel Uclaf's role in a daring way: women seeking nonsurgical abortions and their physicians would be among the company's core stakeholders, and the company would support this constituency through astute political activism. That approach resonated with Sakiz's own core values and with what he thought the majority of employees and other stakeholders wanted. It was clear to him that he needed to find a way to introduce the drug onto the market. The only question was how.

From Vision to Reality   To make their ethical visions a reality, top-level executives must assess their opponents and allies very carefully. What allies do I have inside and outside my company? Which parties will resist or fight my efforts? Have I underestimated their power and tactical skill or overestimated their ethical commitment? Whom will I alienate with my decision? Which parties will retaliate and how? These tactical concerns can be summed up in the question, *What combination of shrewdness, creativity, and tenacity will make my vision a reality?* Machiavelli put it more succinctly: "Should I play the lion or the fox?"

Although we may never know exactly what went through Sakiz's mind, we can infer from his actions that he had no interest in playing the lion. On October 21, 1988, a month after the French government approved RU-486, Sakiz and the executive committee of Roussel Uclaf made their decision. The *New York Times* described the events in this way: "At an October 21 meeting, Sakiz surprised members of the management committee by calling for a discussion of RU-486. There, in Roussel Uclaf's ultramodern boardroom, the pill's long-standing opponents repeated their objections: RU-486 could spark a painful boycott, it was hurting employee morale, management was devoting too much of its time to this controversy. Finally, it would never be hugely profitable because much would be sold on a cost basis to the Third World. After two hours, Sakiz again stunned the committee by calling for a vote. When he raised his own hand in favor of suspending distribution of RU-486, it was clear that the pill was doomed."

The company informed its employees of the decision on October 25. The next day, Roussel Uclaf announced publicly that it was suspending distribution of the drug because of pressure from antiabortion groups. A Roussel Uclaf official explained the decision: "The pressure groups in the United States are very powerful, maybe even more so than in France."

The company's decision and Sakiz's role in it sparked astonishment and anger. The company and its leadership, critics charged, had doomed a promising public-health tool and had set an example of cowardice. Sakiz's colleague and friend, Etienne-Emile Baluieu, whose research had been crucial to developing RU-486, called the decision "morally scandalous" and accused Sakiz of caving in to pressure. Women's groups, family-planning advocates, and physicians in the United States and Europe came down hard on Sakiz's decision. Other critics suggested sarcastically that the company's decision was no surprise because Roussel Uclaf had decided not to produce contraceptive pills in the face of controversy during the 1960s.

Three days after Roussel Uclaf announced that it would suspend distribution, the French minister of health summoned the company's vice chairman to his office and said that if the company did not resume distribution, the government would transfer the patent to another company that would. After the meeting with the minister of health, Roussel Uclaf again stunned the public: it announced the reversal of its initial decision. The company would distribute RU-486 after all.

Sakiz had achieved his goals but in a foxlike manner. He had called out to his allies and rallied them to his side, but had done so in an indirect and shrewd way. He had used the predictable responses of the many stakeholders to orchestrate a series of events that helped achieve his ends, without looking like he was leading the way. In fact, it appeared as if he were giving in to outside pressure.

Sakiz had put into place the three principal components of the third type of defining moment. First, he had secured his own future at the company. The French health ministry, which supported Sakiz, might well have been aggravated if Hoechst had appointed another CEO in Sakiz's place; it could then have retaliated against the German company in a number of ways. In addition, by having the French government participate in the decision, Sakiz was able to deflect some of the controversy about introducing the drug away from the company, protecting employees and the bottom line. Finally, Sakiz had put Roussel Uclaf in a role of technological and social leadership within French, and even international, circles.

A BOW WITH GREAT TENSION

As we have moved from Steve Lewis to Peter Adario to Eduoard Sakiz, we have progressed through increasingly complex, but similar, challenges. These managers engaged in difficult acts of self-inquiry that led them to take calculated action based on their personal understanding of what was right in the given situation.

But the three met with varying degrees of success. Steve Lewis was able to balance his personal values and the realities of the business world. The result was ethically informed action that advanced his career. Peter Adario had a sound understanding of his personal values but failed to adapt them to the realities he faced in the competitive work environment at Sayer Microworld. As a result, he failed to prevent McNeil's firing and put his own career in peril. Eduoard Sakiz not only stayed closely connected to his personal values and those of his organization but also predicted what his opponents and allies outside the company would do. The result was the introduction of a drug that shook the world.

The nineteenth-century German philosopher Friedrich Nietzsche once wrote, "I believe it is precisely through the presence of opposites and the feelings they occasion that the great man—the bow with great tension—develops." Defining moments bring those "opposites" and "feelings" together into vivid focus. They force us to find a balance between our hearts in all their idealism and our jobs in all their messy reality. Defining moments then are not merely intellectual exercises; they are opportunities for inspired action and personal growth.

PART FOURTEEN
Global Dimensions

"The world has become an international marketplace." Has anyone not heard this assertion in the past decade? Does anyone still deny the inevitability of the assertion? Nevertheless, the global arena is a new domain for many organizations, and there are key lessons to be learned. Furthermore, the dynamics generated by organizations doing business in the global arena are leading toward the creation of a "borderless world."

Several contemporary books focus our attention on global issues of managerial interest. Part Fourteen presents two recent books that address global aspects of organization and management.

Kenichi Ohmae challenges some of the ways that managers have historically viewed the world and the way that business has been conducted. Performance standards are being created by those who buy products in the global marketplace; these standards are no longer being created by those who manufacture or those who regulate the manufacturers. As a consequence, organizations need to adjust their structures so that they see and think globally, are focused on customers, and operate as "insiders" in countries around the globe as opposed to operating merely as exporters to these countries. Ohmae proposes that organizations rid themselves of a centralized "headquarters mentality" and their engrained *companyism* (seeking to beat their competition) and instead avoid competition where possible. He also advocates the adoption of a *China mentality*, wherein managers act with the confidence that they understand and can change key markets in the world.

Kenichi Ohmae is the Managing Director of McKinsey and Company, a large international consulting firm. He draws on his experiences with businesses and governments doing business in the emerging global economy to derive suggestions for how companies can win in the new global marketplace.

Many writers, such as co-authors Bolman and Deal (see Part Two) have urged managers to develop the capacity to see and handle paradoxes. John Naisbitt, in *Global Paradox*, points out the seeming contradiction (paradox) that *smaller* players will become increasingly powerful as the world economy gets larger. They are more flexible and agile, less burdened with bureaucracy, and able to react to changing marketplace needs more rapidly. The emergence of giant new markets (e.g., China, Asia, Latin America) and the blurring of nation-state boundaries (e.g., the European Union) will open up immense opportunities to be successful for both small firms and large firms who "act small."

Naisbitt achieved popularity with his early book *Megatrends*, which sold over six million copies. With Patricia Aburdene, he has also published *Megatrends 2000, Megatrends for Women*, and *Re-Inventing the Corporation*. Naisbitt and Aburdene are widely known for their reporting of key trends and their social forecasting that draws from extensive data-gathering of political, economic, technological, and social events.

READING 1

The Borderless World

Kenichi Ohmae
Summary prepared by Robert Wharton

> **Robert Wharton** *received his doctorate from Rutgers University and is a member of several professional associations, including the Academy of Management.*

"An isle is emerging that is bigger than a continent—the Interlinked Economy (ILE) of the Triad (the United States, Europe, and Japan)" (p. xi). Joined by aggressive economies in Taiwan, Hong Kong, and Singapore, the ILE has grown so powerful that it is destroying the old national borders that once defined consumer groups and corporate identities.

The emergence of the ILE has resulted in a great deal of confusion, both for managers and for economic policy makers. Old theories that compared one nation against others simply do not work anymore. When the economy grows stronger, jobs are created abroad and not at home, disappointing the experts. If the government raises interest rates to control inflation, cheaper money rushes in from other countries in the ILE. Statistics on the balance of trade become meaningless when corporations spread their production and distribution functions throughout the ILE. Any managers or politicians who do not understand this new reality risk isolating their companies, or their citizens, from the dynamic economy of the borderless world.

The Borderless World is organized into three parts. First, the strategy and organization of companies operating in the new international environment are discussed. Second, government bureaucrats who are causing great problems for their citizens are attacked, even as these officials are becoming powerless and irrelevant. Finally, Ohmae's vision of the economic world into which we are moving is presented.

STRATEGIES FOR INTERNATIONAL COMPANIES

An Inside-Out View of Macroeconomics

In a borderless world, strategic managers need to understand, and master, five concerns in order to operate effectively in an interlinked economy. Striking the correct balance among these *five Cs* is essential to any successful business.

Customers · Managers must understand the growing power of consumers around the globe. Customers throughout the Triad have few national allegiances; they are only interested in buying the products that offer them value—the best quality at the

---

Kenichi Ohmae, *The Borderless World*. New York, NY: Harper Business, 1990.

best price. Lack of allegiances gives consumers their power, and as news of product performance becomes harder to suppress, consumer power grows greater still. The critical objective for a company, therefore, is to find new ways to create new value for its customers.

Competition   Products on the market today require so many different technologies, and the technologies change so rapidly, that no company can maintain a lead in all of them. Fifty years ago, General Motors could keep in house all the technology involved in building a car. But today, consider what has made the IBM Personal Computer such a success. Lotus, along with many other companies, wrote the application software for an operating system designed by Microsoft. Microsoft wrote the operating system for a microprocessor designed by Intel. Today, no single company can simultaneously master all of the technologies essential to making a product successful. And because companies are forced to cooperate, no technology stays secret for long. Therefore, operating globally means finding partners, some of whom may also be competitors.

Company   A fundamental change has taken place in business over the past ten or fifteen years. Automation has nearly eliminated the labor component of manufacturing a product, so production is increasingly a fixed-cost activity. Because new technologies are so critical and change so rapidly, research and development (R & D) is also becoming a fixed-cost activity. And because maintaining brand recognition for powerful customers is essential, marketing and advertising become fixed costs as well. Managers can no longer boost profits by reducing wages or labor hours or other variable costs. For companies with large fixed costs, the only way to defray their investment is to find more customers and increase sales. This means rising fixed costs are driving companies toward globalization.

Currency   In a borderless world, currency exchange rates are much more volatile than they were just a few years ago. In order to neutralize the effect of currency, managers of global companies are forced to become strong in all areas of the Triad. Then, if currency becomes a negative in one area, positives in another area cancel it out.

Country   Companies move into a country as they seek to neutralize the impact of currency fluctuations. To serve them well, though, they have to move deeply into those countries to get as close to their customers as possible. Managers have to find a way for their companies to benefit from world-scale operations. But at the same time, they must know and serve their customers as well as any local company from the same country. Coca-Cola's success in Japan, for example, is partly a result of introducing unique products for Japanese consumers.

Changes in the five Cs have forced companies to spread out across national borders, but the changes have been so rapid that managers have not always been able to make the necessary adjustments in the way they organize their companies, in the way they think about strategy, or in their assumptions about how to do business.

The Equidistant Manager

Most managers are nearsighted, with their vision dominated by customers in their home countries. Too few try to plan and build companies as if all key customers were equidistant from the corporate headquarters. Honda, for example, has divisions throughout the Triad, but its managers do not act as if the company were divided into Japanese and overseas operations. In fact, the word "overseas" has no place at Honda. The first rule of equidistance is to *see and think globally*.

National boundaries may still be clear on a map, but for managers those boundaries have largely disappeared. With the persistent flow of information around the world, people quickly learn what products are available, and what level of quality they can expect. People have become genuinely global consumers. For managers, this flow of information puts a priority on learning to meet the demands of a borderless world.

This may mean becoming an *insider*, replicating a complete business in every country or key market in which your company does business. Managers cannot hope to run every business in every market around the world from corporate headquarters. They have to become a true insider in each market so they can respond to competitors and provide the value local consumers demand.

Managing effectively in the borderless world means paying central attention to delivering value to customers, and to developing an equidistant perspective on who they are and what they want. First and most important is the strategic need to *see your customers clearly*.

Getting Back to Strategy

For many managers, strategy still means beating the competition. It means doing what your competition does, only better. This belief is wrong, since strategy should first be a process of responding to the needs of customers and delivering value to those customers. Indeed, strategy should include an effort to *avoid* competition whenever possible.

Many Japanese managers have failed to learn this lesson. As these firms went global, they concentrated on differentiating their products from those of their competitors. Today, though, many find themselves trapped between competing customer needs. On the one hand, German companies, such as Mercedes or BMW in automobiles, command high prices by serving the quality end of the market. On the other hand, companies like Korea's Hyundai have tried to satisfy price-conscious consumers on the low end of the market. The result, for Japanese firms, is a painful squeeze caused by their focus on competitors, rather than on customer needs.

How should a manager respond to this squeeze? Consider the strategy of Yamaha, a Japanese maker of pianos. The piano market is in decline, as people simply are not buying many new pianos today, and most of the existing ones are sitting around gathering dust. Yamaha decided to take a hard look at its customers and the product. What they found was fewer and fewer people with the time to play the piano, or even to learn how to play the piano. How does one provide value for these customers? Yamaha worked hard on new electronic technology that could turn existing pianos into sophisticated player-pianos. Now, for $2,500, customers can turn their idle pianos into useful instruments. And instead of a dying market, Yamaha now has the prospect of a $2,500 sale to retrofit up to forty million old pianos.

Like Yamaha, many Japanese companies are talented value-adders. Many others are so intent on beating the competition that whole industries have suffered as a consequence. In the blind pursuit of *companyism* (the desire to beat the competition by *doing more better*), Japanese shipbuilders and producers of semiconductors, color TVs, and watches have relentlessly overbuilt and overproduced in an effort to beat their competitors. Now, these industries are flooded with overcapacity and all companies are robbed of an opportunity to make a profit.

Companyism is not entirely a bad thing, of course. Many American companies suffer from too little company orientation. Japanese firms build loyalty, in part, by nurturing a sense of equal participation throughout the company. In most firms, for example, the total compensation of most Japanese CEOs is no more than ten times that of a factory worker. By contrast, Lee Iacocca of Chrysler had an income that was roughly one thousand times greater than that of one of his factory workers.

What is critical, however, is that managers not be so blinded by company loyalty that they forget to ask whether the system needs to be the way it is. Managers in a borderless world need a certain mindset. They need the freedom to rethink their products and ask whether there is a better way to serve their customers. In a changeable world, very few solutions will work forever.

The China Mentality

In product development, one remedy for companyism is to create multiple product teams, each with the same general direction, and then set these teams free to find their own approaches to a single problem. Managers will then not only have multiple solutions from which they may choose, but they will also be able to offer their customers several solutions to the same problem. At the same time, their companies keep churning out new or improved products at regular intervals. NEC, for example, introduces something new to the market every month. Its competitors do so only once every year or two.

What is necessary for world-class product development is the freedom to keep asking the question "Why?" when attempting to meet customer needs. Unfortunately, too many managers lack the *China Mentality* (China, literally translated, means "center of the universe"). Too many managers fail to believe they are the center of the universe, and hence lack the inner confidence that they can change the world. Lacking this confidence, managers do not allow themselves to be led to answers that deviate far from the company norm. For global players, however, confidence to act on their knowledge of key markets is the secret to success in a borderless world.

Getting Rid of the Headquarters Mentality

Company headquarters often becomes another problem for managers as they begin the process of globalization. Overeager and overanxious corporate managers have frequently destroyed profitable businesses by trying to supervise from a distance. No company can operate globally by centralizing all key decisions at the corporate headquarters. Rather, *decomposing* the corporate center into several regional headquarters is becoming an essential ingredient in the strategy of effective global competitors.

The real challenge in decomposing the corporate center, what Akio Morita of Sony terms *global localization*, is not organizational. The real challenge is psychological, a matter of values. When the mother-country identity of the old corporate headquarters disappears, it must be replaced by a commitment to a single, unified global identity. When managers overcome their headquarters mentality, when they come to believe that they may work *in* different nations but they are *of* the global corporation, then the company will have taken the last step toward true global status. Managers will then be free to decide how best to run their business in their particular market.

The Global Logic of Strategic Alliances

For most managers, management means control. Alliances, though, mean sharing control. So it's not surprising that managers have been slow to experiment with genuine strategic alliances. But in a borderless world, in a world of rapidly changing technologies and escalating fixed costs, true alliances become an essential component of strategy.

Glaxo, the British pharmaceutical company, did not want to establish an extensive sales and service network in every country in which it did business. It could not afford to, given its costly commitment to R & D. So Glaxo decided to develop alliances with major pharmaceutical companies in Japan, trade its best drugs with each partner, and focus its own resources on its base in Europe. Now, for each alliance, Glaxo has two profitable drugs to market without any increase in its fixed investment in R & D or marketing.

True alliances are marriages of equals. They avoid the problems of equity ownership and parental control that have plagued so many joint ventures. Instead, alliances help global companies address the common problem of fixed costs. Nissan distributes for Volkswagen in Japan, and Volkswagen reciprocates in Europe. Ford and Mazda swap cars throughout the Triad. Unless an organization is committed to building a fixed investment in every region of the world, it makes sense to cooperate with someone who already has that force in place.

GOVERNMENTS AND BUREAUCRATS

"Lies, Damned Lies, and Statistics"

The charges are familiar. The United States has an enormous trade deficit, especially with Japan. And while the value of the dollar falls, selfish consumers save virtually none of their incomes. Worse, they insist on buying products manufactured abroad. The country is on an irresponsible binge, in the process of being destroyed by selfishness and short-term thinking.

The charges are familiar, but a different picture can be painted. The United States does not have a trade deficit. In fact, because dollars are the settlement currency in foreign trade, the United States does not have any "foreign" trade at all. Unlike Brazil or France, or even Japan, the United States never has to earn foreign currency to purchase something from abroad. All it has to do is expand its domestic economy across the borders of its trading partners. Because the money used to buy foreign goods is always in dollars, buying cars from Japan is no different than buying PCs from Texas or oranges from California.

Government trade statistics measure goods that cross the national border, but in a borderless world the figures they report are completely meaningless. We act as if they really mean something, when in fact they bear no relation to the real flows of economic activity in the world. Most American corporations have developed a local insider presence in countries around the world, and this is the biggest reason why United States exports have declined statistically. The products they sell to global markets are made in those markets. In fact, any goods they ship back home are recorded as Japanese or European exports to the United States.

The trade deficit is an illusion, created by a system that only measures goods crossing national borders. Consider that in 1985, Japanese purchases of American goods (regardless of where those goods were produced) averaged $580 per person. American per capita purchases of Japanese goods averaged just $298.

Americans also assume that the Japanese have a much higher savings rate. Yet these savings statistics are just as flawed and misleading. A closer examination of the assumptions behind these statistics suggests that there is little or no difference in the savings habits of American and Japanese consumers. In fact, if one looks at the assets we collect rather than the income we put away, Americans may actually be far *better* savers than the Japanese.

Americans worry that the United States has become a debtor nation, that we have mortgaged our future and put ourselves in debt to the rest of the world. But there is no reason to be concerned with most of these "liabilities." The United States is an attractive place for foreigners to invest their money, so foreign investment pours into the country. Most of these investments (the purchase of companies or real estate, for example) carry no interest charges, so the United States incurs no financial obligations. But most foreign investments are recorded at the national border as "external liabilities," so people worry.

Development in a Borderless World

Politicians and policy makers, misled by official statistics and not fully understanding the nature of the borderless world, continue to intervene in the economy with disastrous results. Attempts are made to weaken the value of the dollar in order to make American goods more competitive. But officials succeed only in frightening new investments away. Governments try to "manage" the foreign exchange markets, but accomplish little more than to punish their own domestic companies and consumers.

Perhaps the most murderous effects of confused government policy result from the folly of protectionism. Nations that have been successful at development efforts have made the determination to open the door to the global economy. They have decided to become a part of the global marketplace. Those that fail still harbor the illusion that participation in the interlinked economy is not important.

In a borderless world, the role of a responsible government is to give its people as much choice as possible and to keep its people well informed. The government of India does not do this. Their domestic auto industry is highly protected against foreign products. But cars in India are miserable vehicles, and the auto industry is still sick. Hong Kong, by contrast, has no natural resources and a tiny population. Yet, with a "free port" approach, the people of Hong Kong have achieved a per capita GNP that rivals Great Britain's.

VISION OF THE FUTURE

We need to accept the fact that information and knowledge, not natural resources, are the key to wealth and economic growth. National borders mean little for the real flows of economic activity, and national governments no longer have the ability to produce economic wealth based on what is under the soil, or on what can be taxed, or on the strength of their military. Instead, *wealth emerges from the hard work of well-educated people.*

Given this new reality, what is the role of a modern government? It must educate its people and guarantee them as much information and as much choice as possible. In the interlinked economy, it does not matter who builds this factory or who owns that office building. What is important is that the global corporations that do business in an area give people good work to do and an opportunity to buy the products they want.

It makes no sense for politicians and journalists to be concerned about national industrial competitiveness. Nations are no longer in competition. The only thing that matters is that IBM is in global competition with DEC and Fujitsu, or that Toyota competes worldwide with Honda and Ford. No government should be in the business of dictating choices for their citizens in order to protect domestic firms. In a borderless world, the best companies will be organized on a global scale. Companies that will not, or cannot, compete globally are simply not worth saving.

How close is the ILE to becoming a truly borderless world? Perhaps closer than we think. Certainly, there are still problems. Many companies still suffer from a head-quarters mentality. Too few are ready to take advantage of genuine strategic alliances. National borders are still controlled, and domestic markets are still protected. But more and more corporations are not committed to globalization, and they have bene-fitted from that commitment. And daily, the information age makes consumers more knowledgeable and more demanding. As these trends continue, government leaders may soon realize that their role is not one of dictating choices to their citizens. Governments may provide guidance on such issues as safety and minimum levels of service. But they must step back and allow people the freedom to vote with their pocketbooks.

READING 2

Global Paradox

John Naisbitt
Summary prepared by Kelly Nelson

Kelly Nelson *is the Director of Human Resources for Armco's Mansfield Operations. She has a bachelor's of business administration from the University of Minnesota, Duluth, and is currently pursuing her MBA.*

Although citizens of independent countries want to trade more freely with other countries of the world, they still desire political and cultural independence in their own countries. The *Maastricht Treaty*, calling for the political and economic unification of the European countries, is poised for failure. As countries surrender their currency and replace it with a common currency, a part of their heritage, culture, and independence is relinquished. Further, electronic networks make this loss unnecessary. Electronic networks today connect banks, businesses, and communities worldwide.

THE GLOBAL PARADOX

Although an apparent contradiction, the statement "the bigger the world economy, the more powerful its smallest players" is actually a *paradox* (a statement that seems absurd but is actually valid or true). The expanding world economy makes it possible to study the smallest economic player, the entrepreneur, in an attempt to understand the economic workings of the largest economic entities.

Although large corporations created the American economy, this has changed in recent years. Now 90 percent of the goods exported from the United States come from small- and medium-sized companies. In fact, large U.S. corporations have had to decentralize and downsize in order to survive. By eliminating the bureaucracy, large corporations are becoming more flexible and able to react to the needs of the marketplace more efficiently. By practicing *subsidiarity* (retaining power at the lowest possible level within an organization), corporations are trying to recapture the entrepreneurial spirit of their employees. This results in smaller and stronger units within the organization. However, large corporations have not reached the level of subsidiarity found in small- and medium-sized companies. Because *small companies*, by their nature, retain power at the lowest possible level, they *are poised to dominate more and more of the world economy.*

John Naisbitt, *Global Paradox: The Bigger the World Economy, The More Powerful Its Smallest Players.* New York, NY: Morrow, 1994.

Mergers and takeovers, once commonly viewed as a way to control the marketplace, are being replaced by strategic alliances in which corporations cooperate with their largest competitors. For instance, Nissan purchases automobile parts from Toyota. By creating strategic alliances, corporations take advantage of their competitor's assets, while avoiding the capital investment necessary to improve their own similar products. Strategic alliances fit the large organizations' need to avoid corporate growth and thereby enable small organizations to grow globally. Small corporations can also compete more easily in today's world economy through the removal of trade barriers, the increase in computer and telecommunications, the deregulation of financial markets, and the melding of consumer tastes. A metaphor for the movement from bureaucracies to small, autonomous units is the shift from mainframes to personal computers and then to personal computers networked together.

THE NEW TRIBALISM

Tribalism is the belief in fidelity to one's own kind, defined by ethnicity, language, culture, religion, or profession. Tribalism is surging throughout the world, and a balance must be found between tribal identity and global competition. As the world's economies become more universal, the population begins to act more tribal in an effort to keep the norms it has known. As the world's population becomes more global, traditional nation-states are losing their importance, but the importance of tribalism is growing. The decline of the nation-state is evidenced daily by news reports of countries gaining their independence and the growth of democratic societies out of formerly communistic regimes. This is caused by the tribalistic feelings of citizens within countries, the efficiency created by smaller countries (similar to small corporations), and the revolution of telecommunications; it leads from hierarchical power to networking, from vertical to horizontal emphasis. The demise of the nation-state causes the global paradox to focus on smaller and smaller parts.

POWERING THE PARADOX:
THE TELECOMMUNICATIONS REVOLUTION

Telecommunications will provide the infrastructure on which the global economy will flourish. Through the maturation of telecommunications, technologies have combined, strategic alliances have been formed, global networks have been established, and personal computers have become available for virtually all citizens. The advancement of telecommunications has allowed each individual to become more empowered. Even ordinary citizens without computer programming knowledge can operate computers effectively; cellular phones are accessible and affordable for most; the fax allows individuals to communicate worldwide with virtually the touch of a button.

The progress made in telecommunications is paving the way for strategic alliances between cable, telephone, and computer companies. Telephone companies such as GTE Corp. are partnering with cable companies such as Daniels Cablevision (California) to provide educational, financial, shopping, and travel information on television screens, and Microsoft is developing operating systems for future televisions. The strategic alliances being developed are uniting corporations across nation-state borders. This is possible through deregulation, liberalization, and privatization of telecommunications corporations. Through privatization of formerly public-sector organizations, countries are realizing faster economic growth. Privatization is also encouraging the upgrading of telecommunications systems throughout countries of the former Soviet Union, Eastern Europe, and Asia. The upgrading of telecommunication infrastructure is paving the way for strategic alliances between multinational corporations in both the development and establishment of satellite systems.

The goal of the telecommunications networks, strategic alliances, and developments is to create a global, interconnected, compatible network of telecommunications. The networks will meet the individual's need to communicate in real time, whether across the street or across the world. Through digitalization, all communication—voice, text, image, and video—can be translated into the 1 and 0 language of microprocessors and transmitted via telephone lines around the world. The advancement of this technology will allow individuals to work "at the office" wherever they are, the language barrier will crumble (translation will be done via the terminal); time, distance, and language barriers will be eliminated. The transition to advanced telecommunications is happening now; already, less than half of telecommunications traffic within the United States is via voice. With the global communication possibilities, the pace of change is accelerating. The technology is rapidly changing to accommodate people instead of people accommodating the technology.

TRAVEL: GLOBALIZATION OF THE WORLD'S LARGEST INDUSTRY

Today, travel occupations employ 10.6 percent of the global workforce, contribute 10.2 percent of the world's gross national product, and account for gross output of $3.4 trillion annually. With globalization, travel will grow even larger. As individuals become acquainted with other cultures through telecommunications, the desire to experience those cultures firsthand will grow. The travel industry is already responding to the changing needs of the global individual: deregulation, privatization of state-owned airlines, code-sharing, and co-promotions of airlines are all resulting in less work, worry, and expense for travelers; the travel infrastructure of countries, such as airports, bus lines, railways, and highways, is being built or renovated; and hotels are accommodating business travelers with in-room offices, fax machines, computers, and less-stress international phone calling ability.

Political activities within and between countries are also fueling the growth of global travel. Countries such as the former Soviet Union and the United States have ended the Cold War, and they are forming strategic alliances; China and South Korea have diplomatic relations; countries in the Middle East are pursuing unprecedented peace accords. Individuals are contributing to the increase of global travel as well. Baby boomers and retirees are traveling in ever-increasing numbers, people are becoming more aware of the value of cultural differences, and the global interest in environmental issues fuels individuals' desires to see exotic landscapes and surroundings. As the world's economy integrates, the individual's desire for travel will be fueled, not dampened.

NEW RULES: A UNIVERSAL CODE OF CONDUCT FOR THE TWENTY-FIRST CENTURY

As communication becomes faster and more global, individuals of all nations are insisting on a higher code of ethics for all countries. Through advanced communication, people have a new awareness of cultural diversity and its worth, the health of the environment and its importance to all, and the right of all humans to be treated with dignity. With this new awareness, individuals are holding corporations and governments accountable to a higher, universal code of ethics. Politicians worldwide are resigning under the threat of impeachment or prosecution for dealing in less than an ethical manner. Corporations are facing economic ruin as a result of unethical and environmentally irresponsible decisions. The universal code of ethics that is emerging calls for the respect of tribalism, while respecting the human rights of all. Further, the code of ethics calls for local management of environmental resources for the good of the global population. Corporations are responding to the universal code of ethics by acting in an environmentally responsible manner, by implementing policies that go beyond the letter of the law, and by encouraging other corporations and governments to do the same. Corporations will also see the benefit of these actions in their operations. By acting as responsible corporate citizens, corporations elicit the loyalty of their employees, resulting in higher productivity and better quality work. Corporations are also feeling the pressure from consumers to operate in a socially conscious manner and to deal with suppliers who assist them in creating a reputation for socially conscious operations. As the global paradox widens and the smallest players become more and more powerful, individuals will carry a greater share of the responsibility for an organization's social performance.

THE DRAGON CENTURY: THE CHINESE COMMONWEALTH— GAINING POWER FROM ITS PARTS

The face of China and its place within the global economy is changing. China is in the process of changing its central economy to a "socialist market economy" and in doing so, is allowing its people to use their individual and collective imagination and enthusiasm to become entrepreneurs. Individuals are giving up government-assigned positions in state-owned enterprises, and they are entering private business. Entrepreneurship and making money are now considered respectable. The new Chinese entrepreneur is helping the Chinese economy grow as never before. This economy is also being decentralized, resulting in an increasing number of small players. The larger the Chinese economy becomes, the smaller and more powerful are its parts. By some estimates, almost one-third of the 103 million government employees have given up their positions to start their own businesses. Entrepreneurs are also gaining political influence in China. Rong Yiren, one of China's most prominent entrepreneurs, was elected the country's vice president. The entrepreneurs share values, large numbers, and a quest for money. With money, they know, comes power.

Deng Xiaoping knew that by allowing citizens to become entrepreneurs, productivity would rise. By turning farmers into entrepreneurs, a source of capital for future industrial development was ensured. Throughout the 1980s, the productivity of the Chinese peasant increased more than that of any other workers in the world. By competing with the entrepreneurs, state-run facilities are also streamlining and improving productivity and quality. Further, state-run facilities have improved to better meet the needs of Chinese consumers who have increasing disposable income.

China is also in the process of improving the country's infrastructure to provide the basis for continued expansion. To improve the infrastructure, the Chinese government turned to foreigners for expertise. Improvements in China's airlines, airports, ground transportation, power capacity, and communication network are all underway.

The economic shift to entrepreneurs, the improving infrastructure, and the ever-increasing disposable income of the citizens have taken American businesses to China. Corporations such as Coca-Cola, Procter & Gamble, 7-Eleven, American Express, and Avon are all making inroads into the Chinese economy.

As the Chinese economy reforms, many ask how long it will take before the Chinese political system reforms. Changing from its communistic government is not part of the Chinese plan; communists are very much in power and plan to stay there. The economic reform happening today is not considered by Chinese communists to be outside the realm of communism.

The changes within the Chinese economy are not without downfalls: Unemployment has risen, accompanied by increased corruption and serious inflation have increased, and there has been a lack of attention to the training of human resources. There is also a need for restructuring the financial and taxation relationship between the countrywide and provincial governments. These problems and others notwithstanding, the economic growth of China is a monumentous occasion.

ASIA AND LATIN AMERICA: NEW AREAS OF OPPORTUNITY

For the twenty-first century, the new areas of great economic feasibility are in Asia and Latin America. Countries such as Vietnam, India, Argentina, Chile, Brazil, Uruguay, Paraguay, Bolivia, Colombia, Ecuador, Peru, Venezuela, and Mexico have all demonstrated the will to implement structural reforms necessary to promote free markets as well as to create capital markets and financial infrastructure. In most Latin American countries, private citizens are encouraged to participate in the reform process, and it is generally accepted that the fruits of free-market economy must extend to all citizens and not just to a privileged few.

Asia and Latin America are promising newcomers in the global paradox, while Europe is not. The unification of Europe was heralded as the vehicle by which to make Europe an economic superpower. However, the reunification costs have been staggering, and Europe has suffered a recession. The reunification efforts are further compounded by ethnic tensions, the cost of corruption, and the sluggish economies of the European countries. Further, the countries are burdened by the welfare programs within them.

While Europe flounders, Asia and Latin American countries are replacing their leaders with young, talented, and—many times—American-educated bankers and economists. Their vision is to make deals, facilitate changes, and provide the means necessary for their country's economic growth. Countries in both areas of the world are cooperating with neighbors in a previously unseen manner. Nationalist sentiments are giving way to economic realities. This is evidenced by the *Mercorsor agreement*, whose purpose is to accelerate economic growth by linking Argentina, Brazil, Paraguay, and Uruguay in a common market. Not only did it create Latin America's largest economic base, it also created Latin America's largest industrial base. By capitalizing on the strengths of each country, all countries benefit. By realizing the synergistic effect of such cooperation, these nations are also able to cooperate to facilitate political advantage.

Vietnam has encouraged foreign investment by revising its foreign-investment laws to make them some of the most attractive in the world. Companies from many countries worldwide are investing in Vietnam and are gaining power and income from that investment. Americans need to recover from the Vietnam War and to start looking at Vietnam as a country that offers Americans an economic opportunity.

The Asia Pacific Rim—bounded by Tokyo, Shanghai, Hong Kong, and Singapore—is destined to lead the global economy into the next century. The considerations shaping this global order are (1) the worldwide collapse of communism, (2) the revolution of telecommunications, and (3) the rise of the Asia Pacific region. The countries within this region are an excellent example of the global paradox. Not only are the more prosperous countries investing in the less-developed countries, but also the entrepreneurs are fueling the economies of their own countries as well as neighboring countries. The leaders of these countries must have a clear vision of their own future in order to assert worldwide leadership. A consensus of that vision may be difficult for the countries to attain, however.

CONCLUSION

The end of the Cold War, the fall of communism, decentralization, and the growth of telecommunications are all revolutionizing the economic realities of the world. As nation-state boundaries blur, the global paradox is becoming real: The bigger the world economy, the more powerful its smallest players.

PART FIFTEEN

Managing Personal Effectiveness

Topics of interest to managers are constantly changing and evolving. This section includes a sampling of themes that have received substantial attention in recent years, ranging from one's personal character to moral guidelines to spiritual values at work to the role of "soul" in the workplace. These readings are designed to raise issues, provide an opportunity for reflection on oneself, and stimulate seeking a balance between corporate profits and employee (and personal) needs.

Stephen R. Covey is a well-known speaker, author of several books, and chief executive officer of the Covey Leadership Center. His first book, *Seven Habits of Highly Effective People*, remained on best-seller lists for several years and sold millions of copies. In it, he offers a series of prescriptions to guide managers as they chart their courses in turbulent times. Drawn from his extensive review of the "success literature," Covey urges people to develop a character ethic based on people being proactive, identifying their values, disciplining themselves to work on high-priority items, seeking win-win solutions, listening with empathy, synergizing with others, and engaging in extensive reading and studying.

Covey has also published a "Seven Habits" book that adapts the basic principles for families, *First Things First* (which urges people to manage their time and life well so as to achieve goals consistent with their values), and *Principle-Centered Leadership*. The latter book, summarized in this section as Reading 2, identifies seven human attributes (self-awareness, imagination, willpower, an abundance mentality, courage, creativity, and self-renewal) that, when combined with eight key behaviors (e.g., priority on service, radiating positive energy) help produce effective and principled leaders.

Dorothy Marcic, author of *Managing with the Wisdom of Love: Uncovering Virtue in People and Organizations*, is the president of DM Systems, Ltd. A former Fullbright Scholar and teacher at the Czechoslovak Management Center and the University of Economics in Prague, she has consulted for a variety of organizations, in addition to the U.S. Department of State and the Czech Ministry of Finance.

In her book Marcic challenges us to think about organizations and organizational life in terms of spirituality. She suggests that traditional spiritual values of love, justice, dignity, and respect should become the values of the contemporary workplace. She argues that the absence of trust, low levels of motivation, and failed programs are the result of managerial actions that break spiritual law.

In *Reclaiming Higher Ground: Building Organizations that Inspire Excellence*, Lance H. K. Secretan focuses the reader's attention on "soul" in the workplace. The author argues that employee needs and corporate profits are equally valid goals for the organization. Corporate growth can be attained through the creation of a workplace that is spiritually safe and secure. We encourage readers to reflect upon Dorothy Marcic's *Managing with the Wisdom of Love* as they read Secretan's prescription for reclaiming the "higher ground."

Lance H. K. Secretan is an international business consultant working out of Toronto, Canada. Much of his consulting is focused on coaching managers to inspire and motivate employees, and to create organizational customers for life.

READING 1

The Seven Habits of Highly Effective People

Stephen R. Covey

There are two types of literature on how to succeed. The first type focuses on a *personality ethic*. It claims that you are what you appear to be; appearance is everything. It accents public image, social consciousness, and the ability to interact superficially with others. However, exclusive attention to these factors will eventually provide evidence of a lack of integrity, an absence of depth, a short-term personal success orientation, and a basic deficiency in one's own humanness.

The second type of success literature revolves around a *character ethic*. It provides proven pathways to move from dependent relationships to independence, and ultimately to interdependent success with other people. It requires a willingness to subordinate one's short-term needs to more important long-term goals. It requires effort, perseverance, and patience with oneself. One's character is, after all, a composite of habits, which are unconscious patterns of actions.

Habits can be developed through rigorous practice until they become second nature. There are seven key habits that form the basis for character development and build a strong foundation for interpersonal success in life and at work:

1. *Be proactive*; make things happen. Take the initiative and be responsible for your life. Work on areas where you can have an impact and pay less attention to areas outside your area of concern. When you do respond to others, do so on the basis of your principles.
2. *Begin with the end in mind.* Know where you're going; develop a personal mission statement; develop a sense of who you are and what you value. Maintain a long-term focus.
3. *Put first things first.* Distinguish between tasks that are urgent and not so urgent, between activities that are important and not so important; then organize and execute around those priorities. Avoid being in a reactive mode, and pursue opportunities instead. Ask yourself, "What one thing could I do (today) that would make a tremendous difference in my work or personal life?"
4. *Think "win-win."* Try to avoid competing, and search for ways to develop mutually beneficial relationships instead. Build an "emotional bank account" with others through frequent acts of courtesy, kindness, honesty, and

Stephen R. Covey, *The Seven Habits of Highly Effective People: Restoring the Character Ethic*. New York, NY: Simon & Schuster, 1989.

commitment keeping. Develop the traits of integrity, maturity, and an abundance mentality (acting as if there is plenty of everything out there for everybody).

5. *Seek to understand, and then to be understood.* Practice empathetic communications, in which you recognize feelings and emotions in others. Listen carefully to people. Try giving them "psychological air."

6. *Synergize.* Value and exploit the mental, emotional, and psychological differences among people to produce results that demonstrate creative energy superior to what a single person could have accomplished alone.

7. *Sharpen the saw.* Do not allow yourself to get stale in any domain of your life, and don't waste time on activities that do not contribute to one of your goals and values. Seek ways to renew yourself periodically in all four elements of your nature—physical (via exercise, good nutrition, and stress control), mental (through reading, thought, and writing), social (through service to others), and spiritual (through study and meditation). In short, practice continuous learning and self-improvement, and your character will lead you to increased success.

READING 2

Principle-Centered Leadership

Stephen R. Covey
Summary prepared by Stephen Rubenfeld

Stephen Rubenfeld *is Professor of Human Resource Management in the School of Business and Economics at the University of Minnesota, Duluth. He received his doctorate from the University of Wisconsin, Madison, and was previously on the faculty of Texas Tech University. His professional publications and presentations have covered a wide range of human resource and labor relations topics, including job search behaviors, appeals procedures, employee staffing, and concessionary bargaining. He is a member of the Society for Human Resource Management, the Academy of Management, and the Industrial Relations Research Association.*

In the quest to uncover the secrets of effective leadership, a rapidly expanding body of literature has profiled the successes and failures attributed to organizational leaders. But after decades of research and thousands of publications, a comprehensive understanding of the leadership phenomenon is missing. What are the attributes of effective leaders? Do the charismatic aspects of leadership behaviors make a more significant contribution than the managerial elements? Under what circumstances are leaders successful? The existing literature does offer answers to questions such as these, but the explanations are personalized, situation specific, and technique bound.

The existing literature provides descriptive portraits of what the leader *does* in the organization setting, but fails to shed much light on what the leader *brings* to the organizational setting. This is not merely an oversight, but a fundamental deficiency that limits both the insight and practical value of this literature. Principle-centered leadership approaches leadership from a distinctive perspective. Personal effectiveness and leadership successes are seen as anchored in universal "laws." These laws form the conceptual foundation for a view and practice of leadership that is based on widely held humanistic principles.

Principle-centered leadership is premised on the belief that effective people are guided both in everyday living and in work relationships by universal principles or "natural laws," whereas ineffective people tend to place their energies on finding situation-specific behavioral paths to success as they are confronted by an evolving set of challenges. A principle-centered leadership approach is a natural extension of these habits of effectiveness to interpersonal and organizational settings. In addition

Stephen R. Covey, *Principle-Centered Leadership: Strategies For Personal & Professional Effectiveness.* Bellevue, NY: S & S Trade, 1992.

337

to enhancing the prospects for personal success, this approach to leadership is an essential ingredient in the pursuit of productivity, quality, profitability, and other contemporary organizational goals.

THE NEW PARADIGM

Quick, simple, superficial solutions to organizational problems often fail because they overlook the proven principles that govern human existence. These guiding principles not only endure over time, but serve as the basis for the success of individuals, groups, organizations, and societies. In dealing with challenges and opportunities, we sometimes lose sight of the fact that it is not principles that change, but only their application. The new paradigm introduced by principle-centered leadership suggest that *people must simultaneously center their leadership behaviors and their lives around "true north" principles.*

These laws are believed to be self-evident and self-validating, and unlike values, they represent an objective reality. Like a compass, they always are there to point people in the right direction. In this view, leadership techniques, intricate structural adaptations, and homilies based on someone else's successes are relatively unimportant. They are of value only where they are consistent with, and help people apply, the guiding principles.

An understanding of the "why to do's" provides a necessary foundation for guiding a leader's decisions on the "what to do's." Principle-centered leaders must first be principle-centered people who have a clear vision of the interrelated roles of *wisdom* (perspective on life), *guidance* (direction, identity, conscience), *security* (self-esteem, identity, personal strength), and *power* (the capacity, courage, and will to act). Carried through all facets of life, these four ingredients provide the underpinnings of effective leadership.

CHARACTERISTICS OF PRINCIPLE-CENTERED LEADERS

Seven basic human attributes provide humans with the *capacity* to strive for, and to achieve, personal effectiveness:

- Self-awareness
- Imagination and conscience
- Willpower
- Abundance mentality
- Courage and consideration
- Creativity
- Self-renewal

However, not all people take full advantage of these capabilities in their leadership endeavors. Observation reveals eight behavioral characteristics of effective, principled leaders:

1. *Learn throughout life* Through observation, curiosity, careful listening, reading, and other forms of self-improvement, principle-centered leaders continually extend their knowledge and experience base.

2. *Place a priority on service* Principle-centered leaders view life as a mission of service; they give to others and take responsibility for improving society.
3. *Believe in others* They recognize individual differences, value diversity, and believe in the potential for all people to make meaningful contributions.
4. *Seek balance in life* In attitudes and actions they seek a balanced existence. Principle-centered leaders are neither workaholics nor unidimensional. They are active socially, physically, and intellectually.
5. *Radiate positive energy* They are optimistic, think positively, and are aware of the effects of their energy level and demeanor.
6. *See life as a challenge* Principle-centered leaders are open minded and flexible. They enjoy life and its challenges.
7. *Serve as catalysts* They are change agents and strive to improve any situation of which they are a part.
8. *Exercise for self-renewal* They consistently work to develop and enhance the physical, mental, emotional, and spiritual aspects of their lives.

MASTER PRINCIPLES OF MANAGEMENT AND LEADERSHIP

Although both management and leadership are essential in the organizational setting, it is important to understand the differences between these roles. The primary *management* activities involve implementation, setting up systems and structures to obtain desired results, control, and logistics. In exercising the management role, emphasis is placed on cost-effectiveness, quality measures, rules, procedures, and policies. *Leadership*, on the other hand, deals with bigger and at the same time less tangible issues. Leadership provides vision and direction but also inspires and motivates people to work in diverse ways to achieve a common purpose.

The leadership and management roles must function together effectively for the organization to achieve long-term and lasting success. Nevertheless, owing to emphases on short-term, quantifiable results, it is the management role that predominates in most organizations, while leadership development is neglected. A leader who possesses both strategic and motivational competencies can bring to the organization a sense of direction and purpose, while concurrently building work groups of inspired and motivated employees. Leaders and managers working in tandem represent the marriage of effectiveness and efficiency in the pursuit of organizational goals.

Principle-centered leadership must operate simultaneously at each of four levels:

- *Personal*—self awareness and comfort
- *Interpersonal*—relationships with others
- *Managerial*—responsibility to get the job done
- *Organizational*—need to organize people

At each level, fundamental principles guide behaviors and are the basis for leadership effectiveness. At the personal level, *trustworthiness* is determined by a combination of character and competence. Effectiveness at the interpersonal level requires a high level of *trust*, which grows out of trustworthiness. Trust is also a product of interpersonal experiences and a determinant of future interactions.

At the managerial level, *empowerment* is the desired operating principle. If the level of trust is low, formal control systems are typically required to assure that people do what needs to be done. If trust levels are high, direction based on rank or position can be supplanted by a more constructive system of self-governing work groups. Finally, at the organizational level, when there are trustworthiness, trust, and empowerment, the organization can be structured to reflect *alignment*, or fit. Under these conditions, a flat and flexible structure rather than a rigid, hierarchical system will facilitate the attainment of organizational goals.

PRINCIPLE-CENTERED LEADERSHIP AND TOTAL QUALITY

The pursuit of "total quality" objectives is inextricably related to principle-centered leadership. As already noted, *principled leadership is an all-encompassing philosophy that calls for continuous improvement in the personal, interpersonal, managerial, and organizational domains.* In this respect, "total quality" relies on principles very much in concert with natural laws that provide the conceptual foundation for principle-centered leadership, as well as concepts such as the following:

- Consistency
- Predictability
- Continuous improvement
- Feedback
- Measurement
- Honest and ethical relationships

Without such principles, the techniques and methods of quality improvement are unlikely to provide long-lasting results.

Principle-centered leadership suggests that total quality and continuous system improvement cannot be attained without simultaneously striving to perfect interdependent and interpersonal relationships. When applied to quality initiatives, principle-centered leadership empowers people to pursue improvement in each of the four domains (personal, interpersonal, managerial, organizational), reinforces continuous quality improvement activities, and suggests systems to support quality improvement objectives.

IMPLICATIONS

The principled leader empowers people and their organizations in the pursuit of desired outcomes by extending the natural laws first introduced in *The Seven Habits of Highly Effective People* to the organizational setting. In order to succeed, these laws require complete acceptance of the new paradigm in life and work, along with perseverance and patience. Applied thoroughly and consistently, these principles offer the opportunity for personal and organizational transformation.

Principle-centered leadership is as much a philosophy of life as a guide to becoming an effective leader. While not directly answering the question of whether leaders are born or made, it is clear that one cannot be an effective leader unless an appropriate set of personal beliefs and values is carried into the leadership realm. Adherence to these principles may provide the opportunity to *become* a more effective and successful leader.

The principle-centered leadership perspective helps people to confront change by providing the wisdom and skills to take advantage of opportunities. This perspective is similar to the adage that suggests:

Give [people] fish and you feed [them] for a day.
Teach [people] to fish and you feed [them] for a lifetime.

READING 3

Managing with the Wisdom of Love

Uncovering Virtue in People and Organizations

Dorothy Marcic
Summary prepared by Dorothy Marcic and Marilyn Crawford

Dr. Dorothy Marcic, author of Managing with the Wisdom of Love: Uncovering Virtue in People and Organizations, *is the Director of Graduate Programs in Human Resource Development at Vanderbilt University. She is a former Fullbright Scholar at the University of Economics in Prague and the Czech Management Center. In addition to authoring several books, she has consulted for a variety of public and private organizations, including the U.S. Department of State and the Czech Ministry of Finance.*

Marilyn Crawford is an educational consultant on public school reform and a doctoral student at Vanderbilt University.

CHANGE IS THE NORM FOR BUSINESS

In today's chaotic, unpredictable world, business as usual usually does not work. The traditional modes of hierarchy, strong and controlling leadership, stovepipe departmental structures, and ego-based management do not work as successfully as they did two or three decades ago.

COMPANIES ARE BOUND BY PHYSICAL AND SPIRITUAL LAWS

Physical laws are real. When a ball is thrown, it follows an arc according to the laws of physics. Hydrogen and oxygen combine to make water by the laws of chemistry. Whether someone accepts or understands how these laws work makes no difference to the outcomes. For example, a baseball pitcher cannot decide he does not believe in physics and decide to throw a pitch that defies the laws of gravity.

Dorothy Marcic, *Managing with the Wisdom of Love: Uncovering Virtue in People and Organizations*. San Francisco, CA: Jossey-Bass, Inc., 1997.

Spiritual laws, like physical laws, are also real. If someone tells a lie, the person lied to will lose trust in the liar. The result of lying is as predictable as the laws of gravity. In organizations, when employees are treated poorly or even abused, a predictable result is that employees will pull back and work with less motivation. Perhaps someone will even try to sabotage the work. "Get hurt, get mad, get even," is a common saying.

Laws exist regardless of whether or not we acknowledge them, and ignoring them will not make the laws disappear. They *are*. Just as there are physical laws that we can see, there are spiritual laws that are just as real, despite the fact that we don't "see" them as readily.

Spiritual laws are ancient and multicultural. All the world's religions speak of the consequences of our actions. The Hebrew Bible states, "Reap what ye sow." Buddhism calls it "dharms," Hinduism names it "karma," while Zoroastrians call it the "Law of Asha," with Mizdem being the consequences of our own behaviors.

Not only individuals are bound by these laws, but companies as well. Violation of laws has unavoidable consequences, and the consequences are real both for violating physical laws and spiritual laws. If a company denies a rumor of layoffs, only to have the workforce cut the following day, does anyone believe the workers will have higher levels of motivation after having been deceived?

ORGANIZATIONS HAVE FIVE DIMENSIONS

Organizations operate on five dimensions: material, intellectual, volitional, emotional, and spiritual. The five dimensions are like a tree, with spirituality as the root—the key to life for all the rest of the tree. Volitional ability, the willingness to reach out and change, is defined as the span of the roots. The greater the span, the more capacity the tree has to take in food and nutrients. The trunk is the emotional dimension, providing visible support for the rest of the organization. Branches of the tree represent intellectual development of the organization, and the leaves are the physical evidence most visible to people within the organization and without.

Managers are gardeners that care for the tree, providing conditions that allow the tree to thrive. Despite lack of control of external elements such as storms or drought, the gardener creates optimal opportunity for health within the context of those elements.

THE FIVE DIMENSIONS OF ORGANIZATIONS MUST BE IN BALANCE

We tend to focus on the surface rather than to go deep where the roots are. Most energy from management is directed toward the material and the intellectual, such as earnings, profits, buildings, equipment, training, innovation, and the bottom line (quarterly financial reports). In times of stability and predictability this can be effective. When the profit picture deteriorates, the common response is to cut expenses (material), often including staff and training, both of which reduce the intellectual capital. Rarely do executives look at deeper issues of emotional well being or spiritual connections to the work, in order to assess problem areas.

Some attention may be given to the volitional dimension (desire to change), though infrequently; this is a critical problem, for some studies report that 50 percent of U.S. profits come from goods and services not even invented five years ago. Therefore, intellect, no matter how sharp, without volition allows a company to survive for only a few years.

The emotional dimension is critical to company success. In today's impulsive environment, companies cannot compete in the intensely competitive global marketplace unless they have extremely high levels of motivation, creativity, enthusiasm, and loyalty from workers. These levels of motivation require that the emotional and spiritual needs of human beings be met in the workplace. Employees can no longer be seen as resources to be exploited. The emotional dimension deals with the quality of relationships among employees. How do people feel about one another? How do they resolve conflicts? Is there a sense of community? James Autry found that by helping an Australian publishing company work on building community (emotional), within three years profits had tripled. Previously, without emotional well-being, the company was doing poorly. Similarly, spiritual needs are crucial to healthy organizations. The spiritual dimension, the root of the tree, is fundamental to success and balance in all other dimensions, as this quote from Shoghi Effendi Rabbani suggests:

It is the soul of man which first has to be fed.

Spiritual needs relate to the deeper meanings of workers, such as whether the work has a sense of purposefulness to it. Also important is the extent to which the company practices virtues taught by all the world's religions for thousands of years.

IMBALANCE CREATES FAILURE

Lack of attention to all five levels creates failure in the long run. *The goal is to achieve balance*, with high level of functioning in all the five dimensions of work (physical, intellectual, emotional, volitional, spiritual). There is synergy in balance, and the whole is greater than the sum of the individual parts.

When organizations fail to achieve balance in the five dimensions, serious problems result, such as the following:

- An organization where the most challenging problem of over half the employees was making it through until retirement. It's not hard to imagine the impoverished motivation level of that group.
- Organizations that strip jobs from workers, feel no guilt or remorse, and do not try in more than cursory ways to give retribution.
- Employees who feel exploited or humiliated, who then in return work less or sabotage results, steal office supplies, make long distance telephone calls, or "borrow" other resources. They wait patiently for their chance to get back at their employer.
- The organization exhibiting all the ugly manifestations of control, manipulation, dishonesty, withholding information, and divide-and-conquer tactics, where morale is dismal.
- The employee who feels misunderstood, neglected, unappreciated, exploited, and even abused for years, who one day comes to work with a gun and uses it destructively.

Knowing these problems, managers try one change program after another. Yet, such programs have failure rates of between 55 and 90 percent. Why? The reason is that we do not attend to the real issues of people in organizations. *We pretend that emotional and spiritual needs are irrelevant in the workplace.* No wonder the change programs are doomed!

ORGANIZATIONS CREATE BALANCE BY LIVING ACCORDING TO SPIRITUAL LAW

To achieve balance, organizations must pay greater attention to the spiritual, emotional, and volitional dimensions in the workplace by helping their employees live according to spiritual law. Living according to spiritual law requires a person to become more virtuous. Some of the virtues that are necessary for organizational well-being are trustworthiness, unity, respect, justice, and service. We call these The New Management Virtues, and they are critical interlocking "bricks" in the spiritual path. They provide a well-worn (past-present-future and multicultural, multireligion) path for the journey to spirituality and achieving balance.

Trust is the fundamental virtue. Trustworthy companies build loyalty to customers and employees. Lack of trust has great economic costs. This does not imply that a manager should try being trustworthy in order to achieve greater profits, for such behavior negates the pure intentions needed to truly follow spiritual law. Pure motives are an essential part of living, according to spiritual law. The reality of this concept is that when one does the right thing for the right reason, long-term results tend to be positive. In common terms, "what goes around comes around." Marcus Tullius Cicero (C. 50 B.C.) stated it as

Virtue is its own reward.

Unity provides a foundation for shared vision and commitment, which are sources of power in organizational change. Working with a truly cohesive team with common direction and broad commitment of members is a thrilling experience, and the sense of meaning is a powerful driver for change. Reciprocity (treating others as they want to be treated) creates synergy through setting up a pattern of giving back and forth.

Respect and dignity are the keys to empowering employees to work to their fullest, valuing the contribution all can make to the organization rather than holding on to the old traditional hierarchy. Through treating employees with respect and dignity, managers break down the old paradigms of forcing people to work and allow people to work to their fullest capacity. Sometimes employers talk about employee involvement but actually attempt to maintain control, and this is not the same as real empowerment. Note this warning from Bahai', Baha'u'llah.

Beware . . . lest ye walk in the ways of them whose works differ from their deeds . . . for the professions of most men, be they high or low, differ from their conduct.

The Golden Rule states the concept of justice, the notion of putting oneself in another's place. Justice does not stand alone as a virtue, and there is a sense of fairness and empathy that is necessary for justice to exist. Fairness is situational, and justice is determined over and over again by seeing—and treating—other people as equals. Compensation systems and workforce reduction programs are two areas of organizations where justice, or lack thereof, is often evident.

Service adds meaning to the workplace, giving workers a sense of higher purpose and significance. Work performed in the spirit of service not only helps the company and its customers but also positively impacts other workers and individuals themselves. Here is an example, drawn from Shoghi Effendi Rabbani:

> *Work draws us nearer to God, and enables us to better grasp His purpose for us in this world.*

Humility allows people to admit wrongdoing, feel genuinely sorry for mistakes, and take responsibility for their own errors. Ego-driven managers are incapable of listening to others and learning from them, particularly from workers of lower status, and this is a major problem for business. In contrast, Lao Tsu urges us to

> *Surrender yourself humbly; then you can be trusted to care for all things.*

MANY COMPANIES USE NEW MANAGEMENT VIRTUES

Many successful companies apply spiritual laws, thus illustrating that there are a wide variety of ways of being spiritual. Examples include ServiceMaster with its commitment to diversity and focus on God as a common unifying force, Texas Instruments with its proactive stance on ethics and morality, Meredith Magazine Group's practice of "presume goodwill," and TDIndustries with its focus on employee empowerment.

THE PATH TO ORGANIZATIONAL CHANGE

The quest for spirituality involves change; change is active and action-based rather than just internal. Spirituality is a long journey, not a fact or product, and pure intent (rather than manipulation) is fundamental to the journey.

There are specific ways to make the changes, but determining what is needed is far different from being able to lay out the "how" and from having the will to do it. How to operationalize the New Management Virtues and spirituality is often the tricky question. Bringing about effective and enduring change in values and culture in an organization is a long-term process, as Albert Einstein suggests:

> *The most important human endeavor is the striving for morality in our actions. Our inner balance and even our very existence depend on it. Only morality in actions give beauty and dignity to life.*

There are many paths to "managing with the wisdom of love," but some key fundamentals can assist in putting theory into practice. First, companies must be committed to a long-range plan for success rather than focusing on immediate profit. Second, leaders must be willing to let go of control and share power. Third, leaders must organize ways of communicating and idea sharing as the basis of shared vision. Practices that can assist in this process include consultation, dialogue, and future search.

CONCLUSION

Managers need to build hope and then follow a path toward the goal of spirituality rather than limiting themselves to success or failure as a permanent condition. Numerous stories show that it is possible to have successful organizations grounded in love. Love and virtue carry their own rewards, according to spiritual law. You can become more spiritual by following a spiritual path, but you cannot use spirituality for your own gain. Instead, love, spiritual law, and virtue can help you to see the essential nobility of yourself and others and apply this nobility to the world of business. In doing so, you can understand the beauty and meaning of those things that are invisible and intangible, yet all-pervasive and indispensable. This is the Wisdom of Love.

READING 4

Reclaiming Higher Ground

Creating Organizations That Inspire Excellence

Lance H. K. Secretan
Summary prepared by R. Warren Candy

R. Warren Candy *is Vice President of Generation for Minnesota Power, Inc., a diversified utility located in Duluth, Minnesota, and he has responsibility for the operations of its generating resources in Minnesota and North Dakota. His interests include high-performance organizations, sustainable leadership, and sociotechnical systems implementation. He received his bachelor of science degree in Production Engineering from Swinburne Institute of Technology in Melbourne, Australia.*

As our society, our industries, and our companies move into a more service and technologically oriented economy, we must continually improve our levels of innovation and creativity not only to survive, but also to prosper. Unfortunately, today's approaches to management are grossly ineffective in getting people to be creative and involved on demand.

REACHING FOR THE HIGHER GROUND

To energize people we need to create work environments in which creativity and innovation can flourish through the positive expression of the human spirit, and where employee needs and company profits are seen as equally valid organizational goals. We must restore trust, integrity, emotion, and lifetime learning back into our companies, in an effort to bring both personal and organizational soul into our day-to-day interactions with each other, always reaching to "reclaim the higher ground."

Unfortunately, we have become fixated on the cult of the personality and our desire for ego gratification at the expense of the soul. Companies and people will once again begin to grow and prosper when we restore respect for the soul and create workplaces that are spiritually safe and secure.

Ultimately we must make our work, and our companies, an essential part of our life, and that will be good for our hearts as well as our minds and corporate

Lance H. K. Secretan, *Reclaiming Higher Ground: Building Organizations That Inspire Excellence*. New York, NY: McGraw-Hill Companies, Inc., 1997.

bottom lines. We must be encouraged to bring our whole being to our work. We need to have the place, and the opportunity, to use all of our talents and our gifts in fulfilling our job responsibilities. Just imagine the enormous power available when the full potential of an impassioned individual, in mind, body, and spirit, is released.

However, as we look at today's increasingly competitive work environment, this is not occurring. Our personalities are becoming richer and richer, while our souls are becoming poorer and poorer. We are all being whipped into the frenzied activities of acquiring more, doing more, and being faster, while at the end of the day we feel empty and yearn for renewal. It appears that somewhere along our journey of human and work experience, we have given up our souls in favor of our personalities, and this is leading us down a road that is going nowhere.

Today, the real breakthroughs in organizational performance and organizational life are being made by those who realize that people everywhere are seeking much more from their working lives than they are currently receiving—something that inspires the soul rather than merely focuses on the old questions with their predictable answers and solutions of doing more with less, faster.

For the past 100 years, organizations have succeeded beyond their wildest dreams in meeting the needs of the personality, but in the process, they have abandoned the soul. Percy Barnevik, former chief executive officer and president of Asea Brown Boveri says, "Our organizations are constructed so that most of our employees are asked to use five percent to ten percent of their capacity at work. It is only when those same individuals go home that they can engage the other 90 percent to 95 percent—to run their households, lead a boy scout troop, or build a summer home. We have to be able to recognize and employ that untapped ability that each individual brings to work every day."

Before we can reach the higher ground where we can renew our souls, we must first look inwardly at ourselves. When we open ourselves to self-renewal, self-questioning, and regeneration, acceptance and personal growth can commence. This might enable us to ask the important questions of contemporary life: Why is this happening to me? What is going on? Why is everything so chaotic? How can I protect myself? How can I thrive? What is my purpose? What will my legacy be? How can I contribute? How can I be of service?

PERSONAL EVOLUTION

Answering these questions begins the process of personal evolution that is the path to personal transformation. *Personal evolution* is the result of emotional and spiritual reinvention through the self-generated process of giving ourselves permission to change our attitudes and our skills and make it safe for each other to do so.

The path of personal evolution moves through three stages:

- *Immature*: In this phase, we do not explore consciousness but simply defer to power and penalty.
- *Traditional*: In this phase, our self-doubt and insecurity drive us to behave in ways that are shaped by personality and ego that enable us "to fit in," so that we are accepted by others.

- *Evolving*: This phase is the most advanced human condition in which we gain a measure of consciousness by challenging traditional logic, aligning our beliefs, searching for the connection between soulfulness and work, and seeking deeper meaning in our lives.

To reach the higher ground, we must start with ourselves, becoming more interested in asking the right questions than giving others the right answer, examining for ourselves all of the conventional wisdom and paradigms that have lead us to our emptiness and spiritual poverty.

A MODEL FOR WORK AND LIFE

In its current form, dedicated as it is to results achieved and the people achieving them, the modern organization is heading for an evolutionary dead-end. On the other hand, no other sector of our society has the potential to do so much to bring about the positive changes that would uplift the human spirit. The reinvented modern organization has the global reach, influence, talent, knowledge, assets, and the technology to make the world a better place through service to humanity. More than any other group in society, it has the potential to reclaim higher ground and inspire people by working from personality to soul. Our society is experiencing a paradox of wealth: We have never been so rich, yet we have never been so poor. We are experiencing both the greatest period of material prosperity and scientific achievement as well as the greatest period of social breakdown:

WE ARE GETTING RICHER AND RICHER WITH . . .

Success	Power	Wealth
Consumer choice	Ambition	Technology
Pride	Entertainment	Prestige
Science	Speed	Lower costs
Information	Freedom	Vacations

. . . AS WE GET POORER AND POORER WITH . . .

Burnout	Loss of spirit	Stress
Less wonder	Lack of balance	Crime
Loneliness	Prejudice	Fear
Lack of meaning	Less time	Ecological
Absence of wisdom	Degradation	Unhappiness
Selfishness	Lack of renewal	Less fun

The question before us as managers and participants in the organizations of today is "How do we break this cycle?" that is, how do we move from where we currently are to where we all know we would like to be?

A metaphor that we can use is the bicycle. If our organization, regardless of its type, were thought of as a bicycle, it would first derive its power from the back wheel and then its direction from the front wheel. From the back wheel, we derive the three values that are the life skills that energize individuals, teams, and organizations, as they help us to kickstart personal development and change attitudes: mastery, chemistry, and delivery.

Mastery: **Undertaking Whatever You Do to the Higher Standards of Which You Are Capable**   *Mastery* is possessing a commitment to do what it takes to be the best in whatever you do, being devoted to continuous personal and professional improvements, to setting standards for personal development, enhancing one's skills, competencies, and practices, and respecting knowledge, wisdom, and learning. Mastery embodies a commitment to excellence in everything one does.

Chemistry: **Relating So Well With Others That They Actively Seek to Associate Themselves With You**   People with *chemistry* possess characteristics and attitudes that favor building strong relationships. They place a high value on harmonious interaction with others, taking the initiative to repair, maintain, and build friendships. They know that interest is the most sincere form of respect. Truth-telling and promise-keeping are keystones of chemistry and result in the establishment of emotional bonds with others built on trust.

Delivery: **Identifying the Needs of Others and Meeting Them**   *Delivery* is being respectful of the needs of others and having a passion for meeting them. This focus on the needs of others is motivated by enlightened self-interest and altruism. Delivery is founded on "win-win" deals and relationships that treat customers, employees, and suppliers as partners rather than adversaries.

To become proficient in these primary values we must adopt three other behaviors and habits:

1. Mastery is driven by *learning*: seeking and practicing knowledge and wisdom.
2. Chemistry is dependent on *empathizing*: considering the thoughts, feelings, and perspectives of others.
3. Delivery is supported by *listening*: hearing and understanding the communications of others.

We now have the strength and power of the driving rear wheel of this bicycle, but a bigger question for our life still remains: "Where are we headed?" The values on the back wheel provide power and acceleration to our lives and our organizations. But that energy can become misdirected unless it is tempered by the value shifts of the front wheel, which provides our direction.

To reinvigorate the soul requires us to move, change, and grow as individuals. We must move from

- Me to you,
- Things to people,
- Fear to love,
- Weakness to strength,
- Momentary improvement to continuous growth.

Most of us are not committed practitioners of the values on the front wheel—in fact, we need to shift from "old" values to these "new" ones. That's why they are called "Value Shifts." They represent the major shift from individual personality to spiritual soul.

You before Me   The personality-driven way is dangerously egocentric. The "you before me" value, however, is other-centered and seeks win-win combinations. It assumes that when we help others to win, we all win. It recognizes that a proposition that is good for me but bad for you is ultimately bad for both of us. More importantly, a shift from me to you offers a much-needed balance to the preoccupations flowing from our personalities, by shifting our focus from increasing market share, sales, cash flow, or power, to being of service to others and to our planet.

People before Things   The genius of Western management has been our unsurpassed ability to acquire, measure, analyze, and count things. In revering analysis and acquisition, however, we have forgotten that organizations are the sum of people, not of things. The "things approach" obeys politics, procedures, policies, manuals, formal systems, and salary levels. The "people approach" recognizes the universal desire of people to be trusted, respected, and loved.

Continuous Improvement and Breakthrough   Creativity nourishes the soul and there are two ways to be creative: by *innovating* (finding a *different* way) and by *continuous improvement* (finding a *better* way). The capacity to do the same thing a little better every day may not look like a spectacular achievement in the short run, but it is in the long run. The Japanese call this *kaizen*—continuous improvement in personal life, home life, social life, and work life, involving everyone. Such dedication to continuous improvement builds self-esteem of individuals and teams and propels organizations to excellence. While acknowledging the importance of being a world-class innovator (by finding a different way), this value recognizes that it is just as important to practice *kaizen* (by finding a better way). This subtle difference nourishes the souls of individuals and therefore propels them and their organizations into a unique spiritual plane.

Strengths before Weaknesses   Researchers claim that during an average business meeting each new idea is met with nine criticisms. By mistakenly placing our faith in the Aristotelian notion that by attacking ideas we will strengthen them, we have perfected our mechanical skills of rational thinking and criticism. But imagine if every person and every organization devoted as much passion and time to building on their strengths, as they do dragging down others; our organizations and our souls would reach new, unexpected, and unknown heights.

Love before Competition, Hostility, and Fear   Winning has come to mean defeating one's opponent. From that perspective, it seems that before you can win, there must always be a loser. Life today has become an endless battle, in which we are all competitors at some level, seeking to beat and to vanquish our opponents (who in truth are our colleagues) at school, work, home—even within our own country and society. *In reality, life is not a battleground—it is a playground.*

People are not motivated by war or by the fear of losing. Great performances are romanced from people, not beaten out of them. If we love what we do (mastery), love the people with whom we do it (chemistry), and love the reason for doing it (delivery), would we still call it work? People are inspired to do what they do well by the love they feel for what they do (mastery), by the people with whom they share tasks and relationships (chemistry), and by their commitment to being of service to others (delivery). Our previous notions of leadership and management are being swept away. The Values Bicycle is a model that enables *everyone* to become a missionary responsible for managing and leading, whether he or she sports a managerial title or not. The Values Bicycle assumes that work is not war, but love. The more we decentralize, the more we will depend on the competence and human-relations skills of the individual. We all share the load, the opportunity, and the responsibility.

Building Greatness Is Achieved One Human Being at a Time   Simply put, the difference between whether an organization is mediocre or superb is determined by whether all its individual members are mediocre or superb. The difference between organizations that are mediocre and those that are great is the attitude within each of us—our values and our culture. An inspired organization is simply the sum of inspired souls.

Glossary of Terms

administrative expert The role of managing the firm's infrastructure through reengineering organization processes in an effort to build an efficient infrastructure. (Ulrich)

antecedents Things that precede a behavior, which set the stage for (cue) that behavior. (Daniels)

automatic listening When the listener doesn't actually attempt to hear what the speaker has to say and instead only affirms his or her own unexamined assumptions. (Barrentine)

autopoietec structures Self-organizing or self-creating systems which maintain coherence through a core of values; these values permit the system to respond to challenges from the environment without losing the systemic identity. (Wheatley)

benchmark A measured, "best-in-class" achievement, a reference or measurement standard for comparison; a performance level recognized as the standard of excellence for a specific business practice. (Watson)

benchmarking A systematic and continuous measurement process; a process of continuously comparing and measuring an organization's business process against business leaders anywhere in the world, to gain information that will help the organization take action to improve its performance. (Watson)

benchmarking code of conduct A behavioral convention that describes the protocol of behaviors to be used in conducting benchmarking studies. (Watson)

benchmarking partner A relationship between two parties who associate in a collegial relationship involving close cooperation to conduct benchmarking studies—the protocol of this relationship is summarized by the Benchmarking Code of Conduct. (Watson)

best practice Superior performance within an activity, regardless of industry, leadership, management, or operational approaches, or methods that lead to exceptional performance; a relative term that usually indicates innovative or interesting business practices that have been identified during a particular benchmarking study as contributing to improved performance at the leading organization. (Watson)

bottom-up budgeting Constructing the company's budget by gathering input and feedback from the employees at lower levels in the organization (who will be expected to work within the budget) and involving as many people in the organization as possible. (Case)

business network unit A venture that assigns roles and functions to separate stand-alone speciality businesses to produce or market a product or service. (Galbraith and Lawler)

business strategy Future-focused planning to provide for the long-term success of the organization. (Pfeffer)

capability focus Defining and developing the attributes and competencies that an organization needs to accomplish its strategic objectives. (Ulrich)

change agents Individuals working to facilitate organizational change. Roles may include catalyst and facilitator of change, problem solver, and designer of change processes. (Ulrich)

chaos A stage of group development where individual differences prevail, and crisis management may be required. This mode follows the disintegration of a pseudocommunity. (Barrentine)

character ethic A composite of unconscious patterns of actions (e.g., proactivity; thinking "win-win") that, if practiced with perseverance, help a person become both successful and interdependent with others in their journey. (Covey)

chemistry Relating so well with others that they actively seek to associate themselves with you. (Secretan)

china mentality The conviction that one *can* change the world, motivating one to reject the usual answers and examine old problems in a new light. (Ohmae)

coach The role taken to motivate and direct work units toward activities that will result in the implementation of the vision. (Nanus)

collective work product The performance improvement which is the tangible result of a group effort and not achievable by a single member alone. (Katzenbach)

command-and-control leadership A leadership style which stresses hierarchical lines of authority, the amassing of power and information, a win-lose decision process, and the value of sameness. (Rosener)

community The final stage of group development, in which people feel comfortable about straightforwardly expressing their ideas on both an interpersonal and group level. (Barrentine)

companyism An excessive concern for, or loyalty to, one's company, which leads to the inability to critically examine company strategy or past ways of doing business. (Ohmae)

competitive benchmarking A measure of organization performance compared against competing organizations; studies that tar-

get specific product designs, process capabilities, or administrative methods used by a company's direct competitors. (Watson)

consequence management A management philosophy that rewards and punishes on the basis of the consequences or results of individual action. (Katzenbach)

consequences Things that follow a behavior and change the probability of that behavior recurring. (Daniels)

credibility A combination of honesty, inspiration, and competence in leaders that inspires workers to be motivated, feel valued, and act ethically. (Kouzes and Posner)

credibility gap The difference between what leaders say and what they do. (Kouzes and Posner)

critical numbers The essential operating ratios and numbers that determine a company's success. (Case)

culture The underlying beliefs and values that are taught to new members of the organization that guide activities within the organization. (Nanus)

data A set of discrete, objective facts about an event. (Davenport and Prusak)

deadly diseases A set of chronic ailments that can plague any organization and prevent its success. (Deming)

defensive reasoning Reasoning that occurs when individuals (1) firmly hold premises of questionable validity yet think they are unassailable; (2) make inferences that do not necessarily follow from the premises yet they think they do; and (3) reach conclusions that they believe they have tested carefully yet they have not because the way the conclusions have been framed make them untestable. (Argyris)

defining moments Situations in which one's professional responsibilities unexpectedly come into conflict with their own deepest values, especially with regard to choosing between two apparently "right" courses of action. (Badaracco)

deliverables Outcomes which accomplish their objectives, but also reflect value added by organizational policies, practices, and activities. (Ulrich)

delivery Identifying the needs of others and meeting them. (Secretan)

Deming management theory A set of fourteen steps that managers are advised to take to transform their organizations into more successful systems. (Deming)

design team Group of steering team members; may also include supervisors, human resource personnel, union officials, team members, and other functional representatives. This team plans the implementation of the team strategy and acts as champion of the team effort. (Wellins, Byham, and Wilson)

dissipative structures A scientific phrase describing systems which dissipate their energy to recreate themselves into new forms; organizations can recreate themselves in a similar manner. (Wheatley)

discretionary effort More behavior than is minimally required. (Daniels)

divisional structure A model that organizes the business around a product or products where each division operates much like a separate business entity. (Galbraith and Lawler)

dominator A model of social organization, like a hierarchy, that has a vertical structure in which power means power over people. (Barrentine)

double-loop learning Learning that focuses on the values governing the actions that produced the errors. (Argyris)

effective managers Managers who manage themselves and others so that both employees and the organization benefit. (Blanchard and Johnson)

employee champion The role of managing employee contribution through listening and responding to employees in an effort to increase employee commitment and capability. (Ulrich)

empowerment Providing employees a say in how the organization is run and some degree of control and responsibility for their work domains. (Covey)

empowerment The notion that employees voice ideas, take part in decisions that affect them, and help run their workplace. (Case)

emptying A stage of group development in which individuals develop a critical self-awareness. This differs from the chaos mode in that rather than simply being aware of diversity and differences in others, workers recognize their own weaknesses and strengths. (Barrentine)

enable The process, practices, or methods that facilitate the implementation of a best practice and help to meet a critical-success factor; characteristics that explain the reasons for the achievement of benchmark performance. (Watson)

enlightened management systems Organizations where employees are assumed to be at the highest levels of the need hierarchy, are capable of self-actualization, and are receptive to management practices that keep people informed, provide clarity of direction, and challenge them to stretch and grow. (Maslow)

entropy The natural tendency for systems to expend energy and produce increasing disorder. (Wheatley)

espoused theories The beliefs and values people hold about how to manage their lives. (Argyris)

essential business The basic activities by which an organization defines itself. (Nanus)

executive discipline The implied rules executives follow to enforce individual accountability and consequence management. (Katzenbach)

extinction The absence of reinforcement, with the result that behavior declines and eventually stops. (Daniels)

fancy footwork Actions that permit individuals to be blind to inconsistencies in their actions, to deny that these inconsistencies exist, or to blame other people for their actions. (Argyris)

feedback Information regarding results of one's efforts (how well one is performing). (Blanchard and Johnson)

feminine The characteristics of compassion, loving, and nurturing, which can be found in men as well as women. (Barrentine)

fields Invisible, non-material connections that form the basic structure of the universe (i.e., magnetic field). Organizations need to be permeated with similar, intangible fields of vision and quality. (Wheatley)

first-order errors Errors that are caused by not knowing. (Argyris)

fixed costs Costs that are based on commitments from previous budgets and cannot be altered quickly. (Ohmae)

frame A schemata, map, image, metaphor, tool, or perspective that presents a unique image of organizations and allows managers to gather information, make judgments, and determine how to take action from its vantage point. Four frames are the structural, human resources, political, and symbolic. (Bolman and Deal)

front-end/back-end model A model that organizes separately around a "front-end" that deals with customers and service, and a "back-end" that is organized around product development and manufacturing. (Galbraith and Lawler)

functional benchmarking An application of process benchmarking that compares a particular business function at two or more organizations. (Watson)

functional model A traditional business structure that is organized around functions such as human resource departments, accounting, and manufacturing. (Galbraith and Lawler)

fusion leadership A style which recognizes one's subtle leadership gifts, potentials, and passions and acts from them to lead organizational change and improvement. (Daft and Lengel)

gainsharing Systems of financial rewards in which employee bonuses are based on organizational performance. (Galbraith and Lawler)

game A short-term drive designed to reach a particular goal. (Case)

gap A difference in performance, identified through a comparison between the benchmark for a particular activity and other companies; the measured leadership advantage of the benchmark organization over other organizations. (Watson)

generic benchmarking An application of functional process benchmarking that compares a particular business function at two or more organizations selected without regard to their industry. (Watson)

glass ceiling The invisible barrier women face when moving up the corporate ladder that stops them from attaining executive managerial positions. (Rosener)

global benchmarking The extension of strategic benchmarking to include benchmarking partners on a global scale. (Watson)

global localization The capacity to operate on a global scale while retaining the ability to serve local customers and markets. (Ohmae)

global paradox The strange phenomenon in which the larger the world economy becomes, the more powerful its smallest players are. (Naisbitt)

globalization The standardization of product design and advertising strategy throughout the world. (Ohmae)

goal setting The establishment of targets (goals) for employee performance that facilitate the conscious intentions of employees to perform. (Blanchard and Johnson)

governance strategy Consciously designed movement toward creating a governance system that dramatically rearranges social and power relationships between the organizational leadership and the core employees. (Block)

grounding A process of meditation and relaxation that encourages personal intuition. (Barrentine)

HeroZ Individuals who empower themselves and encourage others to work together to successfully accomplish goals. (Byham and Cox)

hierarchical control A traditional, top-down management style that provides an employee's immediate supervisor with the responsibility and authority to reward/discipline the employee. (Pfeffer)

high-involvement organization An organization that seeks to give all its members access to information, the opportunity to influence decisions, and a share in the rewards of performance. (Galbraith and Lawler)

high-performance team A group that meets all the conditions of real teams and has members who are deeply committed to one another's personal growth and success. (Katzenbach and Smith)

huddle system A series of meetings that take place on regular intervals that are designed to enable employee participation in running the business. (Case)

inductive thinking The ability to first recognize a powerful solution and then seek the problems it might solve. (Hammer and Champy)

information Data that has meaning and makes a difference through changing the way the receiver perceives something. (Davenport and Prusak)

integration Creating conditions at work such that individuals can *best* achieve their own goals by directing their efforts toward the success of the enterprise. (McGregor)

interactive leadership style A leadership style which emphasizes consensus building, comfort with ambiguity, and the sharing of power and information. (Rosener)

interlinked economy The open and deregulated global economy that is currently emerging, encompassing Japan, Europe, the United States, and other aggressive economies. (Ohmae)

internal benchmarking An application of process benchmarking performed within an organization by comparing the performance of similar business units or business processes. (Watson)

job enrichment Creating jobs in which individuals can be responsible for an entire product or service. (Galbraith and Lawler)

kaizen The Japanese term for continuous, incremental improvement. (Hammer and Champy)

knowledge A fluid mix of experience, values, shared context, and expert insight that provides a framework for evaluating and incorporating new experiences and information. (Davenport and Prusak)

knowledge management The capture, distribution, and utilization of knowledge. (Davenport and Prusak)

knowledge map A visual representation of where to locate knowledge. (Davenport and Prusak)

knowledge transfer The transmission, absorption, and use of knowledge. (Davenport and Prusak)

knowledge work The processing of data and exchanging of information. (Case)

lateral unit Organizational unit that brings related tasks or work groups together across divisional and hierarchical lines. (Galbraith and Lawler)

law of maldistribution Eighty percent of the effort expended in a process is caused by only 20 percent of the input, according to Vilfredo Pareto, a twentieth-century economist; also known as the Pareto Principle and the 80-20 rule. (Hammer and Champy)

leadership capacity The amount of leadership time and talent available to a group or organization at a specific point in time. (Katzenbach)

learning disability A way of thinking in organizations that keeps managers and others from making necessary changes and adapting to environmental needs. (Senge)

Maastricht treaty The treaty that calls for European communities to become a united economic power. (Naisbitt)

managing by wandering around (MBWA) The process of having managers spend a substantial portion of their time meeting with customers, vendors, and employees to learn their needs. (Peters and Waterman)

mastery Undertaking whatever you do to the higher standards of which you are capable. (Secretan)

mental models Deeply engrained generalizations, assumptions, or pictures that influence how people see the world. (Senge)

mercorsor agreement An agreement linking Argentina, Brazil, Paraguay, and Uruguay in a common market in order to accelerate their individual and collective economic growth. (Naisbitt)

mission The purpose for with the organization exists; the needs or desires that the organization satisfies for customers or clients. (Nanus)

monitoring Gathering information about how well the vision is being implemented in the organization. (Nanus)

multiskilling Team members are required to learn every job on their team and, in some cases, the jobs on other teams as well. (Wellins, Byham, and Wilson)

negative reinforcement Desired behavior is exhibited and strengthened as a means to avoid punishment. (Daniels)

new-design plants Organization-wide approaches to participative management in which group members participate in selection decisions, the layout facilitates work-group tasks, job design revolves around teams, and pay systems are egalitarian. (Lawler)

nichemanship An organizational strategy of fulfilling a segment of unmet demand in a larger market. (Belasco and Stayer)

objectives Milestones that must be attained in order to implement the vision. (Nanus)

one-best-model Organizational belief that there is only one best way to design, operate, and lead an organization. (Rosener)

organizational defensive routines Actions or policies that protect individuals or segments of the organization from experiencing embarrassment or threat. (Argyris)

organizational fusion The release of subtle forces in a large group in order to build relationships, connections, community, and a positive culture and value system. (Daft and Lengel)

organizational gardening An organic metaphor for a business paradigm that emphasizes the ongoing planning, development, and nurturing of a business. (Barrentine)

paradigm A model or conceptual framework; a mindset for understanding aspects of reality. (Covey)

paradigm A set of rules and regulations (written or unwritten) that does two things: (1) it establishes or defines boundaries; and (2) it tells how to behave inside the boundaries in order to be successful. (Barker)

paradigm effect Process by which practitioners of an established paradigm are forced to reassess their own perceptions as a result of the introduction of new paradigms. (Barker)

paradigm paralysis A description of the state of a paradigm whereby participants are tolerant of the established rules, boundaries, and behaviors, and are intolerant of alternative rules, boundaries, and behaviors. This state is marked by very low levels of expressed creativity and very low levels of innovation. (Barker)

paradigm pliancy A description of the state of a paradigm whereby participants are tolerant of established rules, boundaries, and behaviors, and of alternative rules, boundaries, and behaviors. This state is marked by high levels of expressed creativity and high levels of innovation. (Barker)

paradigm shift A change to a new paradigm having new rules, boundaries, and behaviors. (Barker)

paradox A statement that seems absurd but is actually valid or true. (Naisbitt)

Parkinson's Law Work expands to fill the amount of time available for its completion. The reengineering revision of Parkinson's Law states that "Work expands to fill the amount of equipment available for its completion." (Hammer and Champy)

partnership A model of social organization that, as its name implies, is nonhierarchical. This model of social organization is more supportive and productive than a dominance model. (Barrentine)

patriarchal management Leaders act, and are viewed as, parents of the organization, and the rest of the members are the children looking for structure, guidance, direction, praise, and an appropriate reward for performing desired behaviors. (Block)

peer-based control The power of team members to enforce and to encourage certain behaviors. (Pfeffer)

people-centered management A management philosophy that emphasizes the organization's success will be maximized when employees are treated as partners in the business. (Pfeffer)

performance management Creating the right environment and conditions to bring out the best in people. (Daniels)

personal evolution The result of emotional and spiritual reinvention through the self-generated process of giving ourselves permission to change our attitudes and our skills and making it safe for each other to do so. (Secretan)

pinpointing Specifying tangible results and related behaviors that are observable, measurable, and reliable. (Daniels)

positive reinforcement A consequence that increases the rate or frequency of a behavior, because the performer values that outcome and views it as contingent on the behavior. (Daniels)

praise Verbal reinforcement (e.g., compliment) for desirable employee behavior and performance. (Blanchard and Johnson)

problem The difference between what is actually happening and what you want to happen. (Blanchard and Johnson)

process benchmarking The activity of measuring discrete performance and functionality against organizations whose performance is excellent in analogous business processes. (Watson)

process A set of activities that, taken together, produce a result of value to the customer. (Hammer and Champy)

productivity Employee output in terms of the quantity and quality of work completed. (Blanchard and Johnson)

protectionism The attempt to defend domestic companies from trade or competition with foreign industries. (Ohmae)

pseudo-team A group that has not focused on collective performance and is not really trying to achieve it. (Katzenbach and Smith)

punishment A consequence that causes behavior to diminish in frequency and ultimately stop. (Daniels)

real team A small number of people with complementary skills who are committed to a common purpose, performance goals, and working approach for which they hold themselves mutually accountable. (Katzenbach and Smith)

reengineering The fundamental rethinking and radical redesign of business processes to achieve dramatic improvements in critical, contemporary measures of performance, such as cost, quality, service, and speed; starting over. (Hammer and Champy)

reprimand Negative verbal feedback provided when undesirable employee behavior and performance occur. (Blanchard and Johnson)

reverse engineering A comparison of product characteristics, functionality, and performance with those of similar products made by competitors; the tear-down of competitive products to their fundamental

subassembly level by engineers, in order to evaluate design characteristics. (Watson)

Sapp A force that drains energy from people. (Byham and Cox)

Say's law Supply creates its own demand, as formulated by Jean Baptiste Say, a nineteenth century French economist. (Hammer and Champy)

scenarios Integrated and interrelated sets of possible future events that will have an impact on the organization's success. (Nanus)

scorecard A form of display mechanism devised to allow a company's critical numbers to be clearly presented in a public way (e.g., a cutout of a thermometer, computer generated printouts, or e-mail messages). (Case)

second-order errors Errors that humans actively design and produce. (Argyris)

self-directed work teams (SDWT) An intact group of employees, responsible for a whole work process or segment, that develops a product or delivers a service to an internal or external customer. (Wellins, Byham, and Wilson)

selective adaptation Choice of a method or action that accommodates identified conditions rather than ignoring or going against those facts. (McGregor)

self-actualizing employees Those persons who institute their own ideas, make autonomous decisions, learn from their mistakes, and grow in their capabilities. (Maslow)

semiautonomous teams Small groups of employees who manage many dimensions of their own work affairs. (Byham and Cox)

servant leaders Managers who value the role of serving, and giving to, those with whom they work. (Kouzes and Posner)

sex role spill-over Sex role expectations of women and men carried over from early childhood that spills over into the work place. (Rosener)

sexual static A phenomenon, resulting from gender differences, which causes interference with messages being communicated between men and women. (Rosener)

shared vision The capacity to hold a shared picture of the future. (Senge)

single-loop learning Learning that focuses on the presenting problem (symptom) and ignores the causes of the problem. (Argyris)

spiritual havens Programs of support and education for workers and their spiritual development during periods of transition. (Barrentine)

spiritual needs The desire by workers to have their deeper needs met at work, such as a desire for purposefulness and trustworthiness. (Marcic)

spokesperson The formal role associated with communicating the vision to both internal and external constituents. (Nanus)

status differences Psychological and compensatory differences between layers of an organization. (Pfeffer)

steering committee This group is usually composed of upper and middle management, union representatives, team leaders, and in some cases prospective team members. This group takes the vision and direction provided by senior management and oversees the design effort for self-directed work teams. (Wellins, Byham, and Wilson)

stewardship contract A social agreement that defines and limits what is to be controlled, the boundaries and limitations of a partnership among participants, and the relationship between employees and the organization. (Block)

stewardship contract Definition of the ground rules for employees to participate in the new governance structure, the results that are required, the constraints within which they must live, and the changes that will be made toward greater empowerment, partnership, and service. (Block)

stewardship Empowering people to be accountable for their own actions, predicated on the idea that people in communities and organizations are willing to choose service over self-interest, while not being dependent on managers. (Block)

strategic alliance A mutually beneficial, long-term, cooperative relationship with another firm. (Ohmae)

strategic benchmarking The application of process benchmarking to the level of business strategy; a systematic process for evaluating alternatives, implementing strategies, and improving performances by understanding and adapting successful strategies from external partners who participate in an ongoing business alliance. (Watson)

strategic partner The role of managing strategic human resources through executing strategy and aligning human resource and business strategy. (Ulrich)

Strategic Plans on the Top Shelf (SPOTS) Missions, visions, or strategies that are developed, but ignored as objectives, policies, and practices are determined. (Ulrich)

synergy Working together, cooperating, combining in a cooperative action to yield an outcome that is greater than the sum of its parts. (Covey)

systems thinking The ability to look at the whole and see how one part affects another. (Senge)

targeted interviewing A technique that focuses on gathering facts about the applicant (instead of theoretical information). This approach looks at past behavior as a predictor of future behavior. (Wellins, Byham, and Wilson)

teachable moment The period of time when a person is most likely to understand, and accept, the material being taught. (Wellins, Byham, and Wilson)

teaching organization One in which individual leaders value the competency of developing others, develop a teachable point of view, and devote regular efforts to honing the leadership skills in others. (Tichy and Cohen)

team basics The five elements necessary to achieve real team performance: size, purpose and goals, skills, working approach, and mutual accountability. (Katzenbach)

things gone right (TGR) Product improvements and innovations. (Peters)

things gone wrong (TGW) Defects and other quality errors. (Peters)

theories in use The actual rules or master programs that individuals use to achieve control. (Argyris)

theory of constraints An approach that suggests that by continually identifying and removing bottlenecks, a system will automatically operate more effectively (assuming that the goal is clear and well-known). (Goldratt and Cox)

Theory X A set of assumptions that explains some human behavior and has influenced conventional principles of management. It assumes that workers want to avoid work and must be controlled and coerced to accept responsibility and exert effort toward organizational objectives. (McGregor)

Theory Y A set of assumptions offered as an alternative to Theory X. Theory Y assumes that work is a natural activity, and given the right conditions, people will seek responsibility and apply their capacities to organizational objectives without coercion. (McGregor)

tracking Gathering information about the effectiveness of the vision in the external environment. (Nanus)

transparent company A company in which vital business information is shared with and understood by all employees, not just those in charge. (Case)

triad The combined market of the industrialized world (Japan, Europe, and the United States). (Ohmae)

tribalism The belief in fidelity to one's own kind, defined by ethnicity, language, culture, religion, or profession. (Naisbitt)

"true north" principles Basic truths and natural laws that govern human existence. Like a compass, they always point the way. (Covey)

value chain The suppliers and customers of the organization, the linkages and practices which define these relationships. (Ulrich)

variable costs Costs that are closely associated with the volume of the business. (Ohmae)

virtual organization A disembodied organization that functions as a series of loosely connected networks of specialists that combine to complete a project and then disband. (Peters)

virtual worksite A workplace that does not exist in a physical location but instead is created through the use of computer networks and other information technology. (Galbraith and Lawler)

vision An engaging yet realistic image of what the organization could become. (Nanus)

visionary leadership Developing an engaging image of what an organization can become and then creating organizational systems to attain the vision. (Nanus)

witch doctors Management writers who persuasively put forth "new" ideas riddled with jargon, common sense, and conflicting directions for easy success while avoiding self-criticism. (Micklethwait and Wooldridge)

work teams Groups of employees who are given considerable responsibility to decide how the group will operate. (Galbraith and Lawler)

working group Any small group collaborating together to accomplish a common purpose or goal. (Katzenbach)

world class Leading performance in a process, independent of industry or geographic location, as recognized using process benchmarking for comparison to other worldwide contenders. (Watson)

Zapp A force that energizes people, enabling them to seek and obtain continuous improvement in their jobs. (Byham and Cox)

Bibliography of Inclusions

Argyris, Chris. (1990). *Overcoming Organizational Defenses.* Needham Heights, MA: Allyn and Bacon.

Badaracco, Joseph L. Jr. (1997). *Defining Moments.* New York, NY: Harvard Business School.

Barker, Joel A. (1992). *Paradigms: The Business of Discovering the Future.* New York, NY: HarperCollins.

Barrentine, Pat. (1993). *When The Canary Stops Singing.* San Francisco, CA: Berrett-Koehler.

Belasco, James A. & Stayer, Ralph C. (1993). *Flight of the Buffalo.* New York, NY: Warner Books.

Blanchard, Kenneth & Johnson, Spencer. (1981). *The One Minute Manager.* La Jolla, CA: Blanchard-Johnson.

Block, Peter. (1993). *Stewardship.* San Francisco, CA: Berrett-Koehler.

Bolman, Lee G. & Deal, Terrence E. (1991). *Reframing Organizations: Artistry, Choice, and Leadership.* San Francisco, CA: Jossey-Bass.

Byham, William C. & Cox, Jeff. (1994). *HeroZ: Empower Yourself, Your Co-workers, Your Company.* New York, NY: Harmony Books.

Byham, William C. & Cox, Jeff. (1988). *Zapp! The Lightning Of Empowerment.* New York, NY: Harmony Books.

Case, John. (1995). *Open-Book Management.* New York, NY: HarperCollins.

Case, John. (1998). *The Open-Book Experience.* Reading, MA: Addison-Wesley.

Collins, James C. & Porras, Jerry I. (1994). *Built to Last: Successful Habits of Visionary Companies.* New York, NY: HarperBusiness.

Covey, Stephen R. (1989). *The Seven Habits of Highly Effective People: Restoring the Character Ethic.* New York, NY: Simon & Schuster.

Covey, Stephen R. (1992). *Principle-Centered Leadership: Strategies For Personal & Professional Effectiveness.* Bellevue, NY: S & S Trade.

Daft, Richard L. & Lengel, Robert H. (1998). *Fusion Leadership: Unlocking the Subtle Forces that Change People and Organizations.* San Francisco, CA: Berrett-Koehler.

Daniels, Aubrey C. (1993). *Bringing Out The Best In People.* New York, NY: McGraw-Hill.

Davenport, Thomas H. & Prusak, Laurence. (1998). *Working Knowledge.* New York, NY: Harvard Business School.

Deming, W. Edwards. (1986). *Out Of The Crisis.* Cambridge, MA: MIT Press.

Dunlap, Albert. (1996). *Mean Business: How I Save Bad Companies and Make Good Companies Great.* New York, NY: Simon and Schuster.

Galbraith, Jay R. & Lawler, Edward E. (1993). *Organizing for the Future.* New York, NY: Jossey-Bass.

Goldratt, Eliyahu M. & Cox, Jeff. (1986). *The Goal: A Process of Ongoing Improvement.* New York, NY: North River Press.

Hammer, Michael & Champy, James. (1993). *Reengineering the Corporation*. New York, NY: HarperBusiness.

Katzenbach, Jon R. (1998). *Teams at the Top: Unleashing the Potential of Both Teams and Individual Leaders*. Cambridge, MA: Harvard Business School.

Katzenbach, Jon R. & Smith, Douglas K. (1993). *The Wisdom of Teams*. Cambridge, MA: Harvard Business School.

Kohn, Alfie. (1993). *Punished By Rewards*. Boston, MA: Harvard Business School.

Kouzes, James M. & Posner, Barry Z. (1993). *Credibility*. San Francisco, CA: Jossey-Bass.

Marcic, Dorothy. (1997). *Managing with the Wisdom of Love*. San Francisco, CA: Jossey-Bass.

Maslow, Abraham H. (1998). *Maslow on Management*. New York, NY: John Wiley & Sons, Inc.

McGregor, Douglas. (1985). *The Human Side of Enterprise*. New York, NY: McGraw-Hill.

Micklethwait, John & Woolridge, Adrian. (1996). *The Witch Doctors: Making Sense of the Management Gurus*. New York, NY: Times Business.

Naisbitt, John. (1994). *Global Paradox: The Bigger the World Economy, The More Powerful Its Smallest Players*. New York, NY: Morrow.

Nanus, Burt. (1992). *Visionary Leadership*. San Francisco, CA: Jossey-Bass.

Ohmae, Kenichi. (1990). *The Borderless World*. New York, NY: HarperBusiness.

Peters, Tom. (1994). *The Tom Peters Seminar*. New York, NY: Random House.

Peters, Thomas J. & Waterman, Robert H. Jr. (1982). *In Search of Excellence*. New York, NY: Harper & Row.

Pfeffer, Jeffrey. (1998). *The Human Equation: Building Profits by Putting People First*. Boston, MA: Harvard Business School.

Rosener, Judy B. (1995). *America's Competitive Secret: Women Managers*. New York, NY: Oxford University Press.

Secretan, Lance H. K. (1997). *Reclaiming Higher Ground*. New York, NY: McGraw-Hill.

Senge, Peter. (1990). *The Fifth Discipline*. New York, NY: Doubleday.

Tichy, Noel M. with Cohen, Eli. (1997). *The Leadership Engine: How Winning Companies Build Leaders at Every Level*. New York, NY: HarperCollins.

Watson, Gregory H. (1993). *Strategic Benchmarking: How to Rate Your Company's Performance Against The World's Best*. New York, NY: Wiley.

Wellins, Richard S., Byham, William C., & Wilson, Jeanne M. (1991). *Empowered Teams*. San Francisco, CA: Jossey-Bass.

Wheatley, Margaret. (1992). *Leadership and the New Science: Learning about Organization from an Orderly Universe*. San Francisco, CA: Berrett-Koehler.

Ulrich, Dave. (1997). *Human Resource Champions*. Boston, MA: Harvard Business School.

Index